HIGH COURT CASE SUMMARIES

CRIMINAL LAW

Keyed to Dressler's Casebook on Criminal Law, 4th Edition

Mat #40604624

610 Opperman Drive
St. Paul, MN 55123
1-800-328-9352

Printed in the United States of America

ISBN: 978-0-314-18110-7

Table of Contents

*

Alphabetical Table of Cases

CHAPTER ONE

Introduction: Setting the Stage

Owens v. State

Instant Facts: An intoxicated person, found asleep behind the wheel of a car parked in a driveway, with its motor running and lights on, is convicted of drunk driving, even though there was only circumstantial evidence that the car was driven on the highway.

Black Letter Rule: A conviction based upon circumstantial evidence alone, may be sustained if the circumstances are inconsistent with any reasonable hypothesis of innocence.

State v. Ragland

Instant Facts: A convicted felon charged with possession of a weapon, contends that the judge erred in instructing the jury that they "must" convict, which conflicted with the jury's nullification power.

Black Letter Rule: The power of jury nullification is not a precious attribute of a right to trial by jury.

Owens v. State

(*Drunk Driver*) v. (*Judge*)
93 Md. App. 162, 611 A.2d 1043 (Md. 1992)

A CONVICTION OF DRUNK DRIVING IS UPHELD THOUGH BASED ON CIRCUMSTANTIAL EVIDENCE

■ **INSTANT FACTS** An intoxicated person, found asleep behind the wheel of a car parked in a driveway, with its motor running and lights on, is convicted of drunk driving, even though there was only circumstantial evidence that the car was driven on the highway.

■ **BLACK LETTER RULE** A conviction based upon circumstantial evidence alone, may be sustained if the circumstances are inconsistent with any reasonable hypothesis of innocence.

■ PROCEDURAL BASIS

Appeal to the Maryland Court of Special Appeals, of a conviction by the trial court, sitting without a jury, for driving while intoxicated.

■ FACTS

On March 17, 1991, Christopher Columbus Owens, Jr. (Owens) (D), was asleep in the driver's seat of a truck. The truck was parked in the driveway of a private residence, with its engine running and the lights turned on. At 11 P.M. Trooper Samuel Cottman (Cottman), responding to a complaint about a "suspicious vehicle", approached the truck and found Owens (D) with an open can of Budweiser clasped between his legs, and two more empty beers cans in the back seat. Cottman awakened Owens (D), who appeared lost and confused with a strong odor of alcohol on his breath. Then Owens (D) stumbled out of the truck, with his face flushed and eyes red. When asked to recite the alphabet, Owens (D) mumbled the letters, and failed to recite them in the correct order. His speech was generally slurred and unclear. A check with the Motor Vehicle Administration revealed that Owens (D) had an alcohol restriction on his license. Owens (D) then declined to submit to a blood test for alcohol. At trial, Owens (D) contended that the law he was charged with violating did not extend to driving on a "private driveway," and that there was insufficient evidence of driving while intoxicated. The trial court, sitting without a jury, convicted Owens (D) of driving while intoxicated. Owens (D) appealed.

■ ISSUE

May a conviction based upon circumstantial evidence alone, be sustained when the circumstances are inconsistent with any reasonable hypothesis of innocence?

■ DECISION AND RATIONALE

(Moylan, J.) Yes. A conviction based upon circumstantial evidence alone, may be sustained if the circumstances are inconsistent with any reasonable hypothesis of innocence. We are called upon, here, to examine the circumstantial evidence, and to ascertain whether there were any attendant and ancillary circumstances to render less likely, and therefore less reasonable the hypothesis of innocence. We agree with Owens (D) that he could not properly have been convicted, no matter how intoxicated, for driving back and forth on a driveway. However Owens (D) was convicted not for driving on a private driveway, but for driving on a public highway before coming to rest on a private driveway. It is a classic case of circumstantial evidence. From his presence behind the wheel of a vehicle with its engine running and lights turned on, it can reasonably be inferred that, 1) he just arrived by way of public highway, or 2) was just about to set forth upon the public highway. These two probabilities are strengthened by the lack of evidence of any third reasonable explanation. The first inference would render Owens (D) guilty, while the second would not. With either inference equally likely, a fact finder could not fairly draw the guilty inference and reject the innocent with the requisite certainty beyond a reasonable doubt. For the State to prevail, there has to be some other factor to enhance the likelihood of the first inference and diminish the second. If Owens (D) was parked in someone else's driveway with the motor still running, it would be more likely that he had just driven there a short time before. If Owens (D) was parked in his own driveway it is more likely that he was on his way out. Although it is routine procedure, Owens' (D) license, which showed the alcohol restriction and Owens' (D) address, was not offered into evidence. Therefore for the purposes of the present analysis, Owens' (D) address is not in this case, and we must look for a tiebreaker elsewhere. Three beer cans were in evidence. Since one does not typically drink in the house and then carry the empty cans out to the car, it may be inferred that some significant drinking had taken place while Owens (D) was in the car. One passes out on the steering wheel after one has been drinking for some time. It is not a reasonable hypothesis that one would leave the house, get in the car, turn on the lights and motor, then, before driving off, consume enough alcohol to pass out on the steering wheel. Furthermore, Trooper Cottman came to the scene because of a complaint about a suspicious looking vehicle. The inference is reasonable that the vehicle had been observed driving in some sort of erratic fashion. Had the appellant simply been sitting, with his motor idling, on the driveway of his own residence, it is not likely that someone from the immediate vicinity would have found suspicious the presence of a familiar neighbor in a familiar car sitting in his own driveway. This does not prove guilt in and of itself, but simply makes one of two alternative inferences less reasonable, and its alternative inference thereby more reasonable. The totality of circumstances are inconsistent with a reasonable hypothesis of innocence. It makes the drawing of the inference of guilt more than a mere flip of a coin between guilt and innocence. It makes it rational and therefore within the proper purview of the factfinder. Affirmed.

Analysis:

This case first raises a concern about the sufficiency of evidence needed for a conviction. Because of factors, such as negative social stigma, that necessarily follow a criminal conviction, the burden of proof is necessarily high. Thus prosecutors have the burden of proving every fact of a case necessary for the conviction, beyond a reasonable doubt. This case exemplifies that this burden of proof can be met, even if only circumstantial evidence is available. A second concern deals with the sufficiency of evidence needed to sustain a conviction. The appellate court must assume that the trier of fact, usually the jury, resolved any conflicts between factual claims in favor of the prosecution. Thus, the standard on appeal is whether a rational trier of fact could reasonably have reached the result that it did. Since the conviction in the instant case was based on circumstantial evidence alone, the appellate court was required to find that the circumstances were inconsistent with any reasonable hypothesis of innocence. A third issue this case raises is the Sixth Amendment right to a trial by jury. In the instant case, Owens (D) was convicted by the trial court judge, sitting without a jury. The right to a trial by jury only applies to "non-petty" offenses, usually when imprisonment for more than six months is authorized or the legislature determines that an offense is a "serious one". Therefore, Owens's (D) right to a trial by jury turns upon the penalty that was imposed.

■ CASE VOCABULARY

CIRCUMSTANTIAL EVIDENCE: Particular circumstances or indirect evidence, which would allow the inference that a particular event or action had taken place.

State v. Ragland

(*Jury*) v. (*Felon*)

105 N.J. 189, 519 A.2d 1361 (N.J. 1986)

THE POWER OF JURY NULLIFICATION IS NOT AN ESSENTIAL ATTRIBUTE OF THE CONSTITUTIONAL RIGHT TO A TRIAL BY JURY

■ **INSTANT FACTS** A convicted felon charged with possession of a weapon, contends that the judge erred in instructing the jury that they "must" convict, which conflicted with the jury's nullification power.

■ **BLACK LETTER RULE** The power of jury nullification is not a precious attribute of a right to trial by jury.

■ FACTS

Ragland (D), a previously convicted felon, was prosecuted for various offenses, including armed robbery and possession of a weapon by a convicted felon. At the conclusion of the trial for the latter offense, the judge instructed the jury that if it found that the defendant was in possession of a weapon during the commission of the robbery, it "must" find him guilty of the "possession" charge. The trial court found Ragland (D) guilty. Ragland (D) appealed arguing first, that the judges use of the word "must" in the instruction conflicted with the jury's nullification power, which Ragland (D) claimed was an essential attribute of his constitutional right to a jury trial. Second, Ragland (D) argued that the judge should have informed the jury regarding its power of nullification.

■ ISSUE

Is the jury's nullification power, an essential attribute of the constitutional right to a jury trial, which the jury must be informed of?

■ DECISION AND RATIONALE

(Wilentz, J.) No. The overwhelming weight of authority is contrary to Ragland's (D) argument. Even where the use of the word "must" is discouraged, it is not a result of a constitutional command. It is only relatively recently that some scholars have characterized this power as part of a defendant's right to trial by jury. Like Ragland (D), they take the position that the exercise of the power is essential to preserve the jury's role as the "conscience of the community." Some laws are said to be unfair, while other laws may do injustice in specific applications. Only the jury, it is thought, is capable of correcting that unfairness or injustice through its nullification power. Cast aside is our basic belief that only our elected representatives, may determine what is a crime, what is not, and what laws need revision. Furthermore, it is their belief that a person is entitled to *more* than a fair trial even when such a trial is pursuant to fair law. In other words, a person is entitled to the right to be found guilty beyond a reasonable doubt, but then acquitted and set free because of the beliefs of the jury. If jury nullification has proven to serve society well, that proof has been kept a deep secret. We know so little about this power that it is impossible to evaluate it in terms of result. Since, there is neither constitutional nor other legal authority mandating a change in jury instructions, its ultimate justification must be that it is desirable that a jury should not be compelled to follow the law. If indeed this is a desirable state of affairs, then the jury should be told of its power. Counsel should be told that they may address nullification in summation, and be able to argue to the jury that it should not apply the law given by the court, but rather follow its own conscience. Moreover, juries should only include those people who are capable of exercising their nullification power. There is no mystery about the power of nullification. It is the power to act against the law. In its immediate application, it would confuse any conscientious citizen serving on a jury, by advising the person that after all is said and done, he can do whatever he pleases. Jury nullification is an unfortunate but unavoidable power. It should not be advertised, and to the extent constitutionally permissible it should be limited. Efforts to protect and expand it are inconsistent with the real values of our system of criminal justice and therefore it is not desirable. We conclude that the power of jury nullification is not a precious attribute of a right to trial by jury. The power of the jury to acquit despite overwhelming proof guilt and the juries belief of guilt beyond a reasonable doubt, is not a right that the jury must be informed of. It is nothing more than a power. Reversed on other grounds.

Analysis:

This opinion raises the issue of the jury's role and power in criminal trials. Specifically, this court strongly favors the role of the jury as the fact-finding body, leaving the judge as the law-finding entity. More importantly, it strongly disfavors the power a jury has to disregard the law. Reasons that jury nullification power exists include protection against governmental oppression, and allowing the jury to send a message about some social issue that is more important than a particular case. Moreover, as the "conscience of the community," the jury may use this power to protect against socially undesirable convictions. However, the court strongly opines and sets forth many reasons why the power of jury nullification does more harm then good. Most importantly, it finds that it should be ultimately up to the elected representatives to determine what is a crime and what is not.

■ CASE VOCABULARY

JURY NULLIFICATION: The power of a jury to deliberately disregard the law and acquit a defendant, even if the prosecutor proves beyond a reasonable doubt that the accused committed the offense charged.

CHAPTER TWO

Principles of Punishment

The Queen v. Dudley and Stephens

Instant Facts: Two English seamen are convicted of murder for killing and eating a young crew member.

Black Letter Rule: A person may be punished and convicted of murder, despite killing out of necessity.

People v. Superior Court (Du)

Instant Facts: A liquor store owner is convicted of voluntary manslaughter, after shooting and killing a young customer, believed to be a shoplifter, in the back of the head while the customer was leaving.

Black Letter Rule: The amount of punishment imposed for voluntary manslaughter depends on the facts of each case.

People v. Du

Instant Facts: A liquor store owner is convicted of voluntary manslaughter, after shooting and killing a young customer, and is given probation, even though originally sentenced to ten years in state prison.

Black Letter Rule: Rule: Probation is a permissible punishment for voluntary manslaughter in unusual cases.

United States v. Gementera

Instant Facts: A convicted mail thief was required, as part of his punishment, to stand outside a post office for a day wearing a signboard stating, "I stole mail. This is my punishment."

Black Letter Rule: The Sentencing Reform Act affords courts broad discretion in fashioning conditions of supervised release that are reasonably related to the nature and circumstances of the offense and the history and characteristics of the defendant.

Coker v. Georgia

Instant Facts: A convicted felon is sentenced to death, after escaping from prison, breaking into a house where he robbed a couple, raping and kidnapping the wife, and driving off in the couple's car.

Black Letter Rule: The death penalty is a grossly disproportionate and excessive punishment for the crime of raping an adult woman, prohibited by the Eighth Amendment.

Ewing v. California

Instant Facts: The defendant, convicted of shoplifting three golf clubs, is given a sentence of 25 years to life under California's three strikes law.

Black Letter Rule: The Eighth Amendment does not require strict proportionality between the crime and sentence, but rather, it only prohibits extreme sentences that are grossly disproportionate to the crime.

The Queen v. Dudley and Stephens

(*Society*) v. (*Cannibals*)
14 Q.B.D. 273 (1884)

PUNISHMENT FOR MURDER IS STILL DESERVED DESPITE KILLING OUT OF NECESSITY

■ **INSTANT FACTS** Two English seamen are convicted of murder for killing and eating a young crew member.

■ **BLACK LETTER RULE** A person may be punished and convicted of murder, despite killing out of necessity.

■ PROCEDURAL BASIS

Appeal to the Queen's Bench Division, of a conviction for felony and murder.

■ FACTS

On July 5th, 1884, Thomas Dudley (Dudley) (D1), Edward Stephens (Stephens) (D2), Brooks, and Richard Parker (Parker) (a young seventeen- or eighteen-year-old English boy) set out to sea on the Mignonette, a yacht. Subsequently, they were cast away in a storm at sea, 1600 miles away from the Cape of Good Hope, and were compelled to put into an open boat belonging to the Mignonette. For three days, the four individuals only had two 1-lb. tins of turnips and no water to subsist upon. On the fourth day, they caught a small turtle, which was entirely consumed after twelve days. For eight days after, they had nothing to eat, and no fresh water, except for rain water they were able to catch. On July 24th, Dudley (D1) proposed to Stephen (D2) and Brooks, but not to Parker, that lots should be cast to see who should be put to death and used for food to save the rest. Brooks refused and there was no drawing of lots. The next day, July 25th, when no vessel appeared to save them, Dudley (D1) and Stephens (D2) agreed to kill Parker, despite Brooks dissent. Dudley (D1) offered a prayer asking for forgiveness should any of them be tempted to commit a rash act, and then approached the young boy. The young boy, lying helpless at the bottom of the boat, weakened by famine and by drinking sea water, unable to resist, and never asserting to be killed, was cut in the throat and killed by Dudley (D1). The men fed upon the young boy, and then were rescued by a passing vessel. Dudley (D1) and Stephen (D2) were tried and convicted of murder.

■ ISSUE

Should a person be punished and convicted of murder, for killing out of necessity?

■ DECISION AND RATIONALE

(Coleridge, C.J.) Assuming any necessity to kill anybody, there was no greater necessity than here. If the men had not fed upon the young boy, they probably would have not survived to be rescued. The young boy, being in a much weaker condition, was likely to have died before them. However, if upon the whole matter the court should find that the killing of Richard Parker be felony and murder, then the jurors say that Dudley (D1) and Stephens (D2) were each guilty of felony and murder as alleged in the indictment.

Analysis:

This case raises the issue of who is deserving of punishment. Specifically, it asks whether Dudley (D1) and Stephens (D2) are deserving of punishment for their conduct, and why. Will punishment convince the general community to forego similar conduct, or deter future misconduct by the offenders? Or is the answer based on the retributive principle, that this conduct is deserving of punishment? It may be a combination of both principles. The answer may turn upon whether the murder was really a necessity, seen as a necessity in the eyes of Dudley (D1) and Stephens (D2), or whether necessity can justify the taking of an innocent boy's life. The answer may also turn upon the feelings of remorse, if any, felt by the murderers.

■ CASE VOCABULARY

GENERAL DETERRENCE: A form of utilitarianism, which states that the goal of punishing a person is to convince the general community to forego similar misconduct.

RETRIBUTIVISM: A principle that justifies punishment, by stating that misconduct is deserving of it.

SPECIFIC DETERRENCE: A form of utilitarianism, which states that the goal of punishing a person is to convince that person to forego similar misconduct.

UTILITARIANISM: A principle that justifies punishment as a potential pain and deterrent to anti-social behavior.

People v. Superior Court (Du)

(*Society*) v. (*Judge*)
5 Cal. App. 4th 822, 7 Cal. Rptr. 2d 177 (1992)

LIQUOR STORE OWNER IS CONVICTED OF VOLUNTARY MANSLAUGHTER AFTER KILLING A YOUNG CUSTOMER

■ **INSTANT FACTS** A liquor store owner is convicted of voluntary manslaughter, after shooting and killing a young customer, believed to be a shoplifter, in the back of the head while the customer was leaving.

■ **BLACK LETTER RULE** The amount of punishment imposed for voluntary manslaughter depends on the facts of each case.

■ PROCEDURAL BASIS

Appeal to the California Court of Appeals, of a judgment by the trial court, giving probation for voluntary manslaughter.

■ FACTS

Empire Liquor Market (Empire) is one of two liquor stores owned and operated by Billy Du and wife Soon Ja Du (Du) (D). It is located in a bad area where shoplifting was a usual occurrence. On March 16, 1991, Du (D) worked at Empire, while Du's (D) husband, slept in the family van outside. While Du (D) was with two other customers, she observed fifteen-year-old Latasha Harlins (Latasha) enter the store, take a bottle of orange juice from the refrigerator, place it in her back pack, and proceed to the counter with the juice partially visible. Du (D) had observed many shoplifters in the store, and it was her experience that people who shoplifted would take merchandise, hide it, then approach the counter, pay for a smaller item, then leave. Witnesses testified that when Latasha approached the counter with about two or three dollars in her hand, she was confronted by Du (D), who called Latasha a "bitch" and accused her of stealing. After Du (D) asked Latasha to pay for the juice, Latasha replied "what juice?" A struggle ensued when Du (D) began to pull on Latasha's sweater trying to retrieve the juice, which fell out of the bag and onto the floor. Latasha then hit Du (D) with her fist, twice in the eye, causing Du (D) to fall behind the counter. Du (D), believing that if she was hit one more time she would die, then through a stool from behind the counter that missed Latasha. Subsequently Du (D) reached behind the counter and pulled out a .38-caliber revolver. Latasha then placed the orange juice on the counter, turned to leave and was shot in the back of the head by Du (D). Latasha was killed instantly with two dollars in her hand. At trial, Du (D) testified that she had never held a gun before, nor knew how it worked. Moreover, Du (D) testified that she did not remember firing and that she did not intend to kill Latasha. The gun was purchased in 1981 by Du's (D) husband, but was never fired. In 1988 the gun was stolen from the other liquor store Du (D) owned, but was returned by police in 1990. At trial a ballistics expert testified that the gun had been altered, and that the trigger pull necessary to fire the gun had been drastically reduced, and that the gun could be fired without putting much pressure on the trigger. Furthermore, the safety mechanism did not function properly. The Jury found Du (D) guilty of voluntary manslaughter, which implied that Du (D) had the intent to kill and that the killing was unlawful. Thus the jury rejected the defenses that the killing was unintentional and that Du (D) killed in self-defense. After the conviction, a probation report was prepared. It revealed that Du (D) was a 51-year-old Korean-born naturalized American citizen, who arrived in the United States in 1976. After saving enough money, Du (D) and her husband purchased Empire, despite warnings that it was in a "bad area." The store was plagued with problems from the beginning. The area surrounding the store was frequented by narcotics dealers and gang members. The store itself was burglarized over 30 times and shoplifting occurred 40 times per week. Furthermore, Joseph Du, Du's (D) son, had been threatened over 30 times, and more than 20 times people came into the store and threatened to burn it down. The report also revealed that Latasha had suffered many painful experiences in her life, including the death of her mother. She lived with her extended family in South Central Los Angeles. Latasha had just graduated Junior High where she was an honor student the previous spring. She was involved in activities at a youth center as an assistant cheerleader, member of the drill team, and summer junior camp counselor. She was a good athlete and church member. The probation officer concluded in his report that Du (D) would be most unlikely to repeat this or any crime if she were allowed to remain free, and that Du (D) would not seek to harm another. However, although Du (D) expressed concern for the victim and her family, this remorse was centered largely on the effect the incident had on Du (D) and her own family. Ultimately, the probation officer concluded and recommended that probation be denied, and that the defendant be sentenced to state prison.

■ ISSUE

How much punishment should be imposed upon a person unlikely to repeat similar misconduct?

■ DECISION AND RATIONALE

(Ashby, J.) OMITTED.

Analysis:

This case raises the concern about the amount of punishment to impose. The decision and rationale of the appellate court is purposely omitted, in order to allow the reader to develop his or her own opinion of how much punishment Du (D) is deserving of. Specifically, the reader must decide, based on these facts, whether Du (D) should be given probation or sent to prison. In answering, the reader should first consider the surrounding circumstances, keeping in mind the history of problems that plagued Du (D) and the liquor store. Second, the reader should also keep in mind that fifty-one-year-old Du (D) was assaulted, albeit by a young woman fifteen years of age. Third, the gun was unknowingly altered with a hair pin trigger, giving the contention that the murder was accidental greater strength. Fourth, the reader should consider whether Du (D) overreacted, and if so, whether the overreaction was understandable. Fifth, the reader should consider Latasha's background, and her actions during the incident. Finally, the reader should consider which form of punishment would better serve a societal purpose, based on theories of utilitarianism and retributivism.

■ CASE VOCABULARY

VOLUNTARY MANSLAUGHTER: The intentional killing of another human being without malice aforethought.

People v. Du

(*Society*) v. (*Store Owner*)
No. BA037738

JUDGE SUSPENDS TEN YEAR PRISON SENTENCE AND PLACES LIQUOR STORE OWNER ON PROBATION FOR VOLUNTARY MANSLAUGHTER

■ **INSTANT FACTS** A liquor store owner is convicted of voluntary manslaughter, after shooting and killing a young customer, and is given probation, even though originally sentenced to ten years in state prison.

■ **BLACK LETTER RULE** Rule: Probation is a permissible punishment for voluntary manslaughter in unusual cases.

■ PROCEDURAL BASIS

Sentence hearing after a trial convicting a liquor store owner of voluntary manslaughter.

■ FACTS

(More detailed facts are presented in *People v. Superior Court (Du),* the preceding case.) After being convicted of voluntary manslaughter for killing Latasha Harlins (Latasha), Soon Ja Du (Du) (D) was sentenced to ten years in state prison. However, the sentence was then suspended and Du (D) was placed on probation.

■ ISSUE

Is a sentence of probation for voluntary manslaughter permissible in unusual cases?

■ DECISION AND RATIONALE

(Karlin, J.) Yes. [Trial Court Opinion] Probation is a permissible punishment for voluntary manslaughter in unusual cases. The district attorney suggest that imposing less than the maximum sentence will send a message that a black child's life is not worthy of protection. This is dangerous rhetoric, which serves no purpose other than to pour gasoline on a fire. It is not my job to exact revenge for those who demand it. Justice is never served when public opinion, prejudice, revenge, or unwarranted sympathy are considered by a sentencing court. In imposing a sentence, I must consider the objectives of sentencing: 1) to protect society, 2) to punish the defendant for committing a crime, 3) to encourage the defendant to lead a law-abiding life, 4) to deter others, 5) to isolate the defendant so she can't commit other crimes, 6) to secure restitution for the victim, and 7) to seek uniformity in sentencing. First, because of the unique nature of each crime of voluntary manslaughter, uniformity in sentencing is virtually impossible. Statistics show that sentences imposed upon defendants convicted of voluntary manslaughter range from probation with no jail time to incarceration in state prison. Second, I do not believe that Du (D) needs to be incarcerated in order to protect society. Moreover, I do not believe that state prison is needed in order to encourage Du (D) to lead a law-abiding life, or to isolate her so that she cannot commit other crimes. However, state prison may be needed to punish Du (D). In the instant case, there is a presumption against probation because a firearm was used, as set forth in California Penal Code 1203(e) [which provides that except in unusual cases, probation shall not be granted to any person who used a deadly weapon upon a human being]. Therefore in order to overcome that presumption, the court must find this case to be unusual. There are three reasons that I find this case unusual. First, the statute is aimed at criminals who arm themselves when they go out and commit crimes. It is not aimed at shopkeepers who lawfully possess firearms for protection. Second, Du (D) has no past criminal record. Third, Du (D) participated in the crime under circumstances of great provocation, coercion, and duress. Thus, this case is an unusual case that overcomes the statutory presumption against probation. Finally, Du (D) should be placed on probation. First, the crime was committed because of unusual circumstances, such as great provocation. Second, although Latasha was not armed with a weapon at the time of her death, she had used her fists as weapons just seconds before she was shot. The district attorney argues that Latasha was justified in her assault on Du (D). However, had Latasha not been shot and had the incident which preceded the shooting been reported, it is my opinion that the district attorney would have relied on the store videotape and Du's (D) testimony to make a determination of whether to file charges against Latasha. Third, having observed Du (D), I cannot conclude that there was any degree of criminal sophistication in her offense. Nor can I conclude that she is a danger to others if not incarcerated. Furthermore, I do not believe that Du (D) would be here today if the gun she had grabbed had not been altered. This was a gun that had been stolen and returned to the Du family shortly before the shooting. There is no reason to believe Du (D) knew the gun had been altered in such a way as to, in effect, make it an automatic weapon with a hairpin trigger. Finally, I cannot ignore the very real terror experienced by the Du family before the shooting, and the fear Du (D) experienced as she worked the day of the shooting. On the day of the shooting Du (D) volunteered to cover for her son to save him one day of fear. She may have reacted inappropriately to Latasha, but her over-reaction was understandable.

Analysis:

This trial court opinion provides the reader with an analysis of the question posed in the previous case. In imposing a sentence, the court first states seven objectives to sentencing. It then states that uniformity in sentencing is virtually impossible because of the unique nature of each crime of voluntary manslaughter, but that probation is not an uncommon sentence. The court then goes on to conclude that imprisoning Du (D) serves no utilitarian purpose. Specifically, the court concludes that prison is not a necessary punishment to protect society, to encourage Du (D) to lead a law-abiding life, to isolate Du (D) so that she cannot commit other crimes, and to deter others. Finally, the court concludes that imprisoning Du (D) serves no retributivist purpose for punishment, because the court believed that Du's (D) overreaction to Latasha was understandable, given Du's (D) past experiences.

■ CASE VOCABULARY

PROBATION: A sentence or punishment that allows a convicted person to return to the community, instead of serving time in prison.

United States v. Gementera

(*Prosecuting Authority*) v. (*Mail Thief*)
379 F.3d 596 (9th Cir. 2004)

THIEVES CAN BE FORCED TO DECLARE THEIR CRIMES IN PUBLIC

■ **INSTANT FACTS** A convicted mail thief was required, as part of his punishment, to stand outside a post office for a day wearing a sign-board stating, "I stole mail. This is my punishment."

■ **BLACK LETTER RULE** The Sentencing Reform Act affords courts broad discretion in fashioning conditions of supervised release that are reasonably related to the nature and circumstances of the offense and the history and characteristics of the defendant.

■ PROCEDURAL BASIS

Appellate review of a sentencing decision.

■ FACTS

Gementera (D), although just twenty-four years old, already had a lengthy criminal history when a police officer observed him stealing mail, including a Treasury check, from mail boxes. Gementera (D) pleaded guilty and was sentenced to two months' incarceration and three years supervised release, subject to certain conditions. One of those conditions was that Gementera (D) performs 100 hours of community service, consisting of standing in front of a post office wearing a sandwich board that declared in large letters, "I stole mail. This is my punishment." Gementera (D) filed a motion to have the sandwich-board condition removed from his sentence, and the court modified his sentence, limiting the sandwich-board time to eight hours and adding other conditions that were deemed more in keeping with the aims of the criminal justice system. Gementera (D) appealed the eight-hour sandwich-board portion of his sentence.

■ ISSUE

Did requiring a convicted mail thief to stand in front of a post office wearing a sign that said, "I am a mail thief" violate the Sentencing Reform Act?

■ DECISION AND RATIONALE

(O'Scannlain, J.) No. The Sentencing Reform Act affords courts broad discretion in fashioning conditions of supervised release that are reasonably related to the nature and circumstances of the offense and the history and characteristics of the defendant. In determining whether a condition is appropriate, the reviewing court must ask, first, whether the sentencing judge imposed the condition for a permissible purpose, and second, whether the condition is reasonably related to that purpose. Gementera (D) contends here that the condition at issue was imposed for the impermissible purpose of humiliation. Although it is true that a sentence should not be humiliating to the defendant, here the sentencing court's written order stresses that the goal was not to humiliate for humiliation's sake, but to create a situation in which the public exposure will serve the dual purposes of rehabilitation of the defendant and protection of the public. The defendant's first argument fails.

Gementera (D) next argues that the condition imposed in his case was not related to the court's asserted purposes. He contends that shaming experiences simply are not rehabilitative. In reality, however, criminal penalties nearly always cause shame and embarrassment. The sandwich-board condition could indeed risk social stigmatization, but it was coupled here with more socially useful conditions as well—lecturing at high schools, writing letters of apology, etc.—which could actually promote the offender's social reintegration. In other words, the sandwich-board requirement was not a standalone condition intended to humiliate, but rather a part of a comprehensive plan to allow Gementera (D)—who did not appear to realize the seriousness of his crime and its impact on the victims—to repair his relationship with society. Accordingly, under the specific circumstances of this case, the sandwich-board condition was reasonably related to the legitimate objective of rehabilitation. Affirmed.

■ DISSENT

(Hawkins, J.) All that will be accomplished by the sandwich-board condition is humiliation akin to the pillories and stocks of years past. To sanction such use of sentencing power runs the risk of instilling a sense of disrespect for the criminal justice system itself. I would vacate the sentence and remand for re-sentencing, instructing the district court that public humiliation has no place in our system of justice.

Analysis:

Much of the appellate court's reasoning in this case focused on the trial court's pairing of the signboard condition with other more socially useful conditions of supervised release. The Ninth Circuit concluded that the trial court had, by combining the various conditions, successfully built a regime by which the defendant, although initially pushed away from society, would be drawn back in as a productive, rehabilitated citizen. In other words, a reasonable relationship existed between the sandwich-board condition and a socially acceptable goal because of the shaming provision's relationship to the entire package of sentencing provisions imposed by the court.

Coker v. Georgia

(*Rapist*) v. (*Community*)

433 U.S. 584, 97 S.Ct. 2861, 53 L.Ed.2d 982 (1977)

DEATH PENALTY FOUND TO BE CRUEL AND UNUSUAL PUNISHMENT FOR RAPE

■ **INSTANT FACTS** A convicted felon is sentenced to death, after escaping from prison, breaking into a house where he robbed a couple, raping and kidnapping the wife, and driving off in the couple's car.

■ **BLACK LETTER RULE** The death penalty is a grossly disproportionate and excessive punishment for the crime of raping an adult woman, prohibited by the Eighth Amendment.

■ PROCEDURAL BASIS

Certification to the Supreme Court of the United States, of a sentence of death for rape.

■ FACTS

On September 2, 1974, while serving various sentences for murder, rape, kidnapping, and aggravated assault, Coker (D) escaped from the Ware Correctional Institution near Waycross, Georgia. At 11 o'clock that night, Coker (D) entered into the house of Allen and Einita Carver through an unlocked kitchen door. After threatening the couple with a "board," Coker (D) tied Mr. Carver in the bathroom, obtained a knife from the kitchen, and took Mr. Carver's money and the keys to the family car. Brandishing the knife, Coker (D) then raped Mrs. Carver and drove away in the family car, taking Mrs. Carver with him. Soon after, Mr. Carver freed himself and notified police. Coker (D) was apprehended and Mrs. Carver was unharmed. Coker (D) was charged with escape, armed robbery, motor vehicle theft, kidnapping, and rape. The jury found Coker (D) guilty, rejecting his plea of insanity, and a sentencing hearing was conducted. The jury was instructed that it could consider as aggravating circumstances, whether the rape had been committed by a person with a prior record of conviction for a capital felony. It could also consider whether the rape had been committed in the course of committing another capital felony, namely, the armed robbery of Allen Carver. Although at least one aggravating circumstance must be found before the death penalty may be imposed, the jury was also instructed that even if aggravating circumstances were present, the death penalty need not be imposed if there were circumstances that may be considered as reducing the degree of moral culpability. The jury, finding both of the aggravating circumstances on which they were instructed, sentenced Coker (D) to death by electrocution. Both the conviction and the sentence were affirmed by the Georgia Supreme Court. Coker (D) appealed to the United States Supreme Court.

■ ISSUE

Is the death penalty for the rape of an adult woman, a grossly disproportionate punishment prohibited by the Eighth Amendment as "cruel and unusual"?

■ DECISION AND RATIONALE

(White, J.) Yes. It is now settled that the death penalty is not invariably cruel and unusual punishment within the meaning of the Eighth Amendment. However, the court firmly embraces the holdings and dicta from prior cases to the effect that the Eighth Amendment bars not only those punishments that are "barbaric," but also those that are "excessive" in relation to the crime committed. A punishment is "excessive" and unconstitutional if it either, 1) makes no measurable contribution to acceptable goals of punishment and hence, is nothing more than the purposeless and needless imposition of pain and suffering, or 2) is grossly out of proportion to the severity of the crime. Furthermore, these Eighth Amendment judgements should not be merely the subjective views of individual Justices. Attention must be given to the public attitudes concerning a particular sentence-history and precedent, legislative attitudes, and the response of juries reflected in their sentencing decisions. By 1977, even though numerous states and the federal government had authorized capital punishment for rape, Georgia was the sole jurisdiction authorizing death for rape of an adult woman. Only two other states allowed capital punishment for the rape of a child. Moreover, since 1973 Georgia juries had sentenced rapist to death only six times in 63 rape convictions. Therefore, we conclude that a sentence of death for the rape of an adult woman, is grossly disproportionate and excessive, and is therefore forbidden by the Eighth Amendment. These recent events evidencing the attitude of state legislatures and sentencing juries do not wholly determine this controversy. However, the legislative rejection of capital punishment for rape confirms our own judgment, that death is indeed a disproportionate penalty for the crime of raping and adult woman. We do not discount the seriousness of rape as a crime. Short of homicide, it is the "ultimate violation of self." Rape, without a doubt, is deserving of serious punishment, but does not compare with murder. Although it may be accompanied by another crime, rape by definition does not include the death or even the serious injury to another person. Life is over for the victim of murder. However, life for the rape victim, though it may not be nearly as happy, is not over or normally beyond repair. Although the jury found that two aggravating circumstances existed, which is necessary under Georgia law for the imposition of the death penalty, this does not change our conclusion. Coker (D) may have had prior convictions for capital offenses, but that does not change the fact that the instant crime being punished is a rape not involving the taking of life. Reversed.

■ CONCURRENCE AND DISSENT

(Powell, J.) I concur with the judgment of the court and the plurality's reasoning, supporting the view that ordinarily death is disproportionate punishment for the crime of raping an adult woman. There is no indication that Coker's (D) offense was committed with excessive brutality or that the victim sustained serious or lasting injury. However the plurality does not limit its holding to the case before us or similar cases. Instead, it holds that capital punishment is always a disproportionate penalty for rape. It is unnecessary for the plurality to write in terms so sweeping as to foreclose each of the 50 state legislatures from creating a narrowly defined substantive crime of aggravated rape punishable by death. It is not this court's function to formulate the relevant criteria that might distinguish aggravated rape from the more usual case, but perhaps a workable test would embrace the factors identified by Georgia. A test that includes the cruelty and viciousness of the offender, the manner in which the crime was committed, and the consequences suffered by the victim.

■ DISSENT

(Burger, J.) The "cruel and unusual punishment" clause does not give members of this court license to engraft their conceptions of proper public policy onto the considered legislative judgment of the states. Unlike the plurality, I would narrow the inquiry in this case to the question actually presented. Whether or not the Eighth Amendment prohibits Georgia from executing a person, who in three years raped three women, killing one and attempted to kill another, who is serving prison terms exceeding his probable lifetime, and who did not hesitate to escape at the first available opportunity. In my view, the Eighth Amendment does not prevent the state from taking an individual's "well demonstrated propensity for life-endangering behavior," into account in devising punishment. Although the plurality acknowledges the gross nature of rape, it takes too little account of the profound suffering the crime imposes upon the victims and their loved ones. The plurality's conclusion is based upon the bare fact that murder ends the life of the victim, but rape does not. However, it is not irrational, nor constitutionally impermissible for a legislature to make the penalty more severe than the crime, in order to deter wrongdoers. The test cannot have the primitive simplicity of "life for life, eye for eye, tooth for tooth." The state must be permitted to engage in a more sophisticated weighing of values in dealing with criminal activity, which consistently poses serious danger of grave bodily harm. I see no constitutional barrier in punishing by death all who engage in such activity, regardless of whether the risk comes to fruition in any particular instance.

Analysis:

The Eighth Amendment to the United States Constitution prohibits the imposition of "cruel and unusual" punishments. The Supreme Court has determined that "cruel and unusual" includes punishments that are grossly disproportionate or excessive when compared to the crime committed. Therefore, although it has been established that the death penalty itself is not "cruel and unusual," it may be a punishment grossly disproportionate to the crime of rape. In the instant case the majority argues that while rape is a serious crime, it does not deprive the victims of their lives. In taking into account other sentences given for rape, the majority concludes that the death penalty is an excessively disproportionate punishment for rape, and is therefore prohibited by the Eighth Amendment. The dissent argues that while the punishment may be disproportionate to the crime, it is not so grossly disproportionate that it is prohibited by the Eighth Amendment.

■ CASE VOCABULARY

CRUEL AND UNUSUAL PUNISHMENT: Punishment that inflicts torture, or by its excessive length or severity, is greatly disproportionate to the crime committed.

RAPE: Unlawful sexual intercourse with a non-consenting person, sometimes requiring the use of force.

Ewing v. California

(*Golf Club Thief*) v. (*Prosecutor*)

538 U.S. 11, 123 S. Ct. 1179, 155 L. Ed. 2d 108 (U.S. 2003)

SENTENCE OF 25 YEARS TO LIFE IS NOT GROSSLY DISPROPORTIONATE TO CRIME OF GRAND THEFT UNDER A STATE'S THREE STRIKES LAW

■ **INSTANT FACTS** The defendant, convicted of shoplifting three golf clubs, is given a sentence of 25 years to life under California's three strikes law.

■ **BLACK LETTER RULE** The Eighth Amendment does not require strict proportionality between the crime and sentence, but rather, it only prohibits extreme sentences that are grossly disproportionate to the crime.

■ PROCEDURAL BASIS

United States Supreme Court granted certiorari to review Ewing's (D) life sentence with no chance of parole for 25 years for stealing golf clubs.

■ FACTS

On March 12, 2000, while on parole from a 9–year prison term, Gary Ewing (D) left the pro shop at the El Seguando Golf Course with three golf clubs, priced at $399 each, concealed in his pants leg. A shop employee, noticing Ewing (D) limping to the door, alerted the police and the police arrested Ewing (D) in the parking lot. Prior to the theft of the golf clubs, Ewing (D) had already been convicted of numerous other crimes. In 1984, at the age of 22, Ewing (D) pled guilty to theft. In 1988, he was convicted of felony grand theft auto, which was later reduced to a misdemeanor, and Ewing (D) was allowed to withdraw his guilty plea. In 1990, he was convicted of petty theft and theft. In January 1993, Ewing (D) was convicted of burglary. In February 1993, Ewing (D) was convicted of possessing drug paraphernalia. In July 1993, he was convicted of appropriating lost property. In September 1993, he was convicted of unlawfully possessing a firearm and trespassing. In December 1993, he was arrested for trespassing on the grounds of a Long Beach apartment complex where he had committed a series of burglaries over the preceding few months. A jury convicted Ewing (D) of first-degree robbery and three counts of residential burglary. He was sentenced to nine years and eight months in prison. Ewing (D) was paroled in 1999. Ten months later, Ewing (D) stole the golf clubs involved in this case. He was convicted of one count of felony grand theft of personal property in excess of $400. In sentencing Ewing (D), the court found that Ewing (D) had been convicted previously of four serious or violent felonies based upon the three residential burglaries and the first-degree robbery in the Long Beach apartment complex. Ewing (D) was sentenced under California's three strikes law to 25 years to life. He appeals the sentence on the grounds that it is grossly disproportionate to the crime committed.

■ ISSUE

Does the Eighth Amendment, which prohibits cruel and unusual punishment, bar a State from sentencing a repeat felon to a prison term of 25 years to life under the State's three strikes law?

■ DECISION AND RATIONALE

(O'Connor, J.) No. The sentence of 25 years to life in prison, imposed for the offense of felony grand theft under California's three strikes law, is not grossly disproportionate to the crime committed and therefore does not violate the Eighth Amendment's prohibition on cruel and unusual punishment. The Eighth Amendment contains a narrow proportionality principle that applies to non-death penalty sentences. This principle prohibits sentences that are so disproportionate to the crime committed as to constitute cruel and unusual punishment. In *Rummel v. Estelle* (*Rummel*), we noted that, outside the realm of death penalty cases, successful proportionality challenges have been quite rare. In *Rummel*, we concluded that it did not violate the Eighth Amendment to sentence a three-time offender to life in prison with the possibility of parole. However, three years later, we set aside a sentence to life imprisonment, without the possibility of parole, in *Solem v. Helm* (*Solem*). Eight years later, in *Harmelin v. Michigan*, we upheld a mandatory life sentence without the possibility of parole for a first-time offender convicted of possessing 672 grams of cocaine. In *Harmelin*, this Court could not agree on why the defendant's proportionality argument failed. In his concurring opinion, however, Justice Kennedy identified the following four principles to guide proportionality review: (1) the primacy of the legislature, (2) the variety of legitimate penological schemes, (3) the nature of our federal system, and (4) the requirement that proportionality review be guided by objective factors. Taking into account all of these principles, the Eighth Amendment does not require strict proportionality between the crime and sentence, but rather, it only prohibits extreme sentences that are grossly disproportionate to the crime. These principles guide our resolution of this present case. State legislatures enacted three strikes laws to target the class of offenders who posed the greatest threat to public safety: career criminals. California's Legislature made a deliberate policy choice that individuals who have repeatedly been convicted of serious or violent crimes must be isolated from society in order to protect the public safety. Nothing in the Eighth Amendment prohibits California's policy choice to address recidivism, which is a serious public safety concern in California. California also acted in the interest of deterring crime. It is not this Court's job to second-guess those policy concerns. We find that the State of California has a reasonable basis for believing that enhanced sentences for habitual felons substantially advance the goals of its criminal justice system. In this light, we evaluate Ewing's (D) claim that his sentence of 25 years to life is unconstitutionally disproportionate to his offense of shoplifting three golf clubs. When weighing the gravity of his offense, we look not only to the current felony, but also to Ewing's (D) long history of recidivism. In imposing a sentence under the three strikes law, the State's interest is not just in assigning appropriate punishment for the current offense, but in dealing in a harsher manner with those repeat offenders, like Ewing (D), who have shown themselves to be incapable of conforming to the norms of society. Furthermore, this was not a matter of merely stealing three golf clubs, but a grand theft for stealing nearly $1,200 worth of merchandise after previous convictions for at least two violent or serious felonies. We hold that Ewing's (D) sentence of 25 years to life in prison is not so grossly disproportionate to the crime committed as to constitute cruel and unusual punishment. Affirmed.

■ CONCURRENCE

(Scalia, J.) I do not agree that the Eighth Amendment contains a narrow proportionality principle. Moreover, this case demonstrates that, even if it did, such a principle cannot be intelligently applied. Proportionality is the notion that the punishment should fit the crime and it is a notion tied to the penological goal of retribution. Once the penological goals move towards deterrence and rehabilitation, it becomes most difficult to apply the concept of proportionality. Because the Constitution does not mandate any one penological theory, a sentence may have a variety of justifications. Given the variety of justifications, it no longer makes sense to merely compare the gravity of an offense to the harshness of the penalty. Thus, the plurality must go one step further, analyzing whether Ewing's (D) sentence was justified by the State's other goals, such as incapacitating and deterring recidivist felons. Indeed, while I agree that Ewing's (D) sentence is justified, it is a mystery to me why this has anything to do with the principle of proportionality.

■ CONCURRENCE

(Thomas, J.) I concur in the judgment. In my view, the Cruel and Unusual punishment clause of the Eighth Amendment does not contain a proportionality principle.

■ DISSENT

(Breyer, J.) We dissent in this case because we believe that this is one of those "rare" cases referred to by the plurality, where this Court can say with reasonable confidence that the punishment is "grossly disproportionate" to the crime. In making this determination, we look for guidance to this Court's most recent sentencing decisions that deal with recidivists, *Rummel* and *Solem*. Ewing's (D) claim is stronger than the claim presented in *Rummel*, but weaker than the claim presented in *Solem*. In comparing these sentences, it is helpful to look at three characteristics: (1) the length of the prison term, (2) the sentence-triggering conduct, and (3) the offender's criminal history. The third factor cannot explain the difference between the outcome of *Rummel* and *Solem* because in *Solem*, where the sentence was found to be too long, the prior record was actually worse than it was in *Rummel*, where the sentence was upheld. Likewise, the second factor, the triggering conduct, cannot explain the difference because the monetary loss involved in both crimes was about the same. The only remaining factor that can explain why the sentence in *Rummel* was held constitutional and the sentence in *Solem* was struck down, is the length of the prison term when measured in "real time" (the length of time the offender is likely to actually spend in prison). Here, we also look to the length of the prison term in making our determination as to whether Ewing's (D) sentence is grossly disproportionate to his crime. Ewing's (D) sentence of 25 years to life is less than the life sentence struck down in *Solem*. It is, however, more than twice as long as the sentence at issue in *Rummel*, which, in real terms, amounted to at least 10 or 12 years in prison. In the present case, Ewing's (D) sentence is long enough to consume the productive remainder of his life and is certainly long enough to raise substantial concerns as to its constitutionality. Indeed, while Ewing's (D) sentence is one of the most severe punishments available for a recidivist, his sentence-triggering behavior ranks at the bottom of the criminal conduct scale. It is useful to look at how other jurisdictions would punish the same conduct in determining whether Ewing's (D) punishment is grossly disproportionate. Notably, under the federal Sentencing Guidelines, a recidivist, such as Ewing (D), would normally receive a sentence not exceeding 18 months in prison. Moreover, the law in 33 other jurisdictions would make it legally impossible for an Ewing-type offender to serve more than 10 years in prison, more than 15 years in 4 other States, and more than 20 years in 4 additional States. Outside of the California three strikes context, Ewing's (D) sentence is virtually unique in its harshness. Finally, in making our proportionality review, we must look at whether special criminal justice policy concerns in California might justify what otherwise might seem a disproportionately harsh punishment. California's statutory reasoning for the three strikes law is to reduce serious and violent crimes. Serious and violent crimes are defined under the statute as including crimes against the person, crimes that create danger of physical harm, and drug crimes. The statute does not make reference to even the more serious crimes against property. In our view, California's three strikes law does not contain any special criminal justice needs sufficient to justify this grossly disproportional sentence.

Analysis:

In this case, only a bare majority of the Court upholds the constitutionality of this sentence, based on differing rationales. Only two members of the Court join with O'Connor in her plurality opinion, while four members of the Court join together in the dissenting opinion. Thus, it requires the two concurring opinions of Justice Scalia and Justice Thomas to make up the plurality opinion (of five votes), which upholds Ewing's (D) sentence. Justice Scalia makes it clear in his concurrence, however, that he does not believe that the proportionality principle can be intelligently applied. Previously, in *Harmelin*, Justice Scalia advocated limiting the need for determining proportionality to those cases where the death penalty was involved. Justice Thomas concurs only in the judgment of this case because he believes that the Eighth Amendment does not contain a proportionality principle.

■ CASE VOCABULARY

RECIDIVISM: A chronic relapse into crime; repeatedly offending.

RETRIBUTION: Form of punishment where goal is repayment, as opposed to deterrence or rehabilitation.

THREE STRIKES LAW: These laws vary from State to State, but they share the common goal of protecting the public by providing longer sentences for repeat felons. Under California law, when a defendant has been convicted of two or more serious or violent felonies, she must receive an indeterminate term of life imprisonment.

WOBBLER: Certain offenses, under California law, that may be classified as either felonies or misdemeanors. While some wobblers become felonies based on a defendant's prior record, other crimes, such as grand theft, are wobblers regardless of a defendant's prior record. Wobblers trigger the three strikes law when they are treated as felonies.

CHAPTER THREE

Modern Role of Criminal Statutes

Commonwealth v. Mochan

Instant Facts: The trial court convicted Mr. Mochan (D) for a common law misdemeanor not codified expressly as a statutory offense for telephoning Mrs. Zivkovich several time per week and making lewd and obscene comments to her.

Black Letter Rule: When the conduct alleged is not prohibited expressly by criminal statute, a violation of the legality principle does not exist if a statutory provision permits punishment of common law offenses.

Keeler v. Superior Court

Instant Facts: Mr. Keeler (D) allegedly murdered an unborn but viable fetus by kicking his pregnant wife in the stomach.

Black Letter Rule: There is a violation of the Due Process Clause when a court construes a criminal statute contrary to the legislative intent and applies its expanded definition of the statute retroactively to a person's conduct.

In re Banks

Instant Facts: Banks (D) was charged with violating a Peeping Tom statute.

Black Letter Rule: Prior judicial interpretation of the terms of a statute challenged for unconstitutional vagueness can vitiate the challenge.

City of Chicago v. Morales

Instant Facts: Chicago's (P) anti-loitering ordinance was challenged as unconstitutionally vague because it failed to give adequate notice of what conduct it prohibited and gave police too much discretion.

Black Letter Rule: To meet the requirements of the Due Process Clause and thus survive invalidation due to vagueness, a criminal law must provide sufficiently specific limits on the enforcement discretion of the police and sufficient notice to the public of what conduct is prohibited.

United States v. Foster

Instant facts: Foster (D), a drug trafficker, was convicted of carrying a firearm in relation to a drug trafficking crime.

Black Letter Rule: A simple English word such as carry can require statutory interpretation to ascertain legislative intent.

Commonwealth v. Mochan

(*People of Pennsylvania*) v. (*Man Suggesting Sodomy to a Married Woman that Is Not His Wife*)
177 Pa. Super. 454, 110 A.2d 788 (1955)

SUPERIOR COURT OF PENNSYLVANIA AFFIRMS CONVICTIONS FOR COMMON LAW OFFENSE NOT CODIFIED IN CRIMINAL CODE

■ **INSTANT FACTS** The trial court convicted Mr. Mochan (D) for a common law misdemeanor not codified expressly as a statutory offense for telephoning Mrs. Zivkovich several time per week and making lewd and obscene comments to her.

■ **BLACK LETTER RULE** When the conduct alleged is not prohibited expressly by criminal statute, a violation of the legality principle does not exist if a statutory provision permits punishment of common law offenses.

■ PROCEDURAL BASIS

Appeal from misdemeanor conviction for lewd and obscene conduct not codified in criminal statute but classified as a misdemeanor at common law.

■ FACTS

The People of Pennsylvania (P) indicted Mr. Mochan (D) for intending to debauch, corrupt, embarrass, and vilify Mrs. Zivkovich, a married woman with an outstanding character in the community. Mr. Mochan (D) was a stranger to Mrs. Zivkovich. Several times during each week, Mr. Mochan (D) telephoned Mrs. Zivkovich and made lewd, immoral, and obscene remarks to her. His comments included suggestions of intercourse and sodomy with Mrs. Zivkovich. The Pennsylvania trial court convicted Mr. Mochan for his conduct, and he appealed alleging that his conduct was neither punishable pursuant to statutory or common law.

■ ISSUE

When the conduct alleged is not prohibited expressly by a criminal statute, may the conduct nevertheless be found to be illegal if a criminal statutory provision permits punishment of common law offenses?

■ DECISION AND RATIONALE

(Hirt, J.) No. When the conduct alleged is not prohibited expressly by a criminal statute, conduct may nevertheless be found to be illegal if a criminal statutory provision permits punishment of common law offenses. Mr. Mochan (D) received a trial before a judge. The trial court convicted him of intending to debauch, corrupt, harass, embarrass, and vilify Mrs. Zivkovich, because he telephoned her numerous times. During the telephone conversations, Mr. Mochan (D) made lewd and obscene statements that included suggesting that Mrs. Zivkovich engage in adultery and sodomy. Case precedent that decides whether Mr. Mochan's (D) conduct is criminal does not exist. Notwithstanding, Section 1101 of the Pennsylvania Penal code of 1939 permits punishment of common law offenses. The controlling principles of this court state that the common law is sufficient to punish as a misdemeanor acts that injure or intend to injure the public, affect public morality, and obstruct or pervert public justice. Additionally, conduct that openly outrages decency and is injurious to public morals is a misdemeanor at common law. If conduct is scandalous and affects the morals or health of the community, it is indictable at common law. Even to maliciously vilify the Christian religion is an indictable offense pursuant to the common law. Precedent sustains that an endeavor to persuade a married women to commit adultery is not indictable under the common law of Pennsylvania. However, Mr. Mochan's (D) conduct exceeds mere oral solicitation to commit adultery. His statements, accompanied by lewd, immoral, and filthy language, suggested sodomy. Therefore, his conduct exceeds solicitation of adultery. Not only were his statements injurious to Mrs. Zivkovich, they were potentially injurious to members of the public which include telephone operators, individuals who share Mr. Mochan's (D) four-party telephone line, and two persons in Mrs. Zivkovich's household who heard Mr. Mochan's (D) statements. Mr. Mochan's conduct establishes a common law misdemeanor. Judgment affirmed.

■ DISSENT

(Woodside, J.) The Pennsylvania Legislature determines the conduct that injures or tends to injure the public, because one of its most important functions is to determine the conduct that the State will punish. The majority's delegation to itself the power to apply general principles to conduct that it finds offensive or injurious to the public vitiates the constitutional power of the legislature. The common law is a part of the law of Pennsylvania, and Pennsylvania may punish conduct that violates it. Notwithstanding, the legislature decides the acts that are punishable, even acts that are an offense under the common law. Mr. Mochan's (D) conduct is reprehensible. Nonetheless, it is not conduct punishable under a law of Pennsylvania, as the majority failed to cite such a law.

Analysis:

Conduct is not punishable unless the law defines it as criminal before it occurs. Further, the Due Process Clause of the Fifth Amendment, applicable to the states through the Fourteenth Amendment, prohibits courts from creating offenses by enlarging statutes. The Due Process Clause requires statutory clarity. The clause prohibits conviction and punishment of persons pursuant to a statute that is vague in the instant case, Section 1101 of the Pennsylvania Penal Code authorizes punishing common law offenses that are not codified expressly in the penal code. The Superior Court of Pennsylvania affirms Mr. Mochan's (D) conviction for solicitation of sodomy and filthy language while acknowledging that case law precedent for its decision does not exist. This situation presents perplexing questions. Since the Pennsylvania Legislature did not define expressly Mr. Mochan's (D) conduct as criminal and the Pennsylvania courts had not previously found his conduct to be criminal, was Mr. Mochan (D) convicted for conduct that lacks a criminal definition in violation of the legality principle?

■ CASE VOCABULARY

NULLEM CRIMEN SINE LEGE; NULLA POENA SINE LEGE: A Latin phrase that states no crime without pre-existent law and no punishment without pre-existent law.

Keeler v. Superior Court

(*Murderer of Unborn Fetus*) v. (*Court Alleged to Lack Jurisdiction Over the Murder Charge*)
2 Cal. 3d 619, 87 Cal. Rptr. 481, 470 P.2d 617 (1970)

SUPREME COURT OF CALIFORNIA FINDS THAT UNBORN BUT VIABLE FETUS IS NOT A HUMAN BEING

■ **INSTANT FACTS** Mr. Keeler (D) allegedly murdered an unborn but viable fetus by kicking his pregnant wife in the stomach.

■ **BLACK LETTER RULE** There is a violation of the Due Process Clause when a court construes a criminal statute contrary to the legislative intent and applies its expanded definition of the statute retroactively to a person's conduct.

■ PROCEDURAL BASIS

A writ of prohibition to arrest murder proceedings.

■ FACTS

Mrs. Keeler became pregnant by a man who was not her husband before receiving a divorce from Mr. Keeler (D). After Mr. Keeler (D) learned of the pregnancy, he met Mrs. Keeler while she was driving down a mountain road, blocked the road with his car, and impeded Mrs. Keeler's progress. He then walked over to Mrs. Keeler's car and confronted her about the pregnancy. When Mrs. Keeler did not respond, he assisted her out of her car. Mr. Keeler (D) then looked at Mrs. Keeler's stomach and became extremely upset. He pushed her against the car, shoved his knee into her abdomen, and struck her in the face. The blow to Mrs. Keeler's abdomen caused extensive bruising of the abdomen wall. Medical personnel performed a Caesarian section on Mrs. Keeler. They discovered that the head of the fetus was severely fractured and delivered it stillborn. A pathologist opined that the death was immediate and caused by the skull fracture. He also opined that the injury could have been the result of Mr. Keeler (D) shoving his knee into Mrs. Keeler's stomach. Mrs. Keeler's obstetrician provided evidence that the fetus had developed to a stage of viability prior to its death. The district attorney filed an information that charged Mr. Keeler (D) with murder of the viable but unborn fetus and infliction of traumatic injury and assault upon his wife. Mr. Keeler (D) then filed a writ of prohibition to arrest the murder proceeding against him, and the Supreme Court of California granted review.

■ ISSUE

Is there is a violation of the Due Process Clause when a court construes a criminal statute contrary to the legislative intent and applies its expanded definition of the statute retroactively to a person's conduct?

■ DECISION AND RATIONALE

(Mosk, J.) Yes. There is a violation of the Due Process Clause when a court construes a criminal statute contrary to the legislative intent and applies its expanded definition of the statute retroactively to a person's conduct. Section 187 of California's Penal Code defines murder as the unlawful killing of a human being with malice aforethought. The legislature of 1872 enacted section 187. It took the language for this section from an 1850 enactment. An important question is whether the fetus that Mr. Keeler (D) is alleged to have murdered is a human being under California law. The inquiry begins by examining the intent of the 1850 legislature. This court presumes that the legislature was familiar with the common law in 1850. It further presumes that a legislature intends to continue common law rules in statutory form when it uses common law language in its enactments. Pursuant to the common law of 1850, a child must be born alive to support a charge of murder. Additionally, an infant could not be the subject of homicide at common law unless it had been born alive. The legislature of 1850 used common law language to define murder as the unlawful killing of a human being, and the common law at that time required a person to be born alive to support a charge of murder. Therefore, the legislature of 1850 intended that the term *human being* refer to a person that is born alive. We further find that there is nothing in the legislative history that demonstrates the legislature of 1872 had a different intention when in enacted section 187. It is the policy of California to construe a penal statute as favorably to the defendant as its language and the circumstances of its application permit. Since Mr. Keeler (D) is entitled to the benefit of reasonable doubt as to the true interpretation of section 187, we hold, for the aforementioned reasons, that the legislature did not intend to include the killing of an unborn fetus under the purview of section 187. The People of California (P) argue that science now facilitates the survival of a viable fetus born prematurely. They then conclude that this fact supports the finding that the killing of such a fetus is punishable under section 187. Their argument is unpersuasive. First, the authority to define punishable crimes rest entirely with the legislature. While a court may construe a statute according to a fair import of its terms to promote justice, it lacks authority to create offenses by enlarging a statute. The fair import of the terms in section 187 compels this court to reject enlarging the statute by construing its terms to cover an unborn but viable fetus. Second, even if we enlarge the statute to cover an unborn but viable fetus, the enlargement would not be applicable to Mr. Keeler (D) because the Due Process Clause guarantees him fair notice of punishable acts. California case law does not hold that killing an unborn but viable fetus supports a charge of murder, nor does the case law of our sister states. To apply a new definition of section 187 to Mr. Keeler (D) is not fair notice; it is an application without any notice. The Ex Post Facto Clause's prohibition against retroactive penal legislation supports this reasoning. The People's (P) suggested enlargement as applied to Mr. Keeler (D) violates the Due Process Clause. Therefore, this court refuses to engage in such unconstitutional folly.

■ DISSENT

(Burke, J.) The majority incorrectly suggests that it must confine its reasoning to common law concepts and the common law definition of murder. The California Penal Code defines homicide as the unlawful killing of a human being. The interpretation of the term human being need not remain static or fixed in time. The duty of this court is to render a fair and reasonable interpretation of the term in accordance with present conditions to promote justice and carry out the evident purpose of the legislature when enacting section 187. Human existence is a spectrum that stretches from birth to death. Damaging a corpse is not homicide, because a corpse is not a human being. Nonetheless, medical life revival, restoration, and resuscitation advancements have modified society's understanding of what constitutes a corpse. If the majority would not ignore these advancements nor exonerate a killer of an apparently drowned child simply because the child would have been considered dead in 1850, why does it ignore medical advances that promote the survivability of a fetus? In this case, the issue before the court should have been determined with medical testimony about the survivability of the fetus prior to Mr. Keeler's (D) conduct. The majority states its lack of authority to create new offenses, however, murder is not a new offense. The legislature used the broad term human being and directed the courts to construe the term according to its fair import to promote justice. Do we serve justice by excluding an unborn viable fetus from the definition of a human being given the present conditions of our time? Further, Mr. Keeler (D) knew or should have known that his conduct could cause a homicide. Therefore, contrary to the majority, the potential for a Due Process Clause violation for lack of fair notice that his conduct could constitute a murder does not exist.

Analysis:

Even though most states have abolished common law offenses, this case provides an excellent example of the importance of common law doctrine as it relates to criminal offenses. A dispositive question in this case is whether a viable but unborn fetus is a human being pursuant to California law. As courts are to interpret the law rather than create it, they must determine the intent of their legislatures when construing statutes. Courts use various resources to ascertain the intent of their legislatures, including the legislative history of an act and the circumstances surrounding its enactment, earlier statutes on the same subject, the common law as understood at the time of the act's adoption, and interpretation of the same or similar statutes. In this case, the Supreme Court of California primarily used the common law to ascertain the intent of the 1850 and 1872 legislatures. This case is of interest because of the secondary implications the ruling has on the issue of the legality of abortion. If the court had ruled that the fetus was a human being, what would this mean for a person seeking an abortion?

In re Banks

(*State of North Carolina*) v. (*Peeping Tom*)
295 N.C. 236, 244 S.E.2d 386 (1978)

SUPREME COURT OF NORTH CAROLINA UPHOLDS PEEPING TOM STATUTE EVEN THOUGH ITS LANGUAGE IS VAGUE

■ **INSTANT FACTS** Banks (D) was charged with violating a Peeping Tom statute.

■ **BLACK LETTER RULE** Prior judicial interpretation of the terms of a statute challenged for unconstitutional vagueness can vitiate the challenge.

■ PROCEDURAL BASIS

State (P) appeals of trial court ruling holding Peeping Tom statute unconstitutionally vague.

■ FACTS

The State of North Carolina (P) charged Mr. Banks (D) with violating its Peeping Tom statute. The statute states that any person who secretly peeps into a room occupied by a female person shall be guilty of a misdemeanor. The trial court found the statute to be unconstitutionally vague, and the State (P) appealed its ruling.

■ ISSUE

Can prior judicial interpretation of the terms of a statute challenged for unconstitutional vagueness vitiate the challenge?

■ DECISION AND RATIONALE

(Moore J.) Yes. Prior judicial interpretation of the terms of a statute challenged for unconstitutional vagueness can vitiate the challenge. Pursuant to the principle of statutory clarity, a criminal statute must not be so vague that people of common intelligence must necessarily guess at its meaning and differ as to its application. Conviction and punishment under statutes that lack clarity are a violation of the Due Process Clause. The definiteness requirement insures fair notice of prohibited conduct and a reasonably ascertainable standard of guilt. Mr. Banks (D) alleges that the intended scope of the State's (P) Peeping Tom statute is indefinite and reasonable persons could differ as to its application. He argues that the statute, if taken literally, prohibits conduct the State (P) did not intend to punish. Essentially, he argues that the statute cannot mean that which it states. In North Carolina, if a statute is susceptible to a constitutional and an unconstitutional interpretation, this court should adopt the interpretation that yields a finding of constitutionality. However, courts must strictly construe a criminal statute with regard to the conduct it is suppose to suppress. The intent of the legislature is controlling. Where a statute is ambiguous, courts resort to judicial construction to ascertain the legislative intent. Means and indicia courts use to determine legislative intent include the purposes appearing from a statute taken as a whole, a statutes phraseology and words, the law as it prevailed before the statute, the remedy and the harm to be remedied, the end to be accomplished, statutes in pari materia, and a statute's preamble or title. Legislative history of an act and the circumstances surrounding its enactment, earlier statutes on the subject, the common law at the time of the enactment and previous interpretations of the same or similar statutes provide other indicia to determine legislative intent. In *Wainwright v. Stone* [a case upholding Florida's Crime Against Nature statute against a challenge of vagueness] the United States Supreme Court stated that the judgment of federal courts as to the vagueness of a state statute must be made in the light of prior state constructions of the statute. This language suggests that judging a statute challenged on the ground of unconstitutional vagueness in light of its common law meaning, its statutory history, or prior judicial interpretation of its particular terms is an appropriate course of action. North Carolina derived its Peeping Tom statute from the common law crimes of nuisance and eavesdropping. The commonly understood meaning of Peeping Tom in this country is a person who sneaks up to a window and peeps for the purpose of spying and invading the privacy of others. North Carolina's Peeping Tom statute makes it a crime to peep secretly. In a prior case, this court dealt with the Peeping Tom statute and conduct within the purview of the common law usage of the term Peeping Tom. It interpreted the word peep in a manner that conveys the idea of a Peeping Tom. The court stated that peep means to look cautiously or slyly—as if through a crevice—from chinks and knotholes. In another case, it stated that the word secretly, as used in the Peeping Tom statute, conveys the idea of spying upon another with the intention of invading a female's privacy. These judicial interpretations give the language of the statute meaning. They sufficiently inform a person of ordinary intelligence, with reasonable precision, that the Peeping Tom statute prohibits wrongful spying into a room inhabited by a female with the intent of violating her legitimate expectation of privacy. Therefore, the statute is not unconstitutionally vague as to violate the state constitution or the Due Process Clause. Additionally, Mr. Banks (D) challenges the statute on the ground that it is overbroad because it prohibits innocent conduct. In *Zwickler v. Koota*, the United States Supreme Court stated that the doctrine of overbreadth has not and will not be invoked when a limited construction has been or could be placed on a challenged statute. In *Lemon v. State* [a case upholding Georgia's Peeping Tom Statute], the Supreme Court of Georgia stated that Georgia's statute was narrowed by the requirement of wrongful intent. North Carolina's Peeping Tom statute is narrowed by the judicial interpretation requiring that the act condemned must be a spying for the wrongful purpose of invading the privacy of a female occupant of a room. The interpretation does not condemn innocent conduct. The statute is not unconstitutionally overbroad.

Analysis:

This case illustrates how prior judicial interpretation of the terms in a statute facing constitutional attack can save the statute. If a statute lacks clarity, it violates the Due Process Clause because it fails to give notice of the conduct the statute intends to punish. Mr. Banks (D) challenged the Peeping Tom statute on the ground of unconstitutional vagueness. Using its prior judicial interpretations, the Supreme Court of North Carolina held that the statute is not unconstitutionally vague. The court notes that North Carolina derived its Peeping Tom statute from the common law crimes of nuisance and eavesdropping. Additionally, it notes the commonly understood meaning of the term "Peeping Tom" as a person that peeps through a window for the purpose of spying on and invading the privacy of a female occupant. It then states that in a *prior* case involving the Peeping Tom statute, the court *interpreted* the word "peep" to mean to look cautiously or slyly—as if through a crevice—out from chinks and knotholes. This meaning conveys the idea of a Peeping Tom. Addressing the meaning of the word "secretly" in the Peeping Tom statute, the Supreme Court of North Carolina states that in a prior case it indicated the word conveys the idea of spying upon a female with the intention of invading her privacy. Armed with these prior interpretations, the court finds that the statute prohibits the wrongful spying into a room upon a female with the intent of violating her legitimate expectation of privacy. Therefore, the Peeping Tom statute is not unconstitutionally overbroad.

■ CASE VOCABULARY

INDICIA: Signs, indications, or circumstances that point to the existence of a given fact as probable but not certain.

IN PARI MATERIA: A rule of statutory construction that holds that statutes that relate to the same subject matter should be read, construed, and applied together so that the legislative intention can be gathered from the whole of the enactments.

City of Chicago v. Morales

(*Anti–Loitering City*) v. (*Gang Member*)

527 U.S. 41, 119 S. Ct. 1849, 144 L.Ed. 2d 67 (1999)

THE SUPREME COURT STRIKES DOWN A CITY'S ANTI–LOITERING ORDINANCE FOR VAGUENESS

■ **INSTANT FACTS** Chicago's (P) anti-loitering ordinance was challenged as unconstitutionally vague because it failed to give adequate notice of what conduct it prohibited and gave police too much discretion.

■ **BLACK LETTER RULE** To meet the requirements of the Due Process Clause and thus survive invalidation due to vagueness, a criminal law must provide sufficiently specific limits on the enforcement discretion of the police and sufficient notice to the public of what conduct is prohibited.

■ PROCEDURAL BASIS

United States Supreme Court granted certiorari from judgment declaring City's anti-loitering ordinance unconstitutional.

■ FACTS

Due to concerns over the increase in criminal street gang activity, the Chicago City Council enacted the Gang Congregation Ordinance. This ordinance prohibits "criminal street gang members" from "loitering" with one another or with other persons in any public place. The ordinance creates a criminal offense based upon four predicates: 1) the police officer must reasonably believe that at least one of the two or more persons present in a "public place" is a "criminal street gang member;" 2) the persons must be "loitering," which the ordinance defines as "remaining in any one place with no apparent purpose;" 3) the officer must then order "all" of the persons to disperse and remove themselves "from the area;" and, 4) a person must disobey the officer's order. Whether or not a gang member, any person who disobeys the order is guilty of violating the ordinance. A violation of this ordinance is punishable by a fine of up to $500, imprisonment for not more than six months, and up to 120 hours of community service.

■ ISSUE

Should the City of Chicago's (P) criminal anti-loitering ordinance be invalidated for vagueness under the Due Process Clause?

■ DECISION AND RATIONALE

(Stevens, J.) Yes. The City of Chicago's (P) criminal anti-loitering ordinance must be invalidated for vagueness because it does not provide sufficiently specific limits on the enforcement discretion of the police or sufficient notice to the public to meet the requirements of the Due Process Clause. A criminal law may be invalidated under the vagueness doctrine on two independent grounds. First, a law must provide the kind of notice that will allow an ordinary person to understand what conduct it prohibits. Second, the law must not authorize or encourage arbitrary and discriminatory enforcement. Here, the ordinance in question prohibits loitering. While the term "loiter" may have a common and accepted meaning, the term is defined in this ordinance as,"to remain in any one place with no apparent purpose.'' At the outset, we note that it would be difficult for a person standing with a group of people in a public place to know whether he or she had an ''apparent purpose.'' Clearly, the City (P) did not intend to criminalize each instance where a citizen happens be standing in a public place in the presence of a gang member. Vagueness dooms this ordinance, not because of the normal meaning of loitering, but rather because it doesn't make clear what ''loitering,'' as defined by the ordinance, is suspect. The ordinance is not saved by the requirement that a loiterer must first fail to comply with an order to disperse before violating the ordinance. If the loitering is in fact harmless and innocent, the dispersal order in itself is an unjustified impairment of liberty. Moreover, the terms of the dispersal order raise questions concerning how long the loiterers must remain apart, how far apart they should be, and whether they are subject to arrest if they later reconvene or will they merely be given another dispersal order. For these reasons, this ordinance is vague in that it fails to provide any meaningful standard of conduct. To avoid vagueness problems, a criminal law must also establish minimal guidelines to govern law enforcement. The Chicago (P) anti-loitering ordinance contains no such guidelines. The police may order dispersal without first making any inquiry about the possible purposes of the loitering, and the ordinance applies to everyone in the City who may remain in one place with a suspected gang member, as long as their purpose is not apparent to the observing officer. In fact, the ordinance gives absolute discretion to police officers to determine which activities constitute loitering. The ''no apparent purpose'' standard is inherently subjective because its application depends on whether some purpose is ''apparent'' to the officer at the scene. We find that this ordinance is unconstitutionally vague because it affords too much discretion to the police and too little notice to the citizens who wish to use the public streets. Affirmed.

■ CONCURRENCE

(O'Connor, J.) As it has been construed by the Illinois Court, Chicago's (P) gang loitering ordinance is unconstitutionally vague. I write, however, to emphasize the narrow scope of today's holding. In spite of our holding, there remain open to Chicago (P) reasonable alternatives to combat the very real threat posed by gang activity. In my opinion, the Illinois Courts could have construed the term ''loiter'' to mean ''to remain in any one place with no apparent purpose other than to establish control over identifiable areas, to intimidate others from entering those areas, or to conceal illegal activities.'' This interpretation would avoid the vagueness problems.

Analysis:

This case illustrates the difficulty of drafting an anti-loitering ordinance that can withstand constitutional challenge for vagueness. Chicago's (P) ordinance unfortunately failed in two areas—it did not give the citizens adequate notice of what was meant by ''loitering'' and it gave the police too much discretion in enforcing the law. Indeed, the majority opinion pointed out the irony that, if enforced as dictated, the ordinance might actually exclude most gang conduct from coverage, because most gang conduct would have an ''apparent purpose,'' such as establishing dominance over territories or intimidating nonmembers. In her concurring opinion, Justice O'Connor gave the City (P) guidance as to how the ordinance might be construed so as to avoid vagueness issues. Later, the Chicago City Council redrafted the ordinance, incorporating Justice O'Connor's suggested language.

■ CASE VOCABULARY

ORDINANCE: A municipal law or regulation.

United States v. Foster

(*Drug Trafficking Law Enforcer*) v. (*Drug Trafficker With A Gun*)
133 F.3d 704 (9th Cir. 1998)

UNITED STATES COURT OF APPEALS FOR THE NINTH CIRCUIT INTERPRETS THE SIMPLE ENGLISH WORD "CARRY"

■ **INSTANT FACTS** Foster (D), a drug trafficker, was convicted of carrying a firearm in relation to a drug trafficking crime.

■ **BLACK LETTER RULE** A simple English word such as carry can require statutory interpretation to ascertain legislative intent.

■ PROCEDURAL BASIS

Appeal from conviction of carrying a firearm in relation to a drug trafficking crime.

■ FACTS

Leon Foster (D) manufactured methamphetamine. When the police became aware of his illegal activity, they pulled him over while he was driving his pickup truck and arrested him. Under his truck bed's snap-down tarp, the police found a loaded 9mm semiautomatic firearm and a bucket. A scale, plastic baggies, and handwritten notes with prices were inside the bucket. Mr. Foster was convicted of possessing methamphetamine, in violation of 21 U.S.C. § 844, and "carrying" a firearm during and in relation to a drug trafficking crime, in violation of 18 U.S.C. § 924(c)(1). Mr. Foster (D) appealed the conviction for "carrying" a firearm.

■ ISSUE

Can a simple English word such as "carry" require statutory interpretation to ascertain legislative intent?

■ DECISION AND RATIONALE

(Kozinski J.) Yes. A simple English word such as "carry" can require statutory interpretation to ascertain legislative intent. Section 924(c)(1) states that whoever during and in relation to any crime of violence or drug trafficking crime uses or *carries* a firearm shall in addition to the punishment provided for such crime of violence or drug trafficking crime, be sentenced to imprisonment for five years. The issue before this court is whether Mr. Foster (D) carried a firearm when he drove with it in his truck bed. "Carry" appears to be a simple word, but it has differing relevant uses. It may mean to transport or to arrange for the transportation of an object. It may also mean to hold an object while moving from place to place. The common understanding of the phrase "someone is carrying a firearm" is a person has a firearm on his person. In *United States v. Barber* [a case interpreting the predecessor of § 924(c)(1)], the court gave the verb "carry" a broad definition when it stated that in ordinary usage, "carry" includes transportation or arranging for transportation. In *United States v. Hernandez* [a case interpreting the word "carry" when a vehicle is not involved], the court narrowed its interpretation of the verb by stating that a person must transport a firearm on or about his person to carry it. This interpretation means that the firearm must be immediately available for use. In Black's Law Dictionary, broad and narrow definitions of the verb exist. Additionally, it defines carrying arms and weapons as to wear, bear, or carry them upon the person or in the clothing or a pocket for the purpose of use. This particular narrow definition is more relevant to the issue at hand. There are those who criticize the narrow definition when applied to a defendant who has a firearm readily assessable within the passenger compartment of a moving car rather than on his person because it seems to exonerate the defendant. The critics fail to understand that the essence of the narrow definition is the ease of accessibility of the weapon while it is in motion rather than its location on a person. Therefore, a weapon in a moving car that is within reach can be said to be carried. In *Bailey v. United States* [the leading case on § 924(c)(1)], the United States Supreme Court began its analysis of the verb "use" by considering its ordinary dictionary meaning. Faced with several different interpretations, the Court considered the verb's placement and purpose in the statute. The Court emphasized that since the statute contains two distinct terms, "uses" and "carries," the Court must define them narrowly enough that neither engulfs the other. Since a person may use a firearm without carrying it and carry a firearm without using it, the Bailey Court narrowly defined "use" as active employment. Construing the terms in pari materia, there is no basis to define "carry" broadly when "use" has a narrow definition. Considering "use" in the context within the broader statute, the Bailey Court examined its employment in § 924(d) and argued that the term should have the same meaning in § 924(c)(1). Unfortunately, "carry" does not appear elsewhere within § 924. However, the Bailey Court warned that if the term "use" is defined too broadly, it would become synonymous with "possess," a term appearing elsewhere in the statute. If "carry" is defined broadly, there is a risk that it will become synonymous with "transport", a term appearing in many places in the gun statutes. This court refuses to take this risk. Since there is minimal legislative history on "carry," it is reasonable to speculate about the purpose a prohibition on carrying a firearm during and in relation to a violent or drug trafficking crime serves. Using or carrying a firearm makes those crimes more dangerous and can lead to injury or violence. However, a gun in a bag under the tarp in a truck bed presents substantially less risk. The previous arguments suggest a narrow definition for "carry." Further, where a criminal law is ambiguous, this court is wary of imposing criminal liability for conduct that the law does not clearly prohibit. This cautiousness supports the rule of lenity. Given the narrow definition of "carry," this court finds that Mr. Foster's (D) firearm was not immediately available to him. To use the firearm, he would have to stop and exit his truck, walk to its rear, open a snap-down tarp, and unzip the bag containing the gun. He could access his gun more quickly if it was within easy hand's reach. Judgment of conviction for carrying a firearm reversed and remanded for resentencing.

■ DISSENT

(Trott, J.) Rather than attack in a straightforward and analytical way the meaning of "carry" in a context of a motor vehicle, the majority casts the proposition as a duel between two interpretations of the word. The common word "carry" takes on metaphysical proportions that require the majority to throw the rule of lenity as a life raft to sinking drug traffickers. This court decided *United States v. Barber,* a case that reaches the correct result with respect to the word "carry" in a vehicle case. Barber was arrested with a gun in a locked glove compartment, and the court decided whether the gun was "carried" under the predecessor to § 924(c)(1). That opinion states that Congress never specifically addressed the question whether the term "carries" encompasses "transport" or "possesses," but the ordinary meaning of the term embraces Barber's transportation of the weapon. In ordinary usage, the verb "carry" includes transportation or causing to be transported. This court further stated that there is nothing in the legislative history indicating that Congress intended any hyper-technical or narrow reading of the word "carries." The transportation test announced in that holding is applicable today. The word "carry" derives from a Latin word that means cart or vehicle. The majority cites *Hernandez* to support the narrow definition of "carry;" however, *Hernandez* is not on point because a vehicle was not in issue. Regarding Congress's intend purpose prohibiting carrying guns during drug trafficking crimes, it is doubtful Congress would recognize the broad versus narrow distinction as espousing its purpose. Further, the distinction gives drug traffickers the least exposure to the law's reach when they are more vulnerable to detection by law enforcement. After reading the majority's opinion, drug traffickers will delight in knowing they can carry their guns in the trunk or under the hood of their car's during and in relation to drug trafficking crimes and remain beyond the reach of § 924(c)(1).

Analysis:

Following *Bailey*'s lead, the majority, having rejected the dictionary's transportation-related meaning of "carry," favors the narrow definition of "carry" so that the word will not become synonymous with transportation. Additionally the majority examined the minimal legislative history to ascertain the intended purpose for "carry." Finding little assistance there, it reasons that a gun carried in the manner as Mr. Foster (D) carried his creates substantially less risk than carrying a gun in hand's reach. By contrast, the dissent uses the ordinary definition of the word "carry" to argue for the broad transportation definition. The dissent frames the interpretation issue in the context of a motor vehicle. Framed in this fashion, it argues for the broad transportation definition of "carry" in a straightforward and well-reasoned manner. The majority bootstraps its argument for a narrow definition on its own selection of a narrow definition from the dictionary.

■ CASE VOCABULARY

IN PARI MATERIA: A rule of statutory construction that holds that statutes that relate to the same subject matter should be read, construed, and applied together so that the legislative intention can be gathered from the whole of the enactments.

CHAPTER FOUR

Actus Reus

Martin v. State

Instant Facts: Police officers arrest an intoxicated man at his home, take him onto a highway, and arrested him for public drunkenness.

Black Letter Rule: A defendant must perform the physical act for each element of a crime that has an actus reus component.

State v. Utter

Instant Facts: Intoxicated father with an alleged conditioned response condition fatally stabs his son in the chest.

Black Letter Rule: A voluntary act requires the consent of the actor's will.

People v. Beardsley

Instant Facts: Intoxicated male fails to assist his female friend who was in a stupor from drinking alcohol and ingesting morphine.

Black Letter Rule: A person may be criminally liable if he fails to perform a legal duty and his omission causes harm.

Barber v. Superior Court

Instant Facts: Barber (D), a physician, removed Herbert (a comatose patient with little chance of recovery) from life support at his family's request.

Black Letter Rule: Removal of life support equipment from a comatose patient who is unlikely to recover is not an affirmative act, but an act of omission, that, if in accord with the patient's or surrogate's wishes, does not give rise to criminal liability.

Martin v. State

(*Intoxicated Man*) v. (*People of Alabama*)
31 Ala. App. 334, 17 So. 2d 427 (1944)

THERE MUST BE A VOLUNTARY ACT FOR EACH ELEMENT OF A CRIME THAT REQUIRES AN ACTUS REUS

■ **INSTANT FACTS** Police officers arrest an intoxicated man at his home, take him onto a highway, and arrested him for public drunkenness.

■ **BLACK LETTER RULE** A defendant must perform the physical act for each element of a crime that has an actus reus component.

■ PROCEDURAL BASIS

Appeal from conviction of being drunk in a public place and engaging in conduct manifesting drunkenness.

■ FACTS

Police officers arrested Mr. Martin (D) at his home and took him onto a public highway. While on the highway, Mr. Martin (D) used loud and profane language in a manner that suggested that he was intoxicated. Mr. Martin (D) was convicted for violating a statute that prohibited appearing in a public place in an intoxicated condition and manifesting that condition with indecent conduct or loud and profane language. Mr. Martin (D) appealed the conviction.

■ ISSUE

Must a defendant perform the physical act for each element of a crime that has an actus reus component?

■ DECISION AND RATIONALE

(Simpson, J.) Yes. A defendant must perform the physical act for each element of a crime that has an actus reus component. Mr. Martin (D) was convicted for violating a statute that provides that an individual in an intoxicated condition who appears in a public place where one or more persons are present and manifest his intoxication by boisterous or indecent conduct, or loud and profane language shall be fined upon conviction. On its face, the statute requires voluntary appearance in a public place. The State (P) cannot prove an accusation of public drunkenness by establishing that the arresting officer, while the defendant was in an intoxicated condition, involuntarily and forcibly carried him to a public place. Reversed and rendered.

Analysis:

Alabama's public drunkenness statute has two elements. First, the accused must appear in a public place. Appearance requires a voluntary physical act. Mr. Martin (D) appeared in a public place; however, he did not perform any physical act, voluntary or involuntary, that led to his appearance, since the police officers *took* him onto the public highway. Therefore, the required actus reus for this element does not exist. Second, the accused must manifest his drunken condition at the public place where he appeared. Since Mr. Martin (D) voluntarily used loud and profane language while he was on the highway in an intoxicated condition, the required actus reus for this element exists. But, a crime did not occur, because the statute requires a coincidence of voluntarily appearing in public *and* manifesting an intoxicated condition through certain conduct.

State v. Utter

(*People of Washington*) v. (*Stabber*)
4 Wash. App. 137, 479 P.2d 946 (1971)

A PERSON WHO ACTS UNCONSCIOUSLY MAY NOT HAVE THE REQUISITE ACTUS REUS

■ **INSTANT FACTS** Intoxicated father with an alleged conditioned response condition fatally stabs his son in the chest.

■ **BLACK LETTER RULE** A voluntary act requires the consent of the actor's will.

■ PROCEDURAL BASIS

Appeal from conviction of manslaughter.

■ FACTS

One afternoon, Mr. Utter's (D) son entered the apartment he shared with his father. Shortly thereafter, the son said, "Dad don't." The son, having been stab in the chest, stumbled into the hallway of the apartment building and collapsed. The son stated that his father stabbed him and then died. On the day of the incident, Mr. Utter (D) drank just under a quart of port wine during the morning hours. In the afternoon, he drank whiskey with a friend. Mr. Utter (D) remembers drinking whiskey with his friend and being in jail subsequent to his son's death, but he does not remember the intervening events. Mr. Utter (D) entered the armed services in 1942. He served as a combat infantryman and received an honorable discharge in 1946. During trial, Mr. Utter (D) introduced, through a psychiatrist, evidence on conditioned response, an act or pattern of activity occurring so rapidly and uniformly as to be an automatic response to certain stimulus. Mr. Utter (D) testified that he received jungle warfare training while he was in the armed services. He further testified that on two occasions in the 1950's he reacted violently towards people approaching him unexpectedly from the rear. The trial court ruled that conditioned response was not a defense and instructed the jury to disregard the evidence on the subject. Mr. Utter (D) was convicted of manslaughter, and he appealed.

■ ISSUE

Does a voluntary act require the consent of the actor's will?

■ DECISION AND RATIONALE

(Farris, J.) Yes. A voluntary act requires the consent of the actor's will. The major issue is whether it was error for the trial court to instruct the jury to disregard the evidence on conditioned response. The actus reus for manslaughter is homicide. The statutory definition of homicide is the killing of a human being by the act, procurement, or omission of another. Mr. Utter (D) asserts that he presented the conditioned response evidence during his trial to determine if he committed a homicide. He contends that his evidence, if believed, establishes that he did not commit a homicidal act. It is sometimes said that a crime does not exist unless a voluntary act causes harm. The phrase "voluntary act" is synonymous with the word "act." An act is a willed movement or the omission of a possible and legally required performance. A spasm is not an act. Mr. Utter (D) contends that any alleged acts he committed did not involve mental processes. Instead, they were learned physical reactions to external stimuli that operated automatically on his autonomic nervous system. Further, he contends that a person in an automatistic or unconscious state is incapable of committing a culpable homicidal act. It is important to realize that this is not a question of mental incapacity; rather, it is recognition that the law judges criminal responsibility at the level of conscious. There is authority that supports Mr. Utter's (D) contentions. Criminal liability does not attach in the absence of a voluntary act. The absence of consciousness excludes the possibility of a voluntary act as well as any specific mental state. Without the consent of the will, human actions are not culpable. If there is no will to commit an offense, is there a just reason for a party to receive the punishment designated for the offense? An act committed while a person is unconscious is not really an act. Rather, it is a physical event or occurrence for which there can be no criminal liability. Notwithstanding, unconsciousness does not, in all cases, provide a defense to a crime. Voluntary intoxication that induces unconsciousness is not a complete defense. In a case where there is evidence that the accused has consumed alcohol or drugs, a trial court should give a cautionary instruction with respect to voluntarily induced unconsciousness. Whether, Mr. Utter (D) was in an unconscious or automatistic state at the time he allegedly committed criminal acts is a question of fact. However, the evidence presented at trial was insufficient to present this issue to the jury.

Analysis:

Actus reus is a voluntary act that causes harm. Mr. Utter stabbed his son and his son died. The harm is the death of the son. The issue in this case is whether Mr. Utter's (D) stabbing of his son was a mere physical event or an act. If Mr. Utter (D) was conscious at the time of the fatal stabbing, there was a voluntary act because there was a coincidence of physical movement and an exercise of the will; otherwise, there is no act. No act, no criminal liability. Assume Mr. Utter (D) does not suffer from conditioned response and someone drugs him without his consent. Now, assume that the effect of the drug makes him unconscious (i.e., no consent of the will). Further, assume that in this unconscious state he fatally stabs his son. Did Mr. Utter (D) commit a homicide? No. Now, make the same assumptions, except rather than someone drugging Mr. Utter (D), he voluntarily ingests the drugs. Is there a homicide? What answer does the opinion suggest?

People v. Beardsley

(*People of Michigan*) v. (*Non-actor*)
150 Mich. 206, 113 N.W. 1128 (1907)

MERE MORAL OBLIGATIONS TO ACT DO NOT CREATE LEGAL DUTIES TO ACT

■ **INSTANT FACTS** Intoxicated male fails to assist his female friend who was in a stupor from drinking alcohol and ingesting morphine.

■ **BLACK LETTER RULE** A person may be criminally liable if he fails to perform a legal duty and his omission causes harm.

■ PROCEDURAL BASIS

Appeal from conviction of manslaughter.

■ FACTS

Mr. Beardsley (D) was a married man who lived in a tenant house. Ms. Burns was his close female friend. Frequently, Mr. Beardsley (D) and Ms. Burns drank together, and on two occasions, they had met at a house that facilitates rendezvous for lovers. Ms. Burns met Mr. Beardsley (D) at his residence on a Saturday evening while Mr. Beardsley's (D) wife was out of town. The couple immediately began to drink alcohol together. Except for a portion of Sunday afternoon when Mr. Beardsley (D) was at work, the couple continually drank together until Monday. A young man that worked at Mr. Beardsley (D) place of employment delivered alcohol to Mr. Beardsley's (D) residence. On Monday afternoon, the young man went to Mr. Beardsley's (D) home to determine if he required anything. While there, Mr. Beardsley (D) said they must fix up the rooms and Ms. Burns could not be found at his residence by his wife who would return at any time. Ms. Burns then sent the young man to the drug store to purchase some camphor and morphine tablets. When the young man returned with the requested items, Ms. Burns concealed the morphine tables from Mr. Beardsley (D). Upon returning from a room, Mr. Beardsley (D) and the young man noticed that she was putting morphine tablets in her mouth. Mr. Beardsley (D) struck the box of morphine tablets from her hand and crushed some of the tablets that fell on the floor with his foot. Ms. Burns picked up two of the tablets and swallowed them. Her total consumption of morphine was approximately three or four grains. An hour later, Ms. Burns was in a stupor and failed to respond when Mr. Beardsley (D) spoke to her. Mr. Beardsley (D) telephoned the young man and asked him to return to his home and help him move Ms. Burns to a tenant's basement room. The young man returned and proceeded to take Ms. Burns to the basement room. Mr. Beardsley (D) was too intoxicated to be of any assistance. The basement tenant arrived at the house and helped the young man move Ms. Burns to his basement room. Mr. Beardsley (D) asked the tenant to look after Ms. Burns and have her leave through the back when she awoke. Between 9 and 10 o'clock that Monday evening, the tenant became alarmed about Ms. Burns's condition. He called the city marshal and a doctor. The marshal and doctor examined Ms. Burns and determined that she was dead. Mr. Beardsley (D) was convicted of manslaughter. The prosecution's theory of the case was Mr. Beardsley (D) omitted to perform his duty to care for and protect Ms. Burns. Mr. Beardsley (D) appealed his conviction.

■ ISSUE

May a person be criminally liable if he fails to perform a legal duty and his omission causes harm?

■ DECISION AND RATIONALE

(McAlvay, J.) Yes. A person may be criminally liable if he fails to perform a legal duty and his omission causes harm. The People (P) do not contend that Mr. Beardsley (D) was an active agent of Ms. Burns's death. Instead, the contention is Mr. Beardsley (D) owed Ms. Burns a duty that he failed to perform, thereby causing Ms. Burns's death. Under some circumstances, a person is chargeable with manslaughter if he omits to perform a duty that he owes to another and the omission results in the death of that person. However, the duty neglected must be a legal duty rather than a mere moral obligation. Further, it must be a duty imposed by law or contract, and the omission to perform the duty must be an immediate and direct cause of death. The authorities are in harmony as to the relationships that must exist between the parties to create a legal duty, the omission of which establishes legal responsibility. These relationships include, but are not limited to, husband and wife, parent and child, and master and seaman. If a person in such a relationship knows the other party to the relationship is in peril of life and willfully or negligently fails to take reasonable steps to rescue the party, the person is guilty of manslaughter if his omission to act is the cause of death. Therefore, an individual who from domestic relationship, public duty, voluntary choice, or otherwise has the custody and care of a person who is in a helpless condition must execute his responsibilities with proper diligence or be found guilty of manslaughter if his culpable negligence causes the death of the helpless person. Given the aforementioned principles, consideration of mere moral obligation cannot influence the outcome of the case at bar. The questions are whether Mr. Beardsley (D) owed a duty to Ms. Burns at the time of her death, and if so, whether his omission to perform this duty caused her death. The facts of this case disclose that Ms. Burns was a woman past 30 years of age. She had married twice and was accustomed to visiting saloons and using intoxicants. She had been intimate with Mr. Beardsley at least twice. There is no evidence or claim in the record that Ms. Burns was a victim of fraud or duress. The prosecution contends that at the time of Ms. Burns' death, Mr. Beardsley (D) stood in the shoes of her natural guardian and protector. In this capacity, it alleges that Mr. Beardsley (D) owed Ms. Burns a legal duty that he failed to perform. However, the aforementioned principles establish that a mere moral obligation does not create a legal duty. The fact that Ms. Burns was in Mr. Beardsley's (D) home does not create a legal duty as exists between a husband and wife. Mr. Beardsley had not assumed care or control over Ms. Burns. If two men became intoxicated under similar circumstances and one of them committed suicide, no one would claim that a legal duty existed that could make the other man criminally liable for omitting to make an effort to rescue his companion. The fact that Ms. Burns was a woman does not change the law. Conviction set aside, and Mr. Beardsley is ordered discharged.

Analysis:

This case demonstrates that, in certain circumstances, criminal liability may be predicated on an omission to act when there is a duty to act. The duty to act may be statutorily imposed, or it may result from a status relationship such as husband and wife, parent and child, or master and servant. In the instant case, the prosecution contended that a status relationship existed between Mr. Beardsley (D) and Ms. Burns. It alleged that Mr. Beardsley (D) had the status of a natural guardian and protector. The Supreme Court of Michigan rejected this contention because it was not supported by precedent. A duty to act may also arise from an express or implied contract. For example, a doctor has a duty to provide ordinary medical care to his patient. Additionally, once an individual offers assistance to a person in peril, he has a duty to continue to provide aid if a failure to do so places the person in a worse condition.

Barber v. Superior Court

(*Physician*) v. (*Trial Court*)
147 Cal.App.3d 1006, 195 Cal.Rptr. 484 (1983)

THERE IS A DISTINCTION BETWEEN REMOVAL OF LIFE SUPPORT FROM A COMATOSE PATIENT (WHICH IS NOT A CRIME) AND EUTHANASIA

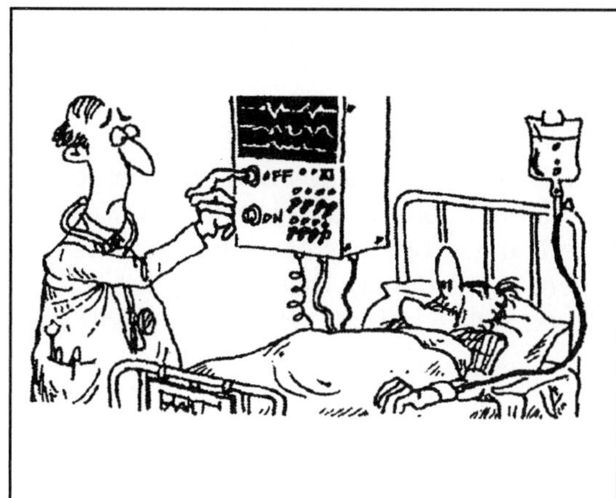

■ **INSTANT FACTS** Barber (D), a physician, removed Herbert (a comatose patient with little chance of recovery) from life support at his family's request.

■ **BLACK LETTER RULE** Removal of life support equipment from a comatose patient who is unlikely to recover is not an affirmative act, but an act of omission, that, if in accord with the patient's or surrogate's wishes, does not give rise to criminal liability.

■ PROCEDURAL BASIS

Appeal from reinstatement of complaint for murder and conspiracy to commit murder.

■ FACTS

Shortly after surgery, Clarence Herbert suffered a cardiac arrest. He was revived and placed on life support. After a few days, Barber (D) and other physicians determined that Herbert was in a deep coma from which he would probably not recover. Herbert had severe brain damage, leaving him in a vegetative state, although there remained some brain activity. Barber (D), Herbert's internist, informed Herbert's family of his opinion and chances for recovery. The family drafted a written request to the hospital, stating that they wished to take Herbert off life support. When they took him off, Herbert continued to breathe without the equipment. After two more days, the family ordered the removal of Herbert's intravenous tubes [just what was in Herbert's will?]. Herbert died some time later.

■ ISSUE

Does removal of life support from a vegetative, but not brain dead, person constitute murder?

■ DECISION AND RATIONALE

(Compton, J.) No. If Barber (D) lawfully and intentionally killed Herbert, malice is presumed regardless of motive. Euthanasia is neither excusable nor justifiable in California. It is conceded by all that Herbert was not dead by either statutory or historical standards, since there was still minimal brain activity. If Herbert were "brain dead," this prosecution could not have been instituted. We conclude that cessation of "heroic" life support measures is not an affirmative act, but a withdrawal of treatment. Although the treatments are self-propelled to a degree, each pulsation of the respirator or each drop of fluid from the IV device is comparable to a manually administered injection or medication. The authority cited by the Government (P) holds that a murder charge may be supported by the failure to feed a child. This case is easily distinguishable. The parent in that case had a clear duty to feed an otherwise healthy child. Here, faced with a vegetative patient with little chance of recovery, the duty of a physician is markedly different. Where it is not possible to ascertain the choice the patient himself would have made when in such a state, the surrogate [usually the family] ought to be guided by their knowledge of the patient's feelings and desires. If the patient's feelings and desires are not known, the surrogate should be guided by the patient's best interests, and the impact on those closest to the patient. There is evidence that Mr. Herbert did not want to be kept alive by machines. Herbert's wife and children decided that Herbert should receive no further treatment—we find no legal requirement that prior judicial approval was necessary. Writ prohibiting prosecution issued.

Analysis:

Gilbert was clearly a euthanasia case, and *Barber* was clearly a case of omission—not an affirmative act like *Gilbert,* right? The court in *Barber* seems to get around the issue of euthanasia by an act/omission analysis, but some scholars are not convinced by the court's reasoning. Herbert was still alive after the respirator was turned off—what killed Herbert was the denial of food and water. Thus, some commentators argue that the physicians caused Herbert's death, just as if Herbert's wife starved her comatose husband at home. Is there a real moral difference between Mr. Gilbert and Mrs. Herbert and the doctors? In *Barber,* the court brings up the issue of omission—a solution to a *Gilbert*-type holding—and the doctor's duty to the comatose patient, asserting that burdens of treatment outweighed the benefits, so that it was not worth continuing treatment. The family made the decision after consulting with the physicians. Clearly, the physician is faced with a difficult task that presents many moral concerns that must be carefully balanced.

■ CASE VOCABULARY

BRAIN DEATH: A condition where the body shows no response to stimuli, shows no bodily function such as breathing or movement, and shows no brain activity.

CHAPTER FIVE

Mens Rea

United States v. Cordoba–Hincapie

Instant Facts: None Stated

Black Letter Rule: To be guilty of a crime which has as one of its elements, "mens rea," the criminal must have a guilty state of mind.

Regina v. Cunningham

Instant Facts: A thief stole a gas meter from the basement of a house, which caused the gas to leak into an adjoining house and partially asphyxiate an elderly woman who lived there.

Black Letter Rule: The mens rea requirement is satisfied by a showing of either intentional or reckless conduct; a showing of malice or wickedness will not suffice.

People v. Conley

Instant Facts: After an altercation at a high school party, two boys got into a fight where one boy hit the other in the face with a wine bottle, which caused extensive injuries to the other boy's mouth and teeth.

Black Letter Rule: A person acts with intent if it is his conscious object to cause a social harm or he knows that such harm is almost certain to occur as a result of his conduct.

State v. Nations

Instant Facts: A nightclub owner was charged with endangering the welfare of a child less than seventeen years old when she hired a sixteen-year-old to dance in her club. She claimed that she had asked the girl for identification and that she thought the girl was eighteen.

Black Letter Rule: Unless the applicable criminal code states otherwise, a requirement that a person commit a certain act "knowingly" with respect to a particular fact will not be satisfied unless the person had actual knowledge of the existence of the particular fact.

United States v. Morris

Instant Facts: A computer hacker intentionally unleashed a worm virus onto the Internet while it was in its nascent stages. Although he did not mean to cause any damage, he underestimated the copy rate of the worm and subsequently caused the crash of several high level government computer systems.

Black Letter Rule: If a statute is ambiguous regarding whether a mens rea term applies to all or only some of the elements of a crime, the court should examine the legislative intent to determine the correct interpretation.

United States v. Cordoba–Hincapie

Instant Facts: None Stated

Black Letter Rule: In some limited circumstances, criminal liability can exist absent any mens rea.

Staples v. United States

Instant Facts: A man was charged with violating a federal statute that required registration of automatic weapons because police found a modified AR–15 civilian rifle (similar to the M–16 military machine gun) in his home.

Black Letter Rule: If a federal crime does not expressly state a mens rea requirement, the determination of the necessary mental state is made by construing the statute itself and by examining the intent of Congress.

Garnett v. State

Instant Facts: 20–year-old man with an I.Q. of 52 has sexual intercourse with a 13–year-old whom he believed was 16.

Black Letter Rule: Mistake of age is not a defense to the strict liability crime of statutory rape.

People v. Navarro

Instant Facts: A man was charged with theft for taking four wooden beams from a construction site and, but argued that he had no intent to steal the beams because he thought they had been abandoned.

Black Letter Rule: With regard to a specific intent crime. a mistake of fact is a defense if the mistake negates the specific intent required in the definition of the crime.

People v. Marrero

Instant Facts: Marrero (D), a federal corrections officer, was convicted for violating a statute which he believed gave him the right to carry a gun.

Black Letter Rule: An erroneous interpretation of the law does not excuse violation of the law, even where the interpretation is reasonable.

Cheek v. United States

Instant Facts: A pilot who had previously filed tax returns stopped filing them because he became influenced by a group who believed that the income tax system was unconstitutional. The IRS charged him with willful tax evasion.

Black Letter Rule: A mistake of law, either reasonable or unreasonable, will be a defense to a crime if it negates the specific intent required for conviction.

United States v. Cordoba–Hincapie

(*Government*) v. (*Accused*)
825 F. Supp. 485 (E.D.N.Y. 1993)

DEFINITION OF MENS REA EVOLVES OVER TIME DUE TO SOCIETY'S CHANGING VIEWS OF MORAL WRONGDOING

■ **INSTANT FACTS** None Stated

■ **BLACK LETTER RULE** To be guilty of a crime which has as one of its elements, "mens rea," the criminal must have a guilty state of mind.

■ **PROCEDURAL BASIS**

None Stated

■ **FACTS**

None Stated

■ **ISSUE**

What is mens rea?

■ **DECISION AND RATIONALE**

(Weinstein, D.J.) A guilty mind, a guilty or vengeful purpose; a criminal intent.

Analysis:

This short excerpt serves as an introduction to the concept of mens rea and the function that it has historically served in the administration of criminal law. It has become axiomatic in modern criminal law systems that for an act to be punishable, it must be committed with a culpable state of mind. This case alerts the student to the fact that mens rea was not always required in order to be held accountable for criminal acts. The English system started out as one based in strict liability. With reference to criminal law, then, at one time it was only necessary to show that the actor had performed the proscribed act (the actus reus). The law was not concerned with the actor's state of mind. Accidental or intentional, blameless or blameworthy, the actor could be convicted if he committed the act, regardless of his state of mind when doing so.

■ **CASE VOCABULARY**

ACTUS REUS: The physical element of a crime; that is, the voluntary, conscious or volitional movement or action that, when combined with the requisite mental frame of mind, makes the actor punishable for having committed a crime.

MENS REA: The mental element of a crime, which encompasses performing the proscribed act with a guilty or morally blameworthy state of mind.

Regina v. Cunningham

(*English Government*) v. (*Thief*)

41 Crim. App. 155, 2 Q.B. 396, 2 All. Eng. Rep. 412 (1957)

MENS REA REQUIRES MORE THAN "WICKEDNESS"

■ **INSTANT FACTS** A thief stole a gas meter from the basement of a house, which caused the gas to leak into an adjoining house and partially asphyxiate an elderly woman who lived there.

■ **BLACK LETTER RULE** The mens rea requirement is satisfied by a showing of either intentional or reckless conduct; a showing of malice or wickedness will not suffice.

■ PROCEDURAL BASIS

Appeal after a conviction for unlawfully and maliciously poisoning a person.

■ FACTS

Cunningham (D) was engaged to Mrs. Wade's daughter. Mrs. Wade owned a house that had been divided into two individual homes. Mrs. Wade lived on one side with her husband and Cunningham (D) was to live on the other side after his marriage to the Wades' daughter. Cunningham (D) was out of work and needed money, so he went into the basement of the unoccupied portion of the house and stole the gas meter. In a statement to the police, Cunningham (D) admitted that he wrenched the gas meter from the wall, stole the money from within (8 shillings) and discarded the meter. Although there was a shut off valve about 2 feet from the meter, Cunningham (D) did not turn off the gas. As a result, gas leaked through the basement wall and into Mrs. Wade's house, where it partially asphyxiated her while she was sleeping in her bedroom. Cunningham (D) was indicted for violating Section 23 of the Offenses against the Person Act [making it a felony to unlawfully and maliciously administer poison to a person, or cause poison to be administered to a person, so as to endanger the person's life]. The trial judge instructed the jury that the term "malicious" in the statute meant "wicked." The jury convicted Cunningham (D) and he appealed, claiming that the judge erroneously instructed the jury as to the meaning of the word "malicious."

■ ISSUE

Will a mens rea requirement of "maliciousness" be satisfied by a finding that the actor acted "wickedly" when he performed the proscribed acts?

■ DECISION AND RATIONALE

(Byrne, J.) No. In order to satisfy the mens rea requirement of maliciousness, the actor must either intentionally set out to cause the harm that resulted, or he must have been reckless with regard to whether the harm would in fact result. If the actor did not intend to bring about the harm, he must at least have been able to foresee that the harm could occur if he persisted in his actions. He would be acting recklessly if he chose to disregard the foreseeable risk of harm and to act anyway. In the instant case, it does not appear that Cunningham (D) intentionally released the gas to poison Mrs. Wade. The trial judge instructed the jury that the statutory concept of "malicious" meant wicked; that is, they could convict if they found that Cunningham (D) was doing something he knew he should not have been doing, something that was wrong. We think that definition was too broad. In the context of this statute, an act is "malicious" if it is done intentionally or recklessly. The jury should have been instructed that Cunningham (D) could have been convicted if he acted "maliciously" in that he intended to cause an injury to Mrs. Wade, or he foresaw that *someone* might be injured by the escaping gas, but recklessly persisted in stealing the meter anyway. Because the jury was erroneously instructed as to the meaning of "malicious," we cannot be sure beyond a reasonable doubt that they found that Cunningham (D) acted with the requisite state of mind. Appeal allowed and conviction quashed.

Analysis:

The trial court in this case followed the "culpability" approach to mens rea, which would support a finding of guilt based on general immoral or improper motives. The offense here required that an actor "maliciously" cause poison to be administered to a person. The trial court's instruction suggested that Cunningham (D) could be convicted if he acted wickedly, that is, if he was morally blameworthy in a general sense for stealing the gas meter, or if he knew he was doing something wrong. But Cunningham (D) certainly knew he was doing something wrong when he stole the meter. The crucial question is whether his knowledge that he was doing something wrong when he stole the meter was enough to constitute the maliciousness that was required to hold him accountable for the much greater offense of endangering a person's life. The appellate court's concern was that the jury may have convicted Cunningham (D) because his act of stealing the meter indicated that he was a "bad" or "immoral" man. Although such a finding may have been sufficient under the "culpability" approach to mens rea, the appellate court clearly found that more was required to constitute the "malice" required by the statute. The appellate court applied the "elemental" approach to mens rea, under which the proper inquiry was whether Cunningham (D) acted intentionally or recklessly to cause the gas to escape and poison someone.

■ CASE VOCABULARY

INTENTIONALLY: A state of mind indicating that a person performed an act purposefully or willfully, and not accidentally.

MALICE: A state of mind showing an evil intent, or one that causes a person to purposely or willfully commit an act with no regard for its effect on others.

RECKLESSNESS: A state of mind indicating a callous disregard for the foreseeable consequences of performing an act.

People v. Conley

(*Government*) v. (*Accused Batterer*)

187 Ill. App. 3d 234, 134 Ill. Dec. 855, 543 N.E. 2d 138 (1989)

INTENT ENCOMPASSES EITHER A DESIRE TO BRING ABOUT SPECIFIC HARM OR KNOWLEDGE THAT HARM IS PRACTICALLY CERTAIN TO OCCUR

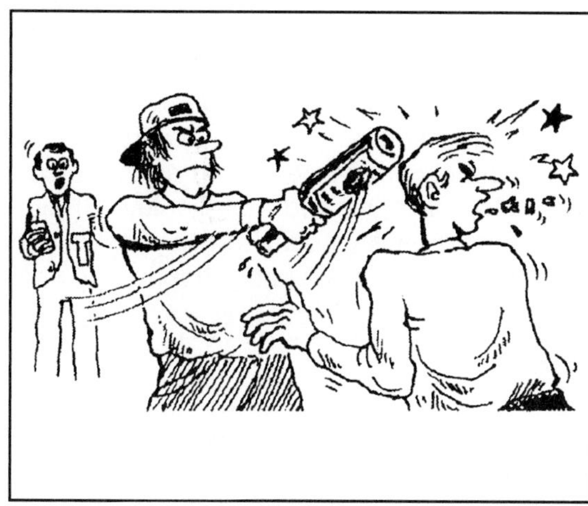

■ INSTANT FACTS After an altercation at a high school party, two boys got into a fight where one boy hit the other in the face with a wine bottle, which caused extensive injuries to the other boy's mouth and teeth.

■ BLACK LETTER RULE A person acts with Intent if it is his conscious object to cause a social harm or he knows that such harm is almost certain to occur as a result of his conduct.

■ PROCEDURAL BASIS

Appeal following a conviction for aggravated battery.

■ FACTS

About 200 high school kids attended a party where they paid admission to drink unlimited beer. Sean O'Connell attended the party with several of his friends, including Marty Carrol. At one point during the party, Sean and his friends were approached by a group of about 20 boys, who accused Sean's group of making derogatory comments. Sean's group denied making the comments, said they wanted no trouble and left the party. On their way to the car, someone across the street yelled "there's those guys from the party." Sean and Marty were approached by a boy who demanded that Marty give him a beer from the six pack Marty was carrying. Marty refused and the boy took a swing at Marty with a wine bottle. Marty ducked and the wine bottle hit Sean in the face. As a result of the blow, Sean's upper and lower jaw were broken, along with four other bones in his face. At trial, Marty identified Conley (D) as the boy who hit Sean. Conley (D) was charged with aggravated battery based on permanent disability and great bodily harm. An expert testified that Sean sustained a permanent condition called "mucosal mouth" and permanent partial numbness in one lip as a result of the blow. Conley (D) was convicted of aggravated battery based on permanent disability. On appeal, Conley contended that the State (P) failed to prove a permanent disability, and alternatively, that the State (P) failed to prove that he intended to inflict a permanent disability. The court addressed the issue whether the injuries inflicted constituted a permanent disability and found that they did.

■ ISSUE

In order to satisfy the requirement of intent, is it necessary to find that the actor consciously desired to bring about a particular harm?

■ DECISION AND RATIONALE

(Cerda, J.) No. Intent is satisfied if it can be shown either that a person consciously desires to bring about a particular harm or that he knows that his conduct is practically certain to cause the harm. Conley (D) argues that it is not enough for the State (P) to prove that he intended to cause some harm. Rather, for his conviction to stand, Conley (D) maintains that the State (P) must have proven that he intended to cause a *permanent disability.* The State (P) contends that such a showing was not necessary; that it had only to prove that Conley (D) intended to strike Sean. We agree that the State (P) was required to show that Conley (D) intended to cause a permanent disability, because that is the standard that is enunciated in the statute. [The statute provides that a person who intentionally or knowingly causes great bodily harm or permanent disability while committing a battery has committed an aggravated battery.] Whether the State (P) has met its burden of proving intent, then, turns on the statutory meaning of the words "intentionally" and "knowingly." The statute provides that a person acts intentionally if it is his conscious desire or purpose to bring about a result. He acts knowingly if he is consciously aware that the result is practically certain to occur from his conduct. Here, the State (P) was required to prove beyond a reasonable doubt that Conley (D) either consciously desired to bring about a permanent disability when he struck Sean with the bottle, or that he knew that his conduct was practically certain to result in such permanent disability. Of course, the jury was permitted to infer intent from the evidence provided and from the surrounding circumstances. Conley (D) introduced no evidence to negate a finding of intent. A jury confronted with the circumstances, such as the force of the blow, the weapon used, and the absence of a warning, could have inferred that Conley (D) either intended to cause a permanent disability or knew that a permanent disability could certainly result. The evidence was therefore sufficient to support a finding of intent beyond a reasonable doubt. Affirmed.

Analysis:

The court alludes in the opinion to the fact that the jury was permitted to infer intent because of the presumption that one intends the natural and probable consequences of his actions. This is called the "natural and probable consequences" doctrine, and it is problematic when used in conjunction with proving causation or intent in criminal cases. The Supreme Court has ruled that a *presumption* that a person intends the natural and probable consequences of his actions unconstitutionally alleviates the prosecution's burden of proving every element of a crime and therefore violates the Due Process Clause. A judge is not constitutionally permitted to instruct the jury that it may presume intent from the resulting outcome. Instead, the jury is permitted to *infer* intent from the surrounding circumstances and from the evidence that is presented. In all probability, the jury is doing the same thing whether you call it a "presumption" or an "inference." The members of the jury are simply using their common sense and collective experiences to decide if it is likely that the actor intended the consequences that resulted from his actions.

■ CASE VOCABULARY

AGGRAVATED BATTERY: A battery committed with a heightened level of violence—usually with a deadly weapon or other extreme circumstances surrounding the act.

BATTERY: An intentional harmful or offensive touching of a person without his or her consent.

State v. Nations

(*Government*) v. (*Nightclub Owner*)

676 S.W.2d 282 (Missouri Court of Appeals, Eastern District 1984)

MENS REA REQUIREMENT "KNOWINGLY" MEANS HAVING ACTUAL KNOWLEDGE OF ATTENDANT CIRCUMSTANCES

■ **INSTANT FACTS** A nightclub owner was charged with endangering the welfare of a child less than seventeen years old when she hired a sixteen-year-old to dance in her club. She claimed that she had asked the girl for identification and that she thought the girl was eighteen.

■ **BLACK LETTER RULE** Unless the applicable criminal code states otherwise, a requirement that a person commit a certain act "knowingly" with respect to a particular fact will not be satisfied unless the person had actual knowledge of the existence of the particular fact.

■ PROCEDURAL BASIS

Appeal from a conviction for endangering the welfare of a child less than seventeen years old.

■ FACTS

Nations (D) owned a nightclub called "Main Street Disco." Police officers entered the disco and observed a scantily clad girl dancing with another female on a stage for tips. After watching the girl for a few minutes, the police approached Nations (D) and questioned her about the girl's age. Nations (D) told the police that both of the girls on the stage were of legal age and that she had checked their identification when she hired them. The police then questioned the young-looking girl about her age. She told them first that she was eighteen but later admitted to being sixteen. She had no identification with her. At trial, the girl testified that Nations (D) had asked her for her identification that night and that she was crossing the stage to get her ID when the police arrived. Nations (D) testified that she had asked the girl for identification that night (the first night she hired the girl) and the girl told her that she would "show it to her in a minute." Nations (D) was convicted of endangering the welfare of a child under seventeen years old. Nations (D) appealed, claiming that the State (P) did not prove that she knew the girl was under seventeen and therefore did not prove that she had the intent to endanger the welfare of a child under seventeen.

■ ISSUE

If a statute requires a person to act "knowingly" with regard to a certain fact, can she be convicted if she does not have actual knowledge of the fact?

■ DECISION AND RATIONALE

(Satz, J.) No. If a statute requires that a person act "knowingly" with respect to an attending circumstance as an element of the offense, the State (P) must prove that the accused had actual knowledge of the circumstance in order to meet its evidentiary burden. Our Criminal Code defines "knowingly" as actual knowledge. A person acts knowingly with respect to attendant circumstances when he is aware that those circumstances exist. Although our Criminal Code is based upon the Model Penal Code ("MPC"), our legislature did not define the term "knowingly" as broadly as does the MPC.

Under the MPC, a person acts knowingly with respect to a particular fact if he has actual knowledge of the existence of the fact *or he is aware of a high probability of the existence of the fact.* Therefore, the MPC contemplates knowledge in cases where the actor willfully blinds himself to the existence of the fact, or when he deliberately chooses to remain ignorant of the fact. We feel that this latter definition of "knowledge" is identical to "recklessness." Under the MPC, then, an accused who recklessly and willfully falls to investigate the existence of a fact is charged with the knowledge of that fact. That is not the case with our Code, however. Our Code restricts the definition of "knowingly" or "knowledge" to those instances where the actor has actual knowledge of the existence of a particular fact. In this case, the State (P) did not prove that Nations (D) knew that the girl was under seventeen years old. As this was a required element of the offense, and the State did not meet its burden of proof, the conviction can not stand. Judgment reversed.

Analysis:

Knowledge of an attending circumstance is a different element of the crime than intent. If knowledge of an attending circumstance is a required element, then the prosecution must prove *both* elements in order to obtain a conviction. Keep in mind, though, that different criminal codes have different definitions of knowledge with respect to attending circumstances. In a jurisdiction that follows the MPC, the prosecution's burden is somewhat lightened because it has to prove either that the accused actually knew of the attending circumstance or that she was aware of a high probability of its existence and deliberately chose *not* to know about it, i.e., to purposefully avoid learning something that she did not want to know. If the criminal code in *Nations* had followed the MPC, it is arguable that the conviction might have been upheld, because whether Nations (D) actually knew or she was aware of a high probability that the girl was underage would have been a question of fact for the finder of fact.

■ CASE VOCABULARY

ATTENDING CIRCUMSTANCES: Facts that surround a particular event; in the criminal sense, it is a required element of some offenses that an actor has knowledge of a particular fact, but chooses to act anyway.

United States v. Morris

(*Government*) v. (*Hacker*)

928 F. 2d 504 (2d Cir. 1991)

AMBIGUITY IN A CRIMINAL STATUTE REQUIRES THAT THE COURT EXAMINE LEGISLATIVE INTENT TO AID IN INTERPRETATION

■ **INSTANT FACTS** A computer hacker intentionally unleashed a worm virus onto the Internet while it was in its nascent stages. Although he did not mean to cause any damage, he underestimated the copy rate of the worm and subsequently caused the crash of several high level government computer systems.

■ **BLACK LETTER RULE** If a statute is ambiguous regarding whether a mens rea term applies to all or only some of the elements of a crime, the court should examine the legislative intent to determine the correct interpretation.

■ PROCEDURAL BASIS

Appeal of conviction for violating the Computer Fraud and Abuse Act of 1986 [adopted by Congress to protect against computer crimes].

■ FACTS

Morris (D) was a graduate student in a Ph.D. program in computer science at Cornell University. He had extensive experience with computers from undergraduate study at Harvard and from various jobs. Morris (D) spoke to some of his fellow students about the ease with which he could infiltrate the security of certain computer networks. In October of 1988, Morris created a virus, or worm, to release on the Internet. At that point, the Internet consisted of a group of national computer networks that connected various governmental agencies, universities, medical research facilities and military operations. Morris (D) created the worm to demonstrate the inadequacies of the security systems on the Internet. He programmed the worm to infect computers quietly and unobtrusively. However, Morris (D) was concerned that computer operators would be able to detect the worm and disable it, so he deliberately made it difficult to kill. In order to ensure that the worm only infected a previously uninfected computer, Morris (D) programmed the worm to ask each computer if it already had a copy of the worm. If the computer answered "no," then the worm would infect it. Morris (D) became concerned that programmers could outsmart the worm by programming their computers to say "yes" automatically, so he placed an override in the program that would automatically re-infect a computer after the worm had received seven consecutive "no" answers. Unfortunately, Morris (D) underestimated the rate of re-infection. After he released the worm onto the Internet on November 2, 1988, many computer systems around the country crashed. At that point, Morris (D) tried to send a message detailing how to kill the worm, but the systems were not functioning properly and could not receive the message. The estimated cost of dealing with the worm ranged from $200 to $53,000 in different facilities. Morris (D) was charged with violating 18 U.S.C. § 1030(a)(5)(A) [making criminally liable anyone who intentionally accesses a federal computer without authorization and damages or destroys information therein and thereby causes damage in excess of $1,000 in one year]. Morris (D) was convicted and appealed, claiming that the statutory language indicated that the government had to prove both that he intended the unauthorized use of a federal interest computer and that he intended to cause a loss. The government (P) contended that the language of the statute was clear and unambiguous, that the adverb "intentionally" modified only the access portion of the statute and that a resort to legislative history was unnecessary.

■ ISSUE

Is a court required to determine the legislative intent behind a criminal statute if it is ambiguous as to whether a mens rea term modifies all or only some of the elements of the offense?

■ DECISION AND RATIONALE

(Newman, C.J.) Yes. In a case such as this one, where the wording of the offense is ambiguous as to the mens rea requirement, resort to the legislative history to determine legislative intent is appropriate. It is true that there is no hard and fast rule here. Some courts have interpreted similar statutes by taking into account sentence structure and the rules of grammar. We are not convinced, however, that punctuation should be the only consideration. Nor are we convinced, as the government (P) would have us be, that the placement of the comma in this statute renders the text so clear as to preclude a review of legislative history. Congress amended the Computer Fraud and Abuse Act of 1986 in 1988 to better reflect its intent. At that point, Congress added the Section now at issue. The old version covered anyone who knowingly accessed a computer without authorization and who knowingly used, modified or destroyed information, thereby causing damage or loss. The 1988 amendment changed the mental state requirement from "knowingly" to "intentionally." Additionally, the 1988 amendment used the scienter requirement only once. The new Section covers anyone who intentionally accesses a government computer without authorization and alters, damages or destroys information, thereby causing damage or loss. The new section does not repeat the scienter requirement after the access phrase. We think the legislative history indicates that Congress intended the mens rea requirement of "intentionally" to modify only the access phrase, and not to apply also to the damages phrase. Judgment of conviction affirmed.

Analysis:

The issue in this case is one that frequently arises with respect to criminal statutes. The modern view is that a mens rea term placed at the beginning of the statute modifies all of the phrases in the statute. That is the view that the Model Penal Code espouses in Section 2.02(4). According to the Model Penal Code, a single mens rea term in a statute modifies each actus reus element of the offense, unless the legislature plainly indicates a contrary purpose. However, courts occasionally come to different conclusions. One common exception occurs when the actus reus term is an attending circumstance. In this case, courts do not always view the mens rea term as modifying the attending circumstance. Thus, a statute that makes it a felony to intentionally break and enter the dwelling house of another would probably be construed as requiring that the defendant intended to break into and enter, but not that he intended the structure to be a dwelling house. Another common exception is when, like in the instant case, the phrase containing the mens rea requirement is set off from the rest of the statute by punctuation. In that case, it may be evident that the mens rea term was intended only to modify the actus reus provision within the set off phrase.

■ CASE VOCABULARY

SCIENTER: Literally, scienter means "knowingly." It is a general mens rea term that sometimes means intent, but more often simply means guilty knowledge.

United States v. Cordoba–Hincapie

(*Government*) v. (*Accused*)

825 F.Supp. 485 (E.D.N.Y. 1993)

MENS REA IS NOT REQUIRED FOR STRICT LIABILITY OFFENSES

■ **INSTANT FACTS** Not Stated.

■ **BLACK LETTER RULE** In some limited circumstances, criminal liability can exist absent any mens rea.

■ **PROCEDURAL BASIS**

Not Stated.

■ **FACTS**

Not Stated.

■ **ISSUE**

Not Stated.

■ **DECISION AND RATIONALE**

(Weinstein, D.J.) In almost every instance, mens rea is a required element for criminal liability to exist. Although the rule used to be that no criminal liability could attach absent mens rea, this rule has undergone significant changes over time. The law now recognizes that a man can be convicted of some kinds of crimes even without a guilty frame of mind—without a mens rea. Probably the most common examples of crimes that do not require a mens rea for conviction are those crimes categorized as "public welfare offenses." Historically, the law has permitted criminal liability to attach without regard to fault with respect to violations of liquor laws, traffic laws, sanitary laws and the like. These so-called "strict liability" crimes generally arise from the need to protect the public welfare through the orderly administration of laws promulgated for the collective good of society. Strict liability crimes permit the wrongdoer to be convicted of the crime regardless of whether he had a guilty mind when he acted. In general, the law has tolerated strict liability crimes that involve fairly light penalties, i.e. fines. When the penalties begin to get more harsh, i.e. imprisonment or hefty fines or forfeitures, our criminal justice system generally requires mens rea for criminal liability to exist. One exception to these general rules is the crime of statutory rape. Historically, statutory rape has been a strict liability crime, despite the fact that conviction for statutory rape carries with it significant penalties and the potential for long-term imprisonment.

Analysis:

One common exception to the requirement of a mens rea is the "strict liability" offense. Although strict liability is a disfavored doctrine in the criminal law, it survives with respect to certain "public-welfare" or regulatory offenses. Common examples include traffic laws, liquor laws, the sanitary code, and building laws. These regulatory offenses generally have light penalties or fines, and they are usually part of a broad regulatory scheme implemented to protect the collective interests of society. A general rule of thumb is that the more severe the penalty involved, the more likely that the court will find that the government must prove the necessary mens rea.

Staples v. United States

(Gun Owner) v. *(Government)*

511 U.S. 600, 114 S.Ct. 1793, 128 L. Ed. 2d 608 (1994)

FOR CRIMINAL LIABILITY TO EXIST, A DEFENDANT MUST KNOW OF THE FACTS THAT MAKE HIS CONDUCT ILLEGAL

■ **INSTANT FACTS** A man was charged with violating a federal statute that required registration of automatic weapons because police found a modified AR-15 civilian rifle (similar to the M-16 military machine gun) in his home.

■ **BLACK LETTER RULE** If a federal crime does not expressly state a mens rea requirement, the determination of the necessary mental state is made by construing the statute itself and by examining the intent of Congress.

■ PROCEDURAL BASIS

Appeal to United States Supreme Court of conviction for violating a federal registration statute.

■ FACTS

Local police and federal agents executed a search warrant at Staples' (D) home where they found a modified AR-15 rifle. The rifle is a civilian version of the military's M-16, except that the AR-15 is a semi-automatic weapon. The M-16 is a selective fire rifle that allows the operator to switch between automatic fire and semi-automatic fire with the flip of a switch. The parts of an M-16 are interchangeable with the parts of an AR-15 and can be used to convert the AR-15 into an automatic weapon. The federal agents observed that Staples' (D) gun had been modified with M-16 parts and that a metal stop that would ordinarily have been on the AR-15 to prevent its being modified into an automatic weapon had either been filed or worn away. The federal agents tested the gun and found that it was capable of fully automatic fire. Staples (D) was charged with violating the National Firearms Act ("Act"), which requires that all statutorily defined "firearms" be registered in the National Firearms Registration and Transfer Record. The Act defines "firearm" as a gun that shoots or can readily be made to shoot more than one shot automatically with one pull of the trigger, without having to manually reload. Violations of the Act are punishable by up to ten years in prison. Staples' (D) weapon was not registered. He insisted that the gun had never been fired automatically when he possessed it. Staples (D) contended that the weapon had only fired semi-automatically—and even then he said that it had sometimes been problematic. Staples (D) requested the trial judge to instruct the jury that the government had to prove that he knew that the gun would fire automatically in order to establish a violation of the Act. The trial court rejected the proposed instruction and Staples (D) was convicted. He was sentenced to five years of probation and a $5,000.00 fine. The Court of Appeals affirmed and Staples (D) petitioned the United States Supreme Court for certiorari.

■ ISSUE

If a federal criminal statute is silent as to the mens rea requirement, will it be construed as a strict liability offense?

■ DECISION AND RATIONALE

(Thomas, J.) No. The requirement of mens rea is firmly embedded within our system of justice. A statute that is silent as to the mens rea requirement should not be construed as dispensing with mens rea absent a clear indication of congressional intent to dispense with the requirement. It is true that we have recognized that mens rea is not always a required element of some crimes. Those offenses that we have labeled "public welfare" or regulatory offenses sometimes do not require a showing of mens rea. Instead, they are typically referred to as "strict liability" offenses. In most cases, we have recognized such offenses only when they involve the regulation of potentially dangerous or harmful items. In those cases, we have charged the possessor of such an item with the knowledge that the item is dangerous and that the responsibility is his to determine whether the law regulates his conduct. But we have not traditionally done away with the requirement of mens rea with regard to statutes that regulate otherwise lawful and innocent conduct. We are confronted with such a statute here. Citizens of our country have traditionally owned guns; within certain boundaries it is perfectly lawful for them to do so. Although guns are potentially dangerous items, the prevalence of gun ownership in this country militates against dispensing with a mens rea requirement that a person know the characteristics of his gun make it illegal. We do not believe that Congress, by remaining silent on the point, intended that there be no requirement of mens rea with respect to this statute. Additionally, the Act imposes a penalty of up to ten years imprisonment. We have historically examined the nature of the penalty provided for by the statute when determining whether the statute subjected the violator to strict liability. Generally, the small penalties that attach to public welfare offenses justify dispensing with the mens rea requirement. Although we do not adopt an absolute rule, we note here that the provision of such a harsh penalty in the statute is inconsistent with a finding that this is a public welfare offense that dispenses with the mens rea requirement. Judgment of conviction reversed.

■ DISSENT

(Stevens, J.) The Act does indicate the express intent of Congress to dispense with a mens rea requirement because it does not contain a knowledge requirement at all. Nor does the statute describe a common law offense. Public welfare offenses are those offenses that have been statutorily created and regulate dangerous items. They heighten the duties of those who possess or use them and they do not depend on the existence of a particular mental state. This Act is silent as to a knowledge requirement, and silence on the part of Congress indicates that it intended to alleviate the burden of proving that the defendant knew that his conduct was unlawful. I would find that this Act fits the description of a public welfare statute.

Analysis:

As this case indicates, one of the reasons that the mens rea requirement is dispensed with in some offenses is to ease the prosecution's burden of proof. That is, while the prosecution usually has to prove every element of the crime beyond a reasonable doubt to obtain a conviction, categorizing an offense as a strict liability crime alleviates the prosecution's burden of having to prove intent or knowledge. With respect to regulatory offenses, doing away with the prosecution's duty to prove the mental element lessens the burden on our court systems and promotes social compliance with regulatory schemes. On the other hand, imposing strict liability sometimes means that people who had no intention of violating the law or did not even know that their conduct was illegal are convicted of crimes. Conviction in such a case seems to run counter to the notion that our criminal justice system only punishes those who perform proscribed acts with a sufficiently culpable state of mind.

■ CASE VOCABULARY

STRICT LIABILITY: A category of criminal offense that does not require a mens rea; only an actus reus is required for conviction.

Garnett v. State

(*Mentally Disabled Man*) v. (*Government*)
332 Md. 571, 632 A.2d 797 (1993)

DESPITE LACK OF MENS REA, MISTAKE IS NO DEFENSE TO STRICT LIABILITY OFFENSES

■ **INSTANT FACTS** A 20-year-old man with an I.Q. of 52 has sexual intercourse with a 13-year-old whom he believed was 16.

■ **BLACK LETTER RULE** Mistake of age is not a defense to the strict liability crime of statutory rape.

■ PROCEDURAL BASIS

Appeal from conviction for statutory rape.

■ FACTS

Raymond Garnett (D) is a 20-year-old, mentally disabled man. He has an I.Q. of 52, and interacts socially at the level of an 11- or 12-year-old. In November or December of 1990, a friend introduced Garnett (D) to Erica Frazier, a 13-year-old girl. On February 28, 1991, Erica invited Raymond into her room, and the two had sexual intercourse. Nine months later, Erica gave birth to a child, of which Raymond is the biological father. Raymond was convicted of one count of second degree rape under Maryland Code § 463, which reads in part, "A person is guilty of rape in the second degree if the person engages in vaginal intercourse with another person . . . [w]ho is under 14 years of age and the person performing the act is at least four years older than the victim." Garnett (D) attempted to offer evidence of his belief that Erica Frazier was 16, but the court explained that a even a good faith mistake as to age was no defense. Maryland Code § 463 does not set a particular mens rea requirement. The Government (P) insists that the statute was designed to impose strict liability. Garnett (D) replies that criminal law exists to punish the morally culpable, and such culpability was absent in his case.

■ ISSUE

Is statutory rape a strict liability offense to which mistake of age is no defense?

■ DECISION AND RATIONALE

(Murphy, J.) Yes. The requirement that an accused must have acted with a culpable mental state is an axiom of criminal jurisprudence. Legislatures have created strict liability statutes dealing with public health and welfare issues, usually imposing fines for misconduct. Statutory rape, on the other hand, imposes a sentence of up to 20 years in prison. Strict liability is a somewhat disfavored doctrine. The Model Penal Code [MPC], for example, requires that a person act with some degree of mens rea to be held criminally liable. The MPC recognizes strict liability solely for offenses deemed "violations," defined as wrongs subject to fines, forfeitures, or other civil penalty. Likewise, commentators disapprove of statutory rape as a strict liability crime, noting that statutory rape prosecutions proceed even when there is evidence supporting the defendant's belief that the complainant was of age. Strict liability for the offense is not justified by the "moral wrong theory," which would hold that Garnett (D), acting without mens rea, nonetheless deserves punishment for having violated moral teachings that prohibit sex outside marriage. Maryland has no law against fornication. Also, the criminality of an act performed without a guilty mind rests uneasily on the subjective, shifting moral norms of some members of the community. Seventeen states have allowed the mistake of age defense in some form. However, Maryland's statute does not require the Government (P) to prove mens rea, and makes no allowance for a mistake of age defense. The silence as to mens rea results from legislative design in drafting the statute. The legislative history also reveals that the statute was viewed as imposing strict liability. Even among states with an available mistake of age defense, most do not allow the defense where the complainant is aged 14 years or less. Any new provision in Maryland law that introduces a mistake of age defense must result from legislative amendment. Judgment Affirmed.

■ DISSENT

(Bell, J.) Despite the legislative history and the majority's interpretation of the statute, I do not believe that the General Assembly can subject a defendant to strict liability in every case. To hold that the Government (P) need not prove mens rea with respect to the age of the complainant, or that Garnett (D) may not offer a defense, offends fundamental principles of justice and is inconsistent with due process. I would hold that Garnett (D) should be allowed the opportunity to produce evidence supporting his claim of mistake of age. If he is able to produce such evidence, the Government (P) must then show beyond a reasonable doubt that the act was committed without any mistake of fact.

Analysis:

The moral wrong theory holds that an actor should be held responsible despite mistake where, if the facts were as the accused believed them to be, the accused's conduct would still be immoral. In the famous case of *Regina v. Prince*, the defendant Prince was found guilty of "taking . . . [an] unmarried girl . . . under the age of sixteen . . . out of the possession . . . of her father." The girl was thirteen, but Prince believed her to be eighteen. Out of *seventeen* judges deciding the case, ten held that the offense was a strict liability crime. Six others held that mens rea had to be proven. The judges relied on the moral wrong theory. Assuming that Prince reasonably believed that the girl was thirteen, he would still be culpable. Although the girl was not thirteen, she was still of "tender years," and Prince knew that he was taking the girl from her father, which is an immoral act. The implication is that Prince knew the act was immoral. Yet as the majority in *Garnett* observes, it is sometimes difficult to ascertain what constitutes moral behavior in a diverse society.

■ CASE VOCABULARY

MALUM PROHIBITUM: Typically refers to offenses that are not wicked per se, such as regulatory offenses.

MORAL WRONG THEORY: Holds that an actor should be held responsible despite mistake where, if the facts were as the accused believed them to be, the accused's conduct would still be immoral.

STRICT LIABILITY: Refers to offenses that do not require any mens rea, but hold an actor responsible regardless of intent.

People v. Navarro

(*Government*) v. (*Accused Thief*)
99 Cal.App.3d Supp. 1, 160 Cal. Rptr. 692 (1979)

A MISTAKE OF FACT IS A DEFENSE TO A SPECIFIC INTENT CRIME WHEN IT NEGATES THE REQUIRED MENS REA

■ **INSTANT FACTS** A man was charged with theft for taking four wooden beams from a construction site and, but argued that he had no intent to steal the beams because he thought they had been abandoned.

■ **BLACK LETTER RULE** With regard to a specific intent crime, a mistake of fact is a defense if the mistake negates the specific intent required in the definition of the crime.

■ PROCEDURAL BASIS

Appeal of a conviction for petty theft.

■ FACTS

Navarro (D) entered a construction site and removed four wooden beams from the site. He was charged with grand theft. The statute provided that any person who feloniously steals the property of another is guilty of theft. The statute was a codification of the common law offense of larceny, which is the "trespassory taking and carrying away of the personal property of another with the intent to steal the property." Navarro (D) presented evidence that he did not intend to steal the beams, but that he thought they had been abandoned and the owner would have no objection to his taking them. Navarro (D) requested a jury instruction to the effect that if he took the beams with a good faith belief that they had been abandoned he could not be convicted, even if the belief was objectively unreasonable. The judge modified the requested instruction, and instead instructed the jury that if Navarro (D) took the beams with a reasonable and good faith belief that they had been abandoned, he could not be convicted. Navarro (D) was convicted of petty theft and appealed. He contended that the judged erred in his instruction of the jury.

■ ISSUE

Does a mistake have to be reasonable in order to negate the mental state required by a specific intent crime?

■ DECISION AND RATIONALE

(Dowds, J.) No. Even an unreasonable mistake will be a defense to a specific intent crime if it negates the specific mens rea requirement. Navarro (D) was charged with theft, which is a specific intent crime. The offense requires that a person feloniously steal the property of another to be convicted; that is, a person must *intend* to steal the property. Navarro (D) presented evidence that tended to show that he lacked the specific intent required by the wording of the offense, i.e. that he thought the beams had been abandoned. The Supreme Court has stated that "where a felonious intent must be proven it can be done only by proving what the accused knew." We understand the Supreme Court's words to mean that it is not enough to show that a reasonable man would have known the true nature of the facts. Instead, where a specific intent is required to convict a person of a crime, the prosecution must show that the accused actually possessed the requisite intent. In these circumstances, it does not matter if the alleged mistake is objectively reasonable or unreasonable. If a mistake as to the facts or law negates the specific intent required by the statute, the accused is entitled to a defense. The trial court erred when it instructed the jury that Navarro (D) could be acquitted only if the jury found that he entertained a reasonable and good faith belief that he had a right to take the beams. Judgment of conviction reversed.

Analysis:

The common law makes a distinction between specific and general intent crimes with regard to mistakes. If the offense is a general intent crime, only a reasonable mistake of fact or law will provide a defense for the accused. This is so because at common law, general intent crimes required only a morally blameworthy state of mind rather than a specific mental state. Recall that the culpability approach to mens rea usually coincided with common law general intent crimes. Therefore, if common law rules are applied, the first step in analyzing a mistake defense is to determine whether the crime is a specific intent or a general intent offense. If it is a general intent offense and the mistake is reasonable, the actor will not have acted with a morally blameworthy state of mind and so should be entitled to a defense. If the mistake is unreasonable, it has no bearing on the blameworthiness of the individual and he will not be entitled to a defense. On the other hand, if the offense is a specific intent crime, any mistake, reasonable or unreasonable, that both relates to the specific intent required and negates the mental state necessary for conviction will entitle the accused to a defense.

■ CASE VOCABULARY

FELONIOUSLY: Done with a deliberate intent to commit a felony or a crime.

THEFT: The taking of another's property without his consent with the intent to permanently deprive the person of the property.

People v. Marrero

(*Government*) v. (*Federal Corrections Officer*)

69 N.Y.2d 382, 515 N.Y.S.2d 212, 507 N.E.2d 1068 (1987)

MISTAKE OF LAW EXCEPTIONS ARE APPLIED EXTREMELY NARROWLY

■ **INSTANT FACTS** Marrero (D), a federal corrections officer, was convicted for violating a statute which he believed gave him the right to carry a gun.

■ **BLACK LETTER RULE** An erroneous interpretation of the law does not excuse violation of the law, even where the interpretation is reasonable.

■ PROCEDURAL BASIS

Appeal after conviction for unlawful possession of a pistol.

■ FACTS

Marrero (D), a federal corrections officer, was convicted of unlawful possession of a pistol under a statute containing an exemption for "peace officers." The statutory definition of "peace officers" included "correction officers of any state correction facility or of any penal correctional institution." The trial court dismissed the charge, but the Appellate Division ruled by a 3–2 vote that only state and not federal officers were covered by the provision. At the ensuing criminal trial, the court refused to instruct the jury that it should acquit Marrero (D) if he reasonably believed himself to be a peace officer under the statutory definition. Marrero (D) claimed that he relied on interpretations of fellow officers and teachers, as well as the language of the statute itself, in forming his belief that he could carry a pistol.

■ ISSUE

Does misinterpretation of a statute excuse its violation, where the statute does not have a mens rea requirement?

■ DECISION AND RATIONALE

(Bellacosa) No. A mistake of law does not excuse the commission of prohibited acts. Contrasted with kidnapping, which allows a showing of good-faith belief in the legality of the conduct to negate intent, a weapons statute violation imposes criminal liability regardless of intent. The mistake of law defense is available to defendants who have relied on an "official statement" of the law, either expressed in a statute or by a public servant or agency charged with administering, enforcing, or interpreting the law. Marrero (D) claims that his conduct was based on an official statement of the law contained in the statute itself. In view of the ambiguous wording, Marrero (D) argues that his "reasonable" interpretation falls under this exception. However, allowing Marrero (D) this exception would make mistake of law a generally applied or available defense, rather than an unusual exception. The Government (P) analogizes New York's *official statement* defense to the Model Penal Code. The Model Penal Code provides that the *official statement* defense only applies when the accused acts in reliance on a statute that actually authorizes his conduct. If the *official statement* of the law is afterward determined to be invalid or erroneous, the *official statement* defense protects those who mistakenly acted in reliance. Reviewing the legislative history, it is evident that the legislature intended the New York *official statement* defense statute to be similarly construed. Marrero's (D) conduct was never authorized by statute; he only thought that it was. If Marrero's (D) arguments were accepted, the exception would swallow the rule. Mistakes of law would be encouraged. Wrong-minded individuals would use the defense to avoid conviction. To avoid these consequences, the conviction is affirmed.

■ DISSENT

(Hancock) In interpreting a statute, a court should look first to the particular words of the statute in question. Here, there is but one natural and obvious meaning: if a defendant founded his interpretation on an official interpretation of the statute, he should have a defense. The precise phrase from the Model Penal Code limiting the defense to reliance on a statute "afterward determined to be invalid or erroneous" was omitted from New York's penal code. How can the legislature be assumed to have enacted the very language that it specifically rejected? Also, the majority suggests that the Legislature intended the defense to be available solely in acts involving mala in se offenses, such as kidnapping. On the contrary, it is with mala prohibita (regulatory) offenses that reasons of policy and fairness call for a relaxation of the rule limiting the mistake of law defense.

Analysis:

The majority is concerned that if Marrero (D) is acquitted, people might get the message that the law is subjective, that the law is whatever the individual believes it to be. Marrero (D) does not argue, however, that he should be able to interpret the statute however he likes, but that the statute is so ambiguous that his interpretation is completely reasonable. The majority possibly exaggerates the effect an acquittal would have. For most statutes, the window of "reasonable" interpretation is fairly narrow, and judges and juries could be trusted to spot the occasional "unreasonable" interpretation. A positive effect of allowing a broader mistake-of-law defense would be that, where a law allows a wide array of reasonable interpretations, legislators might make a better effort to ensure that legislation is clear and understandable.

■ CASE VOCABULARY

ACTING IN RELIANCE: Actions based on trust in another person's words or actions.

MISTAKE OF LAW: An incorrect interpretation of the legal effect of a given law or set of facts.

Cheek v. United States

(*Delinquent Taxpayer*) v. (*Government*)

498 U.S. 192, 111 S.Ct. 604, 112 L.Ed.2d 617 (1991)

A MISTAKE OF LAW THAT RELATES TO THE SPECIFIC MENTAL STATE REQUIRED AND NEGATES SPECIFIC INTENT IS A DEFENSE TO CRIMINAL PROSECUTION

■ **INSTANT FACTS** A pilot who had previously filed tax returns stopped filing them because he became influenced by a group who believed that the income tax system was unconstitutional. The IRS charged him with willful tax evasion.

■ **BLACK LETTER RULE** A mistake of law, either reasonable or unreasonable, will be a defense to a crime if it negates the specific intent required for conviction.

■ PROCEDURAL BASIS

Appeal to United States Supreme Court of conviction for tax evasion.

■ FACTS

Cheek (D) was a pilot for American Airlines. He duly filed his tax returns through the year 1979, but thereafter ceased to file his returns. Beginning in 1980, he began claiming excessive withholding deductions—eventually claiming 60 allowances on his W-2—and also claimed he was exempt from federal income taxes. Cheek (D) did so because he had become associated with and influenced by a group that believed that the federal income tax system was unconstitutional. He was charged with tax evasion under a statute that provided, "any person who willfully attempts . . . to evade or defeat any tax imposed by this title . . . shall be guilty of a felony." Evidence was presented at trial that Cheek (D) was involved in a number of civil lawsuits challenging the constitutionality of the federal income tax between 1982 and 1986. At each of those trials, Cheek (D) and the other plaintiffs were told that their claims were frivolous or had been repeatedly rejected by the courts. At trial, Cheek (D) represented himself and testified that because he had been attending seminars and listening to lectures sponsored by this anti-tax group he believed that the federal income tax laws were invalid. He also believed that his wages were not income under the federal statute. Cheek (D) presented evidence of a letter from an attorney stating that the Sixteenth Amendment did not authorize a tax on wages as income—only profits and gain. [It's probably safe to assume that this attorney is no longer practicing.] His defense was that he sincerely believed that the tax laws were being unconstitutionally applied and that his failure to file income tax returns was therefore lawful. He argued that, based on his belief that he was acting lawfully, he did not possess the willfulness necessary to convict him of tax evasion. The trial court instructed the jury that if it found that Cheek (D) "honestly and reasonably believed he was not required to pay income taxes" then he could be acquitted. When the jury could not make this decision, the trial judge further instructed them that an honest but unreasonable belief is not a defense and does not negate willfulness. The jury convicted Cheek (D). His argument on appeal was that the judge erred by instructing the jury that only a reasonable mistake about the law negated willfulness.

■ ISSUE

Is a mistake of law that relates to the specific intent of a crime a defense to criminal prosecution?

■ DECISION AND RATIONALE

(White, J.) Yes. The general rule is that a mistake of law is no excuse. A limited exception applies when a mistake of law negates the specific mental state required for conviction. The statute makes it a criminal violation to willfully evade federal income tax obligations. Because of the extreme complexity of the modern tax code, our cases have repeatedly interpreted the term "willfully" to mean a voluntary, intentional violation of a *known legal duty*. In order for a mistake of law to negate willfulness, then, the mistake must relate to whether the accused *knows* of a legal duty. If, because of the complexity of the tax laws, an individual does not know of a legal duty, the mistake affords him a defense because it negates the requirement that he voluntarily and intentionally violated a known legal duty. We do not agree with the Court of Appeals that such a mistake must be reasonable. Even an unreasonable mistake would negate a finding that the individual knew of a legal duty. In this case, if the jury believed Cheek's (D) assertion that he did not think the federal tax code treated wages as income, then it could find that he did not know he had a legal duty to pay income taxes on his wages. His mistaken belief as to his duty to pay taxes on his wages would negate any finding that he intentionally violated a known legal duty. With respect to Cheek's (D) constitutional claims, however, the general rule that mistake is no defense applies. Unlike his belief about wages, Cheek's (D) constitutional claims do not arise from a mistaken belief derived from the complexity of the tax code. instead, his claims indicate that he was intimately familiar with the applicable provisions of the federal income tax code. Cheek (D) claims mistake in that he believed that the tax laws were unconstitutional as applied to him. In other words, he was aware that the law imposed upon him a duty to pay taxes, but mistakenly believed that the law itself was unconstitutional. Because of his mistaken belief as to constitutionality, Cheek (D) voluntarily and intentionally did not pay his taxes. We believe that Cheek's (D) views about the constitutionality of the tax code in general would not preclude a finding that he willfully attempted to evade the tax laws. The District Judge did not err by instructing the jury not to consider Cheek's views about constitutionality. Remanded for a new trial.

■ DISSENT

(Blackmun, J.) I fear that the Court's decision today will encourage taxpayers to cling to frivolous views of the law in the hope of convincing a jury of their sincerity.

Analysis:

The common law rule is that ignorance of the law or a mistake of the law is no defense. Because the tax code has grown so complex, though, the courts have had to soften the common law rule with respect to tax offenses. The government is not interested in punishing those individuals who genuinely did not know they were subject to a particular provision of the code. Instead, the government seeks to punish those who know they have a legal duty to pay taxes but purposefully and intentionally do not do so. Thus, the courts have interpreted the statutory requirement of "willfulness" in the tax code as meaning the individual voluntarily and intentionally violated a known legal duty. It is because of this definition of willfulness that the Court finds that the lower courts erred by instructing the jury that only a reasonable mistake on Cheek's (D) part would constitute a defense.

CHAPTER SIX

Causation

Oxendine v. State

Instant Facts: A father is convicted of manslaughter, after beating his six-year-old child who had been earlier pushed into a bathtub (causing injuries) by the father's girlfriend.

Black Letter Rule: Actual causation or causation-in-fact is a necessary prerequisite to the imposition of criminal liability.

Kibbe v. Henderson

Instant Facts: A person is convicted of second degree murder, after robbing, undressing, and abandoning a highly intoxicated individual on a two-lane highway, who was run over by pickup truck.

Black Letter Rule: Proximate or legal causation is a necessary prerequisite to the imposition of criminal liability.

Velazquez v. State

Instant Facts: A "drag racer" is prosecuted for vehicular homicide, after participating in a race on a public road, where the other racer lost control of his car, drove through a guardrail, and died.

Black Letter Rule: Causation is a necessary prerequisite to the imposition of criminal liability.

State v. Rose

Instant Facts: An automobile driver is convicted of negligent manslaughter, after hitting a pedestrian, and dragging the pedestrian who was lodged underneath the vehicle.

Black Letter Rule: Elements of a crime must occur concurrently in order to impose criminal liability for that crime.

Oxendine v. State

(*Child Abuser*) v. (*Community*)
528 A.2d 870 (1987)

PROOF BEYOND A REASONABLE DOUBT OF ACTUAL CAUSATION IS NECESSARY FOR CRIMINAL LIABILITY

■ **INSTANT FACTS** A father is convicted of manslaughter, after beating his six-year-old child who had been earlier pushed into a bathtub (causing injuries) by the father's girlfriend.

■ **BLACK LETTER RULE** Actual causation or causation-in-fact is a necessary prerequisite to the imposition of criminal liability.

■ PROCEDURAL BASIS

Certification to the Supreme Court of Delaware of a conviction for manslaughter.

■ FACTS

On January 18, 1984, Leotha Tyree (Tyree), Jeffery Oxendine's (Oxendine) (D) girlfriend, pushed Jeffrey Oxendine, Jr. (Jeffrey), Oxendine's (D) six-year-old son, into the bathtub causing microscopic tears in his intestines which led to peritonitis. During a break from work that evening, Oxendine (D) telephoned Jeffery, who complained of stomach pains. When Oxendine (D) returned home he saw bruises on Jeffrey and knew that Tyree had beaten the child earlier that day. The next morning, at 7:30 a.m., Oxendine (D) went into Jeffrey's bedroom and began screaming at him to get up. A neighbor testified to hearing sounds coming from Jeffrey's room, of blows being struck, obscenities being uttered by a male voice, and cries from a child saying, "Please stop, daddy, it hurts." After the sounds continued for five to ten minutes, the witness heard a final noise consisting of a loud thump, as if someone had been kicked or punched "with a great blow." Later that day, Jeffrey's abdomen became swollen. When Oxendine (D) arrived home from work around 5:00 p.m., Tyree urged Oxendine (D) to take Jeffrey to the hospital. Oxendine (D), apparently believing that Jeffrey was exaggerating his discomfort, went out, bought a newspaper, and returned home to read it. Upon his return Tyree had prepared to take Jeffrey to the hospital. On the way to the hospital, Jeffrey stopped breathing, and was pronounced dead shortly after his arrival at the hospital. During trial, the State called medical examiners Dr. Inguito and Dr. Hameli, who both testified that Jeffrey's death was caused by intra-abdominal hemorrhage and acute peritonitis, occurring as a result of blunt force trauma to the front of the abdomen. Similarly, each pathologist identified two distinct injuries, one caused more than twenty-four hours before death, and one inflicted less than twenty-four hours before death. Dr. Inguito could not place any quantitative value on, nor tell which of the hemorrhages caused the death. Moreover, Dr. Inguito was not asked, nor did he express any opinion as to whether the second hemorrhage accelerated Jeffrey's death. Dr. Hameli, on the other hand, was of the opinion that the earlier injury was the plain underlying cause of death, although the second hemorrhage was an aggravating circumstance. Furthermore, Dr. Hameli could not give an opinion as to whether the second hemorrhage accelerated Jeffrey's death. As part of her case, co-defendant Tyree called Dr. Hoffman, a medical examiner, who only perceived one injury, inflicted twelve hours before death. However, in answering a hypothetical posed by the prosecutor, Dr. Hoffman opined that, given Jeffrey's weakened state as a result of the significant trauma to his abdominal cavity, another blunt force trauma to the same area, would accelerate death. At the end of trial Oxendine (D) moved for judgment of acquittal.

The motion was denied and the jury was instructed on the elements of recklessness, causation, and on various lesser offenses. The ultimate and only theory of causation that the jury was instructed on, was based on acceleration. Specifically, the trial court was instructed that a defendant who causes the death of another is not relieved of responsibility for causing the death if another later injury accelerates the death of the other person. Contribution without acceleration is not sufficient. Oxendine (D) was convicted of manslaughter, and sentenced to twelve years' imprisonment. Oxendine (D) appealed, arguing that the Trial Court committed reversible error by denying his motion for a judgment of acquittal on the issue of causation. Specifically, Oxendine (D) argued that the State's medical testimony, relating to which of the codefendant's admittedly repeated beating of Jeffrey was the cause of death, was so vague and uncertain as to preclude his conviction of any criminal offense.

■ ISSUE

Is actual causation necessary to the imposition of criminal liability for manslaughter?

■ DECISION AND RATIONALE

(Horsey, J.) Yes. Actual causation or causation-in-fact is necessary for the imposition of criminal liability. In order to convict Oxendine (D) of manslaughter, the State had to show that his conduct caused Jeffrey's death. In the instant case, the evidence established that Oxendine (D) inflicted a non-lethal injury upon Jeffrey after his son had, twenty-four hours earlier, sustained a lethal injury from a previous beating by Tyree. Thus, in order to convict Oxendine (D) of manslaughter, the State was required to show, for the purposes of causation, that Oxendine's conduct accelerated the child's death. The Superior Court correctly instructed the jury that contribution without acceleration is insufficient to establish causation. Although it is possible to make the victim's pain more intense, we do not equate aggravation with acceleration. Thus, the relevant inquiry is, but for Oxendine's infliction of the second injury, would Jeffrey have died when he died? If the second injury caused Jeffrey to die any sooner, Oxendine would be deemed to have caused his son's death. A finding of medical causation, may not be based on speculation or conjecture. Almost anything is possible, and it is improper to allow a jury to consider and base a verdict upon a possible cause of death. Therefore, a doctor's testimony can only be considered evidence when his conclusions are based on reasonable medical certainty that a fact is true or untrue. The State's expert medical testimony, even when viewed in the light most favorable to the State, was insufficient to sustain the State's ultimate theory of causation on which the court instructed the jury. Both Dr. Inguito and Dr. Hameli, were unable to state with any degree of medical certainty that the second injury contributed to the death of the child. Dr. Inguito could only testify that it was possible that the second injury contributed to death. Dr. Hameli testified that the second injury could have, but probably would not cause death. Moreover, he could not give an opinion as to whether the second injury accelerated Jeffrey's death. Similarly, Dr. Inguito was not asked, nor did he offer an opinion about acceleration. The record establishes that the only theory of causation under which the State submitted the case to the jury was the acceleration theory. Although those responsible must be punished, there must be proof as to who, if anyone, inflicted the injuries that resulted in death. However, because there was sufficient evidence for a rational trier of fact to conclude beyond a reasonable doubt that Oxendine (D) was guilty of a lesser included offense, assault in the second degree, the trial court properly denied Oxendine's (D) motion for judgment of acquittal. Therefore, we reverse the conviction of manslaughter, and remand the case to the Superior Court for entry of a judgment of conviction and resentence.

Analysis:

Courts traditionally use the "but for" test in determining actual cause. In the instant case, the court equated "actual cause" with "acceleration." More specifically, Oxendine (D) would be found the actual cause of Jeffrey's death if his contribution to Jeffrey's injuries accelerated Jeffrey's death. Accordingly, contribution without acceleration would not be sufficient to convict Oxendine (D) of manslaughter. Therefore, as the court states, the relevant inquiry is, but for Oxendine's (D) infliction of the second injury, would Jeffrey have died *when he did*? The last three words, "when he did" in the courts "but for" analysis support the conclusion that "acceleration" equals "actual cause."

■ CASE VOCABULARY

ACCELERATION: The bringing about of a prohibited result at an earlier time than it would be expected to occur, which is sufficient to satisfy "but for" determination of causation.

ACTUAL CAUSE (CAUSE-IN-FACT): The first prong of the causation analysis, determined traditionally by the application of the "but for" test.

MANSLAUGHTER: The intentional killing of a human being without malice aforethought.

Kibbe v. Henderson

(*Thief*) v. (*Not Stated*)
534 F.2d 493 (2d Cir. 1976)

PROOF BEYOND A REASONABLE DOUBT OF PROXIMATE OR LEGAL CAUSATION IS NECESSARY FOR CRIMINAL LIABILITY

■ **INSTANT FACTS** A person is convicted of second degree murder, after robbing, undressing, and abandoning a highly intoxicated individual on a two-lane highway, who was run over by pickup truck.

■ **BLACK LETTER RULE** Proximate or legal causation is a necessary prerequisite to the imposition of criminal liability.

■ PROCEDURAL BASIS

Appeal to the United States Court of Appeal, of a conviction for second degree murder.

■ FACTS

On December 30, 1970, Barren Warren Kibbe (Kibbe) (D), and his codefendant, Roy Krall (Krall), met George Stafford (Stafford) at a bar in Rochester, New York. Stafford had been drinking so heavily and was so intoxicated, that by 9:00 p.m. the bartender refused to serve him further, despite Stafford's offer to pay with a hundred dollar bill. At some point that evening, Stafford began soliciting a ride to Canandaigua from the other patrons at the bar. Kibbe (D) and Krall, who confessed to having already decided to rob Stafford, offered a ride. They first stopped at a second bar, where Stafford was again refused any drinks by the bartender because of his inebriated condition. Then the three proceeded to a third bar, where each were served additional drinks. At about 9:30 p.m. that evening, the three left for Canandaigua in Kibbe's (D) car. According to the statements of Kibbe (D) and Krall, as Krall was driving, Kibbe (D) demanded Stafford's money, and upon receiving it, forced Stafford to lower his trousers and remove his boots to prove that he had no more. At some time between 9:30 and 9:40 p.m., Stafford was abandoned on the side of an unlit, rural two-lane highway. His boots and jacket were also placed on the shoulder of the highway, but his eyeglasses remained in the car. There was testimony that it was "very cold" that night, and that there was an open and lighted service station in the general vicinity, no more than one-quarter of a mile away. About half an hour after Stafford was abandoned, Michael Blake (Blake), a college student, was driving his pickup truck northbound on the highway at 50 miles an hour. This was ten miles over the posted speed limit. A car passed Blake on a southbound direction and the driver flashed his headlights at Blake. Immediately thereafter, Blake saw Stafford sitting in the middle of the northbound lane with his hands in the air. Blake testified that he "went into a kind of shock" as soon as he saw Stafford, and did not apply his brakes, nor attempt to avoid hitting Stafford, because he "didn't have time to react." After the collision, Blake stopped his truck and returned to assist Stafford, whereupon he found that the decedent's trousers were around his ankles, and that his shirt was up to his chest. Stafford was wearing neither his jacket nor his boots. Stafford suffered massive head and body injuries as a result of the collision and died shortly after. The Medical Examiner testified that these injuries were the direct cause of death, and an autopsy revealed a high alcohol concentration of .25% in his blood. Among other things, Kibbe (D) was found guilty of murder in the second degree under New York Penal Law § 125.25(2) [which provides that a person is guilty of murder in the second degree when he recklessly engages in conduct which creates a grave risk of death to another, and thereby causes the death of another]. The Appellate Division affirmed the conviction on finding that there was sufficient evidence that Stafford's death was caused by Kibbe's (D) acts. Kibbe (D) appeals to the United States Court of Appeals, contending that the question of causation was a pivotal issue at trial, and that the judge's failure to instruct the jury with respect to that issue, allowed the jury to convict without finding that every element of the crime had been proven beyond a reasonable doubt.

■ ISSUE

Is proximate or legal causation, a necessary element of a criminal conviction?

■ DECISION AND RATIONALE

(Lumbard, J.) Yes. Proximate or legal causation is a necessary prerequisite to the imposition of criminal liability. In the instant case, the judge failed to define or explain the issue of causation, as the term is used in the New York statute, in his charge to the jury. Nor did the judge mention the legal effect of intervening or supervening cause. The omission of any definition of causation, permitted the jury to conclude that the issue was not before them, or that causation could be inferred merely from the fact that Stafford's death succeeded his abandonment by Kibbe (D) and Krall. Even if the jury was aware of the need to determine causation, the court's instruction did not provide the tools necessary to that task. The complexity of the definition of legal causation, requires an explanation of intervening and supervening cause, as essential to the jury's determination. It has been held that where death is produced by an intervening force, such as Blake's operation of his truck, the liability of one who put an antecedent force into action will depend on the difficult determination of whether the intervening force was a sufficiently independent or supervening cause of death. Given the proper standard of causation, the jury could have found that Blake had been so reckless as to absolve Kibbe (D) of legal responsibility for Stafford's death. Similar cases provide that the controlling questions are whether the ultimate result was foreseeable to the original actor and whether the victim failed to do something easily within his grasp that would have extricated him from danger. We conclude that the trial judge's incomplete instructions took a necessary determination of causation of death from the jury and thereby violated Kibbe's (D) constitutional right to have every element of the crime with which he was charged, proven beyond a reasonable doubt.

Analysis:

This well-written opinion provides a good example of the necessity and difficulty of determining "proximate" or "legal causation", the second prong of the causation analysis. Courts make this determination in order to decide who among the "but for" causes should be held liable for a prohibited result. Here, the trial judge did not provide jury instructions with respect to causation. The appellate court recognizes that, when not given the proper "tools," the jury may be overreaching in its decision to impose criminal liability. As the court states, criminal liability for a prohibited result may be absolved if there is a sufficient independent or supervening cause for the prohibited result. The determination may also depend on the foreseeability of the intervening cause of the prohibited result.

■ CASE VOCABULARY

PROXIMATE CAUSE (LEGAL CAUSE): The determination of who, among those that satisfy the "but for" cause, should be held criminally liable or accountable for a prohibited result.

Velazquez v. State

(*Drag Racer*) v. (*Community*)
561 So.2d 347 (Fla. 1990)

CAUSATION IS AN ELEMENT OF CRIMINAL RESPONSIBILITY

■ **INSTANT FACTS** A "drag racer" is prosecuted for vehicular homicide, after participating in a race on a public road, where the other racer lost control of his car, drove through a guardrail, and died.

■ **BLACK LETTER RULE** Causation is a necessary prerequisite to the imposition of criminal liability.

■ PROCEDURAL BASIS

Appeal to the Florida Court of Appeals, of a conviction for vehicular manslaughter.

■ FACTS

Velazquez (D) and the victim, participated in a "drag race" on a public road. After finishing the course of the race, the victim unexpectedly turned his car around and drove at a speed estimated at 123 m.p.h. toward the starting line, with Velazquez (D) following behind at a similar speed. As both reached the starting point at the end of the road, the victim, unable to stop his car, died when his car hurdled through a guardrail. Velazquez (D) was convicted of vehicular homicide under Florida's vehicular homicide statute, § 82.071 [which defines vehicular homicide as the killing of a human being by the operation of a motor vehicle by another in a reckless manner likely to cause the death of, or great bodily harm to, another]. Velazquez (D) appeals.

■ ISSUE

Is causation a necessary element to the imposition of criminal liability?

■ DECISION AND RATIONALE

(Hubbart, J.) Yes. Causation is a necessary prerequisite to the imposition of criminal liability. There are two statutory elements to vehicular homicide: 1) the defendant must operate a motor vehicle in a reckless manner likely to cause the death of, or great bodily harm to, another, and 2) this reckless operation of a motor vehicle must be the proximate cause of the death of a human being. It seems clear that the proximate cause element requires, at the very least, a causation-in-fact test. In other words the defendant must be the cause-in-fact of the death of a human being. In this respect, vehicular homicide is no different than any other criminal offense in which the occurrence of a specified result, caused by a defendant's conduct, is an essential element of the offense. Clearly, there can be no criminal liability for such result-type offenses unless it can be shown that the defendant's conduct was a cause-in-fact of the prohibited result. Courts throughout the country have uniformly followed the traditional "but for" test in determining whether the defendant's conduct was a cause-in-fact of a prohibited consequence. Under this test, a defendant's conduct is a cause-in-fact of a prohibited result if the said result would not have occurred "but for" the defendant's conduct. Thus, a defendant's reckless operation of a motor vehicle is cause-in-fact of the death of a human being, if the subject death would not have occurred but for the defendant's reckless driving, or would not have happened in the absence of such driving. In rare cases, the "but for" test fails. This anomaly occurs when two defendants, acting independently and not in concert with one another, commit two separate acts, each of which alone is sufficient to bring about the prohibited result. It also occurs when two defendants concurrently inflict mortal wounds upon a human being, each of which is sufficient to cause death. In such cases, each defendant's action was not a "but for" cause of death because the deceased would have died even in the absence of either defendant's conduct, although obviously not in the absence of both defendant's conduct considered together. In these rare cases, the courts have followed a "substantial factor" test. Specifically, the defendant's conduct is a cause-in-fact of a prohibited result if the subject conduct was a "substantial factor" in bringing about the said result. Thus, each defendant's conduct in independently and concurrently inflicting mortal wounds on a deceased clearly constitutes a "substantial factor" in bringing about the deceased's death, and consequently, is a cause-in-fact of the deceased's death. The "proximate cause" element embraces more however than the aforesaid "but for" and "substantial factor" causation-in-fact analysis. Even where a defendant's conduct is a cause-in-fact of a prohibited result, courts throughout the country have for good reason declined to impose criminal liability, 1) where the prohibited result of the defendant's conduct is beyond the scope of any fair assessment of the danger created by the defendant's conduct, or 2) where it would otherwise be unjust, based on fairness and policy consideration, to hold the defendant criminally responsible for the prohibited result.

Analysis:

This case introduces the reader to the concept of causation in criminal law. Similar to torts, causation is a necessary element to the imposition of criminal liability. Specifically, a person must be the cause-in-fact and proximate cause of a specific result. In the instant opinion, the court first states that proximate causation is a necessary element to the imposition of criminal liability. It then recognizes that the starting point of this analysis is the determination of "actual cause" or "cause-in-fact."

■ CASE VOCABULARY

CAUSATION: The producing of a prohibited result, which is required for the imposition of criminal liability.

State v. Rose

(*Society*) v. (*Pedestrian Killer*)
112 R.I. 402, 311 A.2d 281 (1973)

CONCURRENCE OF ELEMENTS IS NECESSARY FOR CRIMINAL RESPONSIBILITY

■ **INSTANT FACTS** An automobile driver is convicted of negligent manslaughter, after hitting a pedestrian, and dragging the pedestrian who was lodged underneath the vehicle.

■ **BLACK LETTER RULE** Elements of a crime must occur concurrently in order to impose criminal liability for that crime.

■ PROCEDURAL BASIS

Certification to the Supreme Court of Rhode Island of a conviction for leaving the scene of an accident and manslaughter.

■ FACTS

On April 1, 1970, at about 6:30 p.m., David J. McEnery (McEnery) was struck by the vehicle of Henry Rose (Rose) (D), at the intersection of Broad and Summer Streets in Providence. According to the testimony of a bus driver, who was traveling north on Broad, and stopped at a traffic light at the intersection of Summer Street, McEnery was starting to cross Broad Street. As he reached the middle of the southbound lane, he was stuck by a "dirty white station wagon," that was proceeding southerly on Broad Street. McEnery was thrown up on the hood of the car. The station wagon stopped momentarily while the body of McEnery rolled off the hood, and then immediately drove off along Broad Street. The bus driver exited the bus in order to help McEnery, but was unable to locate the body. At about 6:40, a police officer located a white station wagon on Haskins Street, 610 feet from the scene of the accident. The body of McEnery was discovered wedged beneath the vehicle, when it was found that the vehicle had been registered to Rose (D). Rose (D) was indicted, and found guilty of, 1) leaving the scene of an accident resulting in death, and 2) with negligent manslaughter. Rose (D) moved for a new trial arguing that he could only be convicted if the prosecution could show that McEnery was killed when Rose (D) drove away, not if he was killed from the initial impact. Rose's (D) motion for a new trial was denied. Rose (D) appeals.

■ ISSUE

Must the elements of a crime all occur at the same time in order to impose criminal liability?

■ DECISION AND RATIONALE

(Roberts, J.) Yes. Elements of a crime must occur concurrently in order to impose criminal liability. We first turn to Rose's (D) contention that the trial court erred in denying his motion for a directed verdict. In a criminal case, where the evidence adduced by the state and the reasonable inferences to be drawn therefrom, even when viewed in a light most favorable to the state, are insufficient to establish guilt beyond a reasonable doubt, the court must grant the defendant's motion for a directed verdict. Here, Rose (D) argues that the evidence didn't exclude any reasonable hypotheses or theory of innocence. Concerning the indictment for manslaughter, Rose (D) directs our attention to the fact that the court charged the jury that there was no evidence in the case of culpable negligence on the part of

Rose (D), up to and including the time at which McEnery was struck by the station wagon. The court further charged the jury that, in order to find Rose (D) guilty of manslaughter, it would be necessary to find that McEnerey was alive immediately after the impact (driving away) and that the conduct of defendant following the impact constituted culpable negligence. Rose (D) is contending that if the evidence is susceptible of a finding that McEnery was killed upon impact, he was not alive at the time he was being dragged under Rose's (D) vehicle and Rose (D) could not be found guilty of manslaughter. An examination of the testimony of the medical witness makes it clear that, in his opinion, death could have resulted upon the initial impact, because of a massive fracture of the skull. The medical witness also testified that death could have resulted a few minutes after the impact, but conceded that he was not sure when it did occur. We agree with Rose's (D) contention. The evidence is such that death could have occurred after Rose (D) had driven away with McEnery's body lodged under his car and, therefore, consistent with guilt. On the other hand, the medical testimony is equally consistent with a finding that McEnery could have died instantly upon impact and, therefore, be consistent with a reasonable conclusion other than guilt. It is clear then, that the testimony of the medical examiner lacking any reasonable medical certainty as to the time of the death of McEnery, we are unable to conclude that on such evidence, defendant was guilty of manslaughter beyond a reasonable doubt. We conclude that it was error to deny Rose's (D) motion for a directed verdict. However, we do not reach the same conclusion with respect to Rose's (D) indictment for leaving the scene of an accident.

Analysis:

In the instant case, Rose (D) was charged with manslaughter. The elements of negligent or involuntary manslaughter that needed to be proven beyond a reasonable doubt included culpable negligence and, of course, death. However, it was also necessary to prove that these elements occurred simultaneously, or more specifically, that Rose's (D) culpable negligence was the cause of the ensuing death. If McEnery died immediately after the initial impact, then Rose (D) cannot be guilty of manslaughter, because of the lack of proof of culpable criminal negligence up to that point. If McEnery died because he was dragged underneath the car, however, Rose (D) would be guilty, because his culpable negligence in leaving the scene of the accident was the cause of the ensuing death. Since both situations were equally possible, the trier of fact could not reasonable believe beyond a reasonable doubt that Rose (D) was guilty of manslaughter. This case turns, therefore, upon the time of McEnery's death. Without sufficient proof that the elements of the crime of manslaughter were satisfied concurrently, Rose (D) could not be held criminally liable for manslaughter.

■ CASE VOCABULARY

CULPABLE NEGLIGENCE: Extreme or gross negligence, sufficient for the imposition of criminal liability.

INVOLUNTARY MANSLAUGHTER: An unlawful killing, committed without intent, by an act of criminal or culpable negligence.

NEGLIGENCE: Failure to act as a reasonably prudent person.

CHAPTER SEVEN

Criminal Homicide

People v. Eulo

Instant Facts: Shooter shot the victim who was pronounced brain dead. The hospital then harvested the victim's organs and turned off life support. Shooter claims hospital killed victim, not he.

Black Letter Rule: When a person is brain dead, he is dead for purposes of assigning criminal liability for homicide.

State v. Guthrie

Instant Facts: Guthrie (D) was convicted of first-degree murder and appealed the conviction based on the trial court's instructions to the jury.

Black Letter Rule: Murder in the first degree consists of an intentional, deliberate, and premeditated killing, which means that the killing occurs after a period of time for prior consideration.

Midgett v. State

Instant Facts: A father who had been in the habit of physically abusing and neglecting his son, got drunk and beat him again resulting in the child's death. The father was found guilty of murder 1st by the trial court.

Black Letter Rule: Evidence of intentional child abuse, which eventually resulted in the child's death, is not sufficient by itself to show the premeditated intent to kill necessary to sustain a conviction for murder in the first degree.

State v. Forrest

Instant Facts: Forrest's (D) father was terminally ill and in the hospital with a do not resuscitate order. Forest (D) killed his father by shooting him, stating he did not want his father to suffer any longer.

Black Letter Rule: Killing someone to prevent their further suffering is still murder in the first degree, if it is willful, deliberate, and premeditated.

Girouard v. State

Instant Facts: A husband killed his wife by stabbing her 19 times after she said horrible things, threatened to leave him and told him he would be court-marshaled.

Black Letter Rule: Words alone are not adequate provocation to provoke a reasonable person to kill in the heat of passion, thus they are not enough to mitigate murder to manslaughter.

Attorney General for Jersey v. Holley

Instant Facts: The defendant was convicted of manslaughter for killing his live-in girlfriend, and he appealed, arguing that the jury was improperly instructed on the defense of provocation because it was directed not to consider his intoxication.

Black Letter Rule: Neither evidence of the defendant's chronic alcoholism nor evidence of his intoxication at the time of the crime is a matter to be taken into account by the jury when considering whether, having regard to the actual provocation and their view of its gravity, a person having ordinary powers of self-control would have done what the defendant did.

People v. Casassa

Instant Facts: After dating Casassa (D) the victim told him that she was not interested. He obsessed about her, stalked her, and killed her. His only defense is that he was acting under extreme emotional disturbance caused by her rejection.

Black Letter Rule: The test of whether the extreme emotional disturbance of the killer had a reasonable explanation or excuse depends on a reasonable evaluation of the external circumstances that the killer believed he was facing and not on the killer's personal point of view.

Berry v. Superior Court

Instant Facts: Berry's (D) pit bull attacked and killed a two-year old child.

Black Letter Rule: Relevant law provided by the next case, People v. Nieto Benitz.

People v. Nieto Benitez

Instant Facts: The court determines that using the description "an abandoned or malignant heart" in its instructions to the jury on implied malice is confusing.

Black Letter Rule: A person commits second-degree murder with implied malice when the person performs an act, the natural consequences of which are dangerous to life, and the person deliberately performed the act with conscious disregard for life and with awareness that his or her conduct endangered the life of another.

State v. Hernandez

Instant Facts: Hernandez (D), while drunk, drove his van into a truck killing one person and injuring two others. At trial the drinking slogans that Hernandez used to decorate his van were admitted into evidence over defense objection.

Black Letter Rule: Evidence to show that the accused was aware of the risks of his behavior is not admissible to show mental state when the charge is involuntary manslaughter.

State v. Williams

Instant Facts: The Williams (D), parents of a 17–month-old child with an abscessed tooth, did not supply necessary medical care, and the child died as a result.

Black Letter Rule: A showing of ordinary negligence may be sufficient to support a conviction for manslaughter.

People v. Fuller

Instant Facts: Two guys who were attempting to escape a police officer who had observed them stealing tires got into a high speed chase which resulted in an accident that killed the driver of another car.

Black Letter Rule: The felony-murder rule imposes strict liability for deaths caused by the commission of one of the enumerated felonies, which include burglary, even when the death is accidental.

People v. Howard

Instant Facts: Howard (D) was convicted of second-degree felony murder after killing the occupant of another vehicle while attempting to flee from police in a stolen vehicle, and he appealed his conviction.

Black Letter Rule: The second-degree felony-murder rule provides that, although malice is ordinarily an element of a murder conviction, murder can be committed without malice if the killing occurs during the commission of an inherently dangerous felony.

People v. Robertson

Instant Facts: Robertson (D) fired shots at two men who were burglarizing his vehicle, purportedly trying to scare them but fatally wounding one of them, and he was convicted of felony murder.

Black Letter Rule: A felony-murder instruction is not proper when the predicate felony is an integral part of the homicide, and when, under the prosecution's evidence, it is included in fact within the offense charged.

State v. Sophophone

Instant Facts: The defendant was charged with felony murder after one of defendant's co-burglars was shot and killed by a police officer while fleeing from the scene of the burglary.

Black Letter Rule: A defendant should not be held responsible under the felony-murder doctrine for the death of a co-felon when the killing was the lawful act of a law enforcement officer acting in the line of duty.

Gregg v. Georgia

Instant Facts: Gregg (D) was found guilty of murder and sentenced to death under a new Georgia statute which was designed to reform the state's imposition of the death penalty so that it would be constitutional.

Black Letter Rule: The death penalty as imposed on murderers by the Georgia statute is constitutional because the death penalty is consistent with societal standards, is not an excessive punishment, and the statute provides sufficient safeguards to prevent it from being imposed in an arbitrary or capricious manner.

McCleskey v. Kemp

Instant Facts: A black man found guilty of killing a white man challenges his sentence based on a study that shows that blacks who kill whites get the death more than whites who kill whites, or those who kill blacks.

Black Letter Rule: A statistical study that shows a risk that capital sentencing is influenced by race does not prove that a specific sentence violates the 8th or 14th Amendment.

Payne v. Tennessee

Instant Facts: Three-year-old survived his wounds when his mother and sister were killed. At the sentencing hearing for the killer his grandmother testified about how this had affected him. The killer was sentenced to death.

Black Letter Rule: The 8th amendment does not prohibit the introduction of victim impact evidence at the sentencing phase of a capital trial.

Tison v. Arizona

Instant Facts: The Tison brothers decided to break their father and his cell-mate out of prison, during the escape the father and cell-mate killed a family while the Tison brothers were present.

Black Letter Rule: Major participation in the felony committed combined with reckless indifference to human life is enough to supply the culpability necessary to constitutionally impose the death penalty.

People v. Eulo

(*Prosecutor*) v. (*Shooter*)

63 N.Y.2d 341, 482 N.Y.S.2d 436, 472 N.E.2d 286 (1984)

BRAIN DEAD IS DEAD ENOUGH FOR HOMICIDE

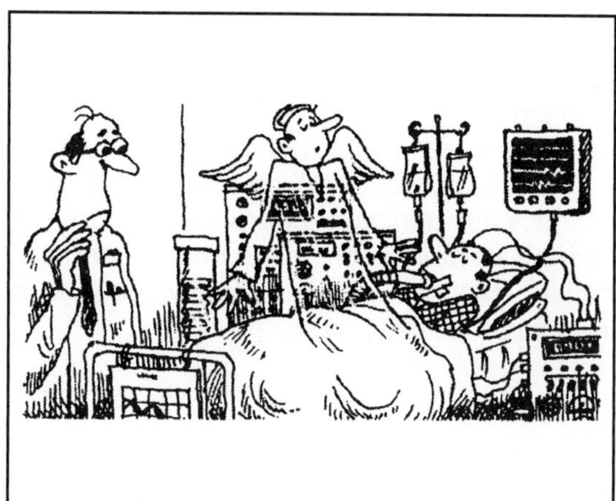

■ **INSTANT FACTS** Shooter shot the victim who was pronounced brain dead. The hospital then harvested the victim's organs and turned off life support. Shooter claims hospital killed victim, not he.

■ **BLACK LETTER RULE** When a person is brain dead, he is dead for purposes of assigning criminal liability for homicide.

■ PROCEDURAL BASIS

Two separate defendants appeal to overturn two separate convictions for manslaughter under similar facts.

■ FACTS

Eulo (D) and Bonilla (D) were separately prosecuted and convicted of manslaughter. Eulo (D) shot his victim in the head. The victim was then taken to the hospital where he was placed on life support. Later the hospital evaluated the victim's condition and determined that his brain was no longer functioning and that he was therefore brain dead. The victim's heart and lungs were still functioning, but only because they were hooked up to machines that kept them that way. With the consent of the victim's family the victim was declared dead. His organs were harvested for donation and life support was terminated. Bonilla's (D) case has substantially the same facts. Both Eulo (D), and Bonilla (D) contend that their actions did not cause the victims' deaths. They argue that in New York death has always been considered to have occurred only when breathing and heartbeat have irreversibly ceased, and that the jury was not properly instructed as to this. This is important, as criminal liability for homicide does not attach until the point of the victim's death. There was extensive testimony at both trials about the victims' having been diagnosed as brain dead. Based on this Eulo (D) and Bonilla (D) contend that the jury may have wrongly concluded that they were guilty of homicide if they were guilty of causing brain death.

■ ISSUE

Is a person criminally liable for homicide if he is criminally liable for causing brain death?

■ DECISION AND RATIONALE

(Cooke, J.) Yes. A person bears responsibility for causing a death, if that person's actions result in brain death, even if it was only after the hospital removed life support that the heartbeat and breathing stopped. To fully address the contentions of Eulo (D) and Bonilla (D) we must examine the correct interpretation of the term. The term has not been expressly defined by the New York State legislature. When a term in a statute is not defined, the court will generally use the ordinary and accepted meaning, and will follow definitions established by judicial precedence. However, definitions may change over time based on changed circumstances, and the court must do its best to support the apparent purpose of the statute. Traditionally death has been defined under common law as the irreversible cessation of breathing and heart rate and the court agrees with that definition as far as it goes. However, circumstances have changed. It is now possible for breathing and heartbeat to be maintained by machines. When these signs are maintained in this way, they are no longer a clear indication of life. Because of this the medical community now considers the cessation of brain activity (brain death) to be a measure of death. This has been recognized by statute in several states. It is considered an extension of the traditional criteria. Though the New York legislature has not yet recognized such an extension, we do not feel that it meant to prevent the court from doing so. Thus a person is dead either when their breathing and heart beat stop irreversibly, or when there is no further brain function (brain death). This interpretation is also consistent with the apparent purpose of the homicide statutes of this state that a person be held responsible for homicide when their actions have caused the victim's total loss of brain function. In these particular cases our affirmation of the convictions is further supported by the fact that even if only the traditional meaning of death was used, and it was found that death did not occur until the machines were turned off, Eulo (D) and Bonilla (D) would still be responsible for the cause of death. Because of the brain death diagnosis, it was medically appropriate to turn the machines off. Thus turning the machines off would not be sufficient intervening cause to interrupt the defendants' liability. Based on all of this there was sufficient evidence for a reasonable juror to find beyond a reasonable doubt that the defendants caused the victims' deaths. Affirmed.

Analysis:

The definition of death is changing. Even the so-called traditional definition of death mentioned in this case marks an evolution from "a person is dead when his heart stops and he isn't breathing," to "a person is dead when his heart stops and he isn't breathing, and he can't be revived." That change reflects advances in medicine, as does the expansion of that definition to include brain death. The definition may change again in the future as we gain a greater understanding of how the body works. To meet their burden, prosecutors must show that a defendant caused the death of the victim beyond a reasonable doubt. In Eulo (D) and Bonilla's (D) case, the court found causation fairly easily. Clearly Eulo (D) and Bonilla (D) caused the victims' brain death by shooting the victims in the head. Even if one disagreed with the court's expanded definition of death, which includes brain death, Eulo (D) and Bonilla's (D) actions still caused the death, because the only reason the life support was turned off, and the organs harvested, is that this is the medically appropriate action once brain death has occurred.

■ CASE VOCABULARY

BRAIN DEATH: Usually, some version of the test: 1) no response to painful stimuli, 2) no spontaneous movement, 3) no reflex reaction and finally 4) a flat EEG reading after a 24 hour period has passed. However, several states have adopted statutory definitions and it is important to check the specific definition for the jurisdiction.

HOMICIDE: A legally neutral term for one person killing another. While homicide clearly includes cases of murder and manslaughter, it also includes post-trail execution by the state, killing in self-defense and other legally sanctioned forms of killing.

STATUTORY CONSTRUCTION: Generally, the interpretation of laws enacted by the legislature. Also a judicial function identifying the correct interpretation of a statute when different interpretations are being argued.

State v. Guthrie

(*Prosecuting Authority*) v. (*Convicted Murderer*)
194 W. Va. 657, 461 S.E.2d 163 (1995)

THE INTENT TO KILL IN FIRST–DEGREE MURDER MUST LAST FOR MORE THAN AN INSTANT

■ **INSTANT FACTS** Guthrie (D) was convicted of first-degree murder and appealed the conviction based on the trial court's instructions to the jury.

■ **BLACK LETTER RULE** Murder in the first degree consists of an intentional, deliberate, and premeditated killing, which means that the killing occurs after a period of time for prior consideration.

■ PROCEDURAL BASIS

Appeal from a conviction for first-degree murder.

■ FACTS

Guthrie (D), a dishwasher, suffered from various psychiatric problems, for which he received treatment. One night at work, he and a co-worker, with whom he normally got along well, were fooling around, and the co-worker snapped a towel at Guthrie (D) several times, telling him to "lighten up." The towel hit Guthrie (D) in the nose and he became enraged, grabbed a knife from his pocket, and stabbed the co-worker in the neck, killing him. Guthrie (D) testified that he had an intense panic attack right before the killing. The jury convicted him of first-degree murder, and Guthrie (D) was sentenced to life in prison. Guthrie (D) appealed.

Guthrie (D) argued on appeal that the trial court's instructions regarding the elements of first-degree murder were improper, because the terms "willful, deliberate, and premeditated" were equated with a mere intent to kill.

■ ISSUE

Did the trial court improperly instruct the jury that in order to find the defendant guilty of first-degree premeditated murder, the intent to kill need only exist for an instant?

■ DECISION AND RATIONALE

(Cleckley, J.) Yes. Murder in the first degree consists of an intentional, deliberate, and premeditated killing, which means that the killing occurs after a period of time for prior consideration. The requisite time varies with the circumstances of each case. Any interval of time between the forming of the intent to kill and the execution of that intent that is of sufficient duration for the accused to be fully conscious of what he intended is sufficient to support a conviction for first-degree murder.

The problem that flows from the instructions given in this case is that they fail to adequately inform the jury of the difference between first-and second-degree murder. Of particular concern is the lack of guidance on the concept of premeditation. Although many states have abandoned the distinction between first-and second-degree murder, given the doctrine of separation of powers, we are not at liberty to rewrite the criminal code. On the other hand, to allow the state to prove premeditation by showing that the intention to kill came into existence for the first time at the instant of a killing completely eliminates the distinction between the degrees. Premeditation and deliberation should be defined more carefully. Accordingly, the court improperly instructed the jury in this case, and the judgment is reversed and the case remanded for a new trial.

Analysis:

"Premeditation" generally requires planning or deliberation, but, as this case demonstrates, the amount of time required for premeditation to exist depends on the particular defendant and the circumstances of the case. Enough time must elapse, after the defendant forms the intent to act, for the defendant to be fully conscious of his intent and for him to fully consider the act. The preparation of weapons may be evidence of premeditation, but not absolute proof of it, since the preparations may have been undertaken for other, legal, purposes, and then suddenly utilized to perform a criminal act. Murder by poisoning, by contrast, is of necessity committed with premeditation.

■ CASE VOCABULARY

SEPARATION OF POWERS: The division of governmental authority into three branches of government—legislative, executive, and judicial—each with specified duties on which neither of the other branches can encroach; the constitutional doctrine of checks and balances by which the people are protected against tyranny.

Midgett v. State

(*Child Abuser*) v. (*Prosecutor*)
292 Ark. 278, 729 S.W.2d 410 (1987)

INTENT TO ABUSE A CHILD IS NOT SUFFICIENT EVIDENCE TO SHOW PREMEDITATED INTENT TO KILL

■ **INSTANT FACTS** A father who had been in the habit of physically abusing and neglecting his son, got drunk and beat him again resulting in the child's death. The father was found guilty of murder 1st by the trial court.

■ **BLACK LETTER RULE** Evidence of intentional child abuse, which eventually resulted in the child's death, is not sufficient by itself to show the premeditated intent to kill necessary to sustain a conviction for murder in the first degree.

■ PROCEDURAL BASIS

Appeal to the Supreme Court of Arkansas of a conviction for murder in the first degree.

■ FACTS

Midgett (D) was the father of several children including Ronnie Midgett, Jr. (Ronnie Jr.), who were living with him. Ronnie Jr.'s mother was not living in the home. Midgett (D) had been beating Ronnie Jr. for some time. This was established both by the fact that bruises had been noticed on Ronnie Jr. at school, and from partially healed injuries discovered during the autopsy. On the day that Ronnie Jr. died, Midgett (D) brought him to the hospital, stating that something was wrong with his child. The autopsy revealed evidence of substantial bruising, rib fractures, undernourishment and poor development. The medical examiner concluded that Ronnie Jr. died from blunt force trauma consistent with having been struck by a large human fist. Ronnie Jr.'s sister testified at the trial that on the day in question Midgett (D) had gotten very drunk and had been hitting Ronnie Jr. all day. Midgett (D) contends that despite the evidence of child abuse, there is no evidence that he had an intent to kill which was premeditated.

■ ISSUE

Is evidence of the intent to abuse a child sufficient to show the premeditated intent to kill that would sustain a conviction for murder in the first degree?

■ DECISION AND RATIONALE

(Newbern, J.) No. The evidence in this case does not show that Midgett (D) intended to kill Ronnie Jr. He had abused the child before without the child dying. There is no evidence showing that this occasion was different. Thus the evidence does not support a leap from an intent to abuse to an intent to kill. In addition, if at sometime during the abuse Midgett (D) did conceive the intent to kill, the evidence shows that he was drunk and enraged at the time. This evidence does not support a finding of premeditation. Therefore, there is no evidence in this case of a premeditated intent to kill, and the conviction for first degree murder can't be sustained. However, there is clearly sufficient evidence here to uphold a verdict of murder in the second. It is understandable that society might seek to punish this kind of child abuse more severely. In some states they have changed the law so that aggravated battery is one of the felonies that can raise a charge of first degree murder. But that is not the case in this state. Because we must follow the laws as they exist at this time, we can not let the jury's verdict stand. There is insufficient evidence to support it. Conviction modified to murder in the second degree and as modified, sustained.

■ DISSENT

(Hickman) This is the case of a child who died as a result of being subjected to deliberate, methodical, intentional and severe abuse. In finding that there is not enough evidence here to sustain a conviction for murder in the first degree, the majority is substituting its judgment for that of the jury. The majority assumes that the father did not intend to kill the child, but simply to subject him to further abuse. It would be just as reasonable for the jury to decide, based on the evidence of Midgett's (D) past behavior, choking, starving and beating the boy, that Midgett had intended to kill him for months. Thus, the jury did have sufficient evidence for murder in the first degree and we should support their verdict.

Analysis:

This case considers the question of what evidence is necessary to show that a murder is willful, deliberate, and premeditated. The majority ruled that evidence of intentional abuse was not enough. The dissent disagreed. This case also raises the question of whether the current criteria that separate these degrees of murder correctly identifies the more culpable party. Is a father who effectively turns his child's life into a living hell, and who kills the child in the process, less culpable for his child's murder just because he didn't actually intend for the child to die? Some state legislatures don't think so, noting that murder is also murder in the first degree if the death is the result of the perpetrator's commission of certain listed felonies. California, for instance, passed a torture murder statute that would make this father guilty of murder without considering what his intent was.

■ CASE VOCABULARY

DELIBERATE: (As used in the context of willful, deliberate and premeditated) Decided after careful, cool consideration.

State v. Forrest

(*Prosecutor*) v. (*Loving Son*)
321 N.C. 186, 362 S.E.2d 252 (1987)

MERCY KILLING, WHEN IT IS PREMEDITATED, IS STILL MURDER IN THE FIRST DEGREE

■ **INSTANT FACTS** Forrest's (D) father was terminally ill and in the hospital with a do-not-resuscitate order. Forrest (D) killed his father by shooting him, stating he did not want his father to suffer any longer.

■ **BLACK LETTER RULE** Killing someone to prevent his further suffering is still murder in the first degree, if it is willful, deliberate, and premeditated.

■ PROCEDURAL BASIS

Appeal to the Supreme Court of North Carolina of a conviction for first degree murder.

■ FACTS

John Forrest (Forrest) (D) brought his father into the hospital on the 22nd of December. Forrest's (D) father was suffering from several severe medical complaints. It was determined that his condition could not be treated and that he was going to die. The hospital agreed that no extreme measures should be taken to prolong his life. On Christmas Eve Forrest (D) went to see his father. A nurses aid was tending to the father, and Forrest asked her to stop, stating that his father was dying. The nurse's aid told him she thought his father was getting better. She noticed that Forrest (D) seemed very upset and was about to cry. She went to get a nurse. The nurse attempted to comfort Forrest (D) by telling him she thought his father was getting better. At this point Forrest (D) became very angry and told her that he had been taking care of his father for years and he would take care of him. The nurse and nurse's aid left. Forrest (D) began to cry, told his father how much he loved him and then shot him four times in the head. He dropped the gun on the floor of the room and then went into the hall and announced that he had "killed his daddy". He stated, "You can't do anything to him now. He's out of his suffering." He also said, "I know they can burn me for it, but my dad will not have to suffer anymore." The gun used was a 22-caliber, and had to be cocked separately for each shot. The jury were provided with four possible verdicts, murder first, murder second, voluntary manslaughter, and not guilty. They found Forrest (D) guilty of murder first. On appeal Forrest (D) contents that the trial court was incorrect in not granting his motion for a directed verdict on the charge of murder in the first-degree. He argues there was insufficient evidence of premeditation and deliberation to support the charge.

■ ISSUE

Is there sufficient evidence of premeditation and deliberation to support a charge of murder in the first degree, if the killing was done to prevent suffering and the perpetrator was clearly upset at the time of the offense.

■ DECISION AND RATIONALE

(Meyer, J.) Yes. Murder in the first degree is the intentional and unlawful killing of a human being with malice and with premeditation and deliberation. In this case there is substantial evidence that the killing was premeditated and deliberate. We previously decided a case where we found that for a killing to have been premeditated there are definable circumstances that should be considered. First, did the victim provoke the killer? Second, how did the killer act during the killing and what did he say. Third, did the killer threaten the victim? Fourth, was there ill will between the parties? Fifth, did the killer continue to attack the victim after he was incapacitated? And sixth, was the killing done in a brutal manner. Clearly Forrest's (D) terminally ill father did nothing to provoke Forrest (D) to kill him. In addition Forrest's (D) father was helpless before Forrest (D) took any action against him. Forrest (D) shot his father four times, cocking the gun separately each time. Forrest (D) took the gun to the hospital. And finally, Forrest's (D) own statements support the idea that he had carefully considered his actions before taking them. He stated that he was aware that he could be "burned" for his actions in killing his father. He stated that he wanted to end his father's suffering. He stated that he had promised his father he would not allow him to continue suffering. All of this points to the fact that he had premeditated his actions. And that he had had time to deliberate about the consequences and benefits of this act. Because premeditation and deliberation are clear in this case, the trial court did not err in submitting the issue of murder first to the jury. Conviction upheld.

Analysis:

The law states that murder that is willful, deliberate, and premeditated is murder in the first degree. In this case the court found that the facts provided sufficient evidence of premeditation. The interpretation of the meaning of the law is very straightforward. Premeditated is defined the same way it would be in the dictionary. What people disagree with here is the law itself, and the results it produces. As discussed in the analysis of *Midgett*, there is a question as to whether premeditation is the correct way to identify what makes one murder worse than another. What is legal is often confused with what is moral. It is true that one of the things that the law is attempting to achieve is the codification of what is morally acceptable behavior in society. However, what society considers to be morally acceptable behavior changes over time. As medical care has advanced, our attitude towards the prolonged process of dying with a terminal illness has changed. Because of this change we are more likely to sympathize with Forrest's (D) motives in this case.

■ CASE VOCABULARY

DIRECTED VERDICT: When the side which carries the burden of proof fails to make a prima facie case the judge may direct that a verdict to be entered without submitting the issue to a jury. The judge may do this because in such a case there is only one verdict that is possible under the law. The verdict that results from this process is a directed verdict.

TERMINAL: In the context of an illness, the stage of the illness that is going to result in death. In some states this is a legally defined term which can be relevant to the consideration of what kinds of treatment can be withdrawn from a dying patient.

Girouard v. State

(*Husband*) v. (*Prosecutor*)

321 Md. 532, 583 A.2d 718 (1991)

WORDS ALONE ARE NOT ENOUGH PROVOCATION TO REDUCE MURDER TO MANSLAUGHTER

■ **INSTANT FACTS** A husband killed his wife by stabbing her 19 times after she said horrible things, threatened to leave him and told him he would be court-marshaled.

■ **BLACK LETTER RULE** Words alone are not adequate provocation to provoke a reasonable person to kill in the heat of passion, thus they are not enough to mitigate murder to manslaughter.

■ PROCEDURAL BASIS

Appeal to the Court of Appeals of Maryland of a conviction for murder.

■ FACTS

Steven S. Girouard (D) (Steven) and Joyce M Girouard (Joyce) got married in August of 1987. Both of them were in the army. The marriage was very tense, and there was some indication that Joyce had been unfaithful. Two months into the marriage Steven (D) overheard Joyce talking on the phone about leaving him. He asked her what that was about and she refused to answer him. He knocked over the food she was eating and left the room. She followed him, hit him on his back and pulled his hair. "The honeymoon is over." She told him that he was a terrible husband, and that she had never wanted to marry him. She said several other things, which were very insulting. This included telling him she had reported him to the JAG for spousal abuse and that he would probably be court-marshaled. Through all of this she continually asked him what he was going to do about it. Steven (D) then went into the kitchen and got a knife which he held under a pillow. He then went back to talk to Joyce and she continued to harangue him. Steven (D) claims that he kept waiting for her to say that she was joking and that when she did not, he stabbed her 19 times. Steven (D) was 6′2″ tall, and weighed over 200 pounds. Joyce was 5′1″ and weighed 115 pounds. After the killing, Steven (D) dropped the knife and took a shower. He attempted to slash his wrists but was unsuccessful. He then called the police and told them he had murdered his wife. He was found wandering, distraught, talking about how much he loved his wife and could not believe what he had done. At his trial a psychiatrist testified that Steven's (D) personality was very fragile, and that he had suffered an extreme explosion of rage combined with intense panic. He was convicted of murder in the second degree. Steven (D) contends that manslaughter should include all criminal homicides that lack the malice essential for murder. And, that the court should thus extend the definition of what constitutes adequate provocation to include cases like his. The prosecutor contends that the court should not extend adequate provocation to any case that involves provocation by words alone because doing so would mean that any domestic argument that ends in murder would be mitigated to manslaughter.

■ ISSUE

Are words alone enough to provoke a reasonable person to kill in the heat of passion and thus constitute adequate provocation to mitigate the charge of murder down to manslaughter?

■ DECISION AND RATIONALE

(Cole) No. The difference between murder and manslaughter is that manslaughter lacks the malice that is present in a murder. This malice is shown to be missing because the killing is done in a sudden heat of passion caused by adequate provocation before there has been a reasonable opportunity for the passion to cool. There are four situations which have been traditionally recognized as adequate provocation: 1) discovering your spouse having sex with someone else, 2) being engaged in mutual combat, 3) having been subjected to assault and batter by the victim, and finally, 4) discovering injury to a family relative or third party. It seems reasonable to suggest that these situations do not cover all the cases that could legitimately be called manslaughter. We are willing to consider expanding the criteria to other situations that fit the Rule of Provocation. The Rule of Provocation requires: 1) adequate provocation, 2) that the killing be the result of a sudden heat of passion, 3) there has been no opportunity to cool off and 4) there must be a causal connection between the provocation and the fatal act. We will assume all of these requirements have been met except for adequate provocation, which is the issue in this case. In order for provocation to be adequate it must be capable of causing a reasonable man to act from passion rather than reason. Maryland case law indicates that words alone are not enough to reach this standard. The only time words have been held to be adequate provocation was when they indicated an immediate intention to inflict injury and were accompanied by a clear ability to carry out the intention. We recognize that the words Joyce used were a significant provocation. However, they do not rise to the level of an adequate provocation. It is not reasonable to suggest that Joyce was threatening Steven (D) with physical harm she had the ability to immediately carry out. She was considerably smaller than Steven (D). She was not armed. Through the testimony at trial an attempt was made to suggest that because of Steven's (D) particular psychology he was particularly vulnerable to Joyce's words, making them adequate provocation. However the standard is what would adequately provoke a reasonable person, it does not take the particular vulnerabilities of the killer into account. Words alone are not enough to provoke a reasonable man to kill in the heat of passion and are thus not an adequate provocation to mitigate murder down to manslaughter. We affirm.

Analysis:

Here the killer is arguing that because the provocation of the victim was so outrageous, the act of killing is not as bad as it would be normally. This defense examines the conduct of the victim and asks society to approve to some degree the killer's conduct. This defense has been recognized by the courts and used as an explanation of why a finding of manslaughter is appropriate. The justification defense has been criticized. It focuses attention on the victim and not on the actions of the killer. This creates a situation where the trial of the killer becomes a trial of the victim. This is particularly distasteful in the long line of cases where a husband kills his wife after discovering her being unfaithful. While society does not approve of adultery, it usually is not something for which a criminal penalty is assessed. Thus it seems strange that the law should continue to consider it any kind of justification for killing someone. The outcome of this case, a refusal to recognize words alone as an adequate excuse for losing control and killing, or as a justification of killing, is very reasonable in light of these considerations.

■ CASE VOCABULARY

ADEQUATE PROVOCATION: Provocation that is so upsetting that it would make a reasonable person so angry that they are no longer capable of reasoned deliberation or premeditation.

MITIGATE: To reduce in severity. Circumstances may mitigate a crime by indicating that the person committing the crime is less culpable. Judges can also mitigate a sentence by making it shorter or otherwise less harsh because of remorse, cooperation with police or other such factors.

MUTUAL COMBAT: A fight that both parties enter into voluntarily, not a case where one party unexpectedly attacks and the other merely defends himself. It is similar to a duel but without formal rules or protocol. Sometimes referred to as a mutual affray.

Attorney General for Jersey v. Holley

(*Prosecuting Authority*) v. (*Convicted Killer*)

UKPC 23, 3 All E.R. 371 (Privy Council 2005)

THE BRITISH DEFENSE OF PROVOCATION IS AKIN TO SELF-DEFENSE

■ **INSTANT FACTS** The defendant was convicted of manslaughter for killing his live-in girlfriend, and he appealed, arguing that the jury was improperly instructed on the defense of provocation because it was directed not to consider his intoxication.

■ **BLACK LETTER RULE** Neither evidence of the defendant's chronic alcoholism nor evidence of his intoxication at the time of the crime is a matter to be taken into account by the jury when considering whether, having regard to the actual provocation and their view of its gravity, a person having ordinary powers of self-control would have done what the defendant did.

■ PROCEDURAL BASIS

Appeal from the defendant's conviction.

■ FACTS

Holley (D) and Mullane lived together for a number of years. They were both alcoholics. Their relationship was stormy, and they engaged in numerous drunken rows, during which Mullane was prone to making derogatory comments to Holley (D) that affected his self-esteem. One afternoon, Holley (D) was drinking at home and chopping wood with an axe. After drinking at a local bar, Mullane returned home and taunted Holley (D) by telling him she had just had sex with another man. Holley (D) claims he picked up his axe to return to his wood chopping, whereupon Mullane said, "You haven't got the guts," and Holley (D) then lifted the axe and repeatedly struck Mullane with it, killing her.

The defendant was tried and convicted of murder, and he appealed, arguing that the jury was improperly instructed on the issue of provocation. The reviewing court agreed and granted a new trial. The only issue at the new trial was that of provocation, and the defendant presented substantial evidence relating to his alcoholism. Nonetheless, the second jury returned a verdict of guilty as well. The defendant appealed again, and the appellate court again found that the jury had been misdirected on the issue of provocation, but given the two preceding trials, it declined to order another one, instead entering a conviction for manslaughter and reducing the defendant's sentence from life to eight years in prison.

■ ISSUE

Should evidence of the defendant's alcoholism or intoxication be taken into account when considering whether a person having ordinary powers of self-control would have done what the defendant did?

■ DECISION AND RATIONALE

(Lord Nichols of Birkenhead.) No. Neither evidence of the defendant's chronic alcoholism nor evidence of his intoxication at the time of the crime is a matter to be taken into account by the jury when considering whether, having regard to the actual provocation and their view of its gravity, a person having ordinary powers of self-control would have done what the defendant did. The court of appeal was wrong in making a distinction between intoxication and alcoholism in this regard. It reasoned that being drunk does not give rise to a reasonable ground for a provocation defense, but that alcoholism is a disease, which must be taken into account when deciding whether a defendant was provoked. This is incorrect.

The defense of provocation has two ingredients. The first is the subjective, or factual, ingredient, which requires that the defendant was provoked into losing self-control, taking into consideration any mental or other abnormalities of the defendant that made it more likely he would lose control. With regard to this factor, the defendant's state of intoxication may be a relevant inquiry. The second is the objective, or evaluative, ingredient, which raises the question of whether the provocation was enough to make a reasonable person do as the defendant did. "Reasonable" is a poor choice of words; in reality, the statutory standard is based on how a person of *ordinary* control would act under the circumstances. It is acceptable to take age and gender into account when determining what is "ordinary" under the circumstances, but other factors, such as intoxication, do not enter into this part of the analysis.

Based on the incorrect jury instruction, the order of the court of appeal would ordinarily be set aside and the defendant's conviction for murder reinstated. But there are procedural oddities in this case. The order of the court of appeal should stand.

Analysis:

The opinion in this case briefly mentions the concepts of "battered woman defense" and the underlying battered person syndrome. Because the defense is most often invoked by women, it is usually characterized in the feminine sense (as battered *woman* syndrome or battered *wife* syndrome), but as the facts of this case indicate, the defense may be implicated for males as well. The courts in both the United States and the United Kingdom have recognized that extensive research shows that battered partners may use force to defend themselves, and sometimes even kill their abusers, because of the abusive circumstances under which they live.

■ CASE VOCABULARY

BATTERED–WOMAN SYNDROME: A constellation of medical and psychological conditions of a woman who has suffered physical, sexual, or emotional abuse at the hands of a spouse or lover. Battered-woman syndrome was first described in the early 1970s by Dr. Lenore Walker. It consists of a three-stage cycle of violence: (1) the tension-building stage, which may include verbal and mild physical abuse; (2) the acute battering stage, which includes stronger verbal abuse, increased physical violence, and perhaps rape or other sexual abuse; and (3) the loving-contrition stage, which includes the abuser's apologies, attentiveness, kindness, and gift-giving. This syndrome is sometimes proposed as a defense to justify or mitigate a woman's killing of a man. Sometimes (more specifically) termed *battered-wife syndrome*; (more broadly) *battered-spouse syndrome*; (broadly) *battered-person syndrome*.

PROVOCATION: The act of inciting another to do something, esp. to commit a crime; something (such as words or actions) that affects a person's reason and self-control, especially causing the person to commit a crime impulsively.

People v. Casassa

(*Prosecutor*) v. (*Killer*)

49 N.Y.2d 668, 427 N.Y.S.2d 769, 404 N.E.2d 1310 (1980)

MODEL PENAL CODE BROADENS APPLICATION OF MANSLAUGHTER DEFENSE, BUT ONLY SO FAR

■ **INSTANT FACTS** After dating Casassa (D) the victim told him that she was not interested. He obsessed about her, stalked her, and killed her. His only defense is that he was acting under extreme emotional disturbance caused by her rejection.

■ **BLACK LETTER RULE** The test of whether the extreme emotional disturbance of the killer had a reasonable explanation or excuse depends on a reasonable evaluation of the external circumstances that the killer believed he was facing and not on the killer's personal point of view.

■ PROCEDURAL BASIS

Appeal of a conviction for murder in the second degree to The Court of Appeals of New York.

■ FACTS

Victor Casassa (D) (Casassa) met Victoria Lo Consolo (Lo Consolo) because they lived in the same apartment complex. They dated a few times casually. Lo Consolo informed Casassa (D) that she was not falling in love with him. Casassa (D) says that this rejection devastated him. After this initial rejection Casassa (D) started doing some odd things. He broke into the apartment below Lo Consolo's so that he could eavesdrop on her while she pursued other relationships. He claims the things he heard further devastated him. He broke into her apartment and lay naked in her bed. He reports having had a knife with him at that time of the break-in. He said he knew he was going to either kill himself or her. Finally on February 28, 1977 he brought several bottles of wine and liquor to her as a gift. When she did not accept this gift he pulled out a steak knife and stabbed her in the throat, after which he pulled her to the bathroom and submerged her body in the tub to make sure she was dead. Casassa (D) does not dispute these facts. He waived a jury trial and had a bench trial before a judge. The defense presented only one witness, a psychiatrist. The psychiatrist testified that Casassa (D) had become obsessed with Lo Consolo and that her rejection combined with his peculiar personality attributes had placed him under the influence of an extreme emotional disturbance at the time of the killing. The state presented several witnesses, among them another psychiatrist. He testified that while Casassa (D) was emotionally disturbed, this should not qualify as an extreme emotional disturbance because his disturbed state was the result of his own twisted mind and not external factors. The trial court found Casassa (D) guilty of murder in the second degree. Casassa (D) appeals arguing that the statute requires the court to examine the case from his point of view and that from his point of view he was suffering from extreme emotional disturbance caused by what he believed was a reasonable explanation or excuse.

■ ISSUE

Is the test of whether an extreme emotional disturbance of the killer was caused by a reasonable explanation or excuse determined from the subjective point of view of the killer?

■ DECISION AND RATIONALE

(Jasen, J.) No. This case is to be decided under section 125.25 of the New York Penal Code, which provides that if the killer can show that he acted under the influence of an extreme emotional disturbance for which there was a reasonable explanation or excuse, he qualifies for an affirmative defense reducing murder in the second degree to manslaughter. Section 125.5 was basically adopted from the Model Penal Code. The "extreme emotional disturbance" defense in the Model Penal Code is an outgrowth of the "heat of passion" defense found in the common law, but it is considerably broader. It eliminates entirely the provision which required that there be no cooling off period between the provocation and the actions which caused the death. It also eliminates the rigid rules concerning what is and what is not adequate provocation. Several incidents can be combined to form the reasonable explanation of the killer's extreme emotional disturbance. The arguments presented by individual defendants can be considered on their own merits. However, it is not a wholly subjective test. It has two separate components. The first component, that the act must have actually been done in a state of "extreme emotional disturbance," is considered subjectively from the killer's point of view. The second component, whether there was a reasonable explanation or excuse for that emotional disturbance, is meant to be more objective. It takes the point of view of a person facing the same circumstances, as the killer believed he was facing, but without any of the particular quirks the killer may have had. "Yes, this is another reworking of the "reasonable man" idea; you didn't really think we were going to escape that, did you?" In this case Casassa (D) has no problem meeting the first component. He was acting out of extreme emotional disturbance. However, the judge, acting here as the finder of fact, reached the conclusion that this emotional disturbance was based on factors peculiar to Casassa (D). And that because these factors were peculiar to him, there was no reasonable explanation or excuse. This conclusion is consistent with the correct application of the law. The definition of manslaughter from the Model Penal Code intentionally leaves the finder of fact with the discretion to make judgmental evaluations of what is reasonable. Here the judge, as finder of fact, has made his decision. Overturning his finding in this case would be inconsistent with the intention of the act. We affirm.

Analysis:

It is very difficult to define the point where we should have compassion for a person who kills after being pushed too far. It has been argued that manslaughter no longer makes sense. The loss of control is not necessarily a good way to identify someone who should spend less time in prison. The fact that a person can lose control and kill someone because of external circumstances does not tend to lessen a person's dangerousness to society. Many have long objected to manslaughter on the basis that it is used as an excuse when abusive men murder their wives. On the other hand, is there anyone who can't imagine a situation in which he or she might be pushed to kill? What if a person came face to face with some modern-day version of Hitler? If a person kills under those circumstances, do we owe him compassion?

■ CASE VOCABULARY

AFFIRMATIVE DEFENSE: A defense that must be raised by the defendant. Some other affirmative defenses in criminal law include self-defense, insanity, alibi, coercion, and duress.

EXTREME EMOTIONAL DISTURBANCE: The phrase, found in the Model Penal Code, used to describe the state of someone who has temporarily lost their self-control because of something external which had a severe emotional effect on them.

FINDER OF FACT: The party charged with determining, when at least some facts are in contention during a trial, what facts are true. In a jury trial the finder of fact is the jury. In a bench trial the judge combines this role with his role as arbitrator of the law.

Berry v. Superior Court

(*Pit Bull Owner*) v. (*Government*)
208 Cal.App.3d 783, 256 Cal.Rptr. 344 (1989)

KEEPING OF A PIT BULL MAY SUPPORT CLAIM OF IMPLIED MALICE SUFFICIENT TO SUPPORT PROSECUTION FOR MURDER

■ **INSTANT FACTS** Berry's (D) pit bull attacked and killed a two-year old child.

■ **BLACK LETTER RULE** Relevant law provided in the case following *Berry*, *People v. Nieto Benitez.*

■ PROCEDURAL BASIS

Petition for a writ of prohibition seeking dismissal of murder charges.

■ FACTS

Berry (D) and the Soto family shared a common driveway. Berry (D) had his pit bull "Willy" tied up on his lot. James Soto, aged two-and-a-half, went near the dog and was mauled. Berry (D) got the dog off the boy, but the child died before the emergency crew arrived on the scene. There was no evidence that Willy had ever attacked a human being before. However, there was considerable evidence that he had been trained as a fighting dog and that he posed a known threat to people. Berry (D) bought Willy from a trainer who informed Berry (D) of Willy's aggressiveness and his exceptionally hard bite. Police found many manuals on dog training and fighting in Berry's (D) possession. Berry (D) had told Mrs. Soto that she needn't be concerned with his other dogs, but that the children should keep away from "the one that he had on the side of the house" which was behind a six-foot fence. Willy was tethered onto a fence on the west side of the house, but was not enclosed. Police found some 243 marijuana plants growing behind defendant's house, and Willy was tethered in such a location that anyone wanting access to the plants would first have to pass by the dog. An animal control expert testified that pit bulls are selectively bred to be aggressive to other animals, and that animal control officers consider a pit bull to be dangerous unless proved otherwise. By petition for a writ of prohibition, Berry (D) seeks dismissal of the murder charges.

■ ISSUE

Could the keeping of a dangerous animal, accessible to the public, support a belief of implied malice?

■ DECISION AND RATIONALE

Relevant law provided in the case following *Berry*, *People v. Nieto Benitez.*

Analysis:

After many attacks, some cities have introduced legislation that effectively prohibits pit bull ownership. One pit bull supporter claims that "if you outlaw pit bulls, only outlaws will have pit bulls." Also, many dog owners, after seeing news of pit bull attacks, bring their dogs to animal shelters to be destroyed, or simply turn them loose. Around forty percent of the stray dogs in Los Angeles County are pit bulls.

What is important about this case, however, is that some conduct can be seen to be so reckless or dangerous as to supply the mens rea element of malice.

People v. Nieto Benitez

(*Prosecution*) v. (*Not given*)

4 Cal.4th 91, 13 Cal.Rptr.2d 864, 840 P.2d 969 (Cal. 1992)

MALICE ELEMENT OF SECOND–DEGREE MURDER MAY BE IMPLIED WHERE ACTION IS TAKEN IN SPITE OF HIGH PROBABILITY THAT IT WILL RESULT IN DEATH, AND ACTOR DEMONSTRATES WANTON DISREGARD FOR HUMAN LIFE

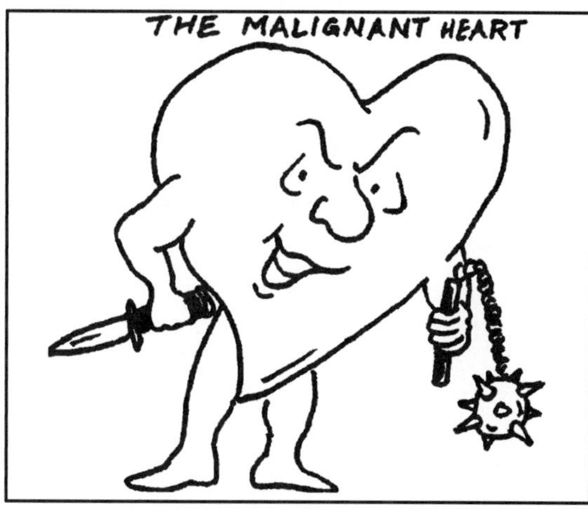

■ **INSTANT FACTS** The court determines that using the description "an abandoned or malignant heart" in its instructions to the jury on implied malice is confusing.

■ **BLACK LETTER RULE** A person commits second-degree murder with implied malice when the person performs an act, the natural consequences of which are dangerous to life, and the person deliberately performed the act with conscious disregard for life and with awareness that his or her conduct endangered the life of another.

■ PROCEDURAL BASIS

Not given.

■ FACTS

The facts of this case are not given. Students are supposed to use the facts of the preceding case, *Berry v. Superior Court*, in conjunction with the law of this case, to analyze *Berry*. The most that we can get from this short excerpt of the opinion is that the Supreme Court of California seems to be contemplating the appropriate manner to instruct a jury on what constitutes malice aforethought in a case where there appears to have been a charge of second degree murder.

■ ISSUE

Should the term "abandoned and malignant heart" continue to be used to instruct a jury on the determination of implied malice in a trial for second-degree murder?

■ DECISION AND RATIONALE

(George, J.) No. The term "abandoned and malignant heart" invites confusion and might lead a jury to equate the malignant heart with an evil disposition, thus leading a jury to convict the defendant if they find him to be a "bad man." Instead, a jury should be instructed that second-degree murder with implied malice has been committed when a person does an act, the natural consequences of which are dangerous to life, and the act was deliberately performed by a person who was aware that his or her conduct endangers the life of another and who acts with conscious disregard for life. In other words, malice may be implied when a defendant takes an action in spite of the high probability that death will result, acting with a base antisocial motive and with a wanton disregard for human life.

Analysis:

Given the basic requirements for a finding of second-degree murder, do you believe that the defendant in *Berry* should be charged with second-degree murder? Do you think that the defendant in *Berry* should have been aware that keeping the pit bull, in the manner that he did, might lead to the death of another person? Did the defendant act with a base antisocial motive or with a wanton disregard for human life? Knowing that there were small children next door, did he have a responsibility to take extra precautions to contain his dog? Does the defendant seem somehow more culpable because he was using the pit bull to protect his marijuana crop?

■ CASE VOCABULARY

DEPRAVED HEART: Term used to describe an actor who takes an action without regard to its life threatening potential and in disregard to social or moral duty.

MALICE AFORETHOUGHT: This term is not synonymous with premeditation, although a finding of malice aforethought may prove sufficient to turn a homicide into a murder. Malice aforethought characterizes action taken with the knowledge that there is a high probability that death will occur.

WANTON: Generally, wanton conduct describes conduct where the actor is aware of the risks of his actions, but is apathetic as to the results.

State v. Hernandez

(*Prosecutor*) v. (*Drunk Driver*)
815 S.W.2d 67 (1991)

WHEN AN INTOXICATED PERSON IS CHARGED WITH INVOLUNTARY MANSLAUGHTER, HIS DISPLAY OF DRINKING SLOGANS IS NOT ADMISSIBLE TO SHOW MENTAL STATE

■ **INSTANT FACTS** Hernandez (D), while drunk, drove his van into a truck killing one person and injuring two others. At trial the drinking slogans that Hernandez used to decorate his van were admitted into evidence over defense objection.

■ **BLACK LETTER RULE** Evidence to show that the accused was aware of the risks of his behavior is not admissible to show mental state when the charge is involuntary manslaughter.

■ PROCEDURAL BASIS

Appeal of a conviction for involuntary manslaughter to the Missouri Court of Appeals.

■ FACTS

On September 12, 1988 Robert Butcher (Butcher) was driving a truck in which Kevin Butcher, his son and Cecil Barrymore were passengers. They were traveling southbound. Pedro M. Hernandez (D) (Hernandez) was driving a van in the opposite direction on the same highway. When Butcher first saw the van it was coming around a curve, on two wheels, and had crossed over into on-coming traffic. Butcher made an effort to avoid the van, which returned to its own side of the line. The van then lurched back across the line and collided with Butcher's truck. As a result of the collision Cecil Barrymore was killed and both Butcher and his son were injured. When Sherry Howard, an employee of the ambulance service tended to Hernandez (D) at the scene of the accident she asked him if he had been drinking. He told her he had had a twelve pack and some whiskey. Hernandez's van was decorated with pins, stickers and signs containing drinking slogans such as: "The more I drink the better you look"; and "Reality is for those who can't stay drunk." Hernandez (D) was charged with involuntary manslaughter. His sun visor, which was covered with the stickers, was admitted into evidence over a defense objection. Hernandez contends that this evidence should not have been admitted because it was not relevant to the charge and was used to show that he was a "bad person" and seeks to overturn his conviction. The state argues that it submitted the evidence to show that Hernandez (D) was aware of the risks of his behavior and approved of excessive drinking.

■ ISSUE

Should evidence which is offered to show that the defendant was aware of the risks of his behavior but which is also prejudicial to his character be admissible when the charge is involuntary manslaughter?

■ DECISION AND RATIONALE

(Per Curiam) No. For evidence to be admissible it must be more relevant than prejudicial. To be relevant it must tend to support or establish a fact or issue between the parties. To prove involuntary manslaughter the prosecutor has to prove 1) that Hernandez (D) acted with criminal negligence and 2) that Cecil Barrymore died as a result of that negligence. Criminal negligence is the least culpable of the mental states that are an element in the commission of a crime. It does not require that Hernandez

(D) be aware of the risk he was creating towards others, but only that he did create such a risk and was criminally negligent in doing so. As a result evidence of his awareness of the risk is not relevant and the prosecution can't put the drinking slogans into evidence. In addition, to admit this evidence to show that the defendant approved of excessive drinking would be to admit character evidence. As Hernandez (D) did not place his character into issue in the case, character evidence from the prosecution is not admissible. Hernandez's (D) conviction for involuntary manslaughter is overturned.

■ DISSENT

(Shrum, J.) The majority argues that it is not necessary to show an awareness of the risk to others, when proving criminal negligence. This is true. However, it is still necessary to prove that the negligence shown by Hernandez (D) in this case rises to a criminal level. In order to do so it is necessary to prove that his conduct was a gross deviation from the standard of care that a reasonable person would show. It must be shown that there is real culpability in Hernandez's (D) failure to be aware of the risk his behavior posed to others. To find Hernandez (D) guilty of involuntary manslaughter, the jury must find 1) that Hernandez (D) created a substantial and unjustifiable risk to the lives of others by driving while intoxicated, 2) that even if he was not aware that by driving while he was intoxicated created this risk he should have been, and 3) that by creating this risk he killed Cecil Barrymore. Some of the stickers with the drinking slogans were relevant to show the second of these elements. The slogan: "The more I drink the better you look" indicates that he knew that drinking affected his perception. "Reality is for those who can't stay drunk," indicates that he was aware that drinking prevented him from being in touch with the world around him. He should have known that these affects of alcohol would prevent him from being able to drive responsibly and that this might place the lives of others at risk. Thus while I agree that this evidence could not be admitted, under this charge, to show that Hernandez was aware of the risk he posed to others, it should be admissible to show that Hernandez's negligent failure to be aware of that risk was criminal.

Analysis:

The basic issue raised by this case is the difference between an unintended murder in the second degree and involuntary manslaughter. Murder in the second degree requires a different mental state, "an abandoned and malignant heart" under common law or "recklessness" under the Model Penal Code, while involuntary manslaughter requires only criminal negligence. For murder in the second degree, the prosecutor must prove that (1) the accused was actually aware that his conduct created a substantial risk of death to others by driving while intoxicated, (2) there was no justification or excuse for that risk, and (3) the risk resulted in the death of the victim. For involuntary manslaughters, he must prove (1) the accused created a substantial and unjustifiable risk; (2) that even if the accused was unaware of this risk, he should have been; and (3) that this risk resulted in the death of the victim. The practical difference comes down to proving whether or not the accused was actually aware that his conduct was creating an unacceptable risk of death.

■ CASE VOCABULARY

CRIMINAL NEGLIGENCE: Negligence that is a gross deviation from a reasonable standard of behavior and is thus culpable. Criminal negligence expands the liability for any damages so that it includes criminal liability as well as civil.

PER CURIAM: Indicates a decision by the whole court instead of just one judge. Sometimes used for opinions from the chief justice.

State v. Williams

(*Government*) v. (*Negligent Parents*)
4 Wash.App. 908, 484 P.2d 1167 (1971)

PARENTS FOUND GUILTY OF MANSLAUGHTER FOR NOT RECOGNIZING THE SEVERITY OF A CHILD'S ILLNESS IN TIME TO SAVE HIS LIFE

■ **INSTANT FACTS** The Williams (D), parents of a 17-month-old child with an abscessed tooth, did not supply necessary medical care, and the child died as a result.

■ **BLACK LETTER RULE** A showing of ordinary negligence may be sufficient to support a conviction for manslaughter.

■ PROCEDURAL BASIS

Appeal from conviction for manslaughter due to ordinary negligence.

■ FACTS

Walter Williams (D) is a 24-year-old Sheshont indian with a 6th grade education. His wife, Bernice Williams (D), is a 20-year-old part-Indian with an 11th grade education. At the time of the marriage, Bernice had two children, the younger of whom was a 14-month-old son. Both Walter and Bernice had a great deal of love for the child. The child became ill on September 1. Both defendants were aware that the child was ill. However, Bernice and Walter "were ignorant," and did not realize how sick he was. They thought he had a toothache, which they did not believe to be life-threatening. They gave the child aspirin in hopes of improving his condition. They did not take the child to a doctor for fear that the Welfare Department would take the baby from them. The abscessed tooth developed into an infection of the mouth and cheeks, eventually becoming gangrenous. This condition, accompanied by the child's inability to eat, brought on malnutrition, which lowered the child's resistance and eventually produced pneumonia, causing death on September 12. The infection lasted about two weeks. A pathologist testified that the infection would have to have been treated within the first 5 days in order to save the child. The Williams (D) were convicted of manslaughter due to their negligence in not seeking medical treatment for the child.

■ ISSUE

May simple negligence support a conviction for manslaughter?

■ DECISION AND RATIONALE

(Horowitz) Yes. There is a parental duty to provide medical care to a dependent, minor child. To prove involuntary manslaughter, the common law requires that a breach of this duty had to amount to more than mere ordinary or simple negligence—a showing of gross negligence was required. In Washington, however, the statutes defining manslaughter require only a showing of simple or ordinary negligence. The concept of ordinary negligence requires a failure to exercise the "ordinary caution" necessary to make out the defense of excusable homicide. Ordinary caution is the kind of caution that a man of reasonable prudence would exercise under the same or similar conditions. If the conduct of a defendant, regardless of his ignorance, good faith, or good intentions, fails to measure up to this standard, he is guilty of ordinary negligence. If such negligence proximately causes the death of the victim, the defendant is guilty of manslaughter. Timeliness in the furnishing of medical care must be considered in terms of ordinary caution. The law does not require that a parent call a doctor at the first sign of illness. However, testimony from the defendants indicates that they noticed the child was ill 10 to 14 days before the child died. In the five critical days in which it would have been possible to save the child's life, the parents noticed that the child was fussy, could not keep food down, and that his cheek turned a "bluish color like." The defendants thought that dentists would not pull a tooth "when it's all swollen up like that." Also, both parents feared that the child would be taken away from them if they took him to a doctor. Thus, there is sufficient evidence that the defendants were put on notice of the symptoms of the illness, and failed to exercise ordinary caution. Judgment affirmed.

Analysis:

Some suggest that the threat of criminal liability does not serve as a deterrent to negligent conduct. The negligent person is unaware of the risk, and cannot be deterred by a thought of possible punishment for taking an unreasonable risk that, in fact, he does not know he is taking. The competing argument contends that the threat of punishment makes people think harder about their conduct generally. When people consider the risks of their conduct, they tend to reduce the risks, and thus create a safer society. Another issue that arises in *Williams* is the cultural issue, though the court does not make much of it. There is a great deal of scholarship on the problem of the reasonable person definition, which is primarily informed by a world view that is white, male, and middleclass. To some extent, a trial by jury consisting of one's peers may counteract some of the potential for injustice in application of the predominant reasonable person standard.

■ CASE VOCABULARY

ORDINARY NEGLIGENCE: Ordinary or simple negligence is the failure to exercise the caution or care that a reasonably prudent person would have exercised in similar circumstances.

People v. Fuller

(*Prosecutor*) v. (*Tire Thieves*)
86 Cal.App.3d 618, 150 Cal.Rptr. 515 (1978)

TIRE THIEVES GUILTY OF MURDER FIRST AFTER CAR CHASE ACCIDENT KILLS OTHER DRIVER

■ **INSTANT FACTS** Two guys who were attempting to escape a police officer who had observed them stealing tires got into a high speed chase which resulted in an accident that killed the driver of another car.

■ **BLACK LETTER RULE** The felony-murder rule imposes strict liability for deaths caused by the commission of one of the enumerated felonies, which include burglary, even when the death is accidental.

■ PROCEDURAL BASIS

Appeal to the Court of Appeal, Fifth District, of the trial court's striking of a murder charge based on the felony-murder rule.

■ FACTS

Two men (the tire thieves) (D) were stealing tires off of cars from a dealer's lot early one Sunday morning. A police officer noticed them acting in a suspicious manner. The police officer made a U-turn to return to the lot at which point the tire thieves (D) got into their car and drove off. A chase followed that covered about seven miles and lasted from 10 to 12 minutes. The chase came to an end when the tire thieves' (D) car ran a red light and struck another car in the middle of an intersection. The driver of the other car was killed. The prosecutor charged the tire thieves with burglary, because they had been breaking into locked cars, and with murder under the felony-murder rule. The trial court struck down the murder charge. The prosecutor appealed that ruling.

■ ISSUE

Can an accidental death caused by a high-speed chase during the commission of a burglary be charged as murder in the first degree under the felony-murder rule?

■ DECISION AND RATIONALE

(Franson, J.) Yes. We are bound by precedent to find that the felony-murder rule applies in this case. Californian law specifically enumerates burglary as one of the felonies that makes a death caused during the commission or attempted commission of the enumerated felonies chargeable as murder in the first degree. The tire thieves (D) committed burglary when they broke into locked vehicles for the purpose of theft. Then they caused the death of the victim by crashing into his car during a high-speed chase. The felony-murder rule imposes strict liability for this death and it does not matter that it was accidental. We do not believe that this is the appropriate outcome, and if we were not bound by precedent we would hold that the tire thieves (D) should not be prosecuted for felony murder because the crime which they intended to commit, car burglary, does not usually pose a danger to human life. However, under current law, the trial court erred in striking the murder charge, and we hold that the tire thieves (D) can be charged with murder.

Analysis:

If the doors to the vehicles in this case had been unlocked so that the tire thieves did not have to break into the cars, then they could only have been charged with theft (probably a misdemeanor) and the felony-murder rule would not have applied. Of course, the reckless behavior involved in engaging in a high speed chase with a police officer might be found to be enough to support murder in the second degree. Considering that breaking into cars on a deserted dealer's lot early Sunday morning, with no weapons, is not something that one would expect to involve violence, and further considering that we have other ways to address reckless driving, does it make sense to apply a rule that makes this conduct equivalent to cold-blooded premeditated murder? When the felony-murder rule first emerged, all felonies were punishable by death; thus the distinction was possibly not that important. England, the country where the rule originated, dropped it in 1957. The United States is the only major western country that still recognizes the rule. Two states, Hawaii and Kentucky, have done away with it, and many others have limited its application.

People v. Howard

(*Prosecuting Authority*) v. (*Criminal Defendant*)

34 Cal.4th 1129, 23 Cal.Rptr.3d 306, 104 P.3d 107 (2005)

AN ACCIDENTAL DEATH OCCURING DURING A POLICE CHASE IS NOT FELONY MURDER

■ **INSTANT FACTS** Howard (D) was convicted of second-degree felony murder after killing the occupant of another vehicle while attempting to flee from police in a stolen vehicle, and he appealed his conviction.

■ **BLACK LETTER RULE** The second-degree felony-murder rule provides that, although malice is ordinarily an element of a murder conviction, murder can be committed without malice if the killing occurs during the commission of an inherently dangerous felony.

■ PROCEDURAL BASIS

Appeal from the defendant's conviction for second-degree felony murder.

■ FACTS

California Highway Patrol officers spotted an SUV without a rear license plate and signaled the driver to pull the vehicle over. When the officers got out of their car to approach the vehicle, the driver sped away and the highway patrol followed. A high-speed chase ensued, primarily in rural areas. As the chase approached downtown Fresno, however, the officers abandoned the pursuit, fearful that the high speeds could result in an accident. About a minute later, the SUV ran a red light and collided with another vehicle, killing the occupant. It turned out that the SUV was stolen. Howard (D), the driver, was arrested and charged with murder under the second-degree felony-murder rule, and with evading a police officer in willful or wanton disregard for the safety of persons or property. The jury convicted him on both counts, and the court of appeal affirmed, rejecting the defendant's contention that he could not be convicted under the second-degree felony-murder rule because the statute he violated was not an "inherently dangerous felony." The defendant appealed to the state supreme court.

■ ISSUE

Is driving with a willful or wanton disregard for the safety of persons or property while fleeing from a pursuing police officer an inherently dangerous felony for purposes of the second-degree felony-murder rule?

■ DECISION AND RATIONALE

(Kennard, J.) No. The second-degree felony-murder rule provides that, although malice is ordinarily an element of a murder conviction, murder can be committed without malice if the killing occurs during the commission of an inherently dangerous felony. In determining whether an underlying felony is inherently dangerous for purposes of the felony-murder rule, the court looks to the elements of the crime in the abstract, and not to the particular facts of the case, i.e., not to the defendant's specific conduct. In other words, the court looks at whether the felony, by its very nature, cannot be committed without creating the substantial risk that someone will be killed.

In concluding that the underlying offense in this case was an inherently dangerous felony, the court of appeal relied on a case that was decided before the statute was amended in 1996. Now, various offenses are given "points" under the current statutory scheme, which points are then tallied to support a conviction. The individual offenses that give rise to points include not only the more dangerous conduct that the defendant here engaged in, but also driving an unregistered vehicle, driving with a suspended license, failing to come to a complete stop, etc. This conduct is not particularly dangerous. Because these violations are not inherently dangerous in the abstract—and despite the fact that this particular defendant's commission of the crime may have been dangerous to human life—a violation of this statute cannot form the basis for second-degree felony murder. Reversed.

■ CONCURRENCE IN PART, DISSENT IN PART

(Brown, J.) Although I agree that the defendant's conviction should be reversed here, I would completely abrogate the second-degree felony-murder rule because its application is irredeemably arbitrary. Second-degree felony murder is a judge-defined crime, and I would leave it to the legislature to define precisely what conduct subjects a defendant to criminal liability.

■ DISSENT

(Baxter, J.) The majority reasons that because some of the offenses for which a defendant gets individual "points" under the subject statute here are not themselves inherently dangerous, one can commit the unitary felony in a way that does not place human life at risk. But driving with reckless indifference to safety in order to elude the police is by its very nature inherently dangerous. It creates a substantial risk that someone will be killed. The requirements of the second-degree felony-murder rule are thus satisfied here, and it makes no sense to refuse to apply that rule simply because some underlying violations of the same statute may not be inherently dangerous. I would uphold the defendant's conviction.

Analysis:

The California Supreme Court held in this case that reckless evasion of a police officer is not an inherently dangerous felony based on the 1998 amendment to Vehicle Code § 2800.2, which added a new subdivision (b). The crime is now statutorily defined to include any flight from an officer in which the driver commits three individual traffic violations having a "point count" under Vehicle Code § 12810, which includes traffic violations that are not particularly dangerous. In other words, because it is *possible* to violate § 2800.2 without engaging in an inherently dangerous activity, violating that section is not inherently dangerous, even if the defendant's conduct *was*. Does the result here serve the purposes of the felony-murder rule, or even make sense for that matter?

People v. Robertson

(*Prosecuting Authority*) v. (*Convicted Murderer*)
34 Cal.4th 156, 17 Cal.Rptr.3d 604, 95 P.3d 872 (2004)

SHOOTING TO SCARE OFF BURGLARS CAN RESULT IN A MURDER CONVICTION

■ **INSTANT FACTS** Robertson (D) fired shots at two men who were burglarizing his vehicle, purportedly trying to scare them but fatally wounding one of them, and he was convicted of felony murder.

■ **BLACK LETTER RULE** A felony-murder instruction is not proper when the predicate felony is an integral part of the homicide, and when, under the prosecution's evidence, it is included in fact within the offense charged.

■ PROCEDURAL BASIS

Appeal from the defendant's conviction for felony murder.

■ FACTS

Riley and Harris, along with two others, were drinking and using drugs as they drove around on the night of December 27, 1998. When they saw Robertson's (D) car parked in front of his residence, they got out and started taking off the hubcaps, making a lot of noise in the process. Robertson (D) heard the commotion and came out onto his porch. He fired shots at Riley and Harris. Harris was only hit in the foot, but Riley was fatally shot in the back. Robertson (D) contended that he did not mean to hurt anyone, but was only trying to scare them by shooting above their heads. Robertson (D) was convicted by a jury of second-degree murder. He appealed, arguing that the "merger doctrine" precluded the use of a violation of § 246.3, discharging a firearm in a grossly negligent manner, as a predicate offense for felony murder.

■ ISSUE

Did the merger doctrine preclude the trial court's instructing the jury that the defendant could be convicted of second-degree felony murder based on the predicate offense of discharging a firearm in a grossly negligent manner?

■ DECISION AND RATIONALE

(George, C.J.) No. A felony-murder instruction is not proper when the predicate felony is an integral part of the homicide, and when, under the prosecution's evidence, it is included in fact within the offense charged. But this concept, first recognized in the *Ireland* case and known as the "merger doctrine," does not apply here. The *Ireland* rule was created so that not every felonious assault could be characterized as felony murder. Such a result would usurp the law of homicide and relieve prosecutors of the burden of providing malice in order to obtain a murder conviction, thereby frustrating the legislative intent to punish intentionally fatal assaults more severely than felonious assaults that happen to result in death. But the merger doctrine has not been applied outside the assault context. As recognized in the later *Mattison* case, it does not apply when the death results from a felony with an independent purpose.

This independent-purpose distinction is consistent with the felony-murder rule's goal of deterrence, since someone who is about to assault another would not likely be deterred by the felony-murder rule, but a defendant with some collateral purpose may be. Here, the defendant's stated purpose was to frighten away the men who were burglarizing his car, which, by his own admission, is a purpose collateral to the resulting homicide. Thus, the crimes did not merge and the felony-murder instruction was permissible. The purpose of deterrence is served by the application of the felony-murder rule in this case, because the rule is intended to deter not only the commission of inherently dangerous crimes, but also carelessness in the commission of a crime. The merger doctrine does not preclude the application of the felony-murder rule in this case, and the court therefore properly instructed the jury.

■ DISSENT

(Kennard, J.) Under the majority's reasoning, the defendant would have been better off here if he had testified that he *tried* to hit the victims when he fired his gun, since that goal would not be a purpose collateral to the resulting homicide and the felony-murder rule would not apply. The defendant's less culpable mental state in this case subjected him to greater criminal liability, which is contrary to basic criminal justice concepts. Moreover, the underlying crime in this case involves gross negligence, but under the felony-murder rule, the prosecution must show that the defendant specifically intended to commit the underlying offense. Gross negligence simply does not require specific intent. In other words, the intent to scare a person by firing a gun at them is not independent of the resulting shooting death, nor is it felonious.

Analysis:

It is noteworthy that this case was decided by a divided California Supreme Court. In fact, three members of the court announced in their separate opinions their willingness to re-examine the legitimacy of California's second-degree felony-murder doctrine. In earlier decisions, second-degree felony-murder had been described as a "disfavored" doctrine that was to be given the "narrowest possible application," and on at least two occasions individual justices suggested that the court should abrogate the doctrine. But then the subject was largely abandoned for about fifteen years, until *Robertson* put it back on the table.

State v. Sophophone

(*Prosecution*) v. (*Co-burglar*)
270 Kan. 703, 19 P. 3d 70 (2001)

A DEFENDANT SHOULD NOT BE HELD LIABLE UNDER THE FELONY-MURDER RULE FOR A POLICE OFFICER'S LAWFUL ACT OF KILLING THE DEFENDANT'S CO-FELON

■ **INSTANT FACTS** The defendant was charged with felony murder after one of defendant's co-burglars was shot and killed by a police officer while fleeing from the scene of the burglary.

■ **BLACK LETTER RULE** A defendant should not be held responsible under the felony-murder doctrine for the death of a co-felon when the killing was the lawful act of a law enforcement officer acting in the line of duty.

■ PROCEDURAL BASIS

Defendant appeals his felony-murder conviction to the Kansas Supreme Court.

■ FACTS

Sanexay Sophophone (D) and three other people broke into a house in Emporia. The resident of the house reported the break-in to the police, who responded to the call. The police observed Sophophone (D) and the others leaving the back of the house and ordered them to stop. Sophophone (D) and the others began to run away. One officer caught up with Sophophone (D), handcuffed him and placed him in a squad car. Another officer chased down Somphone Sysoumphone, one of the other burglars, and ordered him to the ground, telling him not to move. Sysoumphone managed to fire at the officer. The officer returned the fire and killed Sysoumphone. Sophophone (D) was charged with aggravated burglary and with felony murder, for the death of Sysoumphone. He appeals the felony murder conviction.

■ ISSUE

Under the felony murder doctrine, is a defendant responsible for the death of a co-felon that occurred during the course of the felony, when a non-felon lawfully carried out the killing?

■ DECISION AND RATIONALE

(Larson, J.) No. A defendant should not be held responsible under the felony-murder doctrine for the death of a co-felon when the killing was the lawful act of a law enforcement officer acting in the line of duty. The Kansas felony-murder statute states that murder in the first degree occurs when a killing is committed "in the commission of, attempt to commit, or flight from an inherently dangerous felony." Defendant's co-felon, Sysoumphone, was killed during the flight from an aggravated burglary. Aggravated burglary is an inherently dangerous felony. Sophophone (D) does not dispute that he was involved in an inherently dangerous activity when his co-felon was killed. Instead, he asserts that the fact that he was in custody at the time of the killing served as a "break in circumstances" that should insulate him from the reach of the felony-murder statute. He also argues that because the killing was the lawful act of a police officer, done in the line of duty, he should not be held responsible. We disagree with Sophophone's (D) first argument. Time, distance, and the causal relationship between the underlying felony and a killing are factors to be considered in determining whether the killing occurred in the commission of the underlying felony. The evidence of this case indicates that the killing took place during the flight from the burglary, and the fact that Sophophone (D) was in custody at the time does not change this. We must, however, determine whether the felony-murder statute should apply when it was a non-felon whose lawful actions actually caused the death. Under the agency approach, a co-felon cannot be convicted of a homicide carried out by a non-felon because the actor responsible for the killing was not the person with whom she was an accomplice and therefore, her acts cannot be imputed to the co-felon. The "proximate causation" approach holds that the mere coincidence of homicide and a felony is not enough to satisfy the felony-murder doctrine. For liability to hold, the felon must have set in motion the acts that resulted in the death of the co-felon at the hands of the non-felon. No matter how terrible the underlying felon, a person should not have a criminal charge lodged against him for the consequences of the lawful conduct of another person. Here, we believe that it is not the intent of the felony-murder statute to impute the act of killing to Sophophone (D) when the act was the lawful and courageous act of a police officer acting in the line of his duties. Reversed.

■ DISSENT

(Abbott, J.) Sophophone (D) set in motion acts that would have resulted in the death of a law enforcement officer had the alert officer not taken the actions he did. This, in my opinion, is exactly the type of case that the legislature had in mind when it adopted the felony-murder rule. Contrary to the majority's opinion, the felony-murder statute does not require us to adopt the "agency" theory. The statute does not even address the issue at all. The only requirements, pursuant to the statute, are that: 1) there must be a killing, and 2) the killing must occur in the commission, attempt to commit, or flight from an inherently dangerous felony. The circumstances involved in this case satisfy these requirements.

Analysis:

In most jurisdictions, it is now generally accepted that there will be no felony-murder liability when one of the felons is shot and killed by a police officer or a bystander, although it is not easy to explain the rationale for this policy. The court in *Sophophone* seems to struggle to find a theory that will support its decision to reverse Sophophone's (D) felony-murder conviction. In doing so, the court discusses both the agency theory and the proximate cause approach. It is not necessarily clear, however, which theory it actually rests its decision on. Many courts, when presented with similar scenarios, subscribe to the view that when a death is caused by a shot fired by someone other than one of the felons, the killing cannot be said to be in furtherance of the commission of the felony, and therefore, liability will not ensue. How important was it for this court that a police officer lawfully killed Sysoumphone? Would the court's same logic apply if an observant neighbor had stepped outside of his house and killed the escaping burglar without having been first fired upon?

■ CASE VOCABULARY

ACCOMPLICE LIABILITY THEORY: The criminal liability of one who aids, advises or encourages another in the commission of a crime. Being an accomplice to a crime creates an agency relationship for the purposes of that crime.

AGENCY: When one party acts for another and the other is bound by the first party's actions.

Gregg v. Georgia

(*Condemned Man*) v. (*State*)

428 U.S. 153, 96 S.Ct. 2909, 49 L.Ed.2d 859 (1976)

SUPREME COURT FINDS DEATH PENALTY CONSTITUTIONAL

■ **INSTANT FACTS** Gregg (D) was found guilty of murder and sentenced to death under a new Georgia statute which was designed to reform the state's imposition of the death penalty so that it would be constitutional.

■ **BLACK LETTER RULE** The death penalty as imposed on murderers by the Georgia statute is constitutional because the death penalty is consistent with societal standards, is not an excessive punishment, and the statute provides sufficient safeguards to prevent it from being imposed in an arbitrary or capricious manner.

■ PROCEDURAL BASIS

Appeal to the United States Supreme Court of a capital sentence imposed by a court in Georgia.

■ FACTS

Gregg (D) was convicted of murder with intent to kill and armed robbery. At the post-conviction sentencing hearing the jury imposed the death penalty. This was done in accordance with Georgia's new statutory scheme for the imposition of the death penalty. The new Georgia statute requires a bifurcated trial. Guilt is determined in the traditional manner during the first stage, then if the defendant's guilt is established a presentence hearing is held. The defendant is accorded wide latitude in presenting evidence at this hearing. The evidence submitted in the earlier trial is also considered. In order to return a sentence of death the jury must find beyond a reasonable doubt that at least one of 10 listed aggravating factors is present in the crime. Gregg (D) is appealing his sentence.

■ ISSUE

Is the death penalty as imposed by the Georgia Statute constitutional?

■ DECISION AND RATIONALE

(Stewart, J.) Yes. The meaning of the 8th Amendment changes as the standards of what society considers decent evolve. However, this is not a subjective standard. It is necessary to find an objective measure of what society currently considers decent. And beyond current standards of public decency, in order to satisfy the requirements of the 8th Amendment a penalty must accord with the recognition of the dignity of a human being, which is the basic concept, underlying the amendment. This means that the penalty must not be excessive. It must not involve the unnecessary and wanton infliction of pain. And the severity of the punishment must not be grossly out of proportion with the crime. The imposition of the death penalty against murderers has a long history in both the United States and England. The framers accepted it, and it was practiced in every state at the time that the 8th Amendment was included in the Constitution. This court has recognized for nearly 200 years that the death penalty itself is not unconstitutional per se. Since *Furman v. Georgia* [earlier Supreme Court case which found the death penalty as then practiced in Georgia to be unconstitutional] 35 states have enacted new death penalty statutes, and Congress has passed a law authorizing the death penalty for air piracy. In addition, the involvement of juries in these cases directly connects the sentence to the contemporary values of society. Thus the death penalty as imposed here is clearly within society's standards. There must also be penological justification so that it doesn't result in the gratuitous infliction of suffering. The death penalty serves two such purposes, retribution and deterrence. While retribution is no longer the dominant objective of criminal law it is still a legitimate objective. The death penalty serves as an expression of society's moral outrage at particularly heinous crimes. This is somewhat necessary in a civilized society where we deny a victim's family the right to take their own revenge. Statistical studies have been inconclusive on the question of whether the death penalty serves as a deterrent. We feel that the question of deterrence is best left to legislatures who can consider the particular applicability of the studies to their locality and have more creative solutions available to them. As to the death penalty being a disproportionate penalty, we can not believe that that is the case where it is imposed for the crime of murder. Based on all of this we conclude that the death penalty is not unconstitutional per se. The question thus becomes can Georgia impose the death penalty in this case. In *Furman* we recognized that the death penalty is unlike any other punishment and that it must not be inflicted in an arbitrary or capricious manner. However the statutory system Georgia now uses to impose the death penalty successfully addresses those concerns. Georgia now requires a bifurcated proceeding, which ensures that the sentencing authority gets the information relevant to the imposition of the sentence and provides standards for the use of that information in making the sentencing decision. Based on this we uphold the imposition of the death penalty in this case.

■ CONCURRENCE

(White, J.) In effect what Gregg (D) is arguing is that there is an unconstitutional amount of discretion in our entire system of justice. He is arguing that no matter how effective the death penalty may be as a punishment, government created and run by human beings is inevitably too flawed to administer it. We can not accept this as a part of constitutional law. Administering the death penalty is a very serious responsibility and mistakes will be made. However one of society's greatest responsibilities is that of protecting the lives of its citizens from murder, and I will not interfere in Georgia's attempt to meet that responsibility.

■ DISSENT

(Brennan, J.) The cruel and unusual punishment clause must draw its meaning from the evolving standards of decency that mark the progress of a maturing society. In *Furman* I concluded that our civilization and the law had progressed to the point where the punishment of death for whatever crime and under whatever circumstances is cruel and unusual. I won't repeat the whole of my argument in that case here, however I will say that inherent in the clause is the primary moral principle that the state, even as it punishes, must treat its citizens in a manner consistent with their intrinsic worth as human beings. A punishment must not be so severe as to be degrading to human dignity.

■ DISSENT

(Marshall, J.) It is true that 35 states have passed laws providing for imposition of the death penalty since *Furman*, however I do not believe that this is a true indication of the standards of society. I believe, and this has been backed up by recent studies on the subject, that an informed citizenry would find the death penalty as practiced morally offensive. In addition, even if favored by the public the death penalty would remain unconstitutional because it is excessive. The true question here is whether the death penalty is necessary to accomplish a legitimate legislative purpose in punishment when a less severe penalty, life imprisonment, would do as well. The death penalty has not been shown by any study to be an effective deterrent. There is no correlation between capital punishment and lower rates of capital crime. This leaves us with retribution as the only possible justification for capital punishment. The plurality has argued that the death penalty as retribution may be necessary to prevent people from resorting to self-help to get their revenge. But this is not a valid argument; we have other methods for requiring citizens to confine themselves to civilized behavior. Besides this is more of an argument of expediency than a justification of the value of retribution itself. If retribution is to be a justification it must be based on the idea that the death of the murderer is a moral good in itself. This argument is a direct rejection of the 8th Amendment's requirement that we must treat even wrong doers in a manner that is consistent with their intrinsic worth as human beings. Therefore the death penalty is excessive as it fails to advance any legitimate legislative purpose beyond what could be achieved through the less severe punishment of life imprisonment.

Analysis:

Furman v. Georgia, decided in 1972, overturned four death sentences from Georgia. All nine justices wrote opinions in the case, which totaled over 200 pages. Only two of the justices, Brennan and Marshall, the same justices who dissent in *Gregg*, argued that the death penalty was unconstitutional *per se.* They were joined by three other justices, Douglas, Steward and White, in the judgment overturning the Georgia death sentences, but these justices did not agree that the death penalty itself was unconstitutional. Their concern was that Georgia seemed to be imposing the death penalty in a way that was arbitrary, capricious, or discriminatory. The other four justices, C.J. Burger, Blackmun, Powell, and Rehnquist, all dissented, rejecting both the procedural and *per se* attacks on the death penalty. The effect of *Furman* was to invalidate the death penalty in all states, because while the judgment had not found the death penalty unconstitutional per se, none of the statutes then enacted met the standards required to show they were not arbitrary or capricious. As stated in *Gregg*, thirty-five states then went on to adopt new statutes based on the model penal code, so that they could impose the death penalty in a way that would survive a constitutional challenge. The judgment in *Gregg* then held that the death penalty imposed under these new statutes had in fact reached its goal and the death penalty was constitutional once again.

■ CASE VOCABULARY

GRATUITOUS INFLICTION OF SUFFERING: To make someone suffer pain or other distress beyond what is necessary or warranted by the situation.

PENOLOGICAL JUSTIFICATION: Justification based on the theory and practice of criminal rehabilitation.

PLURALITY: An opinion issued by an appellate court that does not represent the majority of the justices but which has more justices joined to it than any concurring opinion.

McCleskey v. Kemp

(*Black Man*) v. (*Person Holding McCleskey in Custody*)
481 U.S. 279, 17 S.Ct. 1756, 95 L.Ed.2d 262 (1987)

U.S. SUPREME COURT SAYS DEATH SENTENCE IS CONSTITUTIONAL, EVEN WHEN STUDY SHOWS BLACKS WHO KILL WHITES ARE DISPROPORTIONATELY SENTENCED TO DEATH

■ **INSTANT FACTS** A black man found guilty of killing a white man challenges his sentence based on a study that shows that blacks who kill whites get the death more than whites who kill whites, or those who kill blacks.

■ **BLACK LETTER RULE** A statistical study that shows a risk that capital sentencing is influenced by race does not prove that a specific sentence violates the 8th or 14th Amendment.

■ PROCEDURAL BASIS

Appeal to the Supreme Court of the United States of the denial of a writ of habeas corpus.

■ FACTS

Warren McCleskey (McCleskey) (D), a black man, was convicted of murdering a white police officer during the course of a robbery. The jury recommended the death penalty and the judge sentenced him to death. McCleskey's (D) sentence was upheld through all state appeals. McCleskey (D) then filed a writ of habeas corpus in federal court. Among other claims this writ raised a claim that in Georgia the death penalty is administered in a racially discriminatory manner in violation of the 14th and 8th Amendments. In support of this claim McCleskey (D) proffered a statistical study by Professors Baldus, Pulaski, and Woodworth. The results of the study are as follows: People (of any race) charged with killing whites got death in 11% of the cases. People (of any race) charged with killing blacks got death in 1% of the cases. Another statistic showed that black defendants got the death penalty 4% of the time, and white defendants got the death penalty 7% of the time. When the race of the victim and defendant are combined, 22% of cases where blacks killed whites resulted in the death penalty. Also, only 8% of whites who killed whites got the death penalty. Only 1% of blacks who killed blacks got death. And, 3% of whites who killed blacks got the death penalty. This data was further analyzed to take account of other variables which resulted in one model that showed that those who kill whites were 4.3 times more likely to get the death penalty than those who kill blacks, and that black defendants were 1.1 times more likely to get the death penalty than other defendants.

■ ISSUE

Can a statistical study that shows a risk that capital sentencing is influenced by race prove that a specific death sentence is unconstitutional under the 8th or 14th amendments?

■ DECISION AND RATIONALE

(Powell, J.) No. McCleskey (D) is arguing, on the basis of the study, that his sentence was influenced by racial discrimination and that this was a violation of his right to equal protection under the 14th amendment and his right not to be subjected to cruel and unusual punishment under the 8th amendment. We first consider his equal protection claim. A successful equal protection claim comes in two parts. First it must be shown that there was purposeful discrimination; then, it must be shown that the discrimination had a discriminatory effect on the person bringing the claim. McCleskey (D) has not offered any specific evidence of discrimination in his case, instead he has offered a general statistical study. The court has accepted statistics as proof of discrimination in some equal protection cases. However, those cases involved the selection of a jury venire in a particular district, and Title VII employment discrimination cases, that are different from the situation here. A capital sentence must be recommended by a properly selected jury. Each of the juries that recommend such a sentence is unique. Each jury is required to consider several factors, which include specific characteristics of the defendant and the facts of the individual case. The cases where we have found statistical studies sufficient have involved fewer entities with fewer variables. In addition because our criminal justice system depends on juries exercising their discretion we would require a higher standard of evidence before we would find that that discretion had been abused. Therefore we find that there is not enough evidence here to support the charge of an equal protection violation. We then turn to McCleskey's (D) 8th amendment claim. A sentence that was definitely based on racial consideration would be a violation of the 8th amendment. However there is no proof here that this particular sentence was racially based. All the statistical study offered here can show is that there is a risk that racial considerations were involved. This risk cannot be completely eliminated because the jury has discretion in reaching its decision. The discretion of the jury is a necessary part of giving each case the individual attention that is an important part of a just system. This discretion also benefits the defendant, because if the jury decides against the death penalty that decision can not be appealed, but a decision for the death penalty is still open to appellate review. Any system that involves human judgment will show some discrepancies; thus the test of constitutionality can't require perfection. Instead we require that the system be surrounded by as many safeguards as possible, a requirement which has been met in this case. In addition, there are two other considerations that influence us against accepting McCleskey's (D) claim. The first is that if McCleskey's (D) argument were to be taken to its logical conclusion it could undermine the entire criminal justice system. The 8th amendment is not limited to capital cases, and as we stated above no realistic system is going to be completely free of discrepancies. Second, we feel that this sort of issue is better addressed by the local legislature as they have a better understanding of how the statistics reflect their local conditions as well as more flexibility to address the problems presented.

■ DISSENT

(Brennan, J.) At some time during the planning of his defense McCleskey (D) must have asked his lawyer about his chances. To answer this question honestly his lawyer would have to tell him that his chances were going to be significantly and negatively influenced by his race and the race of the victim. The majority finds that this is acceptable. This finding is at odds with our consistent concern for rationality in capital sentencing. Rationality in sentencing requires consideration of each individual as a unique human being. Decisions that are influenced by race do not meet this requirement. The greater likelihood that a black defendant will be sentenced to death, and the likelihood that the murder of a black victim will result in less punishment, is a devaluation of the lives of black people. The majority argues that this risk must be greater than what has been shown in this case before we interfere in the discretion of the jury. But the reason the discretion of the jury exists is so that the required individual consideration can happen, and this is just what racist decisions undermine. It is true that a justice system administered by people will always be imperfect. However, that means that we will always be faced with the task of drawing the line at the point where those imperfections become unacceptable. The slippery slope argument used by the majority in refusing to find the imperfections demonstrated by this study unacceptable ignores the special nature of capital punishment and the special repugnance of racial discrimination.

Analysis:

In reading this case it is important to take note of the findings of the study and to understand that race still plays a significant role within the system. If you walk into any Criminal court in a major city in the United States you will see that minority groups are seriously over represented as defendants, while they are seriously under-represented as judges, lawyers, clerks and bailiffs. (Admittedly some progress has been made with court personnel, but the majority remain white.) All of the justices in this case acknowledge that the system is inevitably imperfect. This is a tacit admission that race will always play a role. The question thus becomes, is this an acceptable way to administer the death penalty? Some level of imperfection will have to be accepted in the criminal justice system as a whole because we have to have a criminal justice system, and it has to be run by fallible human beings. But we do not have to have a death penalty. The court split five to four on this case. After his retirement, Justice Powell indicated that he regretted his vote and his opinion in this case. If he had changed his vote at the time, what is currently the dissent would have been the law of the land.

■ CASE VOCABULARY

EQUAL PROTECTION VIOLATION: A violation of the 14th amendment guarantee that no member of one class will be denied the same protection under the law, which is enjoyed by members of other classes.

INVIDIOUS: Stirs up envy and resentment. Used in law to describe discrimination, which is arbitrary, irrational, and not reasonably related to a legitimate purpose.

JURY VENIRE: The group of people, summoned to the court, from which a jury is chosen.

WRIT OF HABEAS CORPUS: In criminal cases a writ to produce the prisoner, which is directed to the party keeping a prisoner in custody. It is used to test the legality of the imprisonment.

Payne v. Tennessee

(*Killer*) v. (*State*)

501 U.S. 808, 111 S.Ct. 2597, 115 L.Ed.2d 720 (1991)

SUPREME COURT OVERRULES ITSELF TO ALLOW VICTIM IMPACT EVIDENCE AT CAPITAL SENTENCING

■ **INSTANT FACTS** Three-year-old survived his wounds when his mother and sister were killed. At the sentencing hearing for the killer his grandmother testified about how this had affected him. The killer was sentenced to death.

■ **BLACK LETTER RULE** The 8th amendment does not prohibit the introduction of victim impact evidence at the sentencing phase of a capital trial.

■ PROCEDURAL BASIS

Appeal to the United States Supreme Court of an earlier ruling on a motion for habeas corpus.

■ FACTS

Pervis Tyrone Payne (D) (Payne) lived in the apartment across the hall from Charisse Christopher (Charisse) and her two children, 2-year-old Lacie and 3-year-old Nicholas. One Saturday, after drinking all morning and injecting cocaine, Payne (D) went to Charisse's apartment and started making sexual advances towards her. She rejected him. Payne (D) became violent. He stabbed Charisse and her daughter Lacie to death. He also attacked Nicholas who only survived after seven hours of surgery. A neighbor called the police after hearing the screams. Payne (D) was found by the first police officer on the scene covered with blood. The scene inside the apartment was very bloody. Charisse had received 84 wounds, none of which was fatal and had most likely bled to death. Payne's (D) defense presented four mitigation witnesses, his mother and father and his girlfriend as well as a psychologist at the sentencing hearing. The psychologist testified that Payne (D) had a low IQ and was mentally handicapped. Charisse's mother also testified at the sentencing hearing. She was asked about how her grandson Nicholas was affected by the murders of his mother and sister. She described him as crying for his mother and being very worried about his little sister. In his closing argument during the sentencing hearing the prosecutor talked about the effect all this was having on Nicholas. He told the jury that Nicholas was conscious throughout the attack and that he was in the same room when his mother and sister were killed. The prosecutor argued that giving Payne (D) the death penalty would be a comfort to Nicholas when he grew up and was able to understand what had happened. The jury sentenced Payne to death.

■ ISSUE

Does the 8th amendment prohibit the introduction of victim impact evidence at the sentencing phase of a capital trial?

■ DECISION AND RATIONALE

(Rehnquist, C.J.) No. We granted certiorari in this case in order to reconsider our holdings in *Booth* and *Gathers* that the 8th Amendment prohibits the presentation of victim impact testimony during the sentencing hearing in a capital case. In Booth we held that victim impact testimony could not be considered because for the death penalty to be constitutional the defendant must be considered as a unique and individual human being. And, the sentencing hearing must thus center around the blameworthiness of the defendant's conduct so that the jury can focus on whether this defendant should receive the death penalty. The blameworthiness in this context is based on the defendant's character and his actions. Factors of which the defendant was not aware, such as the way certain victims would be impacted, or special qualities of the victim, are not relevant to that blameworthiness. We are now reconsidering that decision. The blameworthiness of the defendant is no longer the only thing we feel should be considered at the sentencing hearing. The amount of harm done by an offense has always been relevant under criminal law. Two defendants who performed exactly the same actions in committing a crime would be punished differently if one of those crimes resulted in a death and the other did not. Judges have always considered the amount of harm done in a capital case when they have been given discretion over the sentence. There has been some concern that considering victim impact evidence will lead to the comparison of victims with some being considered less valuable than others. We do not feel that this will actually be the result. We feel that this evidence is instead used to show the unique value of each victim as an individual human being. As it is unconstitutional to prevent the defendant from putting on any evidence that might tend to mitigate his crime in a capital sentencing hearing, mitigation for the defendant can always be heard. It is thus unfair that the prosecutor be prevented from balancing this evidence with evidence about the victim. Therefore we rule that victim impact evidence in capital sentencing hearings is not prohibited by the 8th Amendment and we uphold the sentences in this case.

■ CONCURRENCE

(Souter, J.) Because all victims are unique individuals with family and other human connections, the defendant should be able to foresee the kind of impact his actions will have on victims of his crime. That there would be such impact is inevitable. Because it is inevitable it has moral relevance to the defendant's conduct. Therefore victim impact evidence is relevant to assessing the defendant's blameworthiness and is relevant and appropriate at a capital sentencing hearing.

■ DISSENT

(Marshall, J.) The ruling of the majority in this case is a direct overruling of our previous ruling in *Booth.* There has been no change in the law governing this situation or the factual situation, thus the ruling here is a violation of *stare decisis.*

■ DISSENT

(Stevens, J.) Not only is Marshall correct about this ruling being a violation of *stare decisis.* However, even if we had never decided *Booth* and *Gathers* the ruling of the majority would represent a sharp break with our previous reasoning regarding capital sentencing. There is no support in our previous cases for the presentation at sentencing of evidence that sheds no light on the defendant's moral culpability but rather serves to encourage juror's to make their decision out of emotion rather than sound reasoning. It would clearly be inappropriate to allow the defendant in a capital case to enter evidence that his victim was engaged in immoral behavior of which the defendant was unaware at the time of the killing. The state should be bound by the same limitation and be prohibited from offering positive information about the victim of which the defendant was unaware. In *Locket v. Ohio* we found that those who would be responsible for making the decision to sentence a defendant to death must not be prevented from considering any factor that mitigated the defendant's crime. Victim impact evidence can have the effect of emotionally blinding the jury to the legitimate mitigation offered by the defense. To consider details of the impact of the crime on the victims does not simply balance the mitigation offered by the defendant. The victim is not on trial and is not facing the awesome power of the state. It is true that the consideration of the harm a crime causes is relevant in criminal law, but that is only when that harm is foreseeable. To the extent that the defendant should have known that any such crime would have a foreseeable impact on victims, the jury is also completely capable of comprehending this kind of generic harm with out any specific evidentiary support. In the end specific evidence presented to show special harm suffered by the victim can only serve to support the idea that some victim's lives were more valuable than others. This is as offensive as the idea that prosecutors should seek the death penalty in cases with a white victim, but offer plea bargains in cases where a black person was killed. I recognize that the majority's decision today is likely to be very popular politically, and that it will please many very thoughtful people. However, the court is the one place in a democracy where public opinion should not be the deciding factor. This is the place where the voice of the many should not be able to eliminate the rights of the few.

Analysis:

The basic rule about the admission of evidence is that it must be more relevant than prejudicial. Defense attorneys often argue that especially gory crime scene photos should not be admitted because they are too likely to inflame the jury's emotions and thus be more prejudicial than informative. Of course, the prosecution argues to admit the photos for their informative nature, but also wants this emotional impact. One way this conflict has been resolved is by only allowing the prosecution to submit the evidence in black and white, which avoids some of the emotional impact of the blood. What kind of informational value does the grandmother's testimony have here? The jury already knew that Nicholas had seen his mother and sister murdered and that he had been very seriously wounded himself. Did they have to be told that he was grieving for his mother or sister? The emotionally inflammatory nature of this evidence balanced against its informative value would seem to argue against its admission. The court, however, rules the other way. And it overrules its own previous decisions in order to do so. The dissent argues that the majority was influenced by public opinion. Clearly defending "victim's rights" is much more popular with the public than defending the rights of those facing capital murder charges. Arguably however, it is defending the rights of the unpopular that is the Supreme Court's most important job.

■ CASE VOCABULARY

GUILT PHASE / PENALTY PHASE: A capital trial is divided into two phases. The first, the guilty phase, is the trial where it is decided whether or not the defendant is guilty of the capital offense. If the defendant is found guilty then the trial moves on to the penalty phase, where the sentence is considered.

NON SEQUITUR: A statement, within the context of a conversation, argument or writing, which does not follow the logic of the things that were said before it.

STARE DECISIS: A doctrine that holds that once a matter of law has been carefully considered and decided it will be followed in all future cases. This promotes security and certainty in the law. The decision of a point of law should be strictly followed unless departure is really necessary to vindicate plain and obvious injustice.

Tison v. Arizona

(*Felony-murderers*) v. (*State*)
481 U.S. 137, 107 S.Ct. 1676, 95 L.Ed.2d 127 (1987)

DEATH SENTENCE FOUND CONSTITUTIONAL IN FELONY-MURDER CASE

■ **INSTANT FACTS** The Tison brothers decided to break their father and his cell-mate out of prison, during the escape the father and cell-mate killed a family while the Tison brothers were present.

■ **BLACK LETTER RULE** Major participation in the felony committed combined with reckless indifference to human life is enough to supply the culpability necessary to constitutionally impose the death penalty.

■ PROCEDURAL BASIS

Appeal of two death sentences to the United States Supreme Court.

■ FACTS

Gary Tison (Gary) was sentenced to life imprisonment for murder. His family decided to break him out of jail. He insisted that his cellmate Randy Greenawalt (Greenawalt) also be included in the escape. Three of Gary's sons went to the prison with a large number of weapons. They armed their father, Gary, and his cellmate Greenawalt, and then the five men brandishing weapons were able to flee the prison without any shots being fired. After leaving the prison, the car they were traveling in had a flat tire near an isolated house. The group decided to flag down a passing motorist and steal a car. Raymond Tison (Raymond) (D) stood in front of their disabled car while the others were armed and waiting out of sight. A Mazda being driven by John Lyons (Lyons) pulled over to offer assistance. In the car with Lyons were his wife, his 15-year-old niece and his 2-year-old son. Ricky Tison (D) and Raymond (D) went to fill a water jug some distance away. Gary and Greenawalt killed all of the Lyonses. Both Ricky and Raymond expressed surprise at the killings. They made no effort to aid the victims and continued on with Gary and Greenawalt. They also participated in the final gun battle with the police that ended with all of them being taken into custody. The state tried Ricky (D) and Raymond (D) separately. They were each charged with capital murder of the four victims as well as with armed robbery, kidnapping, and car theft. The capital murder charges were based on Arizona felony-murder law providing that a killing occurring during the perpetration of robbery or kidnapping is capital murder, and that each person participating is legally liable for the acts of his accomplices. Both Ricky (D) and Raymond (D) were found guilty and sentenced to death. The case was appealed to the Arizona Supreme Court and affirmed. United States Supreme Court accepted certiorari.

■ ISSUE

Is it constitutional to impose the death penalty on two major participants in a felony, which resulted in the death of four non-participants, even when they did not personally inflict the fatal injury and did not intend the death?

■ DECISION AND RATIONALE

(O'Conner, J.) Yes. We took certiorari in this case to consider how our previous decision in *Enmund v. Florida* [a getaway driver not eligible for death penalty for the unplanned murders committed by his accomplices while he was waiting in the car] applies to these facts. Only nine states allow the death penalty for accomplices not directly involved in the killing. Studies have shown that juries very rarely find for the death penalty under these situations. We agree that limited participation in a crime, which in itself is not a capital offense and where the death of a non-participant is not expected, is not capital material. Such an offense is unlikely to be deterred by application of the death penalty, as the outcome is not anticipated. Also that is the kind of behavior that does not show a sufficient personal culpability to justify the state in seeking the death penalty for purposes of retribution. In Enmund we found that in order to be eligible for the death penalty the individual defendant must show a high level of personal culpability, and that the state had failed to meet that standard. However, the facts of this case differ significantly from the situation in *Enmund.* We accept that Ricky (D) and Raymond (D) had no intention to kill the victims in this case. Yet, their actions show a much greater involvement in the underlying felony than was the case in *Enmund.* They took lethal weapons into a prison. They then armed two men who had previously been convicted of murder with those weapons and aided them in using the weapons to escape. They were aware that one of these men had killed a prison guard in a previous escape attempt. Raymond (D) flagged down the car containing the victims knowing that they would face an armed ambush when they stopped. Ricky (D) was armed and waiting with the others when the car stopped. They were both at the scene while the murders took place and took no steps to aid the victims. They also participated in the final shootout with the police. While having an intent to kill is obviously relevant to the question of personal culpability it is not the only consideration. A person who kills in self-defense may do so very intentionally but with no culpability. Alternatively someone engaged in the torture of another person who doesn't care whether or not his victim lives or dies is extremely culpable. The mental state displayed in that kind of act would be a reckless indifference to human life, and that is also what is present in the case we are considering here. Ricky (D) and Raymond (D) must have been aware that their actions were very likely to result in someone's death, and they were centrally involved in the events that lead to the deaths. Based on this we find that the capital sentences imposed on Ricky (D) and Raymond (D) are constitutional.

■ DISSENT

(Brennan, J.) The felony-murder doctrine is a holdover from a time when a person could be executed for committing any felony. This made the mental state related to the killing irrelevant, as the intent to commit the underlying felony provided sufficient culpability to justify a death sentence. In most American jurisdictions and practically all European and Commonwealth countries a felon can not be executed for a murder that he or she did not specifically intend to commit. The majority argues that the intent to kill is not a good way to identify the most culpable of murders. They suggest the example of one who tortures someone to death without a care as to whether they lived or died or the robber who shoots indiscriminately during the robbery not caring who might be hit. But there is a crucial element in those cases, which is missing here. In both of those examples the culpability is found in the actions that the perpetrators personally took that caused the death, committing the torture, or firing the gun. Reckless indifference to human life can only rise to the highest level of culpability if there is intentional reckless action. Intent is a central part of what makes an action culpable. Ricky (D) and Raymond (D) did not intend the death of the victims in this case, they were surprised by it. They did not take the actions that resulted In the victim's death. We believe that culpability arises out of the results of a choice made out of an individual's free will. Death, the state's ultimate sanction must be reserved for those whose culpability is greatest.

Analysis:

This case is yet another five-to-four decision. The court is very closely divided here. What is really interesting, however, is what they agree about. Both the majority and the dissent argue that in order to be eligible for the death penalty, the defendant must have a high level of personal culpability and not simply culpability that is transferred to him from an accomplice. While being an accomplice, and participating in a named felony on any level, can make a person guilty of murder, it takes more than that to provide a constitutional basis for a death sentence. The debate is over what specifically makes a defendant sufficiently personally culpable. Being the getaway driver for a robbery where no one is supposed to be killed is not sufficient. The dissent would require either an intent to kill or reckless indifference to human life, combined with direct action to cause the death. The actual ruling in this case is even less definite, requiring major involvement in an underlying felony that has a high likelihood of causing the death of a non-participant. Clearly the majority is using a very fact-specific standard.

■ CASE VOCABULARY

ATTENUATED: Describes something that has been drawn out to the point it has been made thin and weak.

DETERRENT: Anything that prevents, or tends to prevent a person from doing something.

FELONY-MURDER SIMPLICITER: The felony-murder doctrine makes a person guilty of murder because a death resulted from their commission of a felony. Simpliciter is a Latin term for simple, or simplicity. Together in this context they express the idea of the level of a person's culpability created by mere participation, particularly as an accomplice, in an underlying felony which caused a death, as opposed to the greater culpability of someone who actually pulled the trigger or directly killed the victim.

RETRIBUTIVE PURPOSE: A justification of a punishment based on the theory that every crime should be paid for with some kind of equivalent punishment.

TANGENTIAL: Describes relationship that is limited by only connecting at one point, a weak and non-relevant connection.

CHAPTER EIGHT

Rape

State v. Alston

Instant Facts: An ex-boyfriend is convicted of the second rape of his ex-girlfriend, after having intercourse with her at his friends house, despite not using force on the day of the alleged rape.

Black Letter Rule: The element of force of threat of force must occur at the time of the alleged rape, and must be used to obtain sexual intercourse.

Rusk v. State

Instant Facts: A man is convicted of second degree rape, after meeting a twenty-one year old mother of two at a bar, bringing her up to his house, and having sexual intercourse her, despite the lack of force.

Black Letter Rule: Actual force or threat of force is a necessary element of rape.

State v. Rusk

Instant Facts: The Court of Appeals of Maryland affirms the trial courts conviction of second degree rape, finding that the reasonableness of the victim's apprehension of fear was a question of fact for the jury to determine.

Black Letter Rule: An implied threat is sufficient to satisfy the element of force for rape.

Commonwealth v. Berkowitz

Instant Facts: A college student is convicted of raping his girl friend in his dorm room, after the friend voluntarily entered his dorm room and repeatedly said "no" to his sexual advances, although she did not physically resist.

Black Letter Rule: Verbal resistance alone, is not sufficient evidence of rape.

State of New Jersey in the Interest of M.T.S.

Instant Facts: A seventeen-year-old is convicted of the rape of a fifteen-year-old who was asleep at the time of penetration.

Black Letter Rule: Resistance is not a required element of rape.

People v. John Z.

Instant Facts: After initially appearing to consent to sexual intercourse with her boyfriend's friend, John (D), Laura told him that she wanted to go home, but he continued having sexual intercourse with her and, on the basis of this action, was convicted of forcible rape.

Black Letter Rule: A female's withdrawal of consent to sexual intercourse serves to nullify any earlier consent she has given and subjects the male to forcible rape charges if he persists in what has then become nonconsensual intercourse.

Commonwealth v. Sherry

Instant Facts: Three doctors are convicted of rape after taking a nurse to a house and separately having intercourse with her, despite the doctors' mistake-of-fact as to the nurse's consent.

Black Letter Rule: A defense of mistake-of-fact must be based on a reasonable good faith standard.

Boro v. Superior Court

Instant Facts: A man is charged with rape after fraudulently inducing a woman to have sex with him in order to cure her illness, and his motion to dismiss denied, despite the woman's consent to the intercourse.

Black Letter Rule: Fraud-in-the-factum, not fraud in the inducement, will vitiate consent to intercourse.

State v. Herndon

Instant Facts: Opinion by the Court of Appeals of Wisconsin discussing the process of weighing a defendant's Sixth Amendment rights against the interest of rape-shield laws, when determining the admissibility of evidence.

Black Letter Rule: The interest of rape-shield laws (which prohibit the cross-examination of rape victims) and a defendant's Sixth Amendment rights must be weighed in order to determine whether certain evidence should be admissible.

People v. Wilhelm

Instant Facts: After being convicted of third-degree criminal sexual conduct, the defendant appealed, arguing that evidence of the victim's prior provocative behavior should have been admitted on the issue of consent.

Black Letter Rule: Evidence of a victim's sexual conduct with a third party is irrelevant to the issue of whether she consented to sexual intercourse with the defendant.

Garnett v. State

Instant Facts: A mentally disabled twenty-year-old man is convicted of statutory rape, after engaging in sexual relations with a thirteen-year-old girl friend, despite the lack of criminal intent.

Black Letter Rule: Criminal intent or mens rea, is not an element of statutory rape.

State v. Alston

(*Community*) v. (*Ex-boyfriend*)
310 N.C. 399, 312 S.E.2d 470 (1984)

GENERAL FEAR OF FORCE NOT SUFFICIENT FOR A CONVICTION OF RAPE

■ **INSTANT FACTS** An ex-boyfriend is convicted of the second rape of his ex-girlfriend, after having intercourse with her at his friends house, despite not using force on the day of the alleged rape.

■ **BLACK LETTER RULE** The element of force of threat of force must occur at the time of the alleged rape, and must be used to obtain sexual intercourse.

■ PROCEDURAL BASIS

Certification to the Supreme Court of North Carolina of a conviction for second degree rape.

■ FACTS

At the time of the incident Cottie Brown (Brown) and Alston (D) had been in a consensual sexual relationship for six months. Brown testified that although she sometimes enjoyed their consensual sexual relations, she often had sex with Alston (D) just to accommodate him. On those occasions, she would stand still and remain entirely passive while Alston (D) undressed her and had intercourse with her. Furthermore, during the six months, the two had conflicts which, at times, involved some violence. Alston (D) had struck Brown several times during the relationship when she refused to give him money, or refused to do what he wanted. Around May 15, 1981, Alston (D) struck Brown after Brown refused to give Alston (D) money. Brown left the apartment she shared with Alston (D) and moved in with her mother. After Brown left, Alston (D) called her several times and visited her at Durham Technical Institute (DTI) where she was enrolled in classes. When he visited her they talked about their relationship, but Brown never broke off the relationship with Alston (D), because she was afraid that Alston (D) would be angry. She did not have intercourse with Alston (D) after May 15 until the alleged rape on June 15. On June 15, Alston (D) arrived at DTI by taxicab to find Brown standing close to the school door. After blocking Brown's path as she walked toward the door, Alston (D) asked Brown where she had moved. After refusing to tell him, Alston (D) grabbed Brown's arm and told her that she was going with him. Brown testified that it would have taken some effort to pull away. The two walked toward the parking lot and Brown told defendant she would walk with him if he let her go. Alston (D) then released her. Brown testified that she did not run away because she was afraid of him, although other students were nearby. Both began a casually paced walk around the neighborhood of the school while talking about their relationship. Alston talked about Brown's "dogging" him and making him seem a fool and about Brown's mother's interference in the relationship. When the two left the parking lot, Alston (D) threatened to "fix" Brown's face so that her mother could see he was not playing. While walking out of the parking lot, Brown told Alston (D) that she wished to go to class, but Alston (D) replied that she was going to miss class that day. Passing several people, the two walked along several streets and went down a path close to a wooded area where they stopped and talked. Alston (D) again asked where she had moved. Brown asked Alston (D) whether he would let her go if she told him. Alston (D) then asked whether the relationship was over and Brown told him that it was. Alston (D) then said that he had a right to make love to her again, to which Brown did not respond. The two turned around at that point and began walking towards a street they had walked down previously.

Although Alston (D) did not say where they where going, when he said to Brown that he wanted to make love, she knew they were going to the house of a Alston's (D) friend Lawrence Taylor (Taylor), where they have gone on prior occasions to have sex. On the way there the two passed the group of men they had passed previously. However, Brown did not ask for assistance because some of the men were friends of Alston (D), and she assumed that they would not help. When they entered the house, Taylor was inside. Brown sat in the living room while Alston (D) and Taylor went to the back of the house and talked. When asked why she didn't leave at that point, Brown replied, "It was nowhere to go. I don't know. I just didn't." Alston (D) returned and began talking to Brown about another man she had been seeing. By that time, Taylor had left the room and perhaps the house. Alston (D) asked Brown if she was "ready." Brown replied by saying, "no," and informing Alston (D) that she did not consent to going to bed with him. Alston (D) began kissing her, then pulled her from the chair in which she had been sitting and started undressing her. He told her to lie down on the bed which was in the living room. She complied and Alston (D) pushed apart her legs and had sexual intercourse with her. Although Brown cried during the intercourse, she did not attempt to push Alston (D) away. Afterwards, they talked. Brown made a complaint to the police the same day. Alston (D) continued to call Brown after June 15, but she refused to see him. One evening Alston (D) called from a telephone both and told her that he had to talk. When he got to her apartment he threatened to kick her door down and Brown let him inside. Once inside, Alston (D) said that he had intended merely to talk to her, but that he wanted to make love again after seeing her. After Brown sat down and looked at Alston (D), he began kissing her, then picked her up and carried her to the bedroom. He performed oral sex on her and she testified that she did not try to fight him off because she found she enjoyed it. The two stayed together until morning and had sexual intercourse several times that night. Alston (D) was convicted of second degree rape. Alston (D) appeals.

■ ISSUE

Must force or the threat of force occur at the time of the offense and be used to obtain sexual intercourse?

■ DECISION AND RATIONALE

(Mitchell, J.) Yes. The element of force of threat or force must occur at the time of the alleged rape, and must be used to obtain sexual intercourse. Second degree rape involves vaginal intercourse with the victim both by force and against the victim's will. Consent by the victim is a complete defense, unless the consent was induced by fear of violence. If the particular acts of intercourse for which the defendant is charged were both by force and against the victim's will, the offense is rape without regard to the victim's consent given to the defendant for prior acts of intercourse. Here, Brown and Alston (D) have engaged in a prior continuing consensual relationship, making the determination of Brown's state of mind at the time of the alleged rape more difficult. The State ordinarily will be able to show Brown's lack of consent to the specific act charged, only by evidence of statements or actions by the victim which were clearly communicated to Alston (D) and which expressly indicated Brown's withdrawal of any prior consent and lack of consent to the particular act of intercourse. The State did introduce evidence that Brown did not consent to sexual intercourse with the defendant on June 15. Brown's testimony provided substantial evidence that the act of sexual intercourse was against her will. However, the State did not offer substantial evidence of the element of force. Actual physical force need not be shown in order to establish force sufficient to constitute an element of the crime of rape. Threats of serious bodily harm which reasonably induce fear thereof are sufficient. In the present case, there was no substantial evidence of either actual or constructive force. There is evidence that when the two walked out of the parking lot, Alston (D) told Brown he was going to "fix" her face so that her mother could see he was not "playing." However, although this threat and Alston's (D) act of grabbing Brown by the arm at the school may have induced fear, it appears to have been unrelated to the act of sexual intercourse. More important, the record is devoid of evidence that Brown was in any way intimidated into having sexual intercourse with Alston (D) by that threat or any other act on June 15. We note that the absence of an explicit threat is not determinative in considering whether there was sufficient force in whatever form to overcome the will of the victim. It is enough if the totality of circumstances gives rise to a reasonable inference that the unspoken purpose of the threat was to force the victim to submit to unwanted sexual intercourse. Here, although Brown's general fear of Alston (D) may have been justified by his conduct on prior occasions, there was no evidence that Alston (D) used force or threats to overcome the will of Brown. Therefore Brown's general fear was not sufficient to show that Alston (D) used force to support a conviction of rape. Reversed.

Analysis:

This case is important for two reasons. First, it does a very good job of illustrating that consent and force are two separate elements. Thus it shows that lack of consent alone is not enough to support a conviction for rape. Second, the opinion requires that the use of force or threats of force must have occurred at the time of the offense, specifically to obtain sexual intercourse. Therefore, although the court states that it recognizes and understands Brown's "general fear," in consideration of her relationship to Alston (D), this fear is not sufficient absent an explicit threat used to obtain sexual intercourse.

■ CASE VOCABULARY

FORCE / THREAT OF FORCE: Elements, either of which are necessary to a finding of rape, that must occur at the time of the rape, and used to obtain sexual intercourse.

Rusk v. State

(*Light Choker*) v. (*Community*)

43 Md.App. 476, 406 A.2d 624 (1979)

FORCE IS A NECESSARY ELEMENT OF TRADITIONAL RAPE

■ **INSTANT FACTS** A man is convicted of second degree rape, after meeting a twenty-one year old mother of two at a bar, bringing her up to his house, and having sexual intercourse her, despite the lack of force.

■ **BLACK LETTER RULE** Actual force or threat of force is a necessary element of rape.

■ PROCEDURAL BASIS

Appeal to the Court of Special Appeals of Maryland, of a conviction for second degree rape.

■ FACTS

The victim was a twenty-one-year-old mother of a two-year-old son, separated but not divorced from her husband. After leaving her son with her mother, the victim attended a high school reunion, after which she and a female friend went bar hopping in the Fells Point Area of Baltimore, taking separate cars. At the third bar, the victim met Edward Salvatore Rusk (Rusk) (D). After conversing for about five or ten minutes, the victim agreed to give Rusk (D) a ride home. When they arrived at Rusk's home, the victim parked at the curb on the side of the street opposite from Rusk's (D) rooming house, but did not turn off the ignition. Rusk (D) asked the victim numerous times to come up to his apartment, which, as the victim testified, made her afraid. While the victim tried to convince Rusk (D) that she didn't want to go up to his apartment, stating that she was separated and that it might cause her marital problems especially if she was followed by a detective, Rusk (D) took the keys out of the car and walked over to her side of the car. Rusk (D) then opened the door and said, "Now will you come up?" The victim agreed, testifying that at that point, she was scared because she did not know where she was, whether to run, and could not think of anything else to do. After following Rusk (D) to the room, the victim was left alone while Rusk (D) went to the bathroom. However, the victim made no attempt to leave, and while there was evidence that there was a phone inside the room, the victim testified that she did not notice one. When Rusk (D) came back, he sat on the bed and pulled the victim onto the bed. The victim stated that she then removed her slacks and removed his clothes because Rusk (D) asked her to. After undressing, the victim testified that she was still begging Rusk (D) to let her leave, but that Rusk (D) continued to say, "no." At which point the victim stated that she was really scared, more from the look in his eyes. Not knowing what to say, the victim asked Rusk (D), "If I do what you want, will you let me go without killing me?"

The victim then began to cry, and Rusk (D) putting his hands on the victim's throat, began to lightly choke her. At this point the victim asked, "If I do what you want, will you let me go?" After Rusk (D) said yes, the victim proceeded in doing what Rusk (D) desired. After the victim performed oral sex on Rusk (D), they had sexual intercourse. After the incident and upon arriving at home, the victim sat in her car and wondered about what Rusk (D) would have done if she did not assent to his wishes. Believing that the right thing to do was to report the incident, she immediately proceeded to Hillendale to find a police car. Rusk (D) was convicted of rape in the second degree and of assault. Rusk (D) did not challenge the conviction for assault, but appeals the conviction for rape.

■ ISSUE

Is actual force or the threat of force, an essential element to the crime of rape?

■ DECISION AND RATIONALE

(Thompson, J.) Yes. Actual force or the threat of force, is an essential element to the crime of rape. Evidence must warrant a conclusion that the victim resisted and that her resistance was overcome by force, or that she was prevented from resisting by threats to her safety. The victim's testimony offers no evidence of resistance to sex acts, nor any fear that would overcome her attempt to resist or escape. The possession of her keys may have deterred her vehicular escape, but not her departure seeking help in the rooming house or in the street. Furthermore, "the way he looked," fails utterly to support the requirement of fear. The victim argues that the issue of whether or not intercourse was accompanied by force or threats of force is one of credibility to be resolved by the triers of the fact. We cannot follow this argument. The trial judge on ruling on a motion to acquit, must first determine that there is legally sufficient evidence for the jury to find the victim was reasonably in fear. Cases from other jurisdictions have followed the rule that the victim's fear which overcomes her will to resist must be a reasonable fear. We find the evidence legally insufficient to warrant a conclusion that Rusk's (D) actions created in the mind of the victim a reasonable fear, that if she resisted, he would have harmed, or that faced with such resistance, he would have used force to overcome it. Although Rusk (D) lightly choked the victim, we do not believe that "lightly choking" along with all the facts and circumstances in the case, were sufficient to cause a reasonable fear which overcame the victim's ability to resist. At oral argument it was brought out that, "lightly choking," could have been a heavy caress. In the absence of any other evidence showing use of force by Rusk (D), we find that the evidence was insufficient to convict Rusk (D) of rape. Reversed.

■ DISSENT

(Wilner, J.) The majority has effectively substituted their own view of the evidence for that of the judge and jury. In so doing, they have not only improperly invaded the province allotted to those tribunals, but has also perpetuated and given new life to myths about the crime of rape that have no place in our law today. There is clear evidence to show that Rusk (D) had vaginal intercourse with the victim, and that the act was against the victim's will. The point at issue is whether it was accomplished by force or threat of force. Courts often tend to confuse the two elements of force and lack of consent. The cause of this confusion is the notion that the victim must actively resist the attack upon her. Failure to do so entitles a court, as it seems, to find that there was no force or threat of force, that the act was not against the victim's will, or that the victim consented, leading ultimately to the conclusion that the victim was not raped. Thus, the focus is almost entirely on the extent of resistance, or the victim's acts, rather than those of her assailant, in the victim's reaction to the wrongful stimulus. Submission is not the equivalent of consent, and I believe the real test is whether the assault was committed without the consent and against the will of the victim. In the instant case we know nothing about the victim and Rusk (D). We don't know how big they are, what they look like, whether one is bigger and stronger than the other, or what their past life experiences have been. Moreover, we do not know what the inflection was in Rusk's (D) voice as he dangled the car keys in front the victim, or what Rusk's (D) mannerisms were. However, the trial judge and the jury could discern some of these things, by observing the two people in court. If Rusk (D) had desired, and the victim had given, her wallet instead of her body, there would be no question about Rusk's (D) guilt of robbery. Taking the car keys under those circumstances would certainly have supplied the requisite threat of force and negated the element of consent. No one would seriously contend that because she failed to raise a hue and cry she had consented to the theft of her money. Why then is such life-threatening action necessary when it is her personal dignity that is being stolen? A judge and jury observing the witness and hearing the testimony, concluded without dissent that there was sufficient evidence to find beyond a reasonable doubt that Rusk (D) had sexual intercourse with the victim by force or threat of force against her will and without her consent. In other words, they found the extent of her resistance and the reasons for her failure to resist further were reasonable. Furthermore, there is no claim that the jury was misinstructed. Yet the majority of this Court, has simply concluded that the victim's fear was not a reasonable one, brushing aside the judgment of the trial court and jury.

Analysis:

In the instant case, because the use of actual force was not illustrated by the facts, it was essential to a finding of rape that there was a sufficient threat of force. One can infer from the majority opinion that "fear of force" and "threat of force" are not the same. Though the victim may fear that the perpetrator may use force, this fear must be "reasonable." Thus the perpetrator must actually make an affirmative threat. The victim in this case may have believed that she was being threatened, and even asked Rusk (D), "If I do what you want, will you let me go without killing me?" However, this court found that although Rusk answered this question with a "yes," which may be taken as an "implied threat," that was insufficient to satisfy the "threat of force" element of rape. Therefore, it may be inferred that if there is no explicit threat towards the victim, the victim's fear was not reasonable. As the dissent points out, despite the lack of an explicit threat, the "threat of force" may be implicitly based on, among other things, the size of the parties, their history, and the inflection of their voices. Therefore, since these were factors available only to the trial court, perhaps the "threat of force" issue should have been left for the trial court to decide.

■ CASE VOCABULARY

FORCE: A traditional element of rape requiring physical acts sufficient to overcome a victim's resistance.

THREAT OF FORCE: An explicit threat, which would render a victim unable to resist.

State v. Rusk

(*Community*) v. (*Light Choker*)
289 Md. 230, 424 A.2d 720 (1981)

IMPLIED THREAT OF FORCE IS SUFFICIENT FOR A CONVICTION OF RAPE

■ **INSTANT FACTS** The Court of Appeals of Maryland affirms the trial courts conviction of second degree rape, finding that the reasonableness of the victim's apprehension of fear was a question of fact for the jury to determine.

■ **BLACK LETTER RULE** An implied threat is sufficient to satisfy the element of force for rape.

■ PROCEDURAL BASIS

Appeal to the Court of Appeals of Maryland, of a reversal by the Court of Special Appeals, of a conviction of second degree rape.

■ FACTS

(See prior opinion for *Rusk v. State.*)

■ ISSUE

Is an implied threat sufficient to satisfy the element of force for rape?

■ DECISION AND RATIONALE

(Murphy, J.) Yes. An implied threat is sufficient to satisfy the element of force for rape. The reversal by the Court of Special Appeals was in error for the fundamental reason so well expressed in the dissenting opinion. The reasonableness of the victim's apprehension of fear was plainly a question of fact for the jury to determine. Reversed and remanded to the Court of Special Appeals with direction that it affirm the judgment of the Criminal Court of Baltimore.

■ DISSENT

(Cole, J.) I agree with the Court of Special Appeals. Although we no longer require a female to resist to the utmost or resist where resistance would be fool hardy, we do require the victim's submission to stem from fear generated by something of substance. Submission by force is required, as a seducer does not equate with a rapist. The victim must follow the natural instinct of every proud female to resist, by more than mere words. She must make it plain that she regards such sexual acts as abhorrent and repugnant to her natural sense of pride, unless the defendant has objectively manifested his intent to use physical force to accomplish his purpose. In the absence of any verbal threat to do her grievous bodily harm or the display of any weapon and threat to use it, I find it difficult to understand how a victim could participate in these sexual activities and not be willing.

Analysis:

Although resistance may provide clear evidence of "actual force," it places the victim in a position susceptible to physical harm. As stated by the dissent, a woman is required to "follow the natural instinct of every proud female," and "resist" her assailant. However, this may not be realistic, or at the very least, fair. This implicit requirement of resistance requires a woman to take an active role in fighting back. Though many are capable of this, those that are passive are left with no redress for their injuries. It is easy to confuse the elements of consent and force, though the two mean and require different things. Specifically, because resistance is seen as a necessary prerequisite to the finding of actual force, it is easy to mistake lack of resistance for implied consent. It seems to the dissent that only explicit threats would make resistance unnecessary. However, if a victim is in reasonable apprehension of bodily harm, the victim need not resist, despite the lack of an explicit threat. Therefore, as held by the majority, an implied or implicit threat of force may be sufficient to satisfy the "force" element of rape.

■ CASE VOCABULARY

IMPLIED THREAT OF FORCE: A reasonable threat of force that places a victim in apprehension of bodily harm, inferred by the circumstances, which renders the victim unable to resist.

Commonwealth v. Berkowitz

(*State*) v. (*College Student*)

415 Pa.Super. 505, 609 A.2d 1338 (1992)

RAPE CONVICTION IS REVERSED DESPITE THE VICTIM REPEATEDLY SAYING "NO"

■ **INSTANT FACTS** A college student is convicted of raping his girl friend in his dorm room, after the friend voluntarily entered his dorm room and repeatedly said "no" to his sexual advances, although she did not physically resist.

■ **BLACK LETTER RULE** Verbal resistance alone, is not sufficient evidence of rape.

■ **PROCEDURAL BASIS**

Appeal to the Superior Court of Pennsylvania, of a conviction for rape and indecent assault.

■ **FACTS**

In the spring of 1988, Berkowitz (D) and the victim were both college sophomores at East Stroudsburg State University, ages twenty and nineteen years old respectively. At about 2:00 pm on April 19, 1988, the victim returned to her room after class and drank a martini to "loosen up a bit" before going to meet her boyfriend, with whom she had argued with the night before. Ten mintes later she walked to her boyfriend's dormitory lounge to meet him, but he had not yet arrived. Having nothing else to do, she walked up to Berkowitz's (D) room to look for Earl Hassel (Earl), Berkowitz's (D) roommate. Although the victim knocked on the door several times, there was no answer. After writing a note to Earl, the victim knocked again, and upon finding the door unlocked, walked in. She saw someone lying on the bed with a pillow over his head, whom she thought to be Earl. After lifting the pillow from his head, the victim realized it was Berkowitz (D). The victim asked Berkowitz (D) which dresser was his roommate's, and left the note. Before the victim could leave Berkowitz (D) asked the victim to stay and "hang out." She complied because "she had time to kill" and because she didn't really know appellant but wanted to "give him a fair chance." Berkowitz (D) asked her to give him a back rub but she declined, explaining that she did not trust him. Berkowitz (D) then asked the victim to have a seat on his bed, but instead, the victim sat on the floor, and the two conversed about a mutual friend and about the victim's problems with her boyfriend. Thereafter, Berkowitz (D) moved off the bed and down on the floor, and "kind of pushed "the victim" back with his body. It wasn't a shove, it was just kind of a leaning-type thing." Next Berkowitz (D) straddled and began kissing the victim. After the victim responded, "Look I gotta go. I'm going to meet "my boyfriend"," Berkowitz (D) lifted up her shirt and bra and began fondling her. The victim then said "no." After about thirty seconds of kissing and fondling, Berkowitz "undid his pants and moved his body up a little bit." Though the victim kept saying "no," she was unable to move. Berkowitz (D) then tried to put his penis in the victim's mouth. The victim did not physically resist, but continued to verbally protest in a scolding manner. Ten or fifteen seconds later, the two rose to their feet, and Berkowitz (D), ignoring the victim's complaints, locked the door so that no one could enter from outside. However, this lock, as the victim knew, could not lock people inside the room. Berkowitz (D) then put, but did not force the victim onto the bed, removed her sweatpants and underwear from one of her legs, and guided his penis into her vagina. The victim did not physically resist in any way while on the bed, nor did she scream, but testified that she "couldn't like go anywhere," and that, "it was like a dream was happening or something." After Berkowitz (D) was inside the victim, the victim began saying "no, no to him softly in a moaning kind of way... because it was just so scary." After about thirty seconds, Berkowtiz (D) pulled out his penis and ejaculated onto the victim's stomach. Immediately thereafter, Berkowitz (D) got off the victim, and said, "Wow, I guess we got carried away." To this the victim retorted, "No, we didn't get carried away, you got carried away." The victim then quickly got dressed, raced downstairs to her boyfriend who was by then waiting for her in the lounge, and began crying. After the victim and her boyfriend went up to his dorm room and cleaned the seamen off the victim's stomach, the boyfriend called the police. During trial, it was found by defense counsel on cross-examination, that two weeks prior to the incident, the victim attended a school seminar entitled, "Does 'no' sometimes means means 'yes'?" Among other things, the lecturer at this seminar had discussed the average length and circumference of human penises. After the seminar, the victim and several of her friends discussed the subject matter of the seminar over a speaker-telephone with Berkowitz (D) and his roommate Earl. The victim testified that during the conversation, she had spoken to Berkowitz (D) about the size of his penis, to which Berkowitz (D) suggested to the victim that the she "come over and find out." She declined. Furthermore, the victim testified that on two other occasions, she had stopped by Berkowitz's (D) room while intoxicated. During one of those times, she laid down on his bed, but she testified that she did not remember if she asked Berkowitz (D) about his penis size again at that time. According to Berkowitz (D), the victim began communications after the seminar by asking him the size of his penis and whether he would show it to her. Berkowitz (D) suspected that the victim wished to pursue a sexual relationship with him because she had stopped by his room twice after the phone call while intoxicated, laying down on his bed with her legs spread and again asking to see his penis. He believed that his suspicions were confirmed when she initiated the April 19th encounter by stopping by his room, again after drinking, and waking him up. Berkowitz (D) testified that although he did initiate the first physical contact, the victim warmly responded to his advances by passionately returning his kisses. He conceded that she was continually whispering "no," but claimed that she did so while passionately moaning. Thus Berkowitz (D) took such protests to be thinly veiled acts of encouragement, and locked the door so that no one would walk in on them. The two then laid down on the bed, the victim helped him take her clothing off, and he entered her. Berkowitz (D) agreed that the victim continued to say "no" while on the bed, but carefully qualified his agreement, explaining that the statements were "moaned passionately." After hearing both accounts, the jury convicted Berkowitz (D) of rape and indecent assault, and Berkowitz (D) was sentenced to imprisonment of one to four years for rape, and a concurrent term of six to twelve months for indecent assault. Berkowitz (D) appeals his rape conviction.

■ ISSUE

Is verbal resistance alone, sufficient to prove that force was used?

■ DECISION AND RATIONALE

(Per Curiam) No. We contend that upon review, the facts show nothing more than what legal scholars refer as "reluctant submission." The victim herself admits that she was neither hurt nor threatened at any time during the encounter. She never screamed nor attempted to summon help, though the incident occurred in a college dormitory in the middle of the afternoon. There has never been an affirmed conviction for forcible rape under similar circumstances, and the evidence here fails to establish forcible compulsion. The commonwealth's position is that the jury's conclusion that Berkowitz's (D) forcible conduct overcame the victim's will is reasonable. The victim was acquainted with Berkowitz (D) and had no reason to be fearful or suspicious of him, and her resorting to verbal resistance only is understandable. More importantly, perhaps, it is only her lack of consent that is truly relevant. It is entirely reasonable that Berkowitz (D) sat on the victim, pushed her on the bed and penetrated her before she had time to fully realize her plight and raise a hue or a cry. If the law required active resistance, rather than the simple absence of consent, speedy penetration would immunize the most violent attacks. But, contrary to Berkowitz's (D) argument Pennsylvania law says she can "just say no," which is what the victim said repeatedly. The trial court agreed with the commonwealth's position, but we cannot. If the jury could have reasonably determined from the evidence adduced that all of the necessary elements of the crime were established, then the evidence will be deemed sufficient to support the verdict. In Pennsylvania, the crime of rape in the first degree is defined as engaging in sexual intercourse with another person not his spouse, 1) by forcible compulsion, 2) by threat of forcible compulsion that would prevent resistance by a person of reasonable resolution, 3) who is unconscious, or 4) who is so mentally deranged or deficient that such a person is incapable of consent. The alleged victim need not resist. The determination of whether there is sufficient evidence to demonstrate beyond a reasonable doubt that an accused engaged in sexual intercourse by forcible compulsion (which we have defined to include not only force or violence, but also moral, psychological or intellectual force used to compel a person to engage in sexual intercourse against that person's will) or by threat of such forcible compulsion that would prevent resistance by a person of reasonable resolution is, of course, a determination that will be made in each case based upon the totality of the circumstances that have been presented to the fact finder. Significant factors to consider include the ages of the victim and the accused, the respective mental and physical conditions of the victim and the accused, the atmosphere and physical setting in which the incident was alleged to have taken place, the extent to which the accused may have been in a position of authority, domination or custodial control over the victim, and whether the victim was under duress. There existed no significant disparity between the ages of the victim and Berkowitz (D), no physical or mental condition of one party differed from the other in any material way, nor was the atmosphere in any way coercive, as the victim freely walked into Berkowitz's (D) room and voluntarily stayed there. Furthermore, there was no evidence to suggest that Berkowitz (D) was in any position of authority or domination over the victim, nor that the victim was under duress. Indeed, nothing in the record manifests any intent of Berkowitz (D) to impose moral, psychological or intellectual coercion upon the victim. Nor is this a case of a threat of forcible compulsion. The victim herself has admitted during trial that Berkowitz (D) did not threaten her in any manner, and the record fails to reveal any express or even implied threat that would prevent resistance by a person of reasonable resolution. The commonwealth contends that since the victim did not consent to engage in the intercourse, any force used to complete the act of intercourse thereafter constituted "forcible compulsion." The precise degree of actual physical force necessary to prove "forcible compulsion" is a determination that will be made in each case based on the totality of the circumstances. Even in the light most favorable to the commonwealth, the victim's testimony as to the physical aspects of the encounter cannot serve as a basis for "forcible compulsion." The record is devoid of any evidence regarding the respective sizes of the parties. Therefore we can only speculate as to the coercive effects of "leaning" against the victim or placing the "weight of his body" on top of her. Moreover, even if the record indicated some disparity in the respective weights or strength of the parties, such acts are not inconsistent with consensual relations. Thus, there is no evidence that the victim could not have at any time, removed herself from Berkowitz's (D) bed and left the room without any risk of harm or danger to herself whatsoever. These circumstances simply cannot be bootstrapped into sexual intercourse by forcible compulsion. Similarly inconclusive is the fact that the victim testified that the act occurred in a relatively brief period of time. At most, the physical aspects of the encounter establish that appellant's sexual advances may have been unusually rapid. However inappropriate such conduct may be seen to be, it does not, standing alone, prove that the victim was "forced to engage in sexual intercourse against her will." Lastly, we must consider the fact that during the encounter, the victim repeatedly and continually said "no." Unfortunately for the commonwealth, this evidence alone cannot suffice to support a finding of "forcible compulsion." Although evidence of verbal resistance is unquestionably relevant in a determination of "forcible compulsion," it is not dispositive or sufficient evidence of "forcible compulsion". If the legislature had intended to define rape as non-consensual intercourse, it would have done so. However, they defined rape as sexual intercourse by "forcible compulsion," and there is no evidence of such, nor mental coercion or threat in the instant case. Though it may seem that this reasoning is at odds with the "no resistance requirement," this requirement must be applied only to prevent any adverse inference to be drawn against the person who, while being "forcibly compelled" to engage in intercourse, chooses not to physically resist. Since there is no evidence that the victim was at any time "forcibly compelled" to engage in sexual intercourse, our conclusion is not at odds with the "no resistance requirement." We discharge Berkowitz (D) as to the rape conviction, and remand on the case for the indecent assault charge.

Analysis:

Here, the court finds that although the victim did not consent to intercourse, there was no force, threat of force, or mental coercion. What is important to note about this case is the use of the word "no," which was consistently repeated by the victim. It is obvious from the decision that in order to prove force, the use of verbal resistance alone is not sufficient. Although the court purports to follow a "no resistance requirement" in its determination of "force," physical resistance is still required unless the perpetrator uses or threatens the use of force. Thus, as the court states, although verbal protest is relevant evidence in proving that the intercourse was against the victim's will, it is not enough evidence for a finding of "forcible compulsion."

■ CASE VOCABULARY

RESISTANCE: An implicit requirement to the finding of the element of force in rape convictions.

State of New Jersey in the Interest of M.T.S.

(*Community*) v. (*Seventeen-Year-Old*)

129 N.J. 422, 609 A.2d 1266 (1992)

RESISTANCE NOT REQUIRED TO PROVE RAPE

■ **INSTANT FACTS** A seventeen-year-old is convicted of the rape of a fifteen-year-old who was asleep at the time of penetration.

■ **BLACK LETTER RULE** Resistance is not a required element of rape.

■ PROCEDURAL BASIS

Certification to the Supreme Court of New Jersey of a conviction for acquaintance rape.

■ FACTS

On May 21, 1990 fifteen-year-old C.G. was living in a town home with her mother, her three siblings, and several others including M.T.S. (D) and his girlfriend. M.T.S. (D), then age seventeen, was temporarily living at the home with the permission of C.G.'s mother. He slept downstairs on the couch, while C.G. had her own room on the second floor. At approximately 11:30 p.m. C.G. went upstairs after watching television with her mother, M.T.S. (D), and M.T.S.'s (D) girlfriend. According to C.G., earlier that day M.T.S. (D) had told her three or four times that he "was going to make a surprise visit up in "her" bedroom," but she did not take him seriously. She also testified that M.T.S. (D) had attempted to kiss her on numerous other occasions and at least once had attempted to put his hands inside of her pants, but that she had rejected all of his previous advances. On May 22, at approximately 1:30 am, C.G. awoke to use the bathroom. As she got out of bed, she found M.T.S. (D) standing in the doorway fully clothed. C.G. testified that M.T.S. (D) stated that, "he was going to tease "her" a little bit," but that she thought nothing of it. She then walked past him, used the bathroom, and then returned to bed, falling into a "heavy" sleep within fifteen minutes. The next thing C.G. recalled was waking up with M.T.S. (D) on top of her, her underpants and shorts removed, with his penis into her vagina. She immediately slapped M.T.S. (D) in the face and then, "told him to get off "her", and get out." She did not scream or cry out, and M.T.S. (D) complied in less than one minute after being struck. She said she did not know how long M.T.S. (D) had been inside of her before she awoke. C.G. said that after M.T.S. (D) left the room, she "fell asleep crying" because ""she" couldn't believe that he did what he did to "her"." She did not immediately tell anyone of the events that morning because she was "scared and in shock." C.G. was not otherwise harmed. According to M.T.S. (D), he and C.G. had been good friends for a long time, and their relationship "kept leading on to more and more." He testified that three days preceding the incident they had been "kissing and necking," and had discussed sexual intercourse. M.T.S. (D) also stated that C.G. encouraged him to "make a surprise visit up in her room." At exactly 1:15 am on May 22, he entered C.G.'s bedroom as she was walking to the bathroom. When she returned the two began kissing and eventually moved to the bed. After continuing to kiss and touch for about five minutes, the two proceeded to engage in sexual intercourse. According to M.T.S. (D), he "stuck it in" and "did it "thrust" three times, and then the fourth time," C.G. pushed him off and told him "stop, get off," and M.T.S. (D) "hopped off right away." After about one minute, M.T.S. (D) asked C.G. what was wrong and she replied with a slap to his face. He recalled asking her what was wrong a second time, and her replying, "How can you take advantage of me or something like that." The trial court found M.T.S. (D) guilty of second-degree sexual assault. The Appellate Division reversed determining that the absence of force beyond that involved in the act of sexual penetration precluded a finding of second-degree sexual assault. The State appeals.

■ ISSUE

Is resistance a necessary element of rape?

■ DECISION AND RATIONALE

(Handler, J.) No. Resistance is not a required element of rape. The New Jersey Code defines "sexual assault" as the commission "of sexual penetration....with another person" with the use of "physical force or coercion." An unconstrained reading of the statutory language indicates that both the act of "sexual penetration" and the use of "physical force or coercion" are separate and distinct elements of the offense. However, the Code does not provide assistance in interpreting the words, "physical force." Therefore, the initial inquiry is whether the statutory words are unambiguous on their face and can be understood and applied in accordance with their plain meaning. The state asserts that "physical force" entails any amount of sexual touching brought about involuntarily. The Public Defender asserts that "physical force" entails a use of force sufficient to overcome lack of consent. Thus, sexual assault requires the application of some amount of force in addition to the act of penetration. Current judicial practice suggests that "physical force" entails "any degree of physical power of strength used against the victim, even though it entails no injury and leaves no mark." common experience or understanding does not yield a conclusive result. The dictionary provides several definitions of force, including: 1) power, violence, compulsion, or constraint exerted on or against a person or thing, 2) a general term for exercise of strength or power to overcome resistance, or 3) strength or power of any degree that is exercised without justification or contrary to law upon a person or thing. Thus, because of the conflicting interpretations of "physical force," we must turn to the legislative intent, relying on legislative history and the contemporary context of the statute. The origin of the rape statute that the current statutory offense of sexual assault replaced can be traced back to English common law. Under the common law, rape was defined as "carnal knowledge of a woman against her will." Although American jurisdiction generally adopted the English view, over time they added the requirement that the knowledge have been forcible, apparently in order to prove that the act was against the victim's will. As of 1796, New Jersey statutory law defined rape as "carnal knowledge of a woman, forcibly, and against her will. Under traditional rape law, in order to prove that a rape had occurred, the state had to show both that force had been used and that the penetration had been against the woman's will. The presence or absence of consent often turned on credibility. To demonstrate that the victim had not consented to the intercourse, and also that sufficient force had been used to accomplish the rape, the state had to prove that the victim had resisted. Courts and commentators historically distrusted the testimony of victims. Evidence of resistance was viewed as a solution to the credibility problem, because it was an outward manifestation of nonconsent. The judicial interpretation of the pre-reform rape law in New Jersey, with its reliance on resistance by the victim, greatly minimized the importance of the forcible and assaultive aspect of the defendant's conduct, turning the focus to the victim's response. Reformers have emphasized empirical research indicating that women who resisted forcible intercourse often suffered far more serious injury as a result. That research discredited the assumption that resistance to the utmost was the most reasonable or rational response to a rape. Critics of rape agreed that the focus of the crime should be shifted from the victim's behavior to the defendant's conduct, and particularly to its forceful and assaultive, rather than sexual, character. There were, however, differences over the best way to redefine the crime. Some advocated a standard that defined rape as nonconsensual sexual intercourse, while others urged the elimination of any reference to consent from the definition of rape. Nonetheless all proponents of reform shared a central premise, that the burden of showing non-consent should not fall on the victim of the crime. In dealing with the problem of consent, the reform goal was to eliminate the burden that had been placed on victims to prove they had not consented. Similarly, with regard to force, rape law reform sought to give independent significance to the forceful or assaultive conduct of the defendant and to avoid a definition of force that depended on the reaction of the victim. In urging that the "resistance" requirement be abandoned, reformers sought to break the connection between force and resistance. The circumstances surrounding the actual passage of the current law reveal that it was conceived as a reform measure reconstituting the law to address a widely-sensed evil and to effectuate an important public policy. Those circumstances are highly relevant in understanding intent. We are thus satisfied that an interpretation of the statutory crime of sexual assault to require physical force in addition to that entailed in the act of involuntary or unwanted sexual penetration would be fundamentally inconsistent with the legislative purpose to eliminate any consideration of whether the victim resisted or expressed non-consent. Because the statute eschews any reference to the victim's will or resistance, the standard defining the role of force in sexual penetration must prevent the possibility that the establishment of the crime will turn on the alleged victim's state of mind or responsive behavior. We conclude, therefore, that any act of sexual penetration engaged in by the defendant without the affirmative and freely-given permission of the victim to the specific act of penetration constitutes the offense of sexual assault. Therefore, physical force in excess of that inherent in the act of sexual penetration is not required for such penetration to be unlawful. Persons need not expressly announce their consent to engage in intercourse for there to be affirmative permission. Permission to engage in an act of sexual penetration can be and indeed often is indicated through physical action rather than words. It is enough that a reasonable person would have believed that the alleged victim had affirmatively and freely given authorization to the act. We emphasize as well that what is now referred to as "acquaintance rape" is not a new phenomenon. The vast majority of sexual assaults are perpetrated by someone known to the victim. Similarly, contrary to common myths, perpetrators generally do not use guns or knives and victims generally do not suffer eternal bruises or cuts. This more realistic view of rape was a central concern of the proponents of reform in the 1970's. In a case such as this one, in which the State does not allege violence or force extrinsic to the act of penetration, the factfinder must decide whether the defendant's act of penetration was undertaken in circumstances that led the defendant to reasonably believe that the alleged victim had freely given affirmative permission to the specific act of sexual penetration. Such permission can be indicated through words or actions that, when viewed in the light of all the surrounding circumstances, would demonstrate to a reasonable person affirmative authorization for the specific act of sexual penetration. The focus must be on the nature of the defendant's actions. The role of the factfinder is to decide whether the defendant's belief that the alleged victim had freely given affirmative permission was reasonable. In these cases neither the alleged victim's subjective state of mind nor the reasonableness of the alleged victim's actions can be deemed relevant to the offense. In sum, in order to convict under the sexual assault statute in cases such as these, the State must prove beyond a reasonable doubt that there was sexual penetration and that it was accomplished without the affirmative and freely-given permission of the alleged victim. If there is evidence that the defendant reasonably believed that such permission had been given, the State must demonstrate either that defendant did not actually believe that affirmative permission had been freely-given or that such a belief was unreasonable under all of the circumstances. The trial court concluded that the victim had not expressed consent to the act of intercourse, either through her words or actions. We conclude that the record provides reasonable support for the trial court's disposition. Reversed.

Analysis:

This case exemplifies a transition in rape law. Specifically, the opinion in effect does away with the requirement of resistance. Although the element of "force" still expressly exists, the amount of force required amounts to as much force as needed to complete the act of sexual penetration. Therefore, a male commits forcible rape if he has intercourse without securing a consent or a "yes," either by words or actions. The victim is not required to resist, nor to say "no." The court's analysis raises a concern: What conduct short of an express "yes" is sufficient to constitute permission? This case leaves the jury to decide whether the evidence presented leads to the conclusion that the defendant was reasonable in his belief of the victim's consent.

■ CASE VOCABULARY

FORCE: An element of rape satisfied by the use of sufficient physical action needed to complete the act of sexual intercourse.

People v. John Z.

(*Prosecution*) v. (*Teenage boy*)

29 Cal.4th 756, 128 Cal.Rptr.2d 783, 60 P.3d 183 (2003)

EVEN IF CONSENT TO INTERCOURSE IS INITIALLY GIVEN, IF THE CONSENT IS THEREAFTER WITHDRAWN, CONTINUATION OF INTERCOURSE BECOMES FORCIBLE RAPE

■ **INSTANT FACTS** After initially appearing to consent to sexual intercourse with her boyfriend's friend, John (D), Laura told him that she wanted to go home, but he continued having sexual intercourse with her and, on the basis of this action, was convicted of forcible rape.

■ **BLACK LETTER RULE** A female's withdrawal of consent to sexual intercourse serves to nullify any earlier consent she has given and subjects the male to forcible rape charges if he persists in what has then become nonconsensual intercourse.

■ PROCEDURAL BASIS

On appeal to California Supreme Court, defendant asserts that the evidence is insufficient to sustain his forcible rape conviction.

■ FACTS

On March 23, 2000, Laura T., a 17–year old female, received a call from Juan G., whom she had met two weeks earlier. Juan asked her to take him to a party at John Z.'s (D) house that evening. Justin L. and John (D) were present when they arrived at John's (D) house sometime after 6:00 p.m. Justin's brother assisted the group in buying beer. John (D) and Juan drank the beer, but Laura did not drink any. At about 8:00 p.m., Laura decided she was ready to leave. As she was leaving, John (D) asked her if they could talk. She walked back into the house and into his bedroom, which was completely dark. She remained, unrestrained, in his bedroom and did not ask him to turn on the light. John (D) told her that Juan was only using her. He also told her that he really liked her and that she should dump Juan and become his girlfriend. Juan came into the bedroom. The boys then asked Laura if she had ever fantasized about having two guys. She told them that she had not done so, but she remained seated on the bed while the boys undressed her. She said that she felt like there was "no point in fighting" because she had already tried to leave and they had asked her into the bedroom to talk. She lay on the bed with Juan and John (D) at her side. She testified that they engaged in foreplay activities. She testified that she enjoyed these activities "because it was like a threesome." She said she liked being the center of attention. After that, John (D) left the room and Laura had intercourse with Juan, which ended when his condom kept falling off. Then John (D) came back into the room. Laura was still naked because she couldn't find her clothes in the dark. John (D), whose left hand was in a cast, sat on the bed behind her and touched her on the shoulder. He nudged her with one hand and she lay back down on the bed. John (D) began kissing her and she kissed him back. He climbed on top of Laura and penetrated her. She did not say anything or push him away. John (D) did not make any threats, but asked her repeatedly if she would be his girlfriend. Although he only held her with one hand, she stated that she was unable to extricate herself or break the connection. Finally she said "if he really did care about me, he wouldn't be doing this to me and if her really wanted a relationship, he should wait and respect that I don't want to do this." John (D) responded that he really did care about her. At some later point, Laura said, "I should be going now. I need to go home." John (D) asked her to give him a minute. A few minutes later, she once again told him that she needed to go home. He asked her to give him some time. She told him, "No. I have to go home." The third time she was more urgent about it and was starting to cry. She testified that he stayed inside of her for at least a minute thereafter.

■ ISSUE

Is the crime of forcible rape committed when the female victim consents to the initial penetration by the male perpetrator, but then later withdraws her consent during the act of intercourse and the male continues against her will?

■ DECISION AND RATIONALE

(Chin, J.) Yes. A female's withdrawal of consent to sexual intercourse serves to nullify any earlier consent she has given and subjects the male to forcible rape charges if he persists in what has then become nonconsensual intercourse. In so holding, we squarely disagree with the court's decision in *People v. Vela*, where no rape was found after consent had been withdrawn during intercourse. The *Vela* court noted that a woman's outrage at a man continuing with intercourse when she asked him to stop would have to be far less than the outrage she would feel if she didn't consent to the initial penetration. We find the reasoning of *Vela* to be unsound. First of all, we have no way of measuring the level of outrage a victim suffers when she is subjected to continued forcible intercourse after the withdrawal of her consent. We assume that it is substantial. While section 263 does provide that "the essential guilt of rape consists in the outrage to the person," nothing in the statute or case law makes the victim's outrage an element of the crime of rape. Pursuant to section 261, forcible rape occurs when the act of sexual intercourse is accomplished against the will of the victim by force or threat of bodily injury. It is immaterial at what point the victim withdraws her consent, so long as it is communicated to the male and he ignores it. Assuming that Laura gave her initial consent to intercourse with John (D), there is substantial evidence indicating that she withdrew her consent and through both her words and actions, communicated the withdrawal of consent to John (D). John (D) also argues that a male should be allowed a reasonable amount of time to withdraw once the female objects to account for the male's "primal urge to reproduce" which is aroused during intercourse. Nothing in the criminal code or case law supports John's (D) primal urge argument. Moreover, in this case he was clearly given ample time to withdraw but refused to do so, continuing long after she first told him that she needed to go home. We find that John (D) was properly convicted of forcible rape. Affirmed.

■ DISSENT

(Brown, J.) I agree with the majority that clear withdrawal of consent nullifies any earlier consent that has been given to the act of sexual intercourse. I do not believe, however, that the prosecution in this case proved beyond a reasonable doubt that the victim clearly communicated her withdrawal of consent. The facts of this sordid little case create doubt about the withdrawal of consent and use of force. Even if we assume that Laura's statements indicated a clear intent to withdraw consent, the act of rape still is not committed unless intercourse is accomplished forcibly, against the victim's will. Under the facts of this case, there is no evidence that John (D) threatened or forced Laura to stay after she indicated her desire to leave. All that we know is that he didn't instantly respond to her statement that she needed to go home. Moreover, the majority fails to indicate exactly how soon would have been soon enough for John (D) to discontinue the sexual act. Because of these unanswered questions, I respectfully dissent.

Analysis:

The dissent asserts that there was no evidence in this case showing that Laura was "forced" to continue having intercourse after she said that she wanted to go home. The majority, on the other hand, holds that once the victim indicates her withdrawal of consent, the act becomes forcible rape. The majority's view corresponds with that of the *M.T.S.* case, where the court held that lack of consent is enough to show forcible rape was committed. What these courts are essentially saying is that verbal resistance should be the legal equivalent of physical resistance. Do you think that non-consent could ever be indicated through silence?

■ CASE VOCABULARY

CONSENT: Cooperation or voluntary agreement to pursue course of action.

Commonwealth v. Sherry

(*State*) v. (*Doctor*)

386 Mass. 682, 437 N.E.2d 224 (1982)

A REASONABLE MISTAKE-OF-FACT MAY BE A DEFENSE TO RAPE

■ **INSTANT FACTS** Three doctors are convicted of rape after taking a nurse to a house and separately having intercourse with her, despite the doctors' mistake-of-fact as to the nurse's consent.

■ **BLACK LETTER RULE** A defense of mistake-of-fact must be based on a reasonable good faith standard.

■ PROCEDURAL BASIS

Certification to the Supreme judicial court of Massachusetts of a conviction for rape.

■ FACTS

The victim, a registered nurse, and defendants, all doctors, were employed at the same hospital in Boston. On September 5, 1980, Sherry (D1), along with another doctor, was a host at a party for some hospital staff. At this party, the victim had a conversation with Hussain (D2), during which he made sexual advances toward her. Later in the evening, Hussain (D2) and Sherry (D1) pushed her and Lefkowitz (D3) into a bathroom together, shut the door, and turned off the light. They did not open the door until Lefkowitz (D3) asked them to leave her in peace. At various times, the victim danced with both Hussain (D2) and Sherry (D1). Some time later, Hussain (D2) and Sherry (D1) grabbed the victim by her arms and pulled her out of the apartment, as Lefkowitz (D3) said, "We're going up to Rockport." The victim verbally protested but did not physically resist the men because she thought that they were just "horsing around." Nor was she physically restrained as they rode down an elevator with an unknown fifth person, or as they walked through the lobby of the apartment building. The victim testified that once outside, Hussain (D2) carried her over his shoulder to Sherry's car and held her in the front seat as the four drove to Rockport. En route she engaged in superficial conversation with the three defendants. She testified that she was not in fear at this time. When they arrived at Lefkowitz's (D3) home in Rockport, she asked to be taken home. Instead Hussain (D2) carried her into the house. Once in the house, the victim and two of the men smoked marijuana, and all of them toured the house. After being invited by Lefkowitz (D3) to view an antique bureau in a bedroom, all of them entered and the men began to disrobe. Although the victim was frightened and began to verbally protest, the three men proceeded to undress her and maneuver her onto the bed. One of the defendants attempted to have the victim perform fellatio while another attempted intercourse. After the victim told them to stop, two of the defendants left the room temporarily, and each defendant separately had intercourse with the victim in the bedroom. The victim testified, that she felt physically numbed, humiliated, and disgusted and could not fight. After this sequence of events, the victim claimed that she was further sexually harassed and forced to take a bath. Some time later, Lefkowitz (D3) told the victim that they were returning to Boston because Hussain (D2) was on call at the hospital. On their way back, the group stopped to view a beach, eat breakfast, and get gasoline. The victim was taken back to where she left her car and drove herself home. The defendants testified to a similar sequence of events, although details of the episode varied significantly. According to their testimony, Lefkowitz (D3) invited Sherry (D1) to accompany him from the party to a home that his parents owned in Rockport. The victim, upon hearing this, inquired as to whether she could go along. As the three were leaving, Sherry (D1) extended the invitation to Hussain (D2). At no time did the victim indicate her unwillingness to accompany the defendants. Upon arrival in Rockport, the victim wandered into the bedroom where she inquired about the antique bureau. She sat down on the bed and kicked off her shoes, whereupon Sherry (D1) entered the room, dressed only in his underwear. Sherry (D1) helped the victim get undressed, and she proceeded to have intercourse with all three men separately in turn. Each defendant testified that the victim consented to the acts of intercourse. Sherry (D1), Hussain (D2), and Lefkowitz (D3) were convicted of rape without aggravation. Sherry (D1), Hussain (D2), and Lefkowitz (D3) appeal.

■ ISSUE

Must a defense of mistake-of-fact as to whether consent was given be based on a reasonable good faith standard?

■ DECISION AND RATIONALE

(Liacos, J.) Yes. Sherry (D1), Hussain (D2), and Lefkowitz (D3) contend that the judge's jury charge was inadequate and the cause of prejudicial error. However the instructions given by the trial judge placed before the jury the essential elements of the crime required to be proved. The judge instructed the jury that intercourse must be accomplished with force sufficient to overcome the woman's will, or by threats of bodily harm, inferred or expressed, which engendered sufficient fear so that it was reasonable for her not to resist. These instructions correctly stated the elements of proof required for a rape conviction. Sherry (D1), Hussain (D2), and Lefkowitz (D3), appear to have been seeking to raise a defense of good faith mistake on the issue of consent. They would require the jury to "find beyond a reasonable doubt that the accused had actual knowledge of "the victim's" lack of consent." In doing so, they argue that mistake-of-fact negating criminal intent is a defense to the crime of rape. A defense of mistake-of-fact must be based on a reasonable good faith standard. Whether a reasonable good faith mistake-of-fact as to consent is a defense to the crime of rape has never to our knowledge, been decided in this Commonwealth. We do not reach the issue whether a reasonable and honest mistake to the fact of consent would be a defense, for even if we assume it to be, the defendants did not request a jury instruction based on a reasonable good faith standard. We are aware of no American Court of last resort that recognizes mistake-of-fact, without consideration of its reasonableness as a defense, nor do the defendants cite such authority. Affirmed.

Analysis:

This case raises the issue of the mens rea or intent aspect of the crime of rape. Rape is a general-intent offense. Therefore a defendant is guilty of rape if he possessed a morally blameworthy state of mind regarding the female's lack of consent. Thus, as a general rule, a person is not guilty of rape if he entertained a genuine and reasonable belief that the female voluntarily consented to intercourse with him. As you can see, this rule conforms with ordinary common law mistake-of-fact doctrine relating to general-intent offenses. As illustrated by the opinion, the issue of mens rea rarely arises in rape prosecutions. Most likely, the reason for this is because in traditional rape prosecutions, the element of force required to secure intercourse would effectively invalidate a claim that the perpetrator was mistaken with regard to consent. However, the issue of mens rea is more significant in acquaintance-rape prosecutions, in jurisdictions where the resistance rule has been eliminated, and in jurisdictions where a conviction may be obtained in the absence of force beyond that which is necessary for intercourse.

■ CASE VOCABULARY

MISTAKE-OF-FACT: A reasonable or good faith mistake, concerning the existence of an essential element of a crime.

Boro v. Superior Court

(*Donor*) v. (*State*)

163 Cal.App.3d 1224, 210 Cal.Rptr. 122 (1985)

FRAUD IN THE INDUCEMENT WILL NOT INVALIDATE CONSENT

■ **INSTANT FACTS** A man is charged with rape after fraudulently inducing a woman to have sex with him in order to cure her illness, and his motion to dismiss denied, despite the woman's consent to the intercourse.

■ **BLACK LETTER RULE** Fraud-in-the-factum, not fraud in the inducement, will vitiate consent to intercourse.

■ PROCEDURAL BASIS

Appeal to the California Court of Appeal of a denial of a motion to dismiss a charge of rape.

■ FACTS

The rape victim, Ms. R, received a telephone call from a person who identified himself as "Dr. Stevens" and said that he worked at Peninsula Hospital. "Dr. Stevens" told Ms. R. that he had the results of her blood test and that she had contracted a dangerous, highly infectious and perhaps fatal disease, from the use of public toilets. He further explained that there were only two ways to treat the disease. The first was a painful surgical procedure costing $9,000 and requiring uninsured hospitalization for six weeks. The second alternative was to have sexual intercourse with an anonymous donor who had been injected with a serum which would cure the disease. This would cost $4500. When Ms. R. stated that she lacked sufficient funds, "Dr. Stevens" suggested that $1000 would suffice as a down payment. Ms. R. then consented to intercourse with the anonymous donor, believing it was the only choice she had. After discussing her intentions with her work supervisor, Ms. R proceeded to the Hyatt Hotel in Burlingame as instructed, and telephoned "Dr. Stevens." Dr. Stevens became furious when he learned Ms. R. had informed her employer of the plan and threatened to terminate his treatment, finally instructing her to inform her employer she had not decided to go through with the treatment. Ms. R. did so. She then went to her bank, withdrew $1000, and as instructed, checked into another hotel and called "Dr. Stevens" to give him her room number. About a half hour later, Boro (D) the "donor" arrived at her room and the two had sexual intercourse. Boro filed a motion to dismiss Count II, charging him with a violation of Penal Code 261 [which defines rape as an act of sexual intercourse with a person who is at the time unconscious of the nature of the act, and this is known to the accused]. The motion was denied. Boro (D) appeals.

■ ISSUE

Will fraud-in-the-inducement vitiate a victim's consent to intercourse?

■ DECISION AND RATIONALE

(Newsom, J.) No. Fraud-in-the-factum, not fraud in the inducement, will vitiate consent to intercourse. At the time of penetration, it was Ms. R.'s belief that she would die unless she consented to sexual intercourse with the defendant. The People contend that Ms. R. was "unconscious of the nature of the act" because Boro's (D) misrepresentation caused Ms. R. to believe that the intercourse was in the nature of a medical treatment, and not simply an ordinary act of intercourse. Boro (D) contends that

Ms. R. was plainly aware of the nature of the act in which she voluntarily engaged, so that her motivation in doing so is irrelevant. There is sparse California authority on this subject. In one case, the defendant was a physician who "treated" several victims for menstrual cramps. Each victim testified that they were treated in a position with their back to the doctor, bent over a table, with feet apart, in a dressing gown. The treatment consisted of the defendant first inserting a metal instrument, then substituting an instrument which "felt different". The victim did not realize that the second instrument was in fact the doctor's penis. This case is useful to this analysis, because it exactly illustrates certain traditional rules in the area of our inquiry. Thus, as a leading authority has written, if deception causes a misunderstanding as to the fact itself, there is no legally-recognized consent because what happened is not that for which consent was given. This is fraud in the factum. Whereas consent induced by fraud is as effective as any other consent, if the deception relates not to the thing done but merely to some collateral matter. This is fraud in the inducement. The victim in this case consented, not to sexual intercourse, but to penetration by a medical instrument. The consent was to a pathological, and not a carnal, act, and the mistake was therefore in the inducement and not in the factum. The language of our statute could not be plainer. Courts of this state have previously confronted the general rule that fraud in the inducement does not vitiate consent. We can not entertain the slightest doubt that the legislature well understood how to draft a statute to specify fraud in the inducement as vitiating consent. If the legislature had desired to, it could certainly have done so. To so conclude is not to vitiate the heartless cruelty of Boro's (D) scheme, but that it comprised crimes of a different order.

Analysis:

In general, fraud-in-the-factum exists when the act consented to differs from the act that actually took place. In the instant case, the fraud existed in a matter collateral to the act of sexual intercourse. Specifically, fraud was used to obtain consent to the act of sexual intercourse, but the victim knew that she had consented to the sexual intercourse. The court here expressed that if the legislature wished to, it could have included "fraud-in-the-inducement" in the rape statute. The legislature understood that doing so would pose serious concerns about where to draw the line in rape cases. If fraud converted every act of sexual intercourse into rape, could a male be prosecuted every time he falsely claimed love or made promises that he did not intend to keep, in order to secure the female's consent to intercourse?

■ CASE VOCABULARY

FRAUD-IN-THE-FACTUM: Misrepresentation or concealment of the actual act about to occur or occurring.

FRAUD-IN-THE-INDUCEMENT: Misrepresentation or concealment which leads another to enter into a transaction with false or mistaken beliefs.

State v. Herndon

(*Not Stated*) v. (*Not Stated*)

145 Wis.2d 91, 426 N.W.2d 347 (1988)

RAPE-SHIELD LAWS AND SIXTH AMENDMENT RIGHTS WEIGHED TO DETERMINE ADMISSIBILITY OF EVIDENCE

■ **INSTANT FACTS** Opinion by the Court of Appeals of Wisconsin discussing the process of weighing a defendant's Sixth Amendment rights against the interest of rape-shield laws, when determining the admissibility of evidence.

■ **BLACK LETTER RULE** The interest of rape-shield laws (which prohibit the cross-examination of rape victims) and a defendant's Sixth Amendment rights must be weighed in order to determine whether certain evidence should be admissible.

■ PROCEDURAL BASIS

Opinion by the Court of Appeals of Wisconsin discussing rape shield legislation.

■ FACTS

Not Stated.

■ ISSUE

Should the interests of "rape shield" laws be weighed against a defendants constitutional rights in determining the admissibility of evidence?

■ DECISION AND RATIONALE

(Morse, J.) Yes. The Sixth Amendment to the United States Constitution guarantees a defendant a fair trial by providing him with the right to cross-examine all witnesses against him. It also guarantees a defendant the right to compulsory process of witnesses to testify on his behalf. The United States Supreme Court, when addressing a state statute that impinges on these confrontation and compulsory rights, has resorted to a balancing test in which the state's interest in enacting a statute is weighed against the defendants constitutional interests. Rape shield laws have been enacted by almost every state. In general, they deny a defendant in a sexual assault case the opportunity to examine the complainant concerning her prior sexual conduct or reputation. They also deny the defendant the opportunity to offer extrinsic evidence of the prior sexual conduct, or reputation for sexual conduct or practices of the complainant. Rape shield laws were implemented to overcome the invidious and outrageous common law evidentiary rule allowing complainants to be asked in depth about their prior sexual experiences for the purpose of humiliation and harassment and to show unchastity. These statutes reflect the judgment that most evidence about chastity has far too little probative value on the issue of consent to justify extensive inquiry into the victim's sexual history. According to Professor Harriett R. Galvin, rape shield laws can be categorized into four approaches. The Michigan approach are general prohibitions on prior sexual conduct or reputation evidence, but have highly specific exceptions allowing for this evidence in those circumstances in which it is highly relevant and material to the presentation of a defense and therefore constitutionally required. For example, under the

Massachusetts rape shield law, exceptions are made for prior consensual acts with the defendant or recent conduct of the complainant which would explain her physical features, characteristics, or conditions. The evidence is first submitted to the trial court in an in camera hearing so that the court may weigh the relevancy of the evidence against its prejudicial effect on the victim. Policies for this type of rape shield law include: 1) preventing the harassment and humiliation of the complainant, 2) keeping out evidence that has no bearing on the issue of consent at the time in question, 3) excluding evidence in order to keep the jury focused on issues relevant to the case at hand, and 4) promoting effective law enforcement because a victim will more readily report and testify in sexual assault cases if she does not fear that her prior sexual conduct will be brought before the public. Laws written under the Texas approach are purely procedural in nature and often involve "untrammeled judicial discretion." For example, Arkansas' rape shield law provides that, notwithstanding a general prohibition of opinion, reputation or specific sexual conduct evidence, evidence of the complainant's prior sexual conduct with the defendant or any other person, may be used provided certain procedures are followed, and the trial court determines that the probativeness of the evidence outweighs its prejudicial nature. Oregon's rape shield law is a good example of the federal approach. Its key features include: 1) a general prohibition of sexual conduct or reputation evidence, 2) exceptions allowing for this evidence in circumstances where the evidence is undeniably relevant to an effective defense, and 3) a general "catch-basin" provision allowing for the introduction of relevant evidence on a case by case basis. The key feature of the California approach is that the sexual conduct or reputation evidence is separated into two categories. Evidence offered to prove consent is generally inadmissible unless the evidence concerns prior sexual conduct between the complainant and the defendant. However, any sexual conduct or reputation evidence may be used to attack the complainant's credibility as long as the trial court determines that it is relevant to the issue. Since their creation, rape shield laws have generally passed constitutional muster. Because the probativeness of the evidence is so minuscule when compared the potential prejudice, the Sixth Amendment rights must bend to protect the innocent victims. On the other hand, the courts have also universally held that both cross-examination and witnesses brought on behalf of the defendant may show prior consensual sex if that evidence shows a complainant's unique pattern of conduct similar to the pattern of the case at hand, or shows that the complainant may be biased or have motives to fabricate the charges. In such cases, the issues of a witness' bias and credibility are not collateral, and the rape shield laws must give way to the Sixth Amendment.

Analysis:

Rape-shield statutes have been enacted in virtually every state. Although these laws vary, they generally deny the defendant in a rape trial the opportunity to cross-examine the complainant, or to offer extrinsic evidence, concerning her prior sexual conduct or reputation, absent good cause. On the other hand, while protecting the victim's interests, these laws may also increase the risk that an accused person might be denied the opportunity to introduce evidence that would demonstrate his innocence. Furthermore, rape-shield laws may conflict with the defendant's Sixth Amendment right to confront and cross-examine his accusers. This opinion does a good job of illustrating that these constitutional rights are not absolute, and that the interest of the rape-shield laws must be weighed against the defendant's needs in determining which evidence should be admissible.

■ CASE VOCABULARY

RAPE-SHIELD LAW: A statute which prohibits or restricts evidence or cross-examination concerning a victim's prior sexual conduct or reputation.

People v. Wilhelm

(*Prosecuting Authority*) v. (*Convicted Sex Offender*)

190 Mich.App. 574, 476 N.W.2d 753 (1991)

PUBLIC, PROVOCATIVE DISPLAYS MAY OR MAY NOT BE ADMISSIBLE IN RAPE TRIALS

■ **INSTANT FACTS** After being convicted of third-degree criminal sexual conduct, the defendant appealed, arguing that evidence of the victim's prior provocative behavior should have been admitted on the issue of consent.

■ **BLACK LETTER RULE** Evidence of a victim's sexual conduct with a third party is irrelevant to the issue of whether she consented to sexual intercourse with the defendant.

■ PROCEDURAL BASIS

Appellate review of the defendant's conviction.

■ FACTS

After a jury trial, Wilhelm (D) was convicted of third-degree criminal sexual conduct and sentenced to imprisonment. He appealed as of right, arguing that the trial court abused its discretion by refusing to admit evidence of prior acts by the victim. Wilhelm (D) contended that the victim was in the same bar in which he was drinking on the night of the alleged rape, and that she lifted her shirt to expose her breasts to other patrons, and even allowed one man to fondle her breasts. Wilhelm (D) contended that evidence of this behavior should have been admissible to show that the victim consented to have sex with him later that night in the boat parked in his parents' driveway. The trial court did not allow the evidence, and the defendant appealed.

■ ISSUE

Did the rape-shield statute prevent the admission of testimony regarding the victim's provocative conduct toward other men earlier on the night of the sexual assault?

■ DECISION AND RATIONALE

(Per curiam.) Yes. Evidence of a victim's sexual conduct with a third party is irrelevant to the issue of whether she consented to sexual intercourse with the defendant.

Wilhelm (D) argues that another state's similar statute has been held to not prohibit the type of evidence he offered here. In *State v. Colbath*, a New Hampshire case, the victim had engaged in provocative behavior, in a tavern, directed at both the defendant and others. She later accompanied the defendant to his trailer, where they had intercourse. The victim in *Colbath* had, over the course of many hours, engaged in public acts that the defendant argued were relevant to whether the intercourse was consensual. The trial court did not allow the evidence, but the state supreme court ruled that the defendant's right of confrontation required that he be allowed to demonstrate that the probative value of the evidence outweighed its prejudicial effect on the victim.

The defendant here claims, likewise, that the public nature of the victim's activities should remove them from the protection of the rape-shield law, but we disagree. The statute makes no such distinction. One of the purposes of the statute is to encourage victims of rape to come forward, without fearing that criminal proceedings will veer from an impartial examination of the accused's conduct and instead take on the aspects of an inquisition in which the victim is required to justify her own sexual behavior. Moreover, in this case, there is no reason why the victim's behavior toward *other* men would be relevant with regard to her consent to engage in sexual conduct with the defendant. Evidence of a rape victim's unchastity is ordinarily insufficiently probative of her consent to intercourse with a defendant. This is not a case like *Colbath*, in which the victim's behavior constituted a public display of general interest in sexual activity, in which the defendant was directly involved. Because the evidence here was irrelevant, Wilhelm (D) was not deprived of his right of confrontation and the evidence was properly excluded.

Analysis:

Every state has enacted a rape-shield law that prevents the admission in criminal cases of evidence regarding a rape victim's prior sexual behavior. A few states have extended the protection to civil trials. Some states, however, include a "catch-all" provision in their rape-shield statutes that allows for the admissibility of such evidence when it is deemed necessary to protect the constitutional rights of the defendant. Once such a loophole is available, could it become a "slippery slope," enabling defense attorneys to argue that a victim's prior conduct must be admitted into evidence in order to present a complete defense?

Garnett v. State

(Mentally Disabled Man) v. *(Society)*
332 Md. 571, 632 A.2d 797 (1993)

MENTALLY DISABLED MALE CONVICTED OF SECOND DEGREE RAPE DESPITE LACK OF CRIMINAL INTENT

■ **INSTANT FACTS** A mentally disabled twenty-year-old man is convicted of statutory rape, after engaging in sexual relations with a thirteen-year-old girl friend, despite the lack of criminal intent.

■ **BLACK LETTER RULE** Criminal intent or mens rea, is not an element of statutory rape.

■ PROCEDURAL BASIS

Appeal to the Court of Appeals of Maryland of a conviction for second degree rape.

■ FACTS

At the time of the incident, Raymond Lennard Garnett (Garnett) (D) was a twenty-year-old, mentally disabled man, with an I.Q. of 52. According to his guidance counselor, Garnett (D) interacted with others socially at school at the level of someone 11 or 12 years of age. Garnett (D) attended special education classes, and for at least one period of time, was educated at home when he was afraid to return to school due to his classmates taunting. He was unable to complete vocational assignments, or pass any State's functional tests required for graduation. Garnett (D) eventually received only a certificate of attendance rather than a high-school diploma. In November or December 1990, a friend introduced Garnett (D) to Erica Frazier (Erica), then aged 13. The two then subsequently talked occasionally by telephone. On February 28, 1991, Garnett (D), apparently wishing to call for a ride home approached Erica's house at about nine o'clock in the evening. Erica opened her bedroom window, and Garnett (D) took a ladder and climbed up. The two talked and later engaged in sexual intercourse. On November 19, 1991, Erica gave birth to Garnett's (D) baby. Garnett was subsequently convicted of second degree rape under § 463(a)(3) of Maryland's rape statute [which provided that a person is guilty of second degree rape if the person engages in vaginal intercourse with another person who is under 14 years of age, and the person performing the act is at least four years older]. At trial Garnett (D) proffered evidence to the effect that Erica herself and her friends had previously told Raymond that she was 16 years old, and that Garnett (D) acted with that belief. The trial court excluded the evidence as immaterial, opining that the violation was a strict liability offense. Garnett (D) was sentenced to five years probation and ordered to pay restitution. Garnett (D) appeals.

■ ISSUE

Is criminal intent or mens rea a necessary element for a conviction of statutory rape?

■ DECISION AND RATIONALE

(Murphy, J.) No. Criminal intent or mens rea, is not an element of statutory rape. The Maryland statute does not expressly set forth a requirement that the accused have acted with a criminal state of mind, or mens rea. Garnett (D) contends that criminal law exists to assess and punish morally culpable behavior, and essentially asks us to engraft an implicit mens rea requirement to the statute. Modern scholars generally reject the concept of strict criminal liability as unjust, because the actor is subjected to the stigma of a criminal conviction without being morally blameworthy. Thus, criminal sanctions are inappropriate in the absence of a mens rea, whether based on preventive or retributive principles. Dean Singer has articulated some weaknesses of strict criminal liability theory, and has concluded that, "the predicate for all criminal liability is blameworthiness: it is the social stigma which a finding of guilt carries that distinguishes the criminal [penalty] from all other sanctions." If the predicate is removed, the criminal law is set adrift." Accordingly, the Model Penal Code (MPC), conscious of the disfavor of strict criminal liability, requires at a minimum that criminal culpability be followed by acting purposefully, knowingly, recklessly, or negligently, i.e., with some degree of mens rea. In regards to statutory rape, the MPC strikes a compromise with its general policy against strict liability crimes, prohibiting defenses of ignorance or reasonable mistake of age when the victim is below the age of ten, but allowing these defenses when the critical age stipulated in the offense is higher than ten. In addition to these arguments, commentators also observe that statutory rape prosecutions often proceed even when the defendant's judgment as to the age of the victim is warranted by her appearance, her sexual sophistication, her verbal misrepresentations, and the defendant's careful attempts to ascertain her true age. We acknowledge here that it is uncertain to what extent Garnett's (D) intellectual and social retardation may have impaired his ability to comprehend imperatives of sexual morality in any case. We understand that the legislature of 17 states have enacted laws permitting a mistake of age defense in some form in cases of sexual offenses with underage persons. However we think it sufficiently clear that Maryland's second degree rape statute defines a strict liability offense that does not require the State to prove mens rea. It makes no allowance for a mistake-of-age defense, nor any reference to the actor's knowledge, belief, or other state of mind. As we see it, this silence as to mens rea results from legislative design. First, the subsection stands in stark contrast to the provision immediately before it, which expressly provides an element that the actor know or should reasonably know that the victim is mentally defective, mentally incapacitated, or physically helpless. Second, an examination of the drafting history of this statute, reveals that the statute was viewed as one of strict liability from its inception and throughout the amendment process. The legislature explicitly raised, considered, and then explicitly jettisoned any notion of a mens rea element with respect to the complainant's age in enacting the statute. Therefore, we must conclude that the current law imposes strict liability on its violators. This interpretation is consistent with the traditional view of statutory rape as a strict liability crime designed to protect young persons from the dangers of sexual exploitation by adults. The majority of states retain statutes which impose strict liability for sexual acts with under age complainants. Any new provision introducing an element of mens rea should properly result from an act of the Legislature itself, rather than judicial fiat. Affirmed.

■ DISSENT

(Eldridge, J.) Although I agree with the majority that an ordinary defendant's mistake about the age of his or her sexual partner is not a defense to a prosecution under § 463(a)(3) of the Maryland rape statute, I do not believe that the statute contains no mens rea requirement at all. There are pure strict liability offenses that have the purpose of regulation rather than punishment. Also there are other strict liability offenses where the legislature has dispensed with a knowledge requirement, but has not intended to impose criminal liability regardless of the defendant's state of mind. Neither the statutory language nor the legislative history of this subsection of the statute indicate that the General Assembly intended to define a pure strict liability offense. Making the offense punishable by a maximum of 20 years imprisonment, is strong evidence that the General Assembly did not intend to create a pure strict liability offense. In the typical situation, involving older person's engaging in consensual sexual activities with a teenager below the age of consent, which the General Assembly likely contemplated when it enacted this statute, the defendant knows and intends that he or she is engaging in sexual activity with a young person. As the majority points out, the traditional view is that those who engage in sex with young persons do so at their peril, assuming the risk that their partners are underage. It seems to me that the above-mentioned knowledge factors, and particularly the mental ability to appreciate that one is taking a risk, constitute the mens rea of the offense. The General Assembly assumed that a defendant is able to appreciate the risk involved by intentionally and knowingly engaging in sexual activities with a young person. There is no indication that the General Assembly intended to attach criminal liability to a person who is unable to appreciate that risk because of a mental impairment.

(Bell, J.) I do not dispute that the legislative history of section 463 may be read to support the majority's interpretation that subsection (a)(3) was intended to be a strict liability statute. Nor do I disagree that it is in public interest to protect the sexually naïve child from the adverse effects of sexual relations. I do not believe, however, that the General Assembly, in every case, can subject a defendant to strict criminal liability. To hold, as a matter of law that section 463 (a)(3) does not require that the State prove that a defendant possessed the necessary mental state to commit the crime, or that the defendant may not litigate that issue in defense, "offends a principle of justice so rooted in the traditions of the conscience of our people as to be ranked as fundamental," and is therefore, inconsistent with due process.

Analysis:

Strict liability offenses, such as traffic tickets, are usually reserved for crimes where the purpose of punishment is to regulate violators. Also, they are reserved for crimes where punishments are less severe than in cases of rape. On the one hand, protection of society supports statutory rape. Lack of consent is not an element. In this sense, the law concludes that a young person is incapable of giving consent to undertake sexual acts. However, on the other hand, is it fair to convict a perpetrator, and subject him to the same criminal stigma as a person convicted of forcible rape, based on a theory of strict liability? In the instant case, the majority acknowledged that it was uncertain as to what extent Garnett's (D) intellectual and social retardation may have impaired his ability to comprehend imperatives of sexual morality. However, they did not feel the need to delve into the issue, because there was no need to prove any mental aspect of this crime.

■ CASE VOCABULARY

STATUTORY RAPE: Sexual intercourse with another, who is under the statutorily defined age of consent.

CHAPTER NINE

General Defenses to Crimes

Patterson v. New York

Instant Facts: The Supreme Court upheld the second-degree murder conviction (of an estranged husband who killed his (soon-to-be) ex-wife's boyfriend) stating that it did not violate due process for defendant to have to affirmatively show he acted under extreme emotional disturbance [which the jury didn't buy].

Black Letter Rule: A state may require a defendant to bear the burden of proving to a jury that he should not be found guilty of the crime charged because he has a valid affirmative defense.

United States v. Peterson

Instant Facts: Peterson (D) was convicted of manslaughter (over his argument of self-defense) for shooting and killing Keitt whom he caught stealing the windshield wipers off of his wrecked car.

Black Letter Rule: The aggressor in a conflict that results in another's death cannot justify his actions under the right of self-defense.

People v. Goetz

Instant Facts: A frightened (or perhaps angry) man carrying an unlicensed pistol shot and wounded four youths after they approached him on a New York subway train and told him to give them $5.00.

Black Letter Rule: Before a defendant can prevail on a self-defense argument, it must be shown that his "reasonable belief" regarding the necessity to use deadly force comports with a "reasonable man" objective standard.

State v. Wanrow

Instant Facts: Ms. Wanrow (D) shot and killed a neighborhood man in a confrontation after neighbors asserted that the man (who had previously tried to take Ms. Wanrow's son off his bike and into the man's house) was a child molester.

Black Letter Rule: All the facts and circumstances known to a defendant, including those known prior to the incident and the genders of the persons involved, must be taken into consideration when deciding if a defendant's belief of danger was reasonable.

State v. Norman

Instant Facts: Judy Norman (D) shot and killed her sleeping, intoxicated husband after enduring ever-increasing bouts of his abusive behavior.

Black Letter Rule: The fact that an abusive aggressor was passive at the moment of his killing does not necessarily preclude a defendant from claiming self-defense.

State v. Norman

Instant Facts: Trial court did not allow an abused wife to argue self-defense after she killed her sleeping, abusive husband; although the Court of Appeals held she could argue self-defense, it was overturned by the state supreme court, which agreed with the trial court.

Black Letter Rule: A defendant must have a reasonable fear of imminent death or great bodily harm before she is entitled to a jury instruction on self-defense.

People v. Kurr

Instant Facts: After defendant's boyfriend, Pena, punched defendant twice in the stomach, defendant, who was pregnant with quadruplets, stabbed Pena in the chest, killing him.

Black Letter Rule: The "defense of others" doctrine extends to actions taken to protect even a nonviable fetus from an assault against the mother.

People v. Ceballos

Instant Facts: Ceballos (D) set a gun to shoot at anyone who attempted to enter his garage.

Black Letter Rule: An injury or killing by the use of a deadly mechanical device is not justified where the device injures in response to a non-violent burglary.

Tennessee v. Garner

Instant Facts: Unarmed 15–year-old burglar was shot dead by police after he attempted to scale a fence in order to flee the scene of the crime.

Black Letter Rule: Fourth Amendment reasonableness requirement prohibits officers from using deadly force to effect the arrest of a fleeing felon unless it is necessary to prevent the escape and the officer has probable cause to believe that the suspect poses a significant threat of death or serious physical injury to the officer or others.

Nelson v. State

Instant Facts: Nelson (D) raises the defense of necessity as justification for his actions in taking a dump truck and front-end loader from a Highway Department Yard to pull his stuck vehicle from a marshy area.

Black Letter Rule: The defense of necessity may be raised only where the defendant's law-violating actions were necessary to prevent an even greater harm from occurring.

United States v. Schoon

Instant Facts: Schoon (D) and others protested congressional policies at an IRS office, and claimed the necessity defense as a justification for their actions.

Black Letter Rule: Indirect protests of congressional policies can never meet all the requirements of the necessity doctrine, and the necessity defense is therefore unavailable in such cases.

The Queen v. Dudley and Stephens

Instant Facts: English sailors at sea for 20 days (the last 9 days without food or water) killed and consumed a cabin boy for which they were found guilty of murder.

Black Letter Rule: A defendant's actions are not justified under the defense of necessity if he deliberately kills an innocent person in order to save his own life.

United States v. Contento–Pachon

Instant Facts: Contento–Pachon (D), a Colombian national acting under duress, swallows balloons filled with cocaine for transport to the U.S. and is arrested at customs.

Black Letter Rule: A defendant may assert the defense of duress when he acts under a threat of future harm only when the harm is likely to occur so quickly that the defendant cannot escape the situation.

People v. Unger

Instant Facts: Unger (D) escaped from an honor farm (prison) in Illinois and claimed it was necessary for him to do so as he was forced to choose between the lessor of two evils (escaping or being subjected to homosexual attacks and possibly death).

Black Letter Rule: An escaped prisoner may assert the defense of necessary if he can set forth facts that would tend to show that his choice to escape was the lessor of two evils to escape or to remain and be subjected to repeated sexual assault.

People v. Anderson

Instant Facts: Defendant and Ron Kiern kidnapped Margaret Armstrong and Defendant subsequently killed Armstrong at the direction of Kiern, who threatened to harm Defendant if he didn't kill Armstrong.

Black Letter Rule: Duress is not recognized as a valid defense to murder nor will it serve to reduce a murder charge to manslaughter.

Commonwealth v. Graves

Instant Facts: Graves (D), while intoxicated and high, burglarized, robbed, and injured an old man who subsequently died from his injuries; Graves (D) conviction for murder was reversed (and a new trial awarded) by the state supreme court.

Black Letter Rule: Although voluntary intoxication is not an excuse for unlawful actions, evidence thereof may be introduced to negate the intent requirement of the crime charged.

United States v. Freeman

Instant Facts: Freeman (D), a chronic drug abuser and alcoholic, was convicted of the sale of narcotics using the *M'Naghten* Rules to determine his criminal liability.

Black Letter Rule: Model Penal Code Section 4.01, which emphasizes "appreciation" of conduct, rather than simply knowing whether it is right or wrong, should be used in place of the narrow *M'Naghten* Rules to determine whether a defendant lacks criminal responsibility due to mental impairment or defect.

State v. Johnson

Instant Facts: Johnson sets forth the development of the insanity test.

Black Letter Rule: A new standard that allows a jury to consider volitional as well as cognitive impairments before imposing criminal responsibility supercedes the restrictive M'Naghten rule.

State v. Wilson

Instant Facts: Wilson (D) shot to death a friend's father (Jack) because he thought Jack was the mastermind of a huge conspiracy to control everyone's mind, particularly Wilson's (D) mind.

Black Letter Rule: Even if a defendant appreciates that his actions were illegal, if he believes, due to his mental disease or defect, that his actions were morally justified (society would condone his actions if it understood the situation like the defendant understands the situation) then he will not be criminally responsible for his actions.

State v. Green

Instant Facts: Eighteen year old Steven Green's (D) conviction for murder of a police officer was set aside because Tennessee's (P) rebuttal evidence was not sufficient to refute the overwhelming proof of Green's insanity.

Black Letter Rule: Prosecution has the burden to prove beyond a reasonable doubt a defendant's sanity in order to rebut a defendant's evidence of his insanity.

Clark v. Arizona

Instant Facts: The defendant appealed from his conviction for murder, arguing that the evidence he offered as to his mental illness should also have been considered with regard to his ability to form the necessary *mens rea*.

Black Letter Rule: Under Arizona's *Mott* rule, a court will not allow evidence of a mental disorder short of insanity as bearing on a defendant's capacity to form specific intent.

In Re Devon T.

Instant Facts: Devon (D) (almost 14–years-old) was caught at school with twenty zip-lock bags of heroin and was convicted with the equivalent of possession with intent to distribute, despite his claim of incapacity due to infancy.

Black Letter Rule: Rebuttable Presumption of incapacity due to infancy may be overcome with sufficient evidence of a defendant's capacity to distinguish right from wrong.

Latimer v. The Queen

Instant Facts: Latimer (D) killed his seriously ill and disabled daughter and was twice convicted of murder.

Black Letter Rule: In order for the defense of necessity to apply, three requirements must be met: (1) there must be an urgent situation of clear and imminent peril, which is on the verge of transpiring and is virtually certain to occur; (2) there must be no reasonable legal alternative to disobeying the law; and (3) there must be proportionality between the harm inflicted and the harm avoided.

Robinson v. California

Instant Facts: Robinson's (D) misdemeanor conviction and imprisonment for being addicted to narcotics was overturned by the United States Supreme Court.

Black Letter Rule: To the extent that a state law which requires imprisonment for the use of, or addiction to, narcotics is interpreted to allow imprisonment for addiction alone, such law inflicts cruel and unusual punishment in violation of the Fourteenth Amendment.

Powell v. Texas

Instant Facts: Powell's (D) conviction for being drunk in public upheld by the Supreme Court.

Black Letter Rule: The Eighth Amendment prohibition against cruel and unusual punishment is not violated when a state imposes sanctions for public behavior (public intoxication) which violates its law.

State v. Kargar

Instant Facts: In accordance with Afghani custom, Kargar's (D) kissed his young son's penis as a sign of love for his child which was considered by his neighbor, the police, the prosecution, and the trial court to violate Maine's statute prohibiting sexual acts with a child under the age of 14 years.

Black Letter Rule: When a state has a de minimis statute, the court must consider the full range of relevant factors and circumstances surrounding the defendant's admittedly criminal conduct before ruling on his motion to dismiss.

Patterson v. New York

(*Jealous Estranged Husband*) v. (*State*)

432 U.S. 197 (1977)

STATUTE THAT REQUIRES DEFENDANT TO PROVE AFFIRMATIVE DEFENSE DOES NOT VIOLATE DUE PROCESS

■ **INSTANT FACTS** The Supreme Court upheld the second-degree murder conviction (of an estranged husband who killed his (soon-to-be) ex-wife's boyfriend) stating that it did not violate due process for defendant to have to affirmatively show he acted under extreme emotional disturbance "which the jury didn't buy".

■ **BLACK LETTER RULE** A state may require a defendant to bear the burden of proving to a jury that he should not be found guilty of the crime charged because he has a valid affirmative defense.

■ PROCEDURAL BASIS

The Supreme Court upheld New York Court of Appeals judgment finding state statute constitutional and convicting defendant.

■ FACTS

Patterson (D) was estranged from his wife (Roberta) after a short and unstable marriage. Roberta resumed a relationship with John Northrup (Northrup) to whom she was at one time engaged. Patterson (D) borrowed a rifle, went to his father-in-law's house, and through a window saw Roberta (partially undressed) and Northrup together. He entered the house and shot Northrup in the head twice which "of course" killed him. Patterson (D) was charged with second degree murder. There are two elements to New York's (P) statute, 1.) Intent to cause the death of another person, and 2.) Causing the death of such person or of a third person. New York (P) also has a manslaughter statute under which "a person is guilty of manslaughter if he intentionally kills another person under circumstances which do no constitute murder because he acts under the influence of extreme emotional disturbance for which there was a reasonable explanation or excuse." Extreme emotional disturbance is an affirmative defense in New York. Although Patterson (D) confessed to the killing, at trial he raised this defense. The jury was instructed that if it found beyond a reasonable doubt Patterson (D) intentionally killed Northrup but that Patterson (D) had demonstrated by a preponderance of the evidence that he had acted under the influence of extreme emotional disturbance, it had to find Patterson (D) guilty of manslaughter instead of murder. The jury found Patterson (D) guilty of second degree murder. On appeal Patterson (D) argued that New York's (P) statute unconstitutionally shifted the burden of proof. The Court of Appeals did not find the statute unconstitutional and upheld the conviction as did the Supreme Court.

■ ISSUE

Does it violate a defendant's 14th amendment due process rights if a state requires him to bear the burden of proof regarding an affirmative defense?

■ DECISION AND RATIONALE

(White) No. Patterson (D) argues that New York's statute is the same kind of statute that we recently found to be unconstitutional because it improperly placed the burden of proof upon a defendant to disprove an element of the crime charged. In *Mullaney v. Wilbur*, the charge was murder under a Maine statute which included an element of malice aforethought, whether express or implied. Maine's manslaughter statute provided a lesser punishment for "whoever unlawfully kills a human being in the heat of passion, on sudden provocation, without express or implied malice aforethought . . . ." In *Mullaney*, the jury was instructed that malice could be implied from "any deliberate, cruel act committed by one person against another suddenly or without a considerable provocation," in which event an intentional killing was murder unless by a preponderance of the evidence it was shown that the act was committed "in the heat of passion, on sudden provocation." We held that Maine's statute unconstitutionally shifted the burden of proof from the prosecution to the defendant in that it required the defendant to prove that the killing had occurred in the heat of passion on sudden provocation. While we did hold that under the due process clause the prosecution had the burden of proving *each element* of the crime charged beyond a reasonable doubt, we did not find and do not now find, that the prosecution has the burden of proving the nonexistence of all available affirmative defenses. The case here differs from *Mullaney.* In *Mullaney*, the statutory *presumption* was of malice aforethought. Maine's statute required the defendant to prove that he acted without malice. A defendant is not required to disprove any of the elements that constitute the crime for which he is charged. New York's (P) statute does not shift the burden of proving an essential element of the crime charged. New York's (P) statute only requires that the prosecution show that Patterson (D) intended to kill another person, and did kill such person. There is no malice aforethought element. If an intentional killing is shown it is murder. The affirmative defense of extreme emotional disturbance does not negate any of the elements of the crime. It is a separate issue regarding mitigating circumstances. It is the defendant's burden to demonstrate any mitigating circumstances. Just because New York (P) recognizes mitigating circumstances it is not constitutionally required to prove their nonexistence in each case in which the fact is put in issue. The New York Court of Appeals is affirmed.

■ DISSENT

(Powell) The effect of Maine's unconstitutional statute is no different from the effect of New York's (P) statute. The Court is upholding New York's (P) law which requires the defendant to prove extreme emotional disturbance. The Court struck down Maine's law because the defendant was required to show that he acted in the heat of passion, in order to negate the element of malice. We held that this shifting of the burden of proof was unconstitutional. The Court states that because the burden showing extreme emotional disturbance is written as an affirmative defense, it passes constitutional scrutiny. We struck down the statute in *Mullaney* because it required a defendant to disprove an element of the crime charged. Maine's statute was invalid, the Court reasoned, because it defined murder as the unlawful killing of a human being with malice aforethought, either express or implied. Malice, the Court reiterates, in the sense of the absence of provocation, was part of the definition of the crime. The fact of malice was presumed unless the defendant persuaded the jury otherwise by showing that he acted in the heat of passion. Under New York's (P) statute, there is no mention of the element of, or the fact of malice. The absence of malice is written into its statute entitled as an affirmative defense. The defendant is required to show by preponderance of the evidence that he acted under extreme emotional disturbance. The burden in *Mullaney*, which we found unconstitutional, is the same burden here and should be found unconstitutional. The unstated presumption in New York's (P) law is the same presumption we held unconstitutional in Maine's law. Historically, the prosecution bore the burden of proving factors that made a substantial difference in punishment or stigma attached to the defendant's actions. Heat of passion (of which extreme emotional disturbance is a direct descendent) was an important element distinguishing both punishment and stigma. The presence or absence of extreme emotional disturbance makes a critical difference in being convicted of murder or manslaughter. The prosecution should bear the burden in order to gain a conviction. A legislature's ability to "write around" the requisite elements should not provide constitutional protection to this statute.

Analysis:

If a defendant claims that he acted in self-defense in killing another person, should the prosecution, in order to get a conviction, have to prove (beyond a reasonable doubt) the defendant did not act in self-defense, or should the defendant have to prove by a lesser standard (preponderance of the evidence) that he acted in self-defense? According to the reasoning in *Patterson*, it depends on how the statute is written. If written "guilty unless defendant can prove otherwise," it is unconstitutional. However, if just the basic elements are set forth in defining the crime ("a person who causes the death of another human being is guilty of murder"), and the rest of the sentence is written separately ("a person is only guilty of manslaughter, not murder, if he can show that he acted in self-defense") and entitled an affirmative defense, it is constitutionally permissible under the Due Process Clause. There are different burdens of proof in a criminal trial. There is the burden of production, e.g., the prosecution must have enough evidence to bring the charges in the first place. If the court finds enough evidence to support the claim, it may be argued in front of a jury. The next issue is who bears the burden of persuasion, that is, who bears the burden of proving the issue to the jury. The burden of persuasion is what is at issue in *Patterson*.

■ CASE VOCABULARY

AFFIRMATIVE DEFENSE: A legal defense that, when proved, relieves the accused from the responsibility for his otherwise criminal conduct.

MITIGATING CIRCUMSTANCES: The extenuating circumstances which surround illegal conduct which may lessen the severity of the punishment.

United States v. Peterson

(*Federal Prosecutor*) v. (*Windshield Wiper Protector*)
483 F.2d 1222 (D.C.Cir. 1973)

AN AGGRESSOR OF A DEADLY CONFLICT MAY NOT CLAIM SELF-DEFENSE

■ **INSTANT FACTS** Peterson (D) was convicted of manslaughter (over his argument of self-defense) for shooting and killing Keitt whom he caught stealing the windshield wipers off of his wrecked car.

■ **BLACK LETTER RULE** The aggressor in a conflict that results in another's death cannot justify his actions under the right of self-defense.

■ PROCEDURAL BASIS

On appeal to the U.S. Court of Appeals, D.C. Circuit, upholding conviction.

■ FACTS

Peterson (D) came out of his house into his backyard to protest the fact that Keitt (accompanied by two friends) was taking the windshield wipers off of his wrecked car. After a verbal exchange, Peterson (D) went into his house to get a pistol, which he loaded while standing in his back yard yelling at Keitt not to move. At this point Keitt was already in his car about to leave. Peterson (D) walked to the gate holding his pistol and said, "If you come in here I will kill you." Keitt got out of his car, walked to Peterson (D) and said, "What the hell do you think you are going to do with that?" He then walked back to his car and got a lug wrench. With the wrench in a raised position, he advanced toward Peterson (D) who stood with the pistol pointed at him. Peterson (D) warned Keitt not to "take another step," which Keitt did, and Peterson (D) shot him in the face from a distance of about ten feet. Death was apparently instantaneous. Peterson (D) was charged with second-degree murder, but convicted of the lesser included offense of manslaughter. Peterson (D) appeals, arguing that a jury instruction which allowed the jury to consider whether he was the aggressor in the altercation that immediately preceded the homicide was improper. He also argues as improper the jury instruction which allowed the jury to take into consideration when deciding the necessity of his actions, the undisputed fact that at no time did he retreat from Keitt's approach with the lug wrench.

■ ISSUE

Does the instigator of a conflict have the right to claim it was necessary to take a life in order to preserve his own?

■ DECISION AND RATIONALE

(Robinson) No. From the time of English common law *justified* murder has existed in the form of self-defense. Self-defense is a law of necessity. If circumstances exist that require a defensive action, the defensive action must be realistically necessary to alleviate the threat imposed. [The reaction to a threat must be proportional to the threat. You are not justified in killing someone because they hit your backpack while passing you in the hallway.] The only time deadly force is necessary is when one is met with deadly force, i.e., there must be no other way to survive the circumstances than to take a life. The threat must be real and apparent, unlawful and immediate. The defender [this is the defendant, the other guy is dead] must have honestly believed that he was in immediate peril of death or serious bodily harm, and that his response was necessary to save himself. The defender's beliefs must also be objectively reasonable in light of the surrounding circumstances. If a person incites, encourages, or otherwise promotes the circumstances that lead up to his killing another, that person is the aggressor and is not entitled to the claim of self-defense. Only if the aggressor communicates to his opponent his intent to withdraw [walk-away] and in good faith attempts to do so may he claim self-defense. In the majority of jurisdictions one may stand his ground and use deadly force whenever it seems reasonably necessary to save himself. We do not follow the majority rule. Our law is closer to the common law rule requiring "retreat to the wall." This rule forbids the use of deadly force when it is possible to make a safe retreat. Although in modern times there may be exceptions to the concept of walking away from a fight, no such exception applies here. The circumstances that are relevant here begin after Peterson (D) returned to the yard with a pistol as Keitt was about to leave the scene. At this point Keitt was not the aggressor, if he ever had been. Before that only verbal threats had ensued (mere words do not constitute aggression) and a misdemeanor was in progress (the law does not tolerate the use of deadly force in protection of property). After Peterson (D) returned to the yard, he loaded his pistol, walked toward Keitt, dared him to come in, and threatened to kill him if he did. Peterson (D) may not assert self-defense under these circumstances because he is the person who created them. In addition, as noted by the minority rule, Peterson (D) is required to walk-away from the conflict (if he can do so safely). He could have, yet he did not. Peterson (D) argues he was not required to retreat as he was standing in his own yard when Keitt advanced on him. The right of self-defense is not available to the party who provokes or stimulates the conflict. Under the facts, the jury instructions were proper. Judgement of the trial court for conviction affirmed.

Analysis:

The court here noted Peterson's (D) aggressive action was the same type of aggressive action taken by similarly situated defendants who were not allowed the right to self-defense because they put themselves into a fight after they had already reached safety. The defendant in *Laney v. U.S.* escaped from an ensuing mob, then checked a gun he was carrying and returned to the area and shot into the mob (killing one of them). Similarly, in *Rowe v. U.S.*, the defendant left a friend's home where a fight had ensued outside, went to his own apartment, got his gun, and returned to the fight where he was advanced upon by several men at whom he shot, killing two of them. Remember, there must be an honest and *reasonable belief* that someone is about to cause you immediate, unlawful seriously bodily harm or death before you are justified in using deadly force to repel them. Are you required to avoid threatening people in order to claim self-defense? If it means you have to walk home from work by a different route? Although you have a "right" to carry on your daily routine without unlawful interference, the law does not permit you to use unlawful means (killing someone) when you could have avoided the confrontation in the first place.

■ CASE VOCABULARY

CURTILAGE: The area and any buildings immediately surrounding a residence usually enclosed by some kind of fence.

DEADLY FORCE: A force which if taken will cause death or is likely to create a substantial risk of causing death or serious bodily harm.

People v. Goetz

(*State of New York*) v. (*Subway Gunman*)
68 N.Y.2d 96 (1986)

OBJECTIVE "REASONABLE MAN" STANDARD IS THE PROPER STANDARD FOR DETERMINING STATUTORY "REASONABLE BELIEF" REQUIREMENT

■ **INSTANT FACTS** A frightened (or perhaps angry) man carrying an unlicensed pistol shot and wounded four youths after they approached him on a New York subway train and told him to give them $5.00.

■ **BLACK LETTER RULE** Before a defendant can prevail on a self-defense argument, it must be shown that his "reasonable belief" regarding the necessity to use deadly force comports with a "reasonable man" objective standard.

■ PROCEDURAL BASIS

Lower appellate court's dismissal of charges reversed by the Court of Appeals of New York.

■ FACTS

On December 22, 1984, Bernhard Goetz (D) boarded a subway car in Manhattan on which there were, among others, four youths from The Bronx. Two of the youths had screwdrivers inside their coats. One of the youths asked Goetz (D) "how are you," to which Goetz (D) responded "fine." One or two of the youths walked over to Goetz (D) (possibly putting Goetz (D) in-between themselves and the other two youths) and stated to Goetz (D) "give me five dollars." Goetz (D) responded by taking out his unlicensed .38 caliber pistol and shooting in rapid succession one youth in the chest, another in the back, a third in the arm. According to Goetz's (D) statement, he shot at, but missed, one of the youths who was by now sitting on a bench. He said to him, "you seem to be all right, here's another," and fired a shot into the youth's side which severed his spinal chord. According to Goetz's (D) statement, "if I was in a little more under self-control ... I would have put the barrel against his forehead and fired." Goetz (D) also stated that he purchased the gun in 1981 after he had been hurt in a mugging. He stated he subsequently prevented two other assailants simply by displaying the gun. He stated that he knew from the smile on the face of the youth that approached him, they were trying to "play with me." Although he was certain none of them had guns, he was afraid they were going to "maim" him. The lower court held that the objective test submitted to the grand jury to determine the defense of justification was in error; a subjective test should have been utilized. It dismissed the charges of attempted murder, assault, and weapons possession. The Court of Appeals of New York reversed the lower court's dismissal holding that the correct test of reasonableness under New York's (P) law is an objective test, and reinstated the charges against defendant.

■ ISSUE

Before a jury can find that a defendant's use of deadly force was necessity must it determine that not only did defendant reasonably believe his use of deadly force was necessary, but that a "reasonable man" in his situation would find the use of deadly force necessary?

■ DECISION AND RATIONALE

(Wachtler) Yes. New York (P) recognizes the defense of justification. Penal Law § 35.15(1) sets forth the general principles: "[a] person may ... use physical force upon another person when and to the extent he reasonably believes such to be necessary to defend himself or a third person from what he reasonably believes to be the use or imminent use of unlawful physical force by such other person." A limitation is found in Penal Law § 35.15(2): "A person may not use deadly physical force upon another person under circumstances specified in subdivision one unless (a) He reasonably believes that such other person is using or about to use deadly physical force . . . or (b) He reasonably believes that such other person is committing or attempting to commit a kidnapping, forcible rape, forcible sodomy or robbery." The issue turns on the definition of the repeated phrase "reasonably believes." The prosecutor instructed the grand jury that the objective test was to be used in determining whether Goetz (D) reasonably believed he was under one of the triggering conditions set forth above (the youths were using or about to use deadly force or were committing or about to commit one of the stated felonies). The prosecutor told the grand jury they were to consider the circumstances of the incident and determine "whether the defendant's conduct was that of a reasonable man in the defendant's situation." (This is the objective test). The lower court held that because the law is written as "*he* reasonably believes," the correct test is a subjective test, i.e., whether the defendant's beliefs and reactions were reasonable to *him.* The lower court is incorrect. Under the lower court's subjective test any jury would have to acquit a man who claimed he felt his actions were warranted and reasonable. The objective test provided by the prosecutor is the correct test under New York's (P) law. The Model Penal Code which only requires that a defendant show that "he believed that the use of deadly force was necessary" is not New York's (P) law. New York (P) requires that a defendant "reasonably believe" his actions are necessary to defend himself from a force he "reasonably believes" another is committing or about to commit against him. This objective standard does not foreclose a jury from considering the circumstances facing a defendant. The circumstances include, e.g., the action taken by the alleged assailant, the physical characteristics of all persons involved, and defendant's relevant knowledge about the assailant. In addition, the jury may consider any prior experiences of the defendant which would provide a reasonable basis for a belief that another's intentions were to harm or rob him or that the use of deadly force was necessary under the circumstances. The Appellate Division is reversed and the dismissed charges of the indictment reinstated.

Analysis:

Goetz (D) was acquitted of all charges (except for possession of a concealed weapon) by a jury composed of eight men and two women (ten white and two African-American). He served eight months of his one-year jail sentence. He was ordered by a six-member civil jury to pay $18 million in compensatory damages and $25 million in punitive damages to the young man who was paralyzed. Whether Goetz (D) was out-of-control or calculating after he drew his gun depends on one's interpretation of the facts. There was much debate about the racial overtones of the case because Goetz (D) was a middle-aged white male and the young men were African-American. What is the practical difference between what Goetz (D) believed and what a reasonable man in the same situation would have believed? Goetz's (D) fear may have been reasonable, but it is difficult to define his reaction as reasonable. Under the New York law both aspects must be reasonable before a defendant can prevail on self-defense.

■ CASE VOCABULARY

GRAND JURY: A panel of individuals who after hearing the prosecution charges and prosecution witness's testimony determines whether there is probable cause to make a defendant stand trial.

INDICTMENT: The written means by which a defendant is charged with alleged offenses for which he cannot be found guilty unless proven beyond a reasonable doubt.

State v. Wanrow

(*State of Washington*) v. (*Killer Mom*)

88 Wash.2d 221, 559 P.2d 548 (1977)

"REASONABLE PERSON" STANDARD REQUIRES JURY TO VIEW INCIDENT FROM DEFENDANT'S POINT OF VIEW

■ **INSTANT FACTS** Ms. Wanrow (D) shot and killed a neighborhood man in a confrontation after neighbors asserted that the man (who had previously tried to take Ms. Wanrow's son off his bike and into the man's house) was a child molester.

■ **BLACK LETTER RULE** *All* the facts and circumstances known to a defendant, including those known prior to the incident and the genders of the persons involved, must be taken into consideration when deciding if a defendant's belief of danger was reasonable.

■ PROCEDURAL BASIS

On appeal to state supreme court which overturned the lower court's jury's finding for second-degree murder.

■ FACTS

Ms. Wanrow's (D) two children were staying with Ms. Hooper and her seven-year-old daughter. Some months prior to the incident here, Ms. Hooper's daughter had been molested but had not told her mother who had done the molesting. After playing in the neighborhood, Ms. Wanrow's (D) son told Ms. Hooper that a man had tried to pull him off of his bike and drag him into the man's house. Soon thereafter this man, William Wesler (decedent) (Wesler), showed up on Ms. Hooper's front porch saying "I didn't touch the kid, I didn't touch the kid." Upon seeing Wesler, Ms. Hooper's daughter indicated to her mother that he was the man who had molested her. Ms. Hooper's landlord saw Wesler and told Ms. Hooper that Wesler had tried to molest another young boy who had previously lived there and that Wesler had at one time been committed to a state mental hospital. A couple of nights earlier someone had slashed Ms. Hooper's bedroom window and she suspected it was Wesler. The police were called and Ms. Hooper requested they arrest Wesler. She was told they could not arrest him until Monday and she should go to the station on Monday and swear out a warrant. Ms. Hooper's landlord suggested she keep a baseball bat near the door in order to hit Wesler over the head if he should try to enter the house. The police stated, "Yes, but wait until he gets in the house." Being frightened, Ms. Hooper called Ms. Wanrow (D) and asked her to spend the night. Ms. Wanrow (D), being frightened, called her sister and brother-in-law (Chuck Michel) and asked them to spend the night also. Ms. Wanrow (D) arrived with a pistol in her purse. The adults stayed up all night. Around 5:00 a.m., and unknown to the others, Chuck Michel took the baseball bat and went to Wesler's house. When Chuck Michel arrived at Wesler's home, Wesler suggested they go to Ms. Hooper's and clear up the whole thing. Upon arriving at Ms. Hooper's, only Wesler entered the house. Wesler was 6′ 2″ tall, and was visibly intoxicated. He was asked to leave but refused to do so. Much confusion and yelling ensued. Wesler made a comment that one of the boys sleeping on a couch was cute. This, of course, made matters much worse. Ms. Wanrow (D), who is 5′ 4″ tall, and at the time had a broken leg in a cast and was using a crutch, went to the door to call Chuck Michel into the house. Wesler was directly in front of her when she turned around. Ms. Wanrow (D) testified that she was gravely startled by this situation and shot Wesler in a reflex action.

■ ISSUE

Are (1) the genders of the persons involved, and (2) the facts and circumstances learned prior to an altercation, relevant factors that a jury must consider when deciding if a defendant's belief of danger was reasonable?

■ DECISION AND RATIONALE

(Utter) Yes. There are serious errors in the jury instructions defining the justification of self-defense. First, the jury was instructed to consider only the acts and circumstances which occurred "at or immediately before the killing." This is not Washington's (P) law on self-defense. The justification of self-defense is to be evaluated in light of *all the facts and circumstances known to the defendant*, including those known substantially before the killing. In *State v. Ellis* [first-degree murder conviction overturned when trial court instructed the jury that prior threats made by the decedent were insufficient justification for defendant's belief of danger] we stated that the vital question is the reasonableness of the defendant's apprehension of danger. The jury should try to understand the situation from the defendant's point-of-view. It is quite proper for prior experiences to come into play when determining the validity of a claim of self-defense. Second, the instructions are filled with masculine pronouns. The instructions were not only presented as an objective standard, but as a masculine standard. The incident here was not an altercation between two men. The instruction states that a person may not resort to the use of a deadly weapon if *his* assailant has threatened *him* "with naked hands." Even though other instructions note that the relative size and strengths of the persons involved are to be considered, these instructions are not sufficient to inform a jury that Ms. Wanrow's (D) actions are to be judged against her own subjective impressions. In today's society women are rarely provided the means to acquire the skills necessary to protect themselves against attack without using a deadly weapon. The instructions require the jury to compare Ms. Wanrow's (D) point of view with that of a reasonable male finding himself in the same situation. In the context of this case, the instructions violate Ms. Wanrow's (D) right to equal protection of the law. The instructions are improper because they set forth an objective standard of reasonableness, and as written suggest that Ms. Wanrow's (D) conduct should be judged against that of a reasonable man in the same situation. Ms. Wanrow's conviction is reversed.

Analysis:

What would a reasonable man do in this scenario? How about a reasonable man who is 5′ 4″ tall with his leg in a cast and using a crutch? How about a man whose child had been threatened by the 6′ 2″ tall man? What about a man who is suddenly confronted by the 6′ 2″ tall, intoxicated man who had previously physically removed his child from his bike? How much do your stereotypes of women and men (mothers and fathers) play into your definition of reasonable? Remember, even with an objective standard, the definition of "reasonable" includes the circumstances in which the defendant finds herself. The facts known to the defendant and the circumstances that led to and incorporate any altercation necessarily include an element of subjectivity. The jury is to step into the shoes of the defendant and view the altercation from her point of view. The decision here does *not* set forth a broad rule that women are allowed to use deadly force when confronted with less than a deadly threat. It does set forth the idea that gender, as well as other facts, such as prior threats and physical size, may be relevant in determining whether a defendant's perception of danger is reasonable.

State v. Norman

(*North Carolina*) v. (*Abused Killer*)
89 N.C.App. 384, 366 S.E.2d 586 (1988)

BATTERED WOMAN ENTITLED TO PRESENT SELF-DEFENSE ARGUMENT

■ **INSTANT FACTS** Judy Norman (D) shot and killed her sleeping, intoxicated husband after enduring ever-increasing bouts of his abusive behavior.

■ **BLACK LETTER RULE** The fact that an abusive aggressor was passive at the moment of his killing does not necessarily preclude a defendant from claiming self-defense.

■ PROCEDURAL BASIS

On appeal to the Court of Appeals of North Carolina ordering new trial.

■ FACTS

Judy (D) and John Thomas "J.T." Norman (decedent) (Norman) were married for 25 years and had four living children. Starting five years into the marriage, Norman began to drink and beat his wife. When Judy (D) was pregnant with their youngest child, Norman kicked her down a flight of stairs, causing the baby to be born prematurely the next day. Norman required Judy (D) to prostitute herself in order to support him. Norman often threatened to kill Judy, cut off her breasts, and cut her heart out. He often referred to Judy (D) as "dogs," "whores," and "bitches." He often required her to eat cat or dog food from dog bowls, and to sleep on the concrete floor. He often beat Judy (D) with whatever was in his hand, an ashtray, a flyswatter, a beer bottle. He threw food at Judy (D), refused to let her eat, put cigarettes out on her skin, and required her to bark like a dog. All of these activities were accompanied by regular beatings at Norman's whim and sometimes to "show off" for other people. On June 10, 1985, Norman forced Judy (D) to prostitute herself at a truck stop on Interstate 85. Later that day he arrived intoxicated at the truck stop and began to hit Judy (D), slammed the car door into her, and threw hot coffee on her. On the way home he was stopped by police and arrested for driving under the influence. The next morning, Norman was extremely angry after being released from jail and beat Judy (D) throughout the day. Twice, he told her to make him a sandwich. When she brought him the sandwiches, he threw them to the floor. She made the third sandwich using paper towels to cover her hands because he didn't want her to touch the bread. He smeared the third sandwich on her face. That evening police responded to a domestic quarrel reported at the Norman residence. Judy (D) was bruised and crying, but refused to take out a warrant on her husband as advised by the officers because she was afraid if she did, Norman would kill her. Later that evening, the police were dispatched to the Norman residence again. Norman was interfering with emergency personnel who had been called because Judy (D) took an overdose of "nerve pills." Norman, intoxicated, stated they should "let the bitch die." Norman threatened to kill Judy (D), her mother, and her grandmother. After being treated at the hospital, Judy (D) spent the night at her grandmother's house as advised by the therapist at the hospital. The next day, June 12, a friend of Norman's asked him to drive with him to a nearby town to pick up his paycheck. Norman went to his friend's house and Judy (D) drove them. During the trip, Norman slapped Judy (D) for following a truck too closely, poured a beer over her head, and kicked her in the side of the head while she was driving. He told her he would "cut her breast off and shove it up her rear end." Later that day, one of their children informed Judy's (D) mother that

Norman was beating Judy (D) again. Judy's (D) mother called the sheriff's department, but no one arrived at that time. Norman again threatened to kill Judy (D). He smashed a doughnut on her face and put out a cigarette on her chest. In the afternoon, Norman laid down on the larger of two beds in the bedroom to take a nap. Judy (D) tried to lie down on the smaller bed, but Norman told her that she couldn't and that dogs should sleep on the floor. One of their children came into the room and asked if Judy (D) could babysit one of their grandchildren. Norman said Judy (D) could do so. When the baby began to cry, Judy (D) took the baby to her mother's house because she was afraid the crying would wake Norman. She found a .25 automatic pistol at her mother's house. She took the pistol back to her house, loaded it, and shot Norman twice in the head while he slept. "What took her so long?"

■ ISSUE

If a consistently abusive spouse is passive at the moment a battered defendant spouse kills him, is defendant still entitled to claim self-defense?

■ DECISION AND RATIONALE

(Parker) Yes. Judy (D) testified that she could no longer stand things at home. She explained she could not leave Norman because he would find her and kill her. She had left him before and he always found her and beat her. Several witnesses testified to the facts presented here. Two expert witnesses in the field of forensic psychology testified regarding battered spouse syndrome. Dr. Tyson testified that Judy's (D) case had progressed beyond the standard case and had escalated into the kinds of torture and degradation associated with prisoner-of-war camps. Judy (D) was behaving at a basic survival level. When asked if Judy (D) believed it was reasonably necessary to kill Norman, Dr. Tyson stated that Judy (D) believed she had no other choice, that in order to protect herself and her family she had to use deadly force against Norman. Dr. Rollins, who performed the psychiatric evaluation, similarly testified. He stated that Judy (D) believed that Norman was in complete control. That Judy had suffered Norman's abuse for so long she felt worthless and could not see a way to escape. Dr. Rollins testified that Judy's (D) action appeared necessary to her. He did not find any evidence of any psychotic disorder. Judy (D) was not allowed to put forth an argument of self-defense. The basic issue is whether Norman's passivity at the time of the killing *precludes* Judy (D) from asserting self-defense. We hold that the facts presented are sufficient to allow Judy (D) to argue the defense of self-defense to the jury. Self-defense incorporates an objective and subjective standard. The subjective standard relates to what the defendant perceived at the time of the shooting. The question is did the defendant believe it was necessary to kill the deceased in order to save herself from death or great bodily harm. The objective standard relates to what a reasonable person would believe if they were in defendant's circumstances. The record has more than sufficient testimony to support the argument that Judy (D) believed that she would have to kill Norman in order to save her self from death or great bodily harm. In addition, both experts testified that the abusive pattern reduced Judy (D) to a level of "learned helplessness." A defendant's inability to withdraw from the hostile situation and her vulnerability in relation to her abuser are factors to be considered in determining the reasonableness of a defendant's belief in the necessity to kill the abuser. Battered spouse syndrome usually has three phases—the tension-building phase, the violent phase, and the quiet or loving phase [apparently Norman skipped the quiet, loving phase]. During the violent phase, when the traditional concept of self-defense would permit a defendant to protect herself, she is least able to do so because she is immobilized by fear, if not actually physically restrained. Given the expert testimony provided here, it is our opinion that there may be circumstances under which the killing of a passive victim does not preclude the defense of self-defense. Based on the evidence a jury *could* find that Judy (D) believed it necessary to kill Norman to save herself, and that her belief was reasonable under the circumstances. The jury could find that Norman's sleep was but a momentary hiatus in a continuous reign of terror, that Judy (D) merely took advantage of her first opportunity to protect herself, and that there was the kind of provocation required for self-defense. The trial court erred in failing to instruct the jury on self-defense. A new trial is granted.

Analysis:

The appeals court stated, "we do not believe that a battered person must wait until a deadly attack occurs or that a victim [decedent] must in all cases be actually attacking or threatening to attack at the very moment defendant commits the unlawful act [killing] for the battered person to act in self-defense. Such a standard, in our view, would ignore the realities of the condition [battered spouse syndrome]." The appellate court believed that a jury could determine whether, and to what extent, to accept the expert testimony and determine whether Judy (D) was justified in killing Norman. Which justification theory applies to the facts here? It is reasonable to argue that Judy (D) had a right to defend herself against Norman's unlawful interference with her life. Can it also be reasonably argued that Norman's violent actions threatened Judy's (D) life, and thereby Norman forfeited his right to life?

State v. Norman

(*North Carolina*) v. (*Abused Killer*)
324 N.C. 253, 378 S.E.2d 8 (1989)

BATTERED WIFE MUST SHOW EVIDENCE OF *IMMINENT* THREAT OF HARM BEFORE SELF-DEFENSE ARGUMENT ALLOWED

■ **INSTANT FACTS** Trial court did not allow an abused wife to argue self-defense after she killed her sleeping, abusive husband; although the Court of Appeals held she could argue self-defense, it was overturned by the state supreme court, which agreed with the trial court.

■ **BLACK LETTER RULE** A defendant must have a reasonable fear of *imminent* death or great bodily harm before she is entitled to a jury instruction on self-defense.

■ PROCEDURAL BASIS

North Carolina Supreme Court held that defendant could not argue self defense and overturned appellate court holding in favor of defendant's ability to so argue.

■ FACTS

The facts are set forth in the Court of Appeal decision for *State v. Norman* (the previous case).

■ ISSUE

Did the defendant produce sufficient evidence such that the trial court was required to instruct on self-defense?

■ DECISION AND RATIONALE

(Mitchell) No. Before a defendant is entitled to a jury instruction on self-defense, the evidence must show that the defendant killed due to a reasonable fear of *imminent* death or great bodily harm. We conclude that the evidence here would not support such a finding. The trial court properly declined to allow such an instruction. The court of appeals is reversed. Only if defendants are required to show that they killed due to a reasonable belief that death or great bodily harm was *imminent* can the justification for homicide remain clearly and firmly rooted in necessity. A threat is imminent when it must be instantly met and cannot be avoided by calling others for help, including the protection of the law. *All* the evidence tended to show that Judy (D) had plenty of time and opportunity to find other ways to prevent future abuse by Norman. The expert testimony simply showed that Judy (D) felt generally threatened and that she believed her life would, at some point, end because of her abuse. It did not show that Judy (D) killed in the belief that Norman presented a threat of *imminent* death or great bodily harm. To stretch the law of self-defense to fit this case would require changing the imminent requirement. This change would tend to allow the opportune killing of abusive husbands by their wives solely on the basis of the wives' testimony based only on their speculation as to the probability of future assaults by their husbands.

■ DISSENT

(Martin) It must first be noted that the problems of fabricated evidence are not unique to trials of battered wives who kill. The possibility of fabricated evidence arises in all cases in which a defendant seeks the benefit of self-defense. Here, there were several witnesses who substantiated the facts and circumstances supporting a claim of self-defense. There is no reasonable basis to attack the credibility of evidence for the defendant here. This is not an attempt to expand the requirements of self-defense. The proper issue for this court is to determine whether the evidence, viewed in the light most favorable to the defendant, was sufficient to require the trial court to instruct on the law of self-defense. I conclude that it was. Imminence must be viewed from the defendant's point of view. The question is not whether the threat was *in fact* imminent, but whether Judy's (D) belief in the impending nature of the threat, given the circumstances as she saw them, was reasonable. Judy (D) was incarcerated by fear. For the battered wife, if there is no escape, no momentary sense of safety, then the next attack, which could be a fatal one, is imminent. Witnesses' testified as to Judy's (D) intense fear and the events of the last three days of Norman's life which could have led a juror to conclude that Judy (D) reasonably perceived a threat to her life as "imminent," even while her husband slept. Norman had reduced the quality of Judy's (D) life to such an abysmal state that, given the opportunity to do so, the jury might well have found that she was justified in acting in self-defense for the preservation of her tragic life.

Analysis:

In nonconfrontational cases, like the case here, some jurisdictions allow self-defense instructions and some do not. No jurisdiction allows such an instruction when the battered spouse hires a third party to kill her spouse. What purpose does the expert testimony serve in cases where a battered spouse kills? Such testimony can be instrumental in a case where a battered spouse kills her spouse when he is asleep or there is a momentary lull from abuse. It demonstrates a defendant's subjective point of view and allows a jury to understand why she believed it was necessary to take such an action in order to avoid imminent death or great bodily harm. Expert testimony provides an explanation regarding the cycle of abuse in battered-wife syndrome and explains to the jury why the wife didn't "just leave" her abuser. Recall that the deceased's prior behavior may be relevant in determining the reasonableness of the defendant's perception of harm. Whether the case is a confrontational case or nonconfrontational, the decedent's prior behavior demonstrates why a defendant's perception of harm on the occasion of the killing required her to respond with deadly force.

People v. Kurr

(*Prosecution*) v. (*Pregnant Killer*)
253 Mich.App. 317, 654 N.W.2d 651 (2002)

PERSON ACTING TO DEFEND A NONVIABLE FETUS FROM ASSAULT AGAINST MOTHER MAY ASSERT "DEFENSE OF OTHERS" DOCTRINE

■ **INSTANT FACTS** After defendant's boyfriend, Pena, punched defendant twice in the stomach, defendant, who was pregnant with quadruplets, stabbed Pena in the chest, killing him.

■ **BLACK LETTER RULE** The "defense of others" doctrine extends to actions taken to protect even a nonviable fetus from an assault against the mother.

■ PROCEDURAL BASIS

Defendant appeals her voluntary manslaughter conviction.

■ FACTS

On October 9, 1999, defendant and Pena, defendant's boyfriend, argued about Pena's cocaine use. Pena punched defendant twice in the stomach. Defendant, who was 16 or 17 weeks pregnant with quadruplets at the time, warned Pena not to hit her again because she was carrying his babies. When Pena came towards her again, she stabbed him in the chest. He died as a result of the stabbing. Before trial, defendant moved for permission to present testimony and argue that she killed Pena in defense of her unborn children. At trial, testimony was presented regarding both Pena's abusive nature and defendant's pregnancy. Defendant requested that the jury be given an instruction on the "defense of others" doctrine. The trial court did not allow the instruction because, at only 16 or 17 weeks at the time of the stabbing, a fetus would not yet be viable. Defendant was convicted of voluntary manslaughter.

■ ISSUE

Should a nonviable fetus be considered an "other" for purposes of the "defense of others" doctrine?

■ DECISION AND RATIONALE

(Meter, J.) Yes. The "defense of others" doctrine extends to actions taken to protect even a nonviable fetus from an assault against the mother. Case law in Michigan allows a person to use deadly force in the defense of another person. We now believe that this defense should be extended to the protection of a fetus, whether viable or nonviable, based upon Michigan's Fetal Protection Act. This Act sets forth penalties for harming a fetus or embryo during an intentional assault against a pregnant woman. The plain language of the Act shows that the Legislature concluded that fetuses are worthy of protection as living entities. More importantly, the Act makes no distinction between fetuses that are viable or nonviable. Indeed, the Legislature used both the terms "fetus" and "embryo" in the Act. We find it important that the Act reflects a public policy to protect even an embryo from harmful or negligent conduct. We conclude, therefore, that because the Legislature has expressed its intent to provide fetuses and embryos with strong protection from harm, the "defense of others" doctrine should be extended as a defense to those who act to protect a nonviable fetus from an assault against the mother. This defense, however, is limited in scope and applies only in the context of an unlawful assault against the mother. The Legislature has not indicated its intent to extend protections to embryos existing outside a woman's body, such as frozen embryos. Moreover, this defense will not be extended to anti-abortion activists. This defense is only available to those who try to prevent unlawful bodily harm against another. This defense cannot be used to justify action against those who perform abortions, as they are engaging in lawful activity. Because the defendant in this case was not allowed a "defense of others" jury instruction, we find that she was deprived of her due process right to present a defense and a new trial is warranted. Reversed and remanded.

Analysis:

This case introduces students to the "defense of others" doctrine. Although not necessarily explained in the case, this doctrine allows a person to use reasonable force to defend another person when he or she reasonably believes that the other is in immediate danger of unlawful bodily harm and that the use of force is necessary to avoid the harm. Most states will allow a defendant to use the defense as long as he or she reasonably believed that the other was in need of protection, even if that belief was later shown to be erroneous and the person being protected would not have actually had the right of self-defense. Under this defense, the defending party may not use more force than he or she reasonably believes is necessary to relieve the risk of harm. Deadly force is only justified when the person defending another reasonably believes that the attack may be deadly.

■ CASE VOCABULARY

EMBRYO: Term used to describe the result of human conception up until the start of the third month of pregnancy.

NONVIABLE FETUS: A fetus that is not capable of surviving outside of the mother if born early.

People v. Ceballos

(Government) v. *(Garage Gun-Trap Setter)*
12 Cal.3d 470, 116 Cal.Rptr. 233, 526 P.2d 241 (1974)

SPRING GUNS MAY NOT BE USED TO PROTECT PROPERTY, EVEN IF THE OWNER COULD USE THE SAME FORCE WERE HE PRESENT

■ **INSTANT FACTS** Ceballos (D) set a gun to shoot at anyone who attempted to enter his garage.

■ **BLACK LETTER RULE** An injury or killing by the use of a deadly mechanical device is not justified where the device injures in response to a non-violent burglary.

■ PROCEDURAL BASIS

Appeal from conviction of assault with a deadly weapon.

■ FACTS

Don Ceballos (D) lived in a small home with the living quarters above the garage, though Ceballos (D) sometimes slept in the garage. In the garage Ceballos (D) had about $2,000 worth of property. In March of 1970, Ceballos (D) noted that some tools had been stolen from his home. In May he noticed that the lock on his garage door was bent and that there were pry marks on the door. The next day he mounted a .22 pistol in the garage. The pistol was aimed at the center of the garage doors and was connected by a wire to one of the doors so that the pistol would discharge if the door were opened several inches. Two boys, Stephen, aged 16, and Robert, aged 15 came to Ceballos' (D) house while he was away. Both were unarmed with a knife or a gun. Stephen removed the lock with a crowbar, and as he pulled the door outward, was hit in the face with a bullet. Stephen testified that he was not sure if he was going to steal anything, but wanted to go in the garage and look. Ceballos (D) testified that he felt he should set some kind of trap to protect himself and his property. When initially questioned by police, Ceballos (D) stated that he did not have much, and wanted to protect what he did have. The jury found Ceballos (D) guilty of assault with a deadly weapon. Ceballos (D) appealed, contending that under Penal Code section 197, had he been present, he would have been justified in shooting Stephen.

■ ISSUE

Is the use of a deadly mechanical device justified to protect against a non-violent burglary?

■ DECISION AND RATIONALE

(Burke, J.) No. Courts have concluded that a person may be held criminally liable for injuries or death resulting from a deadly mechanical device that he sets on his premises. However, an exception to the rule is recognized where the defendant would have been justified in taking the life or inflicting the injury with his bare hands. However, allowing persons to employ deadly mechanical devices imperils fireman, police officers, and children. When the actor is present, he may realize that deadly force is not necessary, but deadly mechanical devices are without mercy or discretion. Furthermore, even if the rule justifying the use of deadly mechanical devices were applied here, Ceballos (D) would not be justified in shooting Stephen. A killing in defense of property is justified, inter alia, when committed against one who manifestly intends to commit a felony. Furthermore, the felony intended to be committed must be a forcible and atrocious crime, such as murder, mayhem, rape and robbery. Burglary is sometimes included as a forcible and atrocious crime, but only where the burglary creates a reasonable fear of great bodily harm. The burglary in this case did not threaten death or serious bodily harm. Ceballos (D) also contends that another subsection of Penal Code section 197 justifies the homicide since he committed the homicide while attempting to apprehend a felon. However, his testimony indicates that the purpose of the killing was not to apprehend a felon, but to prevent a burglary. Under the common law, extreme force could be used to prevent dispossession of a dwelling house, or against burning of a dwelling. Here we are not concerned with dispossession or burning, but a burglary that did not justify the use of deadly force. We conclude as a matter of law that the exception to the rule of liability for injuries inflicted by a deadly mechanical device does not apply here. Judgment affirmed.

Analysis:

The common law regarding the use of spring guns or trap guns to protect property is changing. Under the old common law rules, a deadly mechanical device could be used where the intrusion was such that the person, if he were present, would be justified in taking the life or inflicting the harm with his own hands. Now many states hold that a resident may not justifiably use a spring gun to repel an intruder, even if he would be justified in inflicting the same harm with his bare hands. As the court in *Ceballos* noted, spring guns kill indiscriminately. Under the old common law rules, the two kids who entered Ceballos's (D) garage committed larceny, not burglary, since they entered during the daytime, and in a typical common-law jurisdiction, Ceballos (D) would not have been allowed to use deadly force. Had they entered at night, their act likely would have constituted burglary, and Ceballos (D) would have been justified in using deadly force.

■ CASE VOCABULARY

DISPOSSESSION: Ejectment or deprivation of a dwelling or other property.

Tennessee v. Garner

(*State*) v. (*Dead Suspect's Father*)

471 U.S. 1, 105 S.Ct. 1694, 85 L.Ed.2d 1 (1985)

POLICE OFFICERS MAY NOT USE DEADLY FORCE TO APPREHEND NONDANGEROUS FLEEING FELONS

■ **INSTANT FACTS** Unarmed 15-year-old burglar was shot dead by police after he attempted to scale a fence in order to flee the scene of the crime.

■ **BLACK LETTER RULE** Fourth Amendment reasonableness requirement prohibits officers from using deadly force to effect the arrest of a fleeing felon unless it is necessary to prevent the escape and the officer has probable cause to believe that the suspect poses a significant threat of death or serious physical injury to the officer or others.

■ PROCEDURAL BASIS

On appeal to the Supreme Court upholding the court of appeals' finding that an officer was not justified in using deadly force against an unarmed, nondangerous, fleeing felon.

■ FACTS

Police Officers Wright and Hymon (D2) responded to a "prowler inside call" placed by a neighbor. Upon arrival, the neighbor was on her porch and indicated to police she heard glass breaking and that someone was inside her neighbor's house. Wright called-in to report they were at the scene while Hymon (D2) went behind the house. After hearing a door slam and seeing someone run across the yard, Hymon (D2) saw, with the aid of his flashlight, Edward Garner (Edward) who appeared to be 5′5″ or 5′7″ and about 17 or 18 years old, crouched at the base of a 6-foot-high chain link fence at the edge of the yard. Hymon (D2) could see Edward's face and hands and saw no weapon. Hymon (D2) called out, "police, halt" and took a few steps toward Edward. Edward began to climb over the fence. Hymon (D2) was convinced that if Edward made it over the fence he would elude capture. Hymon (D2) shot at Edward, hitting him in the back of the head. Edward subsequently died on the operating table. Ten dollars and a purse taken from the house were found on his body. Tennessee's (D1) statute provides, " if, after notice of the intention to arrest the defendant, he either flees or forcibly resists, the officer may use all the necessary means to effect the arrest." The police department policy was slightly more restrictive, but still allowed the use of deadly force in cases of burglary. Although investigated by the Memphis Police Firearm's Review Board and presented to a grand jury, neither took any action. Edward's father (Gamer) (P) brought a 42 U.S.C. § 1983 action [violation of civil rights] in federal court against Hymon (D2) , the police department, the department's Director, the Mayor and the city of Memphis. After a 3-day bench trial the District Court found in favor of the defendants, concluding that Hymon's (D2) actions were authorized by state law and the law was constitutional. The District Court reasoned that Hymon (D2) had used the only reasonable and practicable means of preventing Edward's escape, and that Edward had "recklessly and needlessly attempted to vault over the fence to escape, thereby assuming the risk of being fired upon." The Court of Appeals reversed and remanded. It reasoned that the killing of a fleeing suspect is a "seizure" under the Fourth Amendment, and is constitutional only if reasonable. It also found that the state law failed as applied here because it did not adequately distinguish between felonies of different magnitudes; the facts presented did not justify the use of deadly force. Tennessee (D1) appealed.

■ ISSUE

Is it reasonable under the Fourteenth Amendment to use deadly force against a nondangerous, fleeing felon?

■ DECISION AND RATIONALE

(White, J.) No. We conclude that such force may not be used unless it is necessary to prevent the escape and the officer has probable cause to believe that the suspect poses a significant threat of death or serious physical injury to the officer or others. Whenever an officer restrains the freedom of a person to walk away, he has seized that person. Although it may not be clear when minimal interference by an officer becomes a seizure, there can be no question that apprehension by the use of deadly force is a seizure subject to the reasonableness requirement of the Fourth Amendment. Tennessee (D1) argues that if the requirement of probable cause is met (an officer may arrest a person if he has probable cause to believe that person committed a crime) then there is no Fourth Amendment issue as to how that seizure is made. We do not agree. There are many cases in which this Court, by balancing the extent of the interference by an officer against the need for it, has examined the reasonableness of the manner in which a search or seizure is conducted. Even with probable cause an officer may not always seize a suspect by killing him. The suspect's fundamental interest in his own life and society's interest in a judicial determination of guilt and punishment are up against the government's interest in effective law enforcement. The argument for force is that overall violence will be reduced by encouraging peaceful submission of suspects who know that they may be shot if they flee. Although effective law enforcement and overall reduction of violence are admittedly important goals, we are not convinced that the use of deadly force is a sufficiently productive means of accomplishing these goals to justify the killing of nonviolent suspects. The majority of police departments in this country have forbidden the use of deadly force against nonviolent suspects. In addition, the majority of police department regulations in large cities allow the firing of a weapon only when a felon presents a threat of death or serious bodily harm. Tennessee (D1) has failed to convince us that shooting nondangerous fleeing suspects is so vital as to outweigh the suspect's interest in his own life. Where the suspect poses no immediate threat to the officer or to others, the harm resulting from failing to apprehend him does not justify the use of deadly force to do so. An officer may not seize an unarmed, nondangerous suspect by shooting him dead. The Tennessee (D1) statute is unconstitutional to the extent it authorizes the use of deadly force against such fleeing suspects. However, the statute is not unconstitutional on its face. Where the officer has probable cause to believe that the suspect poses a threat of serious bodily harm, either to the officer or to others, (or the officer has probable cause to believe the suspect has committed a crime involving the infliction or threatened infliction of serious physical harm) it is not constitutionally unreasonable to prevent escape by using deadly force. Our interpretation of the Fourth Amendment in modern times is not limited by the common law rule which allowed for the use of whatever means necessary to arrest a fleeing felon (although most jurisdictions flatly prohibit the use of deadly force to stop a fleeing misdemeanant). When the common law rule was first imposed virtually all felonies were punishable by death. Courts justified the rule by emphasizing the dangerousness of felons. Today, almost none of the crimes previously punishable by death remain so. In addition, numerous misdemeanors involve conduct more dangerous than many felonies (e.g., drunken driving is more physically threatening than white-collar crimes). In addition, handguns were not carried by officers until the latter part of the Nineteenth Century. When the common law rule developed, deadly force meant hand-to-hand struggle during which the safety of the officer was obviously at risk. The changes in technology and legislation mean the common law rule is distorted beyond recognition when literally applied. The District Court concluded that Hymon (D2) was justified in shooting Edward because state law allows, and the Federal Constitution does not forbid, the use of deadly force to prevent the escape of a fleeing felony suspect if no alternative means of apprehension is available. In reversing, the Court of Appeals accepted the District Court's factual conclusions (one of which is that Edward was not armed) and held that "the facts, as found, did not justify the use of deadly force." We agree with the Court of Appeals. Hymon (D2) never attempted to justify his actions on any basis other than the need to prevent escape. Hymon (D2) did not have probable cause to believe that Edward, whom he correctly believed to be unarmed, posed any physical danger to himself or others. We hold that Tennessee's (D1) statute is invalid insofar as it purported to give Hymon (D2) the authority to act as he did.

■ DISSENT

(O'Connor, J.) Household burglaries are serious crimes. According to Department of Justice statistics, 3/5 of all rapes in the home, 3/5 of all home robberies, and 1/3 of home aggravated and simple assaults are committed by burglars. Even if a particular burglary, when viewed in retrospect, does not involve physical harm to others, the harsh potentialities for violence inherent in the forced entry into a home preclude characterization of the crime as "innocuous, inconsequential, minor or nonviolent." Because burglary is a serious and dangerous felony, the public interest in the prevention and detection of the crime is of compelling interest. The legitimate interests of the suspect are adequately accommodated by the Tennessee (D1) statute: to avoid the use of deadly force and consequent risk to his life, the suspect need merely obey the valid order to halt. A proper balancing of the interest involved suggest that use of deadly force as a last resort to apprehend a criminal suspect fleeing from the scene of a nighttime burglary is not unreasonable within the meaning of the Fourth Amendment. The reasonableness of this action for purposes of the Fourth Amendment is not determined by the unfortunate nature of this particular case; instead, the question is whether it is constitutionally impermissible for police officers, as a last resort, to shoot a burglary suspect fleeing the scene of a crime.

Analysis:

The majority appears to view many of the facts in retrospect, e.g., the suspect was fifteen-years-old, he was unarmed, he only stole a minimum amount from the house. But the main issue appears to be that because the suspect appeared nonthreatening at the time the officer fired on him, the officer's use of deadly force was unreasonable. It appears from the lack of any official reprimand that the officer was acting within department policy. However, the point is that under the facts presented, the state law (underlying the policy) was not constitutionally reasonable. To support its finding of unreasonableness, the majority notes that some police departments and the FBI have adopted policies to not use deadly force in similar circumstances. The dissent notes that as regrettable as the circumstances are, the reasonableness of the officer's conduct cannot be viewed after the fact. The dissent points out repeatedly that the officer fired his weapon as a last resort. There was no way for the officer to know, at the time of the crime, whether the suspect stole ten dollars or had murdered the occupants of the house. The dissent claims that the majority has created a Fourth Amendment right for burglary suspects to flee from officers. This goes beyond a realistic reading of the majority opinion. The majority simply holds that officers do not have a blanket constitutional right to kill fleeing burglary suspects.

■ CASE VOCABULARY

42 U.S.C. § 1983: A federal civil rights action brought against a person or entity in which it is alleged that the person or entity, acting under authority of state law, deprived an individual of their Federal Constitutional rights.

Nelson v. State

(*Front-end Loader Wrecker*) v. (*Prosecution*)
597 P.2d 977 (Alaska 1979)

THE DEFENSE OF NECESSITY JUSTIFIES UNLAWFUL ACTIONS TAKEN TO PREVENT AN EVEN GREATER HARM FROM OCCURRING

■ **INSTANT FACTS** Nelson (D) raises the defense of necessity as justification for his actions in taking a dump truck and front-end loader from a Highway Department Yard to pull his stuck vehicle from a marshy area.

■ **BLACK LETTER RULE** The defense of necessity may be raised only where the defendant's law-violating actions were necessary to prevent an even greater harm from occurring.

■ PROCEDURAL BASIS

Nelson (D) appeals his destruction of personal property and joyriding convictions to the Alaska Supreme Court.

■ FACTS

Just after midnight on May 22, 1976, Dale Nelson (D) drove his four-wheel drive truck onto a side road where it became stuck in a marshy area just off the highway. Nelson (D) was worried that the truck might tip over. Nelson (D) and his two companions, Lynette Stinson and Carl Thompson, worked for an hour to try and free the truck. When all efforts failed, Nelson (D) and Stinson began walking down the highway. An acquaintance picked them up and drove Nelson (D) and Stinson to a Highway Department Yard, marked with "no trespassing" signs, where heavy equipment was parked. They waited several hours for someone to show up and then decided to take a dump truck to try pull out Nelson's (D) vehicle. The dump truck also became stuck. At approximately 10:00 a.m. a man named "Curly" appeared. His vehicle was also stuck further down the highway. Curly and Nelson (D) returned to the equipment yard and took a front-end loader, which they used to free the dump truck. They used the dump truck to free Curly's car and returned the truck to the equipment yard. Nelson (D) then tried to use the front-end loader to free his truck. The front-end loader became bogged down too. Thereafter, Nelson (D) and his companions went to sleep, two in a tent and one in the truck. A Highway Department employee found them sleeping and placed them under citizen's arrest. Both the front-end loader and the dump truck sustained considerable damage during Nelson's (D) attempt to free his truck. Nelson (D) was convicted of reckless destruction of personal property and joyriding. Nelson (D) appeals this conviction, arguing that the jury instruction given on the defense of necessity was inadequate.

■ ISSUE

Did the trial court properly instruct the jury that, for the defense of necessity to apply, they must find that defendant's actions were taken to prevent an even greater harm to himself or his property?

■ DECISION AND RATIONALE

(Matthews, J.) Yes. The defense of necessity may be used only where the defendant's law-violating actions were necessary to prevent an even greater harm from occurring. The defense of necessity is based on the policy that the law should promote higher values at the expense of lesser values. This legal doctrine recognizes that there are times where the greater good of society will be promoted by a violation of the criminal law. The three essential elements to this defense are: 1) the act charged must have been done to prevent a significant evil, 2) there must have been no adequate alternative, and 3) the harm caused must not have been disproportionate to the harm avoided. We find that the jury instruction provided by the trial judge properly conveyed these elements. Even if the instructions were not adequately worded, any error would be harmless because Nelson (D) failed to make out a case of necessity. We do not agree that Nelson's (D) vehicle was in "immediate danger" of tipping over. In fact, by the time Nelson (D) took the equipment, it had already been stuck for a few hours. Moreover, 12 hours after being stuck, someone actually slept in the truck. Furthermore, Nelson (D) cannot show an absence of lawful alternatives. On several different occasions people stopped to offer their assistance with rides and offers to telephone the state troopers or a tow truck. Finally, we do not find that the harm Nelson (D) sought to avoid, being the damage to his truck, was greater than the harm caused by his illegal actions. Nelson's (D) fear about the potential damage to his truck did not provide adequate justification for his wrongful appropriation of sophisticated and expensive equipment. Affirmed.

Analysis:

For the defense of necessity to justify a defendant's conduct, the harm prevented must be greater than the harm that occurred as a result of the unlawful conduct. The issue raised by Nelson (D) on appeal involved the proper way to evaluate the harm or emergency presented by the situation. Nelson (D) argues for a subjective, "reasonable person" test, rather than an objective, "after-the-fact" test. The Court in *Nelson* states that the person's actions must be weighed against the harm reasonably foreseeable at the time, rather than the harm that actually occurs. In footnote six, however, the Court notes that the defendant's belief as to the harm that might result is not in itself sufficient. Rather, as an initial matter, the court must make an objective determination as to whether the defendant's value judgment was correct. Thus, the defendant's reasonable belief as to the relative harmfulness of the evil to be avoided and the evil resulting from the actions taken does not control. It is for the court, not a defendant, to weigh the relative harmfulness of the two alternatives.

■ CASE VOCABULARY

APPROPRIATION: The wrongful exercise of control over another's property.

JOYRIDING: Driving another person's vehicle without permission, but without the intent to permanently deprive the owner of the vehicle.

United States v. Schoon

(*Government*) v. (*Indirect Civil Protestor*)
939 F.2d 826 (9th Cir. 1991)

NECESSITY IS NO DEFENSE TO INDIRECT CIVIL DISOBEDIENCE

■ **INSTANT FACTS** Schoon (D) and others protested congressional policies at an IRS office, and claimed the necessity defense as a justification for their actions.

■ **BLACK LETTER RULE** Indirect protests of congressional policies can never meet all the requirements of the necessity doctrine, and the necessity defense is therefore unavailable in such cases.

■ PROCEDURAL BASIS

Appeal from trial court's denial of necessity defense in indirect civil disobedience case.

■ FACTS

Thirty people, including Schoon (D), entered an IRS office in Tucson, where they chanted "Keep America's tax dollars out of El Salvador" [couldn't they come up with a rhyme, or a shorter chant?], splashed simulated blood on the walls [ketchup?], counters, and carpeting, and obstructed the office's operation. Schoon (D) offered evidence of the conditions in El Salvador as the motivation for their conduct. Schoon (D) attempted to assert a necessity defense, arguing that acts in protest of American involvement in El Salvador were necessary to avoid further bloodshed in that country. The district court precluded the necessity defense based on Ninth Circuit precedent. Specifically, the court noted that (1) the requisite immediacy was lacking; (2) the actions taken would not abate the evil; and (3) other legal alternatives existed.

■ ISSUE

Is the necessity doctrine available as a defense to charges stemming from indirect protests of congressional policies?

■ DECISION AND RATIONALE

(Boochever, J.) No. This is a case of indirect civil disobedience, since the protestors were violating a law which is not itself the object of protest. We conclude that the elements of the necessity defense are lacking in indirect civil disobedience cases. Necessity is a utilitarian defense. It justifies criminal acts taken to avert a greater harm, maximizing social welfare. In instances of acceptable necessity defenses, the "crime" averted the occurrence of an even greater "harm." Analyzing the actions of the protestors, we see that there can be no aversion of harm by the protest, since the El Salvador policy cannot be deemed a cognizable harm. The policy does not violate the Constitution, and it was adopted according to appropriate congressional procedure. Also, in political necessity cases involving indirect civil disobedience, the act alone is unlikely to abate the evil precisely because the action is indirect. The IRS obstruction is unlikely to abate the killings in El Salvador, or immediately change Congress' policy. Thus, there is no substantial causal relationship between the criminal conduct and the harm to be averted. Finally, in indirect civil disobedience cases the legal alternatives will never be deemed exhausted when the harm can be mitigated by congressional action. Cases involving protest of congressional policy have implicitly decided that, because Congress can change its mind at any time in response to citizen protest, petitioning Congress is always an adequate legal alternative. Thus, there can never be an absence of legal alternatives where congressional action is the protest's aim. What these cases are really about is gaining notoriety for a cause. Indirect protests of congressional policies can never meet all the requirements of the necessity doctrine. Judgment affirmed.

Analysis:

In *Schoon* the court blocked the necessity defense in all indirect civil disobedience cases. Some advocates of a "political necessity" defense argue that protestors should have the right to such a defense because it allows stifled or unheeded viewpoints to be heard in a public forum. Also, the defense allows the jury to voice its opinion on a controversial subject. However, some believe that allowing the defense would, as Joshua Dressler says, "undesirably erode the principle of traditional civil disobedience, which is that people who are compelled by conscience to violate the law, but who also believe in the democratic system, should accept their punishment (as Gandhi and Martin Luther King did) as part of their protest."

■ CASE VOCABULARY

INDIRECT CIVIL DISOBEDIENCE: A protest in which the participants violate a law which is not itself the object of protest, as opposed to direct civil disobedience, where the participants violate the very law they mean to protest.

POLITICAL NECESSITY DEFENSE: A defense where the protestors attempt to assert a defense based on a need to effect political change or to bring an issue political recognition.

The Queen v. Dudley and Stephens

(*English Prosecutor*) v. (*Hungry Sailors*)
14 Q.B.D. 273 (1884)

DINING ON YE SHIPMATES IS STRICTLY PROHIBITED

■ **INSTANT FACTS** English sailors at sea for 20 days (the last 9 days without food or water) killed and consumed a cabin boy for which they were found guilty of murder.

■ **BLACK LETTER RULE** A defendant's actions are not justified under the defense of necessity if he deliberately kills an innocent person in order to save his own life.

■ PROCEDURAL BASIS

On appeal to the Queen's Bench Division finding from a jury's special verdict for conviction of murder.

■ FACTS

After a storm, three English seaman (sailors) and one, 17-year-old cabin boy (boy) were cast away in an open boat that belonged to the yacht on which they had served. Initially, they had two-one pound tins of turnips which they ate over three days. On the fourth day, they caught and ate a small turtle. They had no fresh water, except occasional rain water they caught in their oilskin caps. After eighteen days at sea, Dudley (D1) and Stephens (D2) began to discuss with the third sailor, Brooks, what should be done if they were not soon rescued. Dudley (D1) suggested one should be sacrificed to save the others, indicating that the boy should be sacrificed. Brooks dissented. No one asked the boy. The next day, Dudley (D1) proposed that lots should be cast to decide who would be put to death to save the rest. Again, Brooks refused to consent, and no one asked the cabin boy. They did not draw lots. Dudley (D1) and Stephens (D2) talked about how they had families and suggested it would be better to kill the boy so that their lives could be saved. They decided that if there was no vessel in sight by the next morning, the boy should be killed. The next day (twentieth day at sea) "the last food was the turtle" Dudley (D1) told Brooks to "have a sleep," and made signs to Stephens (D2) and Brooks that the boy should be killed. Stephens (D2) agreed, but Brooks again dissented. The boy was lying on the bottom of the boat, weak and helpless, and did not assent to be killed. Dudley (D1) offered a prayer asking forgiveness if any of them should be tempted to commit a rash act and that their souls might be saved. He went to the boy, and telling him that his time had come, put a knife into his throat and killed him. The sailors fed upon the body and blood of the boy for four days. On the fourth day they were rescued by a passing vessel. It was set forth in the special verdict that it was likely that the boy, being the weakest, would die before the others; that if the sailors had not fed upon the boy, they probably would not have survived to be rescued; that there was no rescue in sight; that if they did not feed upon the boy or one of themselves soon, they would die of starvation; that there was no appreciable chance of saving life except by killing someone for the others to eat; that assuming any necessity to kill anybody, there was no greater necessity for killing the boy than any of the men. The jury could not determine whether under the circumstances the law would consider Dudley (D) and Stephens (D) guilty of murder and asked the advice of the court.

■ ISSUE

May a person who takes an innocent life in order to save his own claim the defense of necessity?

■ DECISION AND RATIONALE

(Lord Coleridge) No. Under the facts, the jury states that it is unable to determine whether Dudley (D1) and Stephens (D2) are guilty of murder and referred it to this court to determine what are the legal consequences of the facts. In every passage that speaks to necessity the reference is in the ordinary sense, that is, the repelling by violence which is justified so far as it was necessary to repel an unlawful violence against oneself. To quote Lord Hale, "If a man be desperately assaulted and in peril of death, and cannot otherwise escape unless, to satisfy his assailant's fury, he will kill an innocent person then present, the fear and actual force will not acquit him of the crime and punishment of murder, if he commit the fact, for he ought rather to die than kill an innocent." There is no current authority for the proposition of necessity under the circumstances. Now it is admitted that the deliberate killing of this unoffending and unresisting boy was clearly murder, unless the killing can be justified by some well-recognized excuse under the law. It is also admitted that there is no excuse unless the killing was justified by what has been called "necessity." But the temptation to act which existed here was not what the law has ever called necessity. To preserve one's life is generally speaking a duty, but it may be the plainest and highest duty to sacrifice it. War is full of instances in which it is a man's duty not to live, but to die. The duty, in case of shipwreck, of a captain to his crew, of the crew to passengers, of soldiers to women and children; these duties impose on men the moral necessity, not of the preservation, but of sacrifice of their lives for others. It is not correct, therefore, to say that there is any absolute or unqualified necessity to preserve one's life. There is an awful danger of allowing the principle that has been argued. Who is to be the judge of this sort of necessity? By what measure is the comparative value of lives to be measured? Is it to be strength, or intellect, or some other standard? Although we are mindful of the dire circumstances here, a man has no right to declare temptation to be an excuse, nor allow compassion for the criminal to change or weaken in any manner the legal definition of the crime. It is therefore our duty to declare that the act in this case was wilful murder, that the facts as stated in the verdict are no legal justification of the homicide. In our unanimous opinion Dudley (D1) and Stephens (D2) are guilty of murder, and sentence of death is imposed.

Analysis:

People often justify their actions with the thought that "it was him or me." However, the court points out that there are circumstances under which one is supposed to sacrifice one's own life for the greater good of society. The court refers to several legal authorities without finding an easy answer to the issue before it. Although a public opinion poll on the matter might show that many people would forgive the sailors, this does not impact on the legality of their actions. The sailors were not under an immediate threat of death and certainly under no threat from the boy. It would be one thing "morally, legally" to allow the boy to die and then consume him, but it is altogether another thing to kill him in order to consume him. Keep in mind that the facts make all the difference when a jury is determining whether a defendant is justified to take another's life.

■ CASE VOCABULARY

INDIRECT CIVIL DISOBEDIENCE: A protest in which the participants violate a law which is not itself the object of protest, as opposed to direct civil disobedience, where the participants violate the very law they mean to protest.

POLITICAL NECESSITY DEFENSE: A defense where the protestors attempt to assert a defense based on a need to effect political change or to bring an issue political recognition.

United States v. Contento-Pachon

(*Government*) v. (*Unwilling Drug-Runner*)
723 F.2d 691 (9th Cir. 1984)

A THREAT OF FUTURE HARM WILL NOT JUSTIFY A DEFENSE OF DURESS, EXCEPT WHERE THE HARM IS SO LIKELY TO OCCUR THAT THE ACTOR CANNOT ESCAPE THE SITUATION

■ **INSTANT FACTS** Contento-Pachon (D), a Colombian national acting under duress, swallows balloons filled with cocaine for transport to the U.S. and is arrested at customs.

■ **BLACK LETTER RULE** A defendant may assert the defense of duress when he acts under a threat of future harm only when the harm is likely to occur so quickly that the defendant cannot escape the situation.

■ PROCEDURAL BASIS

Appeal from conviction for narcotics transport after motion for exclusion of duress defense is granted.

■ FACTS

Contento-Pachon (D) is a native of Bogota, Colombia, and is employed as a cab driver. One of Contento-Pachon's (D) passengers, Jorge, offered him a job working as a chauffeur. When later he contacted Jorge, however, he was told that the job would consist of swallowing cocaine-filled balloons and transporting them to the United States. Contento-Pachon (D) agreed to consider the job. About a week later, Contento-Pachon (D) told Jorge that he would not accept the job. Jorge responded by telling Contento-Pachon (D) details about his personal life, and informing him that failure to cooperate would result in the death of his wife and his three-year-old child. The pair met again the following day, and Contento-Pachon's (D) life and his family's lives were again threatened. At this point, Contento-Pachon (D) agreed to take the cocaine into the United States. Contento-Pachon (D) swallowed 129 balloons of cocaine. He was informed that he would be watched at all times during the trip, and that if he failed to follow Jorge's instructions he and his family would be killed. When Contento-Pachon (D) arrived in the United States, he consented to have his stomach x-rayed. The x-rays revealed the cocaine. At Contento-Pachon's (D) trial, the Government (P) moved to exclude the defenses of duress and necessity. The motion was granted. Contento-Pachon (D) was convicted of unlawful possession of a narcotic with intent to distribute.

■ ISSUE

May a defendant assert the defense of duress when he acts under a threat of future harm likely to occur so quickly that the defendant cannot escape the situation?

■ DECISION AND RATIONALE

(Boochever) Yes. There are three elements to a duress defense: (1) an immediate threat of death or serious bodily injury; (2) a well-grounded fear that the threat will be carried out; (3) no reasonable opportunity to escape the threatened harm. Factfinding is usually a jury function, and the trial court rarely rules on a defense as a matter of law. Where the trial court finds the evidence insufficient as a matter of law to support a defense, the court may exclude the evidence. The trial court found Contento-Pachon's (D) evidence insufficient. However, the threat of danger was immediate because

Contento-Pachon (D) had reason to believe that Jorge would carry out his threats. Jorge knew where the family lived, and Contento-Pachon (D) contends that he was being watched the entire trip. If Contento-Pachon (D) failed to cooperate, the consequences would have been immediate and harsh. Contento-Pachon (D) had no real opportunity to escape the danger by going to the authorities, since he believed the Bogota police were corrupt and were linked to the drug traffickers. His only other alternative to escape the danger was to flee. To flee, Contento-Pachon (D) would have had to pack all his belongings, leave his job, and take his family beyond the reach of the drug traffickers. Thus, Contento-Pachon (D) presented a triable issue on escapability. The Government (P) argues that the defense of duress also requires that a defendant offer evidence that he attempted to turn himself in to authorities upon reaching a position of safety. However, this element seems to apply only to prison escape cases. In cases not involving prison escape, there seems to be no real difference between this element and the third element as listed above. At the first opportunity to cooperate with authorities without alerting the observer, he consented to an x-ray. We hold that a defendant who has acted under a well-grounded fear of immediate harm with no opportunity to escape may assert the duress defense, if there is a triable issue of fact whether he took the opportunity to escape by submitting to authorities at the first reasonable opportunity. The trial court correctly disallowed Contento-Pachon's (D) use of the necessity defense, because his actions were coerced by human, not physical forces. In addition, he did not act to "promote the general welfare," another instance where the defense of necessity is properly invoked. Because the trier of fact should be allowed to consider the credibility of the proffered evidence as to duress, we reverse. The court correctly excluded Contento-Pachon's (D) necessity defense. Reversed and remanded.

Analysis:

The court distinguishes the duress-defense from a defense of necessity as the one resulting from human coercion, the other resulting from coercion by "physical forces." "Physical forces" are events of nature, such as storms or privations. In some modern cases, however, the distinction is lost—some modern codifications of duress and necessity combine the two doctrines into an overarching "choice of evils" doctrine. The defense of necessity is promoted on utilitarian grounds, upholding the principle that the law ought to encourage the greater good at the expense of the lesser. However, the defense is not absolute. In one case, nine sailors and thirty-two passengers were stranded on a lifeboat after a shipwreck. A storm threatened to sink the lifeboat, and the sailors decided that they must lighten the boat's load to weather the storm. Some of the sailors began throwing unmarried male passengers off the boat, and the boat arrived safely at port. At the trial of one of the sailors, where he was convicted of manslaughter, the court held that the surplus sailors should have sacrificed themselves before the passengers, and that between people in equal situation, those to be sacrificed should be determined by lot.

■ CASE VOCABULARY

NECESSITY DEFENSE: A justification defense where a defendant's actions result from an emergency not of his own creation, and where he commits a harm that is less severe than what would have occurred had he not taken action.

People v. Unger

(*Illinois*) v. (*Escaped Inmate*)

66 Ill.2d 333, 5 Ill.Dec. 848, 362 N.E.2d 319 (1977)

ESCAPED PRISONER MAY ASSERT NECESSITY TO JUSTIFY HIS CHOICE TO FLEE FROM REPEATED INMATE ATTACKS

■ **INSTANT FACTS** Unger (D) escaped from an honor farm (prison) in Illinois and claimed it was necessary for him to do so as he was forced to choose between the lessor of two evils (escaping or being subjected to homosexual attacks and possibly death).

■ **BLACK LETTER RULE** An escaped prisoner may assert the defense of necessary if he can set forth facts that would tend to show that his choice to escape was the lessor of two evils—to escape or to remain and be subjected to repeated sexual assault.

■ PROCEDURAL BASIS

On appeal to the Illinois Supreme Court affirming the judgment of the appellate court to reverse the conviction.

■ FACTS

Francis Unger (D) was serving a one-to three-year term for auto theft. On March 7, 1972, Unger (D) walked off of an honor farm after receiving death threats and threats of homosexual attacks by other inmates. He was caught two days later in a motel room. Unger (D) testified that on the day he walked off the honor farm he received an institutional telephone call in which an unidentified person threatened him with death because the caller believed Unger (D) had reported the assaults to prison officials. Unger (D) had previously been sexually attacked at the honor farm by three inmates whom he named at trial. Prior to his transfer to the honor farm Unger (D) testified that a fellow inmate had brandished a six-inch knife in an attempt to force him to engage in homosexual activities. Unger (D) was 22 years old, 155 pounds, and testified that he was not a particularly good fighter. At no time did Unger (D) report any of the incidences to the proper authorities. Unger (D) said he left the honor farm to save his life and that he planned to return once he found someone who could help him. He stated he was attempting to get enough money from friends to hire an attorney, and after obtaining legal advice, intended to return to the prison.

■ ISSUE

If an escaped inmate asserts that the conditions under which he found himself forced him to choose between escaping or being sexually assaulted is he entitled to assert the defense of necessity?

■ DECISION AND RATIONALE

(Ryan) Yes. The trial court submitted the following jury instruction (People's Instruction No. 9) over the objection of Unger (D): "The reasons, if any, given for the alleged escape are immaterial and not to be considered by you as in any way justifying or excusing, if there were in fact such reasons." The trial court refused to submit jury instructions that provided that for the affirmative defenses of (1) necessity, and (2) compulsion (duress). Illinois (P) contends that as a matter of law neither defense is available to

Unger (D). We agree with the appellate court finding that the giving of People's Instruction No. 9 was reversible error. We also hold that it was reversible error for the trial court to not instruct on the defense of necessity. The defenses of duress and necessity have both been allowed in prison escape situations. In *People v. Harmon*, the defense of duress was held to apply in a case where the defendant alleged that he escaped in order to avoid repeated homosexual attacks by fellow inmates. In *People v. Lovercamp*, a limited defense of necessity was held to be available to two defendants whose escapes were allegedly motivated by fear of homosexual attacks. If Unger's (D) testimony is believed, he was forced to choose between two admitted evils by the situation which arose from actual or threatened homosexual assaults and fears of reprisal. Unger's (D) testimony (of previous attacks, and threatened further attacks, and of death threats) was sufficient to justify the giving of a necessity instruction. Illinois (P) insists that the following test from *Lovercamp* is the appropriate test to follow in order to decide if a necessity instruction is proper: (1) The prisoner is faced with a specific threat of death, forcible sexual attack or substantial bodily injury in the immediate future; (2) There is no time for a complaint to the authorities or there exists a history of futile complaints which make any result from such complaints illusory; (3) There is no time or opportunity to resort to the courts; (4) There is no evidence of force or violence used towards prison personnel or other 'innocent' persons in the escape; and (5) The prisoner immediately reports to the proper authorities when he has attained a position of safety from the immediate threat. These conditions are relevant factors to be considered in assessing a claim of necessity. However, we do not hold that each condition is, as a matter of law, necessary to establish a meritorious necessity defense. These conditions go to the weight and credibility of a defendant's testimony. The absence of one or more of the conditions listed would not necessarily mandate a finding that a defendant could not assert the defense of necessity. The absence of one condition does not alone disprove the claim of necessity and should not, therefore, automatically preclude an instruction on the defense.

Analysis:

The court decides that necessity is an appropriate defense here because (1) Unger (D) was not deprived of his free will by the threat of imminent physical harm (compulsion/duress), and (2) Unger's (D) testimony was sufficient to raise the affirmative defense of necessity. The credibility of Unger's (D) testimony, of course, is left to the jury to determine. The court was not saying that Unger's (D) testimony was believable only that his testimony was sufficient to raise the defense of necessity and entitle him to a jury instruction. The court noted that a defense of compulsion would be applicable in the unlikely event that a prisoner was coerced by the threat of imminent physical harm to perform the specific act of escape. Necessity is a justification defense. Duress is an excuse defense.

■ CASE VOCABULARY

DURESS: To place another person under duress is to unlawfully coerce that person to commit an unlawful act which that person would not otherwise commit.

People v. Anderson

(*Prosecution*) v. (*Murderer of Suspected Child Molester*)
28 Cal.4th 767, 122 Cal.Rptr.2d 587, 50 P.3d 368 (2002)

DURESS IS NO DEFENSE TO MURDER, BUT MAY BE A DEFENSE TO THE UNDERLYING FELONY IN FELONY MURDER CASES

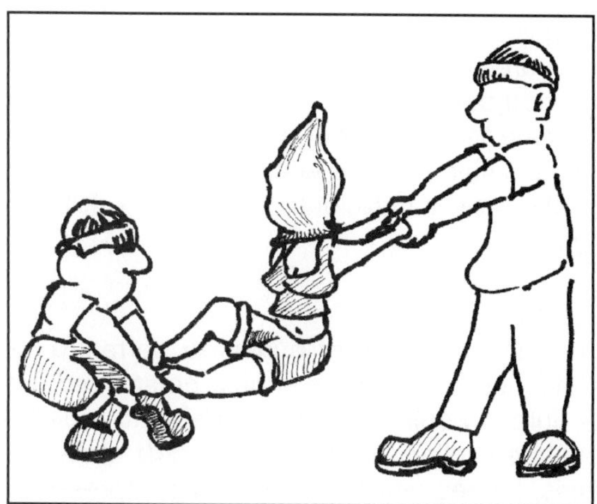

■ **INSTANT FACTS** Defendant and Ron Kiern kidnapped Margaret Armstrong and Defendant subsequently killed Armstrong at the direction of Kiern, who threatened to harm Defendant if he didn't kill Armstrong.

■ **BLACK LETTER RULE** Duress is not recognized as a valid defense to murder nor will it serve to reduce a murder charge to manslaughter.

■ PROCEDURAL BASIS

Defendant appeals his first-degree murder conviction.

■ FACTS

Ron Kiern and Defendant strongly suspected Margaret Armstrong of molesting two girls, one of whom was Kiern's daughter. Defendant and Kiern kidnapped Armstrong. Defendant killed Armstrong at a camp area near Eureka, but claimed that he did it because Kiern threatened to "beat the shit out of him" if he didn't do it. Kiern pled guilty to second-degree murder. Defendant's case proceeded to a jury trial where he was convicted of first-degree murder and kidnapping.

■ ISSUE

Will the existence of duress create either a defense to first-degree murder or serve to reduce the offense of murder to the lesser crime of manslaughter?

■ DECISION AND RATIONALE

(Chin, J.) No. Duress is not recognized as a valid defense to murder nor will it serve to reduce a murder charge to manslaughter. Common law doctrine dictates that duress is never an excuse for murder because a person threatened with his own demise ought to die himself rather than escape by the murder of an innocent person. The rationale behind allowing a duress defense is that, when faced with two evils, a defendant should be allowed to choose the lesser evil, even if it means taking unlawful action. This rational breaks down, however, when a defendant commits murder under duress because the resulting harm, the death of an innocent person, is at least as great as the harm threatened, presumably the death of the defendant. We find that the better policy, in such a situation, is to require people to resist rather than to kill an innocent person. Defendant argues that when the California Legislature adopted the Penal Code in 1872, it made duress a defense to some murders. Section 26, on which Defendant relies, indicates that persons under duress are not capable of committing crimes, but creates an exception for those crimes punishable by death. Under Defendant's argument, those crimes that allow the defense of duress would fluctuate with changes to the State's death penalty law. In 1850, all murder was punishable by death. In 1872, when the current Penal Code was adopted, only first-degree murder was punishable by death. Today, only first-degree murder, with special circumstances is punishable by death. We do not believe that the Legislature intended that the substantive law of duress should change every time there were changes to the death penalty law. Nor do we see any reason for the Legislature to have silently overruled the common law. Indeed, there are perhaps even more reasons today to encourage a person to resist rather than kill an innocent person. Without this interpretation of section 26, many gang-related murders could be justified under the duress defense. We find that accepting the duress defense for any form of murder would encourage killing. Absent stronger language than that found in section 26, we do not believe that the Legislature intended to remove killing under duress from the typical sanctions of criminal law. We conclude that duress is not a defense to any form of murder. Defendant also argues that duress should, at the very least, serve to reduce a murder charge to manslaughter because it negates the malice element. Although we do understand Defendant's argument, we find that because duress can often arrive in a criminal gang context, any changes made to the law of duress are best addressed by the Legislature. Often too, as Defendant argues, the existence of duress may serve to negate the element of premeditation. While we agree that this is true, in this case the jury found that premeditation was present. This is an issue best left to the jury to decide. Until the Legislature determines otherwise, a malicious, premeditated killing, is first-degree murder, even when duress is involved. Affirmed.

■ CONCURRENCE

(Kennard, J.) In that the Defendant failed to present substantial evidence of duress to warrant a jury instruction on this matter, I agree with the majority that Defendant's conviction should be affirmed. I do not, however, agree with the majority that the defense of duress would never be available to a person charged with murder. Here, it is not unreasonable to construe section 26 in a manner that makes the defense of duress available to all but capital murder crimes. Indeed, such a construction represents a moderate approach that is very much in keeping with mainstream legal thinking. Indeed, the Model Penal Code allows the defense of duress to be asserted against all criminal charges, including murder. I find that, in enacting section 26, the Legislature could reasonably have concluded that the same small category of offenses that warrant the death penalty are the only ones to which duress should not be a defense. It would also be perfectly reasonable to conclude that the Legislature worded section 26 so that this subsection of crimes could change as public policy shifted views as to which crimes should be punished by death.

Analysis:

In the absence of a statute addressing duress as a defense, most case law has held that duress will not excuse murder, although it may excuse the underlying felony that would otherwise support felony murder. The *Anderson* Court notes that the trial court did, in fact, instruct the jury that duress could be a defense to the kidnapping charge. In spite of the instruction, the jury still found the defendant guilty of kidnapping. If, however, the jury had found the defendant not guilty of the kidnapping charge, then they could not find that he killed during the commission of the underlying felony. Under the court's reasoning, the Defendant would not be guilty of felony murder for killing during the commission of a felony for which he was found not guilty. Do you think the court is correct in its analysis?

■ CASE VOCABULARY

DURESS: Traditionally used to mean a threat of confinement, but now broadened to mean any threat used to compel a person to do something against his will.

WILLIAM BLACKSTONE: (1723–80) Sir William Blackstone was a famous English judge and writer on law; he wrote what is referred to as "Blackstone's Commentaries," a commentary on the common law of England often referred to in Anglo-American courts.

Commonwealth v. Graves

(Pennsylvania) v. *(Drunk, High, and Forgetful Robber)*
461 Pa. 118, 334 A.2d 661 (1975)

VOLUNTARY INTOXICATION DOES NOT EXCUSE, BUT MAY NEGATE THE INTENT ELEMENT OF THE CRIME CHARGED

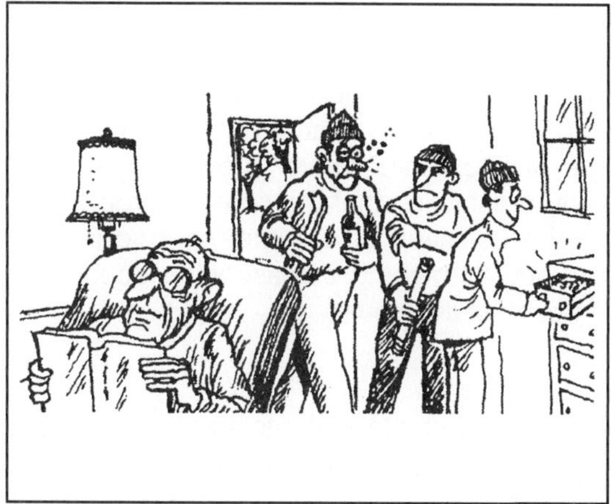

■ **INSTANT FACTS** Graves (D), while intoxicated and high, burglarized, robbed, and injured an old man who subsequently died from his injuries; Graves' (D) conviction for murder was reversed (and a new trial awarded) by the state supreme court.

■ **BLACK LETTER RULE** Although voluntary intoxication is not an excuse for unlawful actions, evidence thereof may be introduced to negate the intent requirement of the crime charged.

■ PROCEDURAL BASIS

On appeal to the Pennsylvania Supreme Court which reversed the conviction for murder and ordered a new trial.

■ FACTS

Pursuant to a prior conceived plan, Daniel Graves (D) (Graves) and his cousins Thomas and Edward Mathis burglarized the home of 75-year-old Sebastiano Patiri, and robbed him. Mr. Patiri later died from injuries sustained in the robbery. Graves (D) testified that on the day of the incident he drank a quart or more of wine and took a pill which was LSD. He testified that this caused him to hallucinate (seeing such things as cars jumping over each other), and that he became unconscious and suffered limited amnesia. He contended that he had no recollection of the occurrence at Mr. Patiri's home. A professional psychiatrist (doctor) testified that he gave Graves (D) a polygraph and a sodium amytal test which confirmed that Graves (D) was telling the truth about ingesting the wine and LSD. The doctor testified that in his opinion, because Graves (D) was under the influence of these intoxicants that "he wasn't able to form the proper conscious intent to take a life, to assault." Graves' (D) counsel than asked the doctor his opinion as to whether Graves (D) could, at the time of the incident, form the specific intent to take or steal from a person. The court sustained Pennsylvania's (P) objection to this question. The court rejected Graves' (D) request for a jury instruction that set forth that if they found Graves (D) incapable of forming the intent to commit burglary or robbery because of the consumption of wine or the ingestion of the drug, or both, he could not be guilty of these offenses.

■ ISSUE

Can evidence of voluntary intoxication be admitted to negate an element of the crime charged?

■ DECISION AND RATIONALE

(Nix, J.) Yes. The trial court erred in denying Graves (D) the opportunity to introduce evidence of the effect of intoxication on his ability to form the requisite intent of the crimes of burglary and robbery. The trial court relied on a previous opinion of this court which we now reverse to the extent that it suggests that evidence of intoxication offered for the purpose of negating the presence of specific intent may not be used in cases other than felonious homicide. The trial court incorrectly held that the evidence of intoxication was irrelevant as to the robbery and burglary charges. For many years we have admitted testimony of intoxication in the most serious crime in this commonwealth, i.e., murder in the first degree. To now contend that it would be less reliable in lesser offenses would be the height of absurdity. We also find that the trial court committed reversible error when it refused to permit evidence and to charge the jury as to the possible effect of Graves' (D) consumption of alcohol and ingestion of drugs upon his capacity to form the requisite intent required in the charges of robbery and burglary. In addition, in view of the fact that the jury was given the option to consider the case under a theory of felony-murder, the finding of murder in the first degree is overturned. The sentence is reversed and a new trial awarded. It is fundamental law in this jurisdiction that voluntary intoxication neither exonerates nor excuses criminal conduct. The only permissible probative value evidence of intoxication may have in criminal proceedings is where it is relevant to the question of the capacity of the defendant to have possessed the requisite intent of the crime charged. Evidence of intoxication becomes relevant if the degree of inebriation has reached that point where the mind was incapable of attaining the state of mind required. It must be emphasized that although evidence of intoxication never provides a basis for exoneration or excuse, it may in some instances be relevant to establish that the crime charged in fact did not occur. When the legislature has included within the definition of a crime, specific intent or deliberation and premeditation, then this element must be proved beyond a reasonable doubt. The defendant must be allowed to produce relevant evidence to contest the issue.

■ DISSENT

In the instances where an individual has voluntarily placed himself in a state of intoxication so as to be incapable of conceiving any intent, we have permitted evidence of such intoxication to lower the degree of guilt within a crime, but only where the legislature has specifically provided for varying degrees of guilt within a crime. Thus, murder in the first degree may be reduced to murder in the second degree. There exist no analogous degrees of robbery. The majority has adopted a new position which, in effect, will allow voluntary intoxication to serve as an excuse for criminal responsibility. An individual who places himself in a position to have no control over his actions must be held to intend the consequences. It matters little that the majority regards such evidence as only bearing upon an element of the crime, the specific intent of the perpetrator, rather than serving as a defense to the crime. The end result is the same and no amount of legal jargon will make it otherwise.

Analysis:

The felony-murder option given to the jury goes to the question of Graves's (D) ability to form the specific intent to take or steal from a person. That is why his attorney asked the doctor if, in his opinion, Graves (D) could form the intent necessary to steal from a person. The court did not allow the doctor to answer. Upon retrial, the testimony of intoxication was allowed so that Graves (D) could argue he did not have the *intent* to commit the crimes which he *in fact* committed. Of course, Mr. Patiri is still dead, whether Graves (D) "meant to" harm him or not. Here, the court is allowing a person who voluntarily placed himself in the situation that caused the harm to argue he was not responsible for the harm because he was too drunk.

■ CASE VOCABULARY

COMMONWEALTH: Used in the sense of a "State," i.e., a group of people choosing self-government, and which is local in nature, but also a necessary part of a nation.

SODIUM AMYTAL TEST: An hypnotic, sedative drug used to elicit feelings and/or memories; it is commonly, but incorrectly, referred to as a truth serum.

United States v. Freeman

(*Government*) v. (*Chronic Drug Abuser*)

357 F.2d 606 (2d Cir. 1966)

THE MODEL PENAL CODE STANDARD REPLACES *M'NAGHTEN* AND ITS UPGRADES AS THE TEST FOR CRIMINAL RESPONSIBILITY

■ **INSTANT FACTS** Freeman (D), a chronic drug abuser and alcoholic, was convicted of the sale of narcotics using the *M'Naghten* Rules to determine his criminal liability.

■ **BLACK LETTER RULE** Model Penal Code Section 4.01, which emphasizes "appreciation" of conduct, rather than simply knowing whether it is right or wrong, should be used in place of the narrow *M'Naghten* Rules to determine whether a defendant lacks criminal responsibility due to mental impairment or defect.

■ PROCEDURAL BASIS

Appeal from a conviction for two counts of selling narcotics.

■ FACTS

Charles Freeman (D) was tried and found guilty on two counts of selling narcotics, and he was sentenced to concurrent five year terms for each count. At trial Freeman (D) alleged that, at the time of sale of the narcotics, he did not possess sufficient capacity and will to be held responsible for the criminality of his acts. The District Court rejected this contention and relied on the *M'Naghten* Rules which allow acquittal only when it is proved that "at the time of committing the act, the party accused was laboring under such a defect of reason, from disease of the mind as not to know the nature and quality of the act he was doing, or, if he did know it, that he did not know he was doing what was wrong." Freeman (D) consumed large amounts of heroin over a fourteen-year period, and was in the habit of consuming one or two bottles of wine per day to increase the effect of the drugs. Freeman (D) also drank six to nine shots of whiskey each day. A psychiatrist, Dr. Denber, observed that Freeman (D) displayed no variation in his emotional reactions, speaking in a flat monotone. As a result of taking impure narcotics for so long, Freeman (D) suffered from frequent episodes of toxic psychosis, characterized by an inability to know what he was doing or where he was. Freeman (D) also boxed for a period of time, and suffered three knock-outs, which led to a general vagueness about details [details like where he was, or what his name is]. Denber noted that Freeman (D) had suffered innumerable brain traumata, which over time resulted in the destruction of brain tissue. Denber initially testified that Freeman (D) was incapable of knowing right from wrong. Later, he acknowledged that Freeman (D) had an awareness of what he was doing in the sense that he knew that he was selling heroin. A psychiatrist called by the Government (P), Dr. Carson, testified that Freeman (D) was able to distinguish between right and wrong within the meaning of the *M'Naghten* test despite his heavy use of narcotics and alcohol. He noted that Freeman (D) possessed the capacity to enter into purposeful conduct and recognized that it was wrong, as evidenced by the fact that Freeman (D) was fearful of being apprehended and sought to conduct the sale in a private location [the men's room]. Carson acknowledged that Freeman (D) had some limitations on his ability to distinguish right from wrong, but not to the degree required by the *M'Naghten* test. The court held that Freeman's (D) condition did not satisfy the requirements of this test, and he was found guilty as charged.

■ ISSUE

Should the trial court have applied a less rigid test than the *M'Naghten* rules, so that psychiatric testimony could have been directed towards the defendant's capacity to appreciate the wrongfulness of his conduct, rather than being confined to *M'Naghten's* narrow "right-wrong" inquiry?

■ DECISION AND RATIONALE

(Kaufman, J.) Yes. Before the *M'Naghten* test was established, the concepts of phrenology and monomania were being developed, and had significant influence on *M'Naghten's* right and wrong test. The rule of *M'Naghten's* case froze these concepts into the common law just as they were becoming obsolete. *M'Naghten* focuses on the ability to know right from wrong, so it does not permit the jury to identify those who can distinguish between right and wrong but cannot control their behavior. The test is also unrealistic because it does not recognize degrees of incapacity. Our mental institutions are filled with people who to some extent can differentiate between right and wrong, but lack the capacity to control their actions. A fatal defect in the *M'Naghten* rules stems from the excessive limitations placed on expert psychiatric testimony—the expert is compelled to test guilt or innocence by a concept which bears little relation to reality. The "irresistible impulse" test was created as a substitute to the *M'Naghten* rules. However, the irresistible impulse rule is inherently inadequate and unsatisfactory. The irresistible impulse test is unduly restrictive because it excludes the far more numerous instances of crimes committed after excessive brooding and melancholy by a person who is unable to control his conduct. The *Durham* test, articulated in 1954, stated that a defendant is not criminally responsible "if his unlawful act was the product of mental disease or mental defect." *Durham* eliminated the *M'Naghten* "right-wrong" dichotomy. However, the *Durham* rule also fails to give the fact-finder any standard by which to measure the competency of the defendant. As a result, psychiatrists testifying that the defendant suffered from a mental disorder effectively usurped the jury's function as the fact-finder. In 1962, the American Law Institute adopted Section 4.01 of the Model Penal Code. Unlike the *M'Naghten* rules, the Model Penal Code formulation is in harmony with modern medical science, since it views the mind as a unified entity and recognizes that mental disease may impair its functioning in numerous ways. The use of the word "substantial" to modify "incapacity" emphasizes that "any" capacity is not sufficient to avoid criminal responsibility but that "total" incapacity is also unnecessary. The choice of the word "appreciate," rather than "know," is significant because mere intellectual awareness that conduct is wrongful, when separated from understanding of the moral import of the behavior, can have little significance. Since Freeman's (D) responsibility was determined under the rigid standards of the *M'Naghten* Rules, we are compelled to reverse his conviction and remand the case for a new trial using Model Penal Code Section 4.01 to determine his responsibility. We wish to emphasize, however, that mere recidivism or narcotics addiction will not justify acquittal under Section 4.01. We also emphasize that those suffering from mental disease or defect, while relieved from criminal responsibility, should not be set free to continue to pose a threat to life and property. Those adjudged criminally irresponsible should be turned over to state officials for commitment to a mental hospital pursuant to state procedures. Conviction reversed and remanded.

■ CONCURRENCE

(Waterman, J.) We have now been persuaded that we should be dissatisfied with the *M'Naghten* Rules because of the discoveries which have, over the course of the 120 years since *M'Naghten*, changed our concepts of mental disease. It is nevertheless true that the scope of serious expert inquiry into the control of conduct has not halted. Tomorrow we may find that Section 4.01 needs further judicial adjustment in light of tomorrow's further discoveries.

Analysis:

The Model Penal Code formulation was repudiated in 1984 in favor of a right-wrong, *M'Naghten*-style test. Nevertheless, a number of states have accepted the Model Penal Code test, some by statute and some by court decision. The "substantial capacity" test, though appreciated by the court in *Freeman*, has been criticized as refurbishing the *M'Naghten* and irresistible-impulse rules. Generally, the words "substantial capacity" and "appreciate" have been criticized because they do not have a stable meaning, and jurors and experts are bound to have various competing interpretations. Overall, the Model Penal Code formulation has been praised by commentators as achieving two important goals of a test of responsibility: the formulation gives expression to an intelligible principle, and it fully discloses that principle to the jury.

■ CASE VOCABULARY

PHRENOLOGY: A rejected science that believed character could be determined by the shape and contours of the skull.

RECIDIVISM: A chronic relapse into crime; repeatedly offending.

State v. Johnson

(*Rhode Island*) v. (*Not Stated*)
121 R.I. 254, 399 A.2d 469 (1979)

HISTORY OF THE INSANITY DEFENSE: M'NAGHTEN TO THE MODEL PENAL CODE, BACK TO M'NAGHTEN (SORT OF)

■ **INSTANT FACTS** *Johnson* sets forth the development of the insanity test.

■ **BLACK LETTER RULE** A new standard that allows a jury to consider volitional as well as cognitive impairments before imposing criminal responsibility supercedes the restrictive M'Naghten rule.

■ PROCEDURAL BASIS

Not Stated.

■ FACTS

Not Stated.

■ ISSUE

Should the M'Naghten test be abandoned in favor of a new standard for determining the criminal responsibility of those who claim they are blameless by reason of mental illness?

■ DECISION AND RATIONALE

(Doris, J.) Yes. Any legal standard designed to determine criminal responsibility must satisfy several objectives, among which are the following: It must accurately reflect the underlying principles of substantive law and community values; it must comport with the realities of scientific understanding and the scientific information must be articulated in such a way that the experts, lawyers, and jury understand it; the definition of such standard must preserve to the trier of fact its full authority to render a final decision on the issue of criminal responsibility. The time has arrived to modernize our rule. We set forth below a brief evolution of criminal responsibility and its criticisms, and adopt "a version" of the Model Penal Code (MPC) which has received widespread and evergrowing acceptance. We believe it represents a significant, positive improvement over our existing rule. It acknowledges that volitional as well as cognitive impairments must be considered by the jury in its resolution of the responsibility issue. Additionally, the test employs vocabulary sufficiently in the common ken that its use at trial will permit a reasonable three-way dialogue between the law-trained judges and lawyers, the medical-trained experts, and the jury. The "knowledge of good and evil" test of criminal responsibility had its inception in England in the 1500's with an emphasis on the "good and evil" part. It shifted in the 1700's to emphasize the "knowing" part. These tests were evolving during a time when beliefs in demonology and witchcraft were widespread; a time when psychiatry was hardly a profession, let alone a science. The psychological theories of phrenology and monomania thrived and influenced the development of the "right and wrong" test. Both of these compartmentalized concepts have been soundly rejected by modern medical science which views the human personality as a fully integrated system. The celebrated and controversial case of Daniel M'Naghten (tried in 1843) froze these concepts into the common law just at the time they were beginning to come into disrepute. The M'Naghten rule

(M'Naghten) is the following two-pronged test: "To establish a defense on the ground of insanity it must be clearly proved that, at the time of committing the act, the party accused was laboring under such a defect of reason, from disease of the mind, as not to know the nature and quality of the act he was doing, or if he did know it, that he did not know that what he was doing was wrong." The test's emphasis upon knowledge of right and wrong refuses to recognize volitional or emotional impairments, viewing the cognitive element as the singular cause of conduct. This requires the psychiatrist to testify in terms of unrealistic concepts having no medical meaning. The rule calls for the psychiatrist to render a moral or ethical judgment, not a scientific opinion, and takes away the jury's function as the decision maker. The M'Naghten rule was supplemented by the "irresistible impulse" test. It adds a volitional component to the cognitive component of M'Naghten, but still in absolute terms. The irresistible impulse is considered in terms of a complete destruction of the governing power of the mind. It misleadingly suggests that such impulses only happen in sudden bursts, and ignores the more common instances of crimes committed after excessive brooding and melancholy by one who is unable to resist sustained physic compulsion. The "Durham" test, although subsequently abandoned, was a significant break with M'Naghten. The Durham test was designed to allow full and complete testimony and allow the jury to consider all relevant evidence. The basic idea of the Durham test is that "an accused is not criminally responsible if his unlawful act was the product of mental disease or mental defect." The undefined scope of "product" of mental disease did not give enough guidance to the jury, and the expert testimony infringed upon the jury's role. Although the test created a great deal of commentary and helped recast the law of criminal responsibility, it was unworkable in practice. After years of criticism of these tests, a new test of criminal responsibility which we have adopted "a version of" today, was provided by the MPC.

Analysis:

The commentary to § 4.01 of the MPC sets forth a standard that "relieves the defendant of responsibility under two circumstances: (1) when, as a result of mental disease or defect, the defendant lacked substantial capacity to appreciate the criminality or wrongfulness of his conduct; and (2) when, as a result of mental disease or defect, the defendant lacked substantial capacity to conform his conduct to the requirements of law. Notice the use of the word "appreciate" as opposed to "know" in part 1 of the MPC standard. The capacity to conform one's conduct is the volitional aspect of the standard. The MPC standard was adopted by a majority of the states. After John Hinckley's attempted assassination of President Reagan and his subsequent insanity acquittal, at least four states eliminated the defense of insanity. Several states reverted to M'Naghten. In 1984, Congress adopted the Insanity Defense Reform Act which allows the affirmative defense of insanity when, as a result of a severe mental disease or defect the defendant was unable to appreciate the nature and quality or the wrongfulness of his acts. Mental disease or defect does not otherwise constitute a defense.

■ CASE VOCABULARY

KEN: "Barbie's significant other, a.k.a., boy toy" Within the range of what one knows; knowledge or consciousness.

MONOMANIA: A mental state characterized by an obsessive interest in a particular idea.

PHRENOLOGY: A theory that the brain was divided up into various sections, each section impacted a different mental function.

VOLITION: The willful exercise of choosing or deciding to act.

State v. Wilson

(*Connecticut*) v. (*Delusional ["gonna save the world"] Shooter*)

242 Conn. 605, 700 A.2d 633 (1997)

DEFINITION OF "WRONGFULNESS" FOR INSANITY DEFENSE INCLUDES NOT ONLY APPRECIATION OF LEGAL WRONG, BUT ALSO OF MORAL WRONG

■ **INSTANT FACTS** Wilson (D) shot to death a friend's father (Jack) because he thought Jack was the mastermind of a huge conspiracy to control everyone's mind, particularly Wilson's (D) mind.

■ **BLACK LETTER RULE** Even if a defendant appreciates that his actions were illegal, if he believes, due to his mental disease or defect, that his actions were morally justified (society would condone his actions if it understood the situation like the defendant understands the situation) then he will not be criminally responsible for his actions.

■ PROCEDURAL BASIS

On appeal to the Supreme Court of Connecticut reversing the conviction and remanding for a new trial.

■ FACTS

Wilson (D) and Jack Peter's (Jack) son, Dirk Peters (Dirk) had attended high school together. On August 5, 1993, Wilson (D) went to Jack's home, argued with him, then shot Jack numerous times with a semiautomatic revolver which he had purchased two days prior. Jack died. Wilson (D) went to the police after the shooting and gave a sworn statement which included the following: (1) his life had been ruined by Dirk, who had drugged, hypnotized and brainwashed him; (2) Jack had assisted Dirk in these activities; (3) Dirk and Jack were responsible for his schizophrenia; (4) the conduct of Dirk and Jack required "drastic action" and "drastic retribution"; and (5) he had shot Jack repeatedly at Jack's home earlier that day. Wilson (D) believed that Jack was the mastermind of a large organization bent on controlling the minds of others and was responsible for Wilson's (D) pathetic life (mom dead, pets dead, girlfriend gone, unemployed, sexually inadequate, physically weak, and drug addicted). Wilson (D) had, during the first half of 1993, repeatedly called police to inform them of Jack's evil plans, but the police told Wilson (D) that it was impossible for them to investigate his allegations. At trial, Wilson (D) requested (and was denied) a jury instruction which incorporates a moral element into the definition of "wrongfulness" such that "an accused is not criminally responsible for his offending act if, because of mental disease or defect, he believes that he is morally justified in his conduct—even though he may appreciate that his act is criminal." The jury rejected Wilson's (D) claim of insanity and convicted him for murder. He was sentenced to sixty years imprisonment. Upon appeal, Wilson (D) argues that the trial court's denial to instruct the jury on the moral component of the insanity defense is reversible error. Wilson (D) argues that the morality element of "wrongfulness" must be defined in purely personal terms. Connecticut (P) argues that morality must be defined by an objective societal standard.

■ ISSUE

Is a defendant criminally responsible for his illegal actions if, because of his mental disease or defect, he believes that he is morally justified in his conduct, although he may appreciate that his actions are legally criminal?

■ DECISION AND RATIONALE

(Palmer, J.) No. Our statute, § 53a-1(a), which is modeled after the Model Penal Code (MPC) allows for the affirmative defense of insanity. It states that "in any prosecution for an offense, it shall be an affirmative defense that the defendant, at the time he committed the proscribed act or acts, lacked substantial capacity, as a result of mental disease or defect, either to appreciate the wrongfulness of his conduct or to control his conduct within the requirements of the law." Three features of the MPC are noteworthy. First, similar to, but not exactly like, our prior common law standard, this test incorporates both a cognitive (to appreciate the wrongfulness of his conduct) and volitional (to control his conduct within the requirements of the law) prong. Second, the test focuses on the defendant's actual appreciation of, not merely his knowledge of, the wrongfulness of his conduct. To *appreciate* the wrongfulness of one's conduct is to understand beyond the bare abstraction of the fact that a certain action is wrong, but to grasp the importance and reality of the conduct. Third, and most important here, is the juxtaposition in the MPC of the word "criminality" with the bracketed word "wrongfulness." The drafters of the MPC did this in order to allow the individual states to decide which of these two standards to adopt to describe the nature of the conduct that a defendant must be unable to appreciate in order to qualify as legally insane. The history of the MPC indicates that "wrongfulness" incorporates a moral element. It is without dispute Connecticut's (P) legislature intended to include this moral element in its insanity statute. We do not agree with Wilson (D) that the standard is completely personal, and although we do agree with Connecticut (P) that there is a societal moral standard involved in the statute, it is not as narrow as Connecticut (P) insists. (Connecticut (P) argued for an objective standard which would mean that "criminality" and "wrongfulness" would be interpreted the same way, which would render meaningless the legislature's choice of the term "wrongfulness.") We need to point out that Wilson's (D) attempt to define morality in purely personal terms are inconsistent with the MPC, judicial precedent, and the assumptions underlying our criminal law. The text accompanying the MPC indicates that a person who appreciates *both* that his conduct violates the criminal law and society's moral standards, should not be allowed the defense of insanity just because of his personal, albeit delusional, moral code. In addition, the large majority of jurisdictions that have considered this cognitive prong of the defense, follow a societal, rather than a personal, standard. Finally, defining the moral element of wrongfulness according to a purely personal standard would undermine the moral culture on which our societal norms of behavior are based. We conclude that a defendant may establish that he lacked substantial capacity to appreciate the "wrongfulness" of his conduct if he can prove that, at the time of his criminal act, as a result of mental disease or defect, he substantially misperceived reality and harbored a delusional belief that society, *under the circumstances as the defendant honestly but mistakenly understood them*, would not have morally condemned his actions. [Highlight the sentence you just read; it is the court's rule for the definition of "wrongfulness."] If a defendant appreciated that his conduct violated the criminal law, yet sincerely believed (due to his mental disease or defect) that society *would* approve of his conduct *if* it shared his understanding of the circumstances underlying his actions, he would be entitled to prevail on the defense. Connecticut (P) argues that Wilson (D) did not provide sufficient evidence to support an instruction on the definition of "wrongfulness." Connecticut (P) claims that Wilson's (D) evidence only tended to show that he followed his own purely personal moral standard. Three expert witnesses who all examined Wilson (D) testified to the effect that he actually believed that by killing Jack he was saving the world from Jack's evil plans. On the basis of this testimony, we conclude that Wilson (D) presented sufficient evidence to support the instruction because a jury reasonably could have found, by a preponderance of the evidence, that Wilson (D) misperceived reality and acting on the basis of that misperception, did not substantially appreciate that his actions were contrary to societal norms. The judgment for conviction is reversed and the case is remanded for a new trial.

■ CONCURRENCE

(Katz, J.) I concur in the result reached by the majority. I am concerned, nonetheless, that the test as interpreted by the majority may exclude certain defendants who are obviously impaired and for whom the interests of justice would not be served by a criminal conviction; specifically, those defendants who, *because of their mental illness*, adhere to a personal code of morality. In declaring that a defendant who, despite his mental illness, has the substantial capacity to appreciate social boundaries, yet nonetheless, chooses to transgress those boundaries must be held criminally responsible, the majority seeks to exclude those otherwise sane individuals who would use the insanity defense as a shield when seeking to satisfy personal grudges, or impose personal political beliefs. I wholeheartedly agree with this goal. I disagree with the majority, however, that the defense should not apply to an individual who is mentally ill and *because of that illness* believes that society's rules do not apply to his or her actions. It is my belief that such a person is not *capable of appreciating* the legal and social import of his or her acts, and therefore, should not be held criminally responsible.

■ DISSENT

(McDonald, J.) The majority approves a jury instruction that provides a definition of wrong as something against societal morality, but not objectively so. Under this formula, a person who knows murder is wrong in the eyes of society and knows that society does not share his perception that the victim needs to be killed may be excused if he believes, because of mental illness, that society would condone the killing if it, too, saw the need. This should not be written into our law. If a defendant recognizes his conduct is both criminal and wrong in the eyes of society, as murder clearly is, public safety demands that he be held responsible for his actions. It is hoped that we can still rely on the common sense of jurors, coping with these enigmatic instructions, to safeguard us.

Analysis:

The majority includes the phrase, *"under the circumstances as the defendant honestly but mistakenly understood them"* within its rule. This certainly reads like a subjective, personal standard. One study of juror behavior has shown that juries come to the same conclusion regardless of the instruction given. Another study indicates that juries use their own sense of justice to evaluate the testimony and determine if the defendant is not guilty by reason of insanity. The majority notes that a person who was following a delusional "deific command" might fall within a category of cases in which a person's delusional personal beliefs so clouded his cognition as to render him incapable of recognizing the broader moral implications of his actions. This person, the majority states, would be entitled to an acquital under the cognitive prong of the insanity defense. Can a person who believes that he is *morally justified* in his actions, despite appreciating the illegality of his actions, be deterred (this time or next) by the prospect of criminal punishment? Will criminal punishment rehabilitate such a person? A person who is incapable of understanding that his delusion is in fact a delusion is probably not going to be deterred.

■ CASE VOCABULARY

DEIFIC: Making divine; a deific command is an instruction from God.

DELUSIONAL: To hold a steadfast belief in an idea that is contrary to facts and logic.

ENIGMATIC: Puzzling or mysterious.

JUXTAPOSITION: Words or things which are next to each other, or placed side by side in order to compare them.

TRANSGRESS: To violate the law; to go beyond the established boundaries.

State v. Green

(*Tennessee*) v. (*Unbathed, Ousiograph-hunting Cop Killer*)
643 S.W.2d 902 (1982)

ONCE A DEFENDANT PRODUCES EVIDENCE OF INSANITY, PROSECUTION MUST PROVE SANITY BEYOND A REASONABLE DOUBT

■ **INSTANT FACTS** Eighteen year old Steven Green's (D) conviction for murder of a police officer was set aside because Tennessee's (P) rebuttal evidence was not sufficient to refute the overwhelming proof of Green's insanity.

■ **BLACK LETTER RULE** Prosecution has the burden to prove beyond a reasonable doubt a defendant's sanity in order to rebut a defendant's evidence of his insanity.

■ PROCEDURAL BASIS

On appeal to the Court of Criminal Appeals of Tennessee setting aside the conviction for murder because of Green's insanity.

■ FACTS

Steven Green (D) (Green), beginning at the age of seven years, had sudden outbursts of anger and violence, both institutionalized and out-patient psychiatric treatment, and a need to find a machine he called an "oustograph" or "ousiograph" which he believed could detect who was attempting to send messages to his brain and "direct" him. He refused to bathe, stayed in bed during the days, and walked the streets at night. He carried a bag around with him which he told his parents kept him company. He laughed at inappropriate times and would stare into space and move his mouth without saying anything. He complained that the television talked back to him. By the age of sixteen he dropped out of school, but then enrolled in a Navy reserve program, returned to school and managed to graduate in June 1978. He reported to Navy training but a few weeks later he was discharged for failure to adapt to regulations. Between this time and January 1979, his whereabouts were often unknown. He did stay with various relatives during part of this time (he stayed with an uncle for six to seven weeks, and an aunt for two weeks) who testified to Green's (D) bizarre behavior. On January 18, 1979, Chattanooga police found the body of Officer Harry Wilcox (Wilcox) lying face down in a pool of blood in a restroom at Warner Park. He had been shot twice in the head, and his police revolver was missing. On his back, officer's found a plastic bag containing a note. The note, addressed to Agent Ray Hanrahan (Hanrahan) of the FBI, contained a meaningless string of words and phrases, including reference to an "ousiograph." Police were led to Green (D) by contacting Hanrahan who Green (D) had previously contacted about finding an "ousiograph" to help detect who was sending messages to his brain. At trial, Green (D) offered both lay and expert testimony to establish that he was insane at the time he committed the offense. Tennessee (P) disputed the fact that Green (D) suffered from a mental disease or disorder. Upon appeal, Tennessee (P) argues that Green (D) had the capacity to know right from wrong and to control his behavior at will.

■ ISSUE

To rebut a defendant's evidence of insanity, must the prosecution (here, Tennessee) prove beyond a reasonable doubt that the defendant is sane?

■ DECISION AND RATIONALE

(Daughtrey, J.) Yes. Green (D) was arrested on January 20, 1979, and charged with the murder of Wilcox. In March 1979, John Littleton was hired as local counsel for Green (D). After attempting to talk with Green (D), he immediately asked for a psychiatric evaluation which the court ordered. Dr. Speal, a forensic psychologist diagnosed Green (D) as paranoid schizophrenic, a condition which is characterized by irrational thinking, feelings inappropriate to the situation, an overly suspicious nature, hostility, and delusions of grandeur and of persecution. Dr. Speal's test of Green (D) in March 1979, showed that Green (D) was psychotic at the time and suffering from auditory hallucinations. He saw Green (D) over a period of 18 months. By May 1979, it was necessary to hospitalize Green (D). He was found incompetent to stand trial. Six months later, he was found to be "greatly improved." Both Dr. Pieper and a clinical nurse who evaluated Green (D) testified that at the time Green (D) killed Wilcox he was acting under the control of delusions or hallucinations or both, that he therefore did not understand that his act was wrong and could not conform his conduct to the requirements of law. Tennessee's (P) rebuttal evidence offered to establish Green's (D) sanity at the time of the offense, consisted of testimony by five Chattanooga police officers and a former county employee. The arresting officer, who spent about two hours with Green (D), testified he was "cooperative," "coherent," and "intelligent," but did not want to talk about the shooting. The other officers (one of whom had been Wilcox's friend), who either took Green (D) to a rescue mission or arrested him for vagrancy, both before and after the killing, testified that Green (D) was cooperative, coherent, and not operating under any delusions, but was unkept and that he smelled. A former county employee gave Green (D) a ride in his van the day Wilcox was shot. He testified that he and Green (D) engaged in small talk for about 45 minutes and that he noticed nothing out of the ordinary about him. From this testimony, Tennessee (P) took the position that Green (D) was "not insane and crazy and bizarre at the time the killing happened," but was just a "little bit different." However, the testimony that described him as normal is not inconsistent with a determination that Green (D) was insane at the time of the offense. The medical experts unrefuted testimony is that a paranoid schizophrenic can operate in a seemingly normal way. Dr. Pieper testified that such a person could appear quite normal, until someone says something, or something happens which the person regards as threatening and it can set them off. Given the nature of the evidence offered by Green (D), the burden of proof in this case squarely fell upon Tennessee (P) to establish Green's (D) sanity beyond a reasonable doubt. Tennessee (P) argues that the nature of Green's (D) condition was not sufficient to meet the two prong test for insanity. It argues that evidence that Green (D) fled the scene and hid the weapon proves he knew the wrongfulness of his acts. The most obvious response to this argument is that the record shows only that Green (D) left the scene at some point and the revolver was never recovered; neither of these facts establishes beyond a reasonable doubt that Green (D) was attempting to conceal his identity nor complicity from the police, or that he otherwise was able to appreciate the wrongfulness of what he had done. Even if we conceded that this behavior evidenced some appreciation of the wrongfulness of his conduct, the record is wholly devoid of any evidence that at the time he shot Wilcox, Green (D) was able to conform his conduct to the dictates of law. Tennessee's (P) only argument in response to overwhelming evidence of Green's (D) incapacity in this respect is that he failed to react violently to the other officers he came into contact with showing his ability to conform his conduct to the law with respect to Wilcox. This argument, of course, not only begs the question (that is, whether under this analysis any initial violent behavior could ever be the product of insanity), but it also ignores the nature of paranoid schizophrenia, as described by experts in this case. Tennessee (P) points out that the jury is not bound by expert testimony. However, the Tennessee Supreme Court has clearly delineated what proof the State must produce to meet and overcome evidence of insanity. The test basically sets forth that the State can introduce evidence by expert testimony on insanity, or relevant lay testimony, or through the showing of acts or statements of the defendant, at or near the time of the commission of the crime, which are consistent with sanity and inconsistent with insanity. In this case, although the acts of Green (D) at or near the time of the killing were arguably "consistent with sanity," quite obviously they were not also "inconsistent with insanity." We have no choice but to set aside Green's (D) conviction.

Analysis:

Notice that Tennessee (P) did not offer any expert testimony to rebut Green's (D) expert testimony. Expert testimony is not required and lay testimony seemed to satisfy the jury. The expert's role is to provide information to the jury about the defendant's medical condition. It is the jury's role to determine whether the defendant in his condition should be held responsible for his actions. The appeals court noted that a reviewing court should be most wary of disturbing a jury verdict. However, it also quotes from a Supreme Court case that notes there are rare cases "where the facts adduced as to the existence and impact of an accused's mental condition may be so overwhelming as to require a judge to conclude that no reasonable juror could entertain a reasonable doubt." One commentator believes that we (society, jurors) can determine whether an individual is "crazy" without expert medical testimony, and that the decision whether to punish a "crazy" person is a social and moral judgment, not one that should be determined by an expert's opinion. His point is that medical opinions change over time as to what is a mental disorder, and that experts are often given too much authority in the courtroom, i.e., they usurp the function of the jury.

■ CASE VOCABULARY

COMPLICITY: To participate (as the actual actor or with another person) in a criminal plan or act.

DELUSIONS OF GRANDEUR: A fixed false belief that you are exalted above all other people or things (e.g., that you are royalty or a god.)

DELUSIONS OF PERSECUTION: A fixed false belief that someone or something is persistently pursuing, harassing, and/or oppressing you [like your civil procedure professor or the financial aid officer].

FORENSIC PSYCHOLOGIST: That branch of psychiatry dealing with mental disorders as they relate to legal principles.

LAY TESTIMONY: [Not expert testimony.] Given by a witness who is not an expert on the matter at hand, but generally, is testimony which is "first-hand knowledge" of the witness.

Clark v. Arizona

(*Convicted Murderer*) v. (*Prosecuting State*)
548 U.S. ___, 126 S. Ct. 2709, 165 L. Ed. 2d 842 (2006)

MENTAL–ILLNESS EVIDENCE DOES NOT BEAR ON *MENS REA*

■ **INSTANT FACTS** The defendant appealed from his conviction for murder, arguing that the evidence he offered as to his mental illness should also have been considered with regard to his ability to form the necessary *mens rea*.

■ **BLACK LETTER RULE** Under Arizona's *Mott* rule, a court will not allow evidence of a mental disorder short of insanity as bearing on a defendant's capacity to form specific intent.

■ PROCEDURAL BASIS

Supreme Court review of the defendant's conviction.

■ FACTS

A uniformed police officer responded to complaints of a pickup truck driving through a residential neighborhood in the early morning hours with loud music blaring. When he spotted the truck, the officer pulled it over, then exited his patrol car and approached the vehicle driven by seventeen-year-old Clark (D). Less than a minute later, Clark (D) shot and killed the officer and then fled on foot, but he was apprehended later that same day. Clark (D) was charged with first-degree murder under Ariz. Rev. Stat. § 13–1105(A)(3) for intentionally or knowingly killing a law enforcement officer in the line of duty.

Clark (D) was found incompetent to stand trial and was committed to a state hospital for treatment, but two years later the same court found his competence restored and ordered Clark (D) to stand trial. Clark (D) waived his right to a jury trial and argued to the court that, due to his paranoid schizophrenia, he could not have formed the requisite intent to commit the crime for which he was charged. The trial court ruled that Clark (D) could not rely on insanity evidence to negate the intent requirement and convicted Clark (D) of first-degree murder, sentencing him to life in prison. Clark (D) moved to vacate the judgment and sentence, arguing that Arizona's *Mott* rule, which the court applied in his case, violates due process. The court denied the motion and Clark (D) appealed.

■ ISSUE

Is due process violated by restricting the consideration of mental-illness evidence to its bearing on a claim of insanity, thus eliminating its significance as relating to the *mens rea* element of the crime charged?

■ DECISION AND RATIONALE

(Souter, J.) No. Under Arizona's *Mott* rule, a court will not allow evidence of a mental disorder short of insanity as bearing on a defendant's capacity to form specific intent. If a jury were free to decide how much evidence of mental disease and incapacity was enough to counter evidence of *mens rea*, to the point of creating reasonable doubt as to the defendant's guilt, that would in functional terms be analogous to allowing jurors to decide on some degree of diminished capacity to obey the law, which would then prevail as a standalone defense.

Three categories of evidence have a bearing on *mens rea*. First, there is *observational evidence*, which includes testimony from those who observed what the defendant did and said at and around the time of the incident in question. In this case, for example, it included the evidence that Clark (D) thought local residents' bodies were inhabited by aliens. Observation evidence can be presented by either expert or lay witnesses. Second, *mental-disease evidence* is offered in the form of opinion testimony that a defendant, such as Clark (D) here, suffered from a mental disease. This evidence usually comes from an expert such as a psychiatrist. In this case, a doctor testified that Clark (D) was psychotic at the time in question and that he suffered from schizophrenia. And third, there is *capacity evidence*, which relates to the defendant's capacity to form a moral judgment, which goes to the ability to form the necessary *mens rea*. Here, as is usual, this testimony came from the same experts who testified about the defendant's mental condition. The *Mott* rule imposes no restrictions on the consideration of observational evidence; rather, it applies only to mental-disease and capacity evidence. Although the trial court apparently applied the rule to all three categories of evidence in this case, Clark (D) does not contest that aspect of the ruling.

Clark (D) argues instead that the rule violates the Fourteenth Amendment's guarantee of due process. He asserts that the rule's application runs counter to the presumption that a defendant is innocent until proven guilty beyond a reasonable doubt on each element of the offense charged, including *mens rea*. But there is also a presumption under the Fourteenth Amendment of sanity. The traditional presumption of sanity varies across state and federal jurisdictions. Legislatures are given wide latitude in defining the presumption's strength, and Arizona acted within that latitude here. Moreover, the traditional right to introduce relevant evidence may be curtailed if there is a sufficiently good reason for doing so. Arizona had such a good reason in this case because it has the authority to define its presumption of sanity and place the burden of persuasion on the defendant. Moreover, the *Mott* rule serves to avoid juror confusion. Accordingly, the *Mott* rule does not violate due process, and we therefore affirm the ruling of the Arizona Court of Appeals.

■ DISSENT

(Kennedy, J.) The Court incorrectly ruled that Arizona may convict Clark (D) of first-degree murder for the intentional or knowing of a police officer when Clark (D) was not permitted to introduce reliable evidence showing he did not have that intent or knowledge. Either Clark (D) knew he was killing a police officer or he did not. If his mental illness bears on this issue, evidence thereof should have been admissible on the issue of *mens rea*. The Court's evidentiary framework is simply unworkable and unjust as applied here.

The fact that mental-illness evidence may be considered in deciding criminal responsibility does not compensate for its exclusion from consideration on the *mens rea* element of the crime. The Court's decision forces the jury to decide guilt in a fictional world with undefined and unexplained behavior, but without mental illness. This rule has no rational justification and imposes a significant burden on a straightforward defense: Clark (D) did not commit the crime with which he was charged.

Analysis:

Courts have recognized for centuries that criminal defendants who lack understanding of their actions also lack moral culpability, and therefore should be treated differently by the legal system than other, more culpable defendants. In recent years, however, some cases have raised concerns that the insanity defense goes too far. When John Hinckley was found not guilty by reason of insanity for shooting then-President Ronald Reagan, for instance, some thought that the law was too liberally applied, which led to widespread reassessment of the insanity defense. Courts continue to struggle with balancing the need for uniformity in the enforcement of criminal justice standards against the recognition that mentally ill persons must, in appropriate cases, be afforded special treatment.

■ CASE VOCABULARY

MENS REA: The state of mind that the prosecution, to secure a conviction, must prove that a defendant had when committing a crime; criminal intent or recklessness. *Mens rea* is the second of two essential elements of every crime at common law, the other being the *actus reus*.

In Re Devon T.

(*Maryland*) v. (*13-Year-Old Heroin Dealer*)
85 Md.App. 674, 584 A.2d 1287 (1991)

EVIDENCE OF KNOWLEDGE OF RIGHT AND WRONG OVERCOMES REBUTTABLE PRESUMPTION OF INFANT'S INCAPACITY

■ **INSTANT FACTS** Devon (D) (almost 14 years old) was caught at school with twenty zip-lock bags of heroin and was convicted with the equivalent of possession with intent to distribute, despite his claim of incapacity due to infancy.

■ **BLACK LETTER RULE** Rebuttable Presumption of incapacity due to infancy may be overcome with sufficient evidence of a defendant's capacity to distinguish right from wrong.

■ PROCEDURAL BASIS

On appeal to the Court of Special Appeals of Maryland affirming juvenile court's finding for delinquency (conviction).

■ FACTS

Devon T. (D) (Devon) was 13 years, 10 months, and 2 weeks of age the day a security guard at his middle school directed him to empty his pockets (the Assistant Principal was there too) which revealed a brown bag containing twenty zip-lock plastic bags which contained heroin. Devon (D) was charged with an act which, if committed by an adult, would have constituted the crime of possession of heroin with intent to distribute. He was found to be delinquent by the juvenile court. Devon (D) timely raised the defense of infancy.

■ ISSUE

Does the prosecution's evidence that the defendant knew the difference between right and wrong and knew, moreover, that what he was doing was wrong overcome the rebuttable presumption of incapacity due to infancy?

■ DECISION AND RATIONALE

(Moylan, J.) Yes. Our defense of infancy follows from the traditional M'Naghten test, from which the relevant question here relates to the cognitive question of whether Devon (D), at the time of the offense, had the cognitive capacity to distinguish right from wrong. At common law the conclusive presumption was that a child under the age of seven was incapable of criminal intent, at age fourteen was fully responsible, and for those in-between there was a rebuttable presumption of criminal incapacity. It is generally considered that the criminal law only imposes sanctions upon those who are blameworthy—those who know they are doing wrong but nonetheless persist in their wrongdoing. Our juvenile courts began as a place where rehabilitation intervention could begin. Over time, the juvenile courts took on the appearance, sanctions, and defenses of criminal courts. A finding of delinquency, unlike other proceedings in juvenile court, unmistakably exposes the delinquent to the possibility of unpleasant sanctions. Clearly, the juvenile would have the available defenses of insanity, mental retardation, and involuntary intoxication. It would be inconceivable that he could be found blameworthy and suffer sanctions, notwithstanding precisely the same lack of understanding and absence of moral accountability, simply because the cognitive defect was caused by infancy rather than by one of the other incapacitating mechanisms. The defense of infancy in a juvenile delinquency adjudication is thus available just as it would be in a criminal trial. Initially, Devon (D) had the benefit of presumptive incapacity. Maryland (P) had the burdens (of both production and persuasion) of rebutting that presumption. It had to produce evidence permitting the reasonable inference that Devon (D) at the time of doing the act knew the difference between right and wrong. In short, when Devon (D) walked around school with twenty zip-lock bags of heroin, apparently for sale or other distribution, could he pass the M'Naghten test? Was there legally sufficient data before the judge to infer that Devon (D) knew the difference between right and wrong and knew, moreover, that what he was doing was wrong? The applicable common law on doli incapax (a mind doli incapaz is incapable of malice or criminal intent, as opposed to a mind doli capax which is capable of malice and criminal intent) with relation to the infancy defense establishes that on the day before their seventh birthday, no persons possess cognitive capacity. (0 per cent). It also establishes that on the day of their fourteenth birthday, all persons possess cognitive capacity. (100 per cent). This places Devon (D) at 98.2 per cent of the way along that continuum. Statistically, this places Devon (D) with other people of his age group wherein 98.2 percent would be expected to possess cognitive capacity. [Remember your LSAT score?] The fact that the quantum of proof necessary to overcome presumptive incapacity diminishes in substantially the same ratio as the infant's age increases only serves to lesson Maryland's (P) burden, not to eliminate it. We hold that Maryland (P) successfully carried its burden. The report of the juvenile master shows that Devon (D) was within his age group for his grade level (although he had flunked the sixth grade twice due to truancy and lack of motivation), that he acknowledged he understood his attorney's advice and the significance of the fact that if he testified he could be asked about his offense. Devon (D) indicated he wished to remain silent. The exchange between Devon (D) and his attorney suggests that an observer could infer some knowledge on Devon's (D) part of the significance of incrimination. After he had been adjudicated and no further risk of incrimination was possible, the juvenile master asked Devon (D) (and a companion who had also been adjudicated delinquent) if they had any statement to make. Neither responded. The permitted inference was that the two were not mere babes caught up in a web they did not understand, but were following a well-established "Code of Silence" and were fully conscious of the ongoing war between lawful authority and those who flout it and had deliberately chosen to adhere to the latter camp. The circumstances here are significant to Devon's (D) knowledge of right and wrong. The case broke when a grandmother (who had to have her own live-in grandson institutionalized) complained to the school that several of her grandson's classmates used her home (while she was at work) as a "hide out" from which to sell drugs. Children who are unaware that what they are doing is wrong have no need to hide out or to conceal their activities. There were no needle marks or other indications of personal use on Devon's (D) body. Devon's (D) charge was not mere possession, it was possession with intent to distribute. This was the finding of the court and it was supported by the evidence. We hold that the surrounding circumstances here were legally sufficient to overcome the slight residual weight of the presumption of incapacity due to infancy. The conviction if affirmed.

Analysis:

In adult criminal trials a jury can be instructed that it may not infer guilt (or anything else for that matter) from the fact that the defendant did not testify. However, the procedural and evidentiary rules are not the same in juvenile proceedings. The court notes that the common law principle underlying the defense of infancy is an unwillingness to punish someone who is not capable of forming criminal intent. And in order to form criminal intent, a person has to know the difference between right and wrong. This is all linked to the idea of blameworthiness of the criminal actor. The court notes that Maryland (P) has adopted the Model Penal Code for the insanity defense, but that the language of the M'Naghten test had traditionally been the common denominator for a whole category of defenses based upon mental incapacity, including infancy.

■ CASE VOCABULARY

DELINQUENT: A child (under a specific age)who has violated a law.

INCRIMINATION: To be exposed to criminal charges or sanctions.

MASTER: A person who is appointed by a court to carry out certain duties on behalf of the court, such as discover evidence or take testimony, and file a report of his findings with the court.

Latimer v. The Queen

(*Convicted Murderer*) v. (*Prosecuting Authority*)

1 S.C.R. 3, 193 D.L.R. (4th) 577 (Supreme Court of Canada 2001)

"MERCY KILLING" IS MURDER

■ **INSTANT FACTS** Latimer (D) killed his seriously ill and disabled daughter and was twice convicted of murder.

■ **BLACK LETTER RULE** In order for the defense of necessity to apply, three requirements must be met: (1) there must be an urgent situation of clear and imminent peril, which is on the verge of transpiring and is virtually certain to occur; (2) there must be no reasonable legal alternative to disobeying the law; and (3) there must be proportionality between the harm inflicted and the harm avoided.

■ PROCEDURAL BASIS

Appeal from the defendant's second conviction for murder.

■ FACTS

Robert Latimer's (D) twelve-year-old daughter, Tracy, suffered from a severe form of cerebral palsy. She was quadriplegic, bedridden, epileptic, and had the mental capacity of a four-month-old. She was thought to be in pain, but pain medications would have interfered with her seizure medications, and even with the drugs, Tracy had five to six seizures per day. Tracy had to be spoon-fed, but lacked adequate nutrients. A feeding tube would have ensured better nutrition, and possibly even better pain control, but her parents refused it as too intrusive and one step toward artificially preserving Tracy's life, which they did not wish to do. Tracy had a serious disability, but was not terminally ill and did appear to enjoy certain aspects of life.

Tracey had undergone several surgeries in her short life. She developed scoliosis, which required the surgical implantation of metal rods to support her spine. Tracy's hip became dislocated, and she was scheduled to undergo yet another surgery to correct that condition, which would have been just one in a series of operations to address recurring joint problems. Tracy's parents were told the hip surgery would cause her great pain.

One day, while Tracy's mother and siblings were at church, Robert Latimer (D) placed Tracy in the front seat of his pickup and inserted a hose connected to the exhaust pipe into the cab. Tracy died from the carbon monoxide. Latimer (D) was twice convicted of second-degree murder for Tracy's death and appealed.

■ ISSUE

Should the jury have been entitled to consider the defense of necessity?

■ DECISION AND RATIONALE

(By the court.) No. In order for the defense of necessity to apply, three requirements must be met: (1) there must be an urgent situation of clear and imminent peril, which is on the verge of transpiring and is virtually certain to occur; (2) there must be no reasonable legal alternative to disobeying the law; and (3) there must be proportionality between the harm inflicted and the harm avoided. The first requirement is not met here. There was no emergency, but rather a long-standing state of affairs. Even the proposed surgery did not pose an imminent threat to Tracy's life. In fact, her health could have improved if the Latimers had not declined the feeding tube. Second, there was a reasonable legal alternative here. Latimer (D) could have struggled on with Tracy's care, or placed her in the group-home setting that they had investigated. And third, even if homicide can *ever* be justified by the defense of necessity—a question which we decline to answer here—in this case, the harm inflicted was immeasurably greater than the pain that would have resulted from Tracey's next operation. Thus, there was no air of reality to any of the three requirements for necessity here. If even one of the requirements has no air of reality, the trial judge is correct in removing the defense from the jury's consideration. Appeal dismissed.

Analysis:

The Canadian court mentions that American jurisdictions are divided on the issue of whether the defense of necessity is ever available in a homicide case. The American Model Penal Code proposes that it should be. "Mercy killings" and "doctor-assisted suicides" became the subject of great debate and media attention when the notorious Dr. Kevorkian publicized his efforts to help terminally ill persons end their lives with dignity. But contrast this case with those involving the famous—or infamous—doctor, in that here the victim was not terminally ill, nor did she make a life-ending decision on her own behalf. Even so, should the defendant here be sentenced as harshly as one who kills under other circumstances?

■ CASE VOCABULARY

NECESSITY: A showing, in court, of a sufficient reason why a defendant did what the prosecution charges the defendant to answer for. Under the Model Penal Code, the defendant must believe that the action was necessary to avoid a harm or evil and that the harm or evil to be avoided was greater than the harm that would have resulted if the crime had been committed. Model Penal Code § 3.02.

Robinson v. California

(*Needle-Marked Narcotic Addict*) v. (*California*)
370 U.S. 660, 82 S.Ct. 1417, 8 L.Ed.2d 758 (1962)

IMPRISONMENT FOR DRUG ADDICTION CONSTITUTES CRUEL AND UNUSUAL PUNISHMENT

■ **INSTANT FACTS** Robinson's (D) misdemeanor conviction and imprisonment for being addicted to narcotics was overturned by the United States Supreme Court.

■ **BLACK LETTER RULE** To the extent that a state law which requires imprisonment for the use of, or addiction to, narcotics is interpreted to allow imprisonment for addiction alone, such law inflicts cruel and unusual punishment in violation of the Fourteenth Amendment.

■ PROCEDURAL BASIS

On appeal to the United States Supreme Court overturning conviction.

■ FACTS

Robinson (D) was convicted by a jury of violating a California (P) health and safety statute which states (in relevant part) that "no person shall use, or be under the influence of, or be addicted to the use of narcotics," unless administered under the supervision of a person licensed by the State to prescribe and administer narcotics. The statute imposes a sentence of not less 90 days and no more than one year in the county jail for those convicted of violating the statute. The judge instructed the jury that Robinson (D) could be convicted under a general verdict if the jury agreed *either* that he was of the "status" *or* had committed the "act" denounced by the statute, and that the prosecution only had to show *either* that Robinson (D) used a narcotic in Los Angeles County, *or* that while in the City of Los Angeles he was addicted to the use of narcotics. Officer Brown testified that he had occasion to examine Robinson's (D) arms one evening on a street in Los Angeles some four months before the trial and had observed scar tissue and discoloration on Robinson's (D) right arm, and numerous needle marks and scabs approximately three inches below the crook of the elbow on his left arm. He also testified that, upon questioning, Robinson (D) admitted to occasional use of narcotics.

■ ISSUE

Does it constitute cruel and unusual punishment to imprison a person solely because of their narcotic addiction?

■ DECISION AND RATIONALE

(Stewart, J.) Yes. The broad power of a State to regulate the narcotic drugs traffic within its borders is undoubtedly a broad one, and is not at issue. The issue here is whether the statute as construed by the California court in this case is repugnant to the Fourteenth Amendment to the Constitution. The courts could have, but did not, construe the statute as requiring actual drug use within the State's jurisdiction. Although there is evidence that Robinson (D) had used narcotics in Los Angeles, the jury was instructed that they could convict him even if they did not believe that evidence. It is impossible to know from the jury's verdict that Robinson (D) was not convicted solely for his "status" of being "addicted to the use of narcotics." This statute is not one which punished for the use of narcotics, for their purchase, sale or possession, or for antisocial or disorderly behavior resulting from their use.

Rather, we deal with a statute which makes the "status" of narcotic addiction a criminal offense for which the offender may be prosecuted at any time. It is unlikely that any State at this time in history would make it a criminal offense for a person to be mentally ill, or a leper, or to be afflicted with a venereal disease. Although a State may find it necessary to require such a victim be dealt with by compulsory treatment, or involuntary quarantine, a law which made a criminal offense of such a disease would doubtless be universally thought to be an infliction of cruel and unusual punishment in violation of the Eighth and Fourteenth Amendments. California's (P) statute is such a statute. Even counsel for California (P) recognizes that narcotic addition is an illness which it is possible to be contracted innocently (use of prescribed drugs) or involuntarily (addicted from the moment of birth). We hold that a state law which imprisons a person thus afflicted as a criminal, even though he has never touched any narcotic drug within the State or been guilty of any irregular behavior there, inflicts a cruel and unusual punishment in violation of the Fourteenth Amendment. Even one day in prison would be cruel and unusual punishment for the "crime" of having a common cold. The conviction is reversed.

■ CONCURRENCE

(Douglas, J.) I wish to make more explicit the reasons why I think it is cruel and unusual punishment in the sense of the Eighth Amendment to treat as criminal a person who is a drug addict. We "as in, humanity" have a long history, going at least back to the New Testament, of believing and treating those who are afflicted with a disease, mental or physical, of being punished for some sin. Various horrid treatments, such as bleeding, water cures (dunking a person under water for long periods of time), and early forms of electric shock, were imposed to drive from the body the evil spirit or toxin. This attitude continues in respect to drug addicts. The impact of addicts on a community causes alarm and often leads to punishment. Cruel and unusual punishment results not from confinement, but from convicting the addict of a crime. The stigma and irreparable damage that attaches to a conviction for addiction cannot be justified as a means of protecting society, where civil commitment would do as well.

■ CONCURRENCE

(Harlan, J.) Insofar as addiction is identified with the use or possession of narcotics within a State's jurisdiction, it may be reached by the State's criminal law. But in this case the trial court's instructions permitted the jury to find Robinson (D) guilty on no more proof than that he was present in California while he was addicted to narcotics. Since addiction alone cannot reasonably be thought to amount to more than a compelling propensity to use narcotics, the effect of this instruction was to authorize criminal punishment for a bare desire to commit a criminal act.

■ DISSENT

(White, J.) I do not consider Robinson's (D) conviction to be a punishment for having an illness or for simply being in some status or condition, but rather a conviction for the regular, repeated or habitual use of narcotics immediately prior to his arrest and in violation of the California law. The evidence was that Robinson (D) lived and worked in Los Angeles. He admitted before trial that he had used narcotics for three or four months, three or four times a week, usually at his place with his friends. He stated to police that he had last used narcotics in the City of Los Angeles 8 days before his arrest. [How high do you have to be to admit to an officer the last time you shot-up?]

Analysis:

The jury was given a general verdict form as opposed to a special verdict form. With a special verdict they could have been asked point by point what they found to be the facts, or for specific violations of the statute. For example, a special verdict could have presented a series of questions, e.g., "do you find that Robinson (D) used narcotics within the City of Los Angeles," and/or "do you find that Robinson (D) was in possession of narcotics," and/or "do you find that Robinson was addicted to narcotics." Instead the jury was given a general verdict from which they could answer "yes or no" to only one question asked in the alternative, that is, "do you find that *either* Robinson (D) had the 'status' of being addicted, *or* committed the 'act' of using narcotics?" Since it is unknown under which theory Robinson (D) was convicted, the Supreme Court held that because it is possible that Robinson (D) was convicted only because of his status of being addicted, the resulting imprisonment constituted cruel and unusual punishment. The Eighth Amendment prohibits the infliction of cruel and unusual punishment, and the Fourteenth Amendment prohibits *the states* from inflicting cruel and unusual punishment.

■ CASE VOCABULARY

EIGHTH AMENDMENT: "Excessive bail shall not be required, nor excessive fines imposed, nor cruel and unusual punishments inflicted."

NEW TESTAMENT: A part of the Christian Bible consisting of several books.

Powell v. Texas

(*Publicaly Intoxicated Alcoholic*) v. (*Texas*)
392 U.S. 514, 88 S.Ct. 2145, 20 L.Ed.2d 1254 (1968)

CHRONIC ALCOHOLISM NOT A DEFENSE TO ACTOR'S CRIMINAL CONDUCT

■ **INSTANT FACTS** Powell's (D) conviction for being drunk in public upheld by the Supreme Court.

■ **BLACK LETTER RULE** The Eighth Amendment prohibition against cruel and unusual punishment is not violated when a state imposes sanctions for public behavior (public intoxication) which violates its law.

■ PROCEDURAL BASIS

On appeal to the United State Supreme Court affirming conviction.

■ FACTS

Leroy Powell (D) (Powell) was arrested, charged, convicted, and fined $50.00 for being found in a state of intoxication in a public place. A psychiatrist (Dr. Wade), after examining Powell (D), testified that Powell (D) is a "chronic alcoholic," who by the time he is intoxicated is not able to control his behavior, and who has reached this point because he has an uncontrollable compulsion to drink. When asked, on cross-examination, whether Powell's (D) act in taking the first drink when he was sober was a "voluntary exercise of his will," Dr. Wade answered yes. He qualified his answer, however, by stating that "these individuals have a compulsion, and this compulsion, while not completely overpowering, is a very strong influence, an exceedingly strong influence, and this compulsion coupled with the firm belief in their mind that they are going to be able to handle it from now on causes their judgment to be somewhat douded." He admitted that when Powell (D) is sober he knows the difference between right and wrong. Powell (D) testified regarding the history of his drinking problem, his many arrests for drunkenness, that he was unable to stop drinking, that when he was intoxicated he could not control his behavior, and that he did not remember his arrest on the occasion for which he was being tried. He admitted, on cross-examination, that he had one drink on the morning of the trial and had been able to discontinue drinking. Texas (P) made no attempt to obtain expert psychiatric testimony of its own. It did nothing to examine the scope of Dr. Wade's reference to "compulsion" which was "not completely overpowering," but which was "an exceedingly strong influence," or to inquire into the question of the proper role of such a "compulsion" in constitutional adjudication. The trial judge disallowed the claimed defense, finding as a matter of law that chronic alcoholism was not a defense to the charge. Powell's (D) counsel submitted, and the trial court entered, the following "findings of fact": (1) That chronic alcoholism is a disease which destroys a person's will power to resist the constant, excessive consumption of alcohol; (2) That a chronic alcoholic does not appear in public by his own volition but under a compulsion symptomatic of the disease; (3) That Powell (D) is a chronic alcoholic.

■ ISSUE

May a state court interpreting a state law find as a matter of law that chronic alcoholism (even if it is a disease) is not a defense to the crime of public intoxication?

■ DECISION AND RATIONALE

(Marshall, J.) Yes. The "findings of fact" are not findings of fact in any recognizable, traditional sense in which that term has been used in a court of law. They are nothing more than disguised premises designed to bring this case within the scope of this court's decision in *Robinson v. California.* There is no agreement in the medical community for a definition of alcoholism. We will not extend our decision in *Robinson* which only dealt with the addiction or sickness of a person, to this situation where the conviction is for the act of being in public while intoxicated. In *Robinson*, this court held as unconstitutional a state law which imposed jail time on a defendant solely based upon his "status" of being a drug addict. On its face the present case does not fall within that holding, since Powell (D) was convicted, not for being a chronic alcoholic, but for being in public while drunk on a particular occasion. The criminal sanction is imposed on public behavior which may create substantial health and safety hazards, both for Powell (D) and the public, and which offends the moral and esthetic sensibilities of a large segment of the community. The dissent suggests that *Robinson* stands for the principle that "criminal penalties may not be inflicted upon a person for being in a condition he is powerless to change." However, the entire point of *Robinson* is that criminal penalties may be inflicted only if the defendant has committed some act, has engaged in some behavior, which society has an interest in preventing. It does not deal with the question of whether certain conduct cannot constitutionally be punished because it is, in some sense, "involuntary" or "occasioned by compulsion." The record from below is woefully inadequate to support the contention that Powell (D) was unable at the time of the incident to control either his drinking or his being in public when drunk. It is easily admitted that a system which provided for the adequate treatment of alcoholics would be good for society, not to mention the alcoholic, however, such a system does not exist on the necessary scale. The criminal system of jail time and/or fines for petty offenses such as public drunkenness is minimal. The criminal system in place, although an unpleasant reality, cannot be said to be irrational. Without a better rehabilitation system in place, it is difficult to say that the criminal process is utterly lacking in social value. The doctrines of criminal law that are utilized to assess the moral accountability of an individual for his antisocial needs cannot be set aside here. The elements of a crime, (e.g., the intent, the act) and the defenses (e.g., insanity, mistake, justification, duress) work together and are adjusted over time to reflect the evolving goals of criminal law and the changing religious, moral, philosophical, and medical views of the nature of man. This process has always been thought to be the province of the States. Conviction affirmed.

■ CONCURRENCE

(Black, J.) Texas (P) law serves many state purposes, e.g., it gets alcoholics off the street and into a jail where they are provide food, clothing, and shelter long enough to sober up, thus keeping the public and themselves safe. A State should not be held constitutionally required to make the inquiry as to what part of a defendant's personality is responsible for his actions and to excuse anyone whose action was, in some complex, psychologic sense, the result of "compulsion." We are asked to apply *Robinson*, but it is not applicable here because it involved punishment for the mere propensity, or the desire to commit an offense, evidence of which is considered relatively unreliable and difficult for a defendant to rebut. Laws which require the State to prove that the defendant actually committed some proscribed act involve none of the problems encountered in *Robinson,* and the requirement of a specific act provides some protection against false charges. The question of whether an act is "involuntary" is an inherently elusive question, and one which Texas (P) may treat as irrelevant.

■ CONCURRENCE

(White, J.) The chronic alcoholic with an irresistible urge to consume alcohol should not be punished for drinking or for being drunk. Powell's (D) conviction was for the different crime of being drunk in a public place. Many alcoholics do make it a point to begin and end their drinking binges in private. It is possible that such an alcoholic will lose his power to control his movement and appear in public. The Eighth Amendment might forbid conviction in such a circumstance, but only on a record satisfactorily showing that is was not feasible for him to have made arrangements to prevent him being in public when drunk and that his extreme drunkenness sufficiently deprived him of his faculties on that occasion. Alcoholics without homes "sounds like a support group, doesn't it" are not only unable to resist drinking, but are then necessarily drunk in public. If such facts were sufficiently proved, punishment would be for the single act of unresistible drunkenness for which punishment would violate the Eighth Amendment.

■ DISSENT

(Fortas, J.) Criminal penalties may not be inflicted upon a person for being in a condition he is powerless to change. In this case, Powell (D) is charged with a crime composed of two elements—being intoxicated and being found in a public place while in that condition. The crime, so defined, differs from that in *Robinson.* The statute covers more than a mere status. But the essential constitutional defect here is the same as in *Robinson,* for in both cases the particular defendant was accused of being in a condition which he had no capacity to change or avoid. A person may not be punished if the condition essential to constitute the defined crime is part of the pattern of his disease and is brought about by a compulsion symptomatic of the disease. Such punishment violates the Eighth Amendment prohibition against cruel and unusual punishment.

Analysis:

Powell (D) was asking the court to apply the rule in *Robinson*, that is, to find the sanctions for being intoxicated in public to be cruel and unusual punishment. The Court refused to extend the rule to the facts presented here. It did not consider the "status" of "being addicted" to be the same thing as the "act" of "being drunk in public." Justice White, although attempting to provide constitutional protection to at least some chronic alcoholics, also seems to think that while they are drunk they should be more responsible. Justice Stewart, who penned *Robinson*, joined the dissent.

State v. Kargar

(*Maine*) v. (*Overly Affectionate Dad*)
679 A.2d 81 (1996)

CUSTOM AND PRACTICE ARE RELEVANT FACTORS IN RULING ON A DEFENDANT'S MOTION TO DISMISS THE CHARGES AGAINST HIM

■ **INSTANT FACTS** In accordance with Afghani custom, Kargar's (D) kissed his young son's penis as a sign of love for his child which was considered by his neighbor, the police, the prosecution, and the trial court to violate Maine's statute prohibiting sexual acts with a child under the age of 14 years.

■ **BLACK LETTER RULE** When a state has a *de minimis* statute, the court *must* consider the full range of relevant factors and circumstances surrounding the defendant's admittedly criminal conduct before ruling on his motion to dismiss.

■ PROCEDURAL BASIS

On appeal to the Supreme Judicial Court of Maine vacating the conviction for gross sexual assault.

■ FACTS

Mohammand Kargar (D) (Kargar) and his family were Afghani refugees who had been in this country for approximately three years. They were babysitting a neighbor's daughter who saw Kargar (D) kiss his 18-month-old son's penis and also saw a picture of the same. She told her mother this and her mother contacted the police. The police legally searched Kargar's (D) apartment and found the picture. Kargar (D) admitted to kissing his son's penis and told the officer that it is accepted as common practice in his culture. He was arrested. At the court trial Kargar (D) moved for a dismissal of the case pursuant to Maine's (P) *de minimis* statute. By agreement, the trial phase was held first, followed by the *de minimis* hearing. Kargar (D) and other Afghani people who were familiar with Afghani practice and custom testified that kissing a young boy (up to the age of three, four or five) on all parts of the body was to show love for the child. Kargar (D) testified that his culture views the penis of a child as not the holiest or cleanest part of the body because it is from where the child urinates. He stated that kissing his son there shows how much he loves his child precisely because it is not the holiest or cleanest part of his body. The witnesses testified that under islamic law any sexual activity between an adult and a child results in the death penalty for the adult. Kargar (D) also submitted statements from a professor of Near Eastern Studies at the University of Arizona who was also a religious teacher and Director of Afghan Mujahideen Information Bureau in New York which supported the testimony of the other witnesses. Maine (P) did not present any witnesses at the *de minimis* hearing. The court denied Kargar's (D) motion and found him guilty of two counts of gross sexual assault.

■ ISSUE

Are culture, lack of harm, and innocent state of mind relevant factors that must be considered by a court before ruling on a defendant's motion to dismiss?

■ DECISION AND RATIONALE

(Dana, J.) Yes. Maine's (P) *de minimis* statute allows the court to dismiss a prosecution if it finds that the defendant's conduct, among other things, did not actually cause the harm sought to be prevented or did so in only a way too trivial to warrant condemnation, or is not the type of conduct envisioned by the Legislature in defining the crime. In determining whether the prosecution should be dismissed, the court is required to view the defendant's conduct "having regard to the nature of the conduct alleged and the nature of the attendant circumstances.". This analysis is, by necessity, case-specific. The purpose of the statute is to allow a court to dismiss charges which although they amount to a criminal act, do not under the circumstances involve any moral turpitude. An objective consideration of the surrounding circumstances is authorized and include such issues as (1) the defendant's background, experience and character; the defendant's knowledge of the existence of the crime; (2) the consequences to him, the victim, and society of the crime; (3) the possible mitigating circumstances which might lesson the punishment; (4) and any other data which might reveal the nature and degree of culpability in the offense. Our review of the record reveals that the court denied Kargar's (D) motion without considering the full range of relevant factors. The court focused on whether the conduct met the definition of gross sexual assault which nullified the effect of the *de minimis* statute. The focus is on whether the admittedly criminal conduct was envisioned by the Legislature when it defined the crime. Because the statute allows for the presentation of other "extenuations" that cannot be regarded as envisioned by the Legislature, the trial court was required to consider the possibility that the result of a conviction *in this case* could not have been anticipated by the Legislature when it defined the crime of gross sexual assault. Prior to 1985, this type of act (genital-mouth contact) included an element requiring that the act be done to satisfy sexual gratification. The Legislature amended the statute by removing this element. The Legislature stated at the time that there was not a concern that the definition would exclude "innocent" touching. This illuminates the fact that an "innocent" touching such as occurred in this case has not always been recognized as inherently criminal under our law. The Legislature's inability to comprehend "innocent" touching is highlighted by reference to another criminal sexual act (the touching of genitals involving direct contact with an instrument or devise manipulated by another). The Legislature kept the requirement that in order for this act to be criminal, it must be done to satisfy sexual gratification or to cause bodily injury or offense contact. The Legislature's stated reason for such requirement was to exclude "innocent" contacts, such as for a proper medical purpose or "other valid reason." All of the evidence presented at the hearing supports the conclusion that there was nothing "sexual" about Kargar's (D) conduct. There is no real dispute that what Kargar (D) did is accepted practice in his culture. Although the court entirely suspended Kargar's (D) sentence, the two convictions expose him to severe consequences including his required registration as a sex offender and the possibility of deportation. We agree with Kargar (D) that the court erred as a matter of law because it found culture, lack of harm, and his innocent state of mind irrelevant to its *de minimis* analysis. The convictions are vacated.

Analysis:

Maine (P) was concerned with the potential harm caused by courts using the factors of this case to allow even more exceptions to the criminal statutes. It thought the Legislature was better suited to collect data, debate the social costs and benefits, and clearly define what conduct constitutes criminal activity. The court noted that the crime here was already clearly defined, but that the Legislature had also allowed for the adjustment of criminal statutes by courts in extraordinary cases. A lively debate could ensue about the extent to which culture should be considered in excusing admittedly criminal conduct. There is an argument that a newly arrived immigrant will not know all the laws of this country that someone raised here would know. While this may not completely excuse the crime, it might be a mitigating factor in culpability or punishment. Also, a person raised in a foreign culture will have religious and moral norms that he or she might feel compelled to follow, even if it violates the law.

■ CASE VOCABULARY

DE MINIMIS STATUTE: Based upon the concept that the law does not pay attention to trivial matters.

EXTENUATIONS: Circumstances which make the criminal conduct less offensive, less loathsome; "extenuating circumstances" may also reduce the punishment.

VACATE: To void or rescind a judgment.

CHAPTER TEN

Inchoate Offenses

People v. Gentry

Instant Facts: Gentry (D) was convicted of attempted murder after spilling gasoline on his girlfriend during a fight which then ignited as she passed the stove.

Black Letter Rule: Only the specific intent to kill satisfies the intent element of the crime of attempted murder.

Bruce v. State

Instant Facts: Bruce (D) was convicted of attempted felony murder, as well as other charges, for shooting a storekeeper he was attempting to rob at gunpoint.

Black Letter Rule: Attempted felony murder is not a crime in Maryland.

United States v. Mandujano

Instant Facts: The court clarifies the definition of "attempt" as used in Section 846 of Title 21.

Black Letter Rule: For the crime of attempt, preparation alone is not enough, there must be some appreciable fragment of the crime committed.

Commonwealth v. Peaslee

Instant Facts: Peaslee (D) concocted a plan to burn a building and all its contents, but he changed his mind before the plan was accomplished.

Black Letter Rule: Collection and preparation of materials in a room for the purpose of setting fire to them, accompanied with a solicitation of another to set the fire, is near enough to the accomplishment of the substantive offense to be punishable.

People v. Rizzo

Instant Facts: Rizzo (D) and three others planned and looked for a man to rob a payroll from, but they were unable to find him before being arrested.

Black Letter Rule: For an act to constitute an attempt it must come very near to the accomplishment of the crime.

People v. Miller

Instant Facts: Miller (D) was convicted of attempted murder for threatening to kill Jeans and then later approaching him with a loaded rifle.

Black Letter Rule: Whenever the design of a person to commit crime is clearly shown, slight acts done in furtherance of this design will constitute and attempt.

State v. Reeves

Instant Facts: Reeves (D) and a friend devised and tried to carry out a plan to kill their homeroom teacher and steal her car.

Black Letter Rule: When an actor possesses materials to be used in the commission of a crime, at or near the scene of the crime, and where the possession of those materials can serve no lawful purpose of the actor under the circumstances, the jury is entitled, but not required, to find that the actor has taken a "substantial step" toward the commission of the crime if such action is strongly corroborative of the actor's overall purpose.

United States v. Alkhabaz

Instant Facts: Alkhabaz (D) was arrested for posting fictional stories involving the abduction, rape, torture, mutilation, and murder of women and young girls on the Internet.

Black Letter Rule: To constitute "a communication containing a threat" under 18 U.S.C. Sec. 875(c), a communication must be such that a reasonable person (1) would take the statement as a serious expression of an intention to inflict bodily harm (the mens rea), and (2) would perceive such expression as being communicated to effect some change or achieve some goal through intimidation (the actus reus).

People v. Thousand

Instant Facts: A Sheriff's Deputy logged into a chat room, posing as a 14–year-old female, and chatted with Thousand (D), who was later charged with attempted distribution of obscene materials to a minor.

Black Letter Rule: A defendant is guilty of attempt if he attempted to commit an offense prohibited by law and engaged in conduct in furtherance of the intended offense, whether or not an element of the underlying offense could not be satisfied due to legal or factual impossibility.

Commonwealth v. McCloskey

Instant Facts: Prisoner planned a prison breach but abandoned the plan before leaving the prison and attempting the escape.

Black Letter Rule: A prisoner contemplating a prison breach, but still within a prison having not yet attempted the act, is in a position to abandon the criminal act voluntarily, thereby exonerating himself from criminal responsibility.

State v. Mann

Instant Facts: None Stated

Black Letter Rule: The solicitor conceives the criminal idea and furthers its commission via another person by suggesting to, inducing, or manipulating that person.

State v. Cotton

Instant Facts: Cotton (D) wrote letters to his wife, which she never received, trying to get her to convince his stepdaughter not to testify against him at trial.

Black Letter Rule: If a solicitor's message never reaches the person intended to be solicited, the act is criminal, but it must be prosecuted as an attempt to solicit.

People v. Carter

Instant Facts: None Stated.

Black Letter Rule: A defendant may be convicted and punished for both the conspiracy and the substantive crime.

Pinkerton v. United States

Instant Facts: Two brothers were convicted of both conspiracy and the substantive offense even though only one actually participated in committing the offense.

Black Letter Rule: Participation in the conspiracy is enough to sustain a conviction for the substantive offense in furtherance of the conspiracy.

People v. Swain

Instant Facts: Swain (D) was convicted of conspiracy to commit murder after his friend killed a young boy in a drive-by shooting.

Black Letter Rule: A conviction of conspiracy to commit murder requires a finding of intent to kill, and cannot be based on a theory of implied malice.

People v. Lauria

Instant Facts: Lauria (D) ran a telephone answering service, which he knew was used by several prostitutes in their business ventures; Lauria (D) was indicted with the prostitutes for conspiracy to commit prostitution.

Black Letter Rule: The intent of a supplier who knows his supplies will be put to criminal use may be established by (1) direct evidence that he intends to participate, or (2) through an inference that he intends to participate based on (a) his special interest in the activity, or (b) the felonious nature of the crime itself.

Commonwealth v. Azim

Instant Facts: Azim (D) was the driver of a car which two friends jumped out of in order to beat and rob a man walking on the street.

Black Letter Rule: Once conspiracy is established and upheld, a member of the conspiracy is also guilty of the criminal acts of his co-conspirators.

Commonwealth v. Cook

Instant Facts: Cook (D) and his brother met a girl and partied a bit, after which Cook's (D) brother forcibly raped her in the woods while Cook (D) watched.

Black Letter Rule: While proof of a tacit agreement to commit a crime may be enough to establish a conspiracy, a defendant cannot be convicted of conspiracy solely on evidence tending to show his complicity as an accomplice in the commission of the substantive crime.

People v. Foster

Instant Facts: Foster (D) devised a plan to rob an old man, however his co-conspirator really had reported him to the police and was just feigning agreement.

Black Letter Rule: The Illinois legislation encompasses the bilateral theory of conspiracy, which requires the actual agreement of at least two participants.

Kilgore v. State

Instant Facts: Kilgore (D) was convicted of shooting Norman twice in the head, killing him, while he was driving down the interstate.

Black Letter Rule: Hearsay testimony can only be admissible under the exception to the hearsay rule which provides that the out-of-court statements of one conspirator are admissible against all conspirators.

Braverman v. United States

Instant Facts: Braverman (D) and others were convicted of violating several statutes in the illicit manufacture, transportation, and distribution of distilled spirits.

Black Letter Rule: A single agreement to commit acts in violation of several penal statutes must be punished as one conspiracy.

Iannelli v. United States

Instant Facts: Iannelli (D) was convicted and sentenced under both the substantive and conspiracy counts for gambling violations.

Black Letter Rule: There is a recognized exception to Wharton's Rule which permits prosecution and punishment for both the substantive offense and the conspiracy.

Gebardi v. United States

Instant Facts: Gebardi (D) and a woman agreed to go across state lines for illicit purposes in violation of the Mann Act, and the two were charged with conspiracy to violate the Mann Act.

Black Letter Rule: A woman cannot be held criminally liable for conspiring to transport herself across state lines for illicit purposes, even where she consents to the substantive offense.

People v. Sconce

Instant Facts: Sconce (D) hired someone to kill a man but before the murder was carried out he changed his mind and called it off.

Black Letter Rule: Withdrawal from a conspiracy avoids liability only for the target offense, or for any subsequent act committed by a co-conspirator in pursuance of the common plan, but liability for forming the conspiracy remains.

People v. Gentry

(*State*) v. (*Firestarter*)

157 Ill.App.3d 899, 109 Ill.Dec. 895, 510 N.E.2d 963 (1987)

SPECIFIC INTENT TO KILL MUST BE SHOWN TO PROVE ATTEMPTED MURDER

■ **INSTANT FACTS** Gentry (D) was convicted of attempted murder after spilling gasoline on his girlfriend during a fight which then ignited as she passed the stove.

■ **BLACK LETTER RULE** Only the specific intent to kill satisfies the intent element of the crime of attempted murder.

■ PROCEDURAL BASIS

Appeal from defendant's conviction by a jury.

■ FACTS

Gentry (D) and his girlfriend, Ruby Hill, were arguing in the apartment they shared together. They were both highly intoxicated and Gentry (D) spilled gasoline on Hill [*accidentally*, no doubt]. Hill passed by the stove and the gasoline ignited. Gentry (D) was able to smother the flames with a coat, but only after Hill had been severely burned. Hill testified to these events at Gentry's (D) trial. At the close of the presentation of evidence in this case, the court defined "attempt" as it relates to murder stating, a person "commits the offense of murder when he, *with intent to commit the offense of murder* does any act which constitutes a substantial step toward the commission of the offense of murder. The offense attempted need not have been completed." It also defined the crime of murder, including four culpable mental states. The court instructed the jury that a person commits the crime of murder "where he kills an individual if, in performing the acts which cause the death, he intends to kill *or* do great bodily harm to that individual; *or* he knows that such acts will cause death to that individual; *or* he knows that such acts create a strong probability of death or great bodily harm to that individual."

■ ISSUE

Is a finding of specific intent to kill a necessary element of the crime of attempted murder?

■ DECISION AND RATIONALE

(Linn, J.) Yes. Gentry (D) contends that the inclusion of all the alternative states of mind in the definitional murder instruction was erroneous because the crime of attempted murder requires a showing of specific intent to kill. Gentry (D) posits that inclusion of all four alternative states of mind permitted the jury to convict him of attempt upon a finding that he intended to harm Hill, or acted with knowledge that his conduct created a strong probability of death or great bodily harm to Hill, even if the jury believed that Gentry (D) did not act with specific intent to kill. We agree with Gentry's position that the jury was misinstructed in this case. Our supreme court has repeatedly held that a finding of specific intent to kill is a necessary element of the crime of attempted murder. Indeed, a trial court instructing a jury on the crime must make it clear that specific intent to kill is the pivotal element of that offense, and that intent to do bodily harm, or knowledge that the consequences of Gentry's (D) act may result in death or great bodily harm, is not enough. The State would read the attempt instruction as requiring a showing of any of the alternative mental states sufficient for a conviction of murder. In other words, the

State makes no distinction between the mental state required to prove murder and the mental state required to prove attempted murder. We find the State's analysis and conclusion to be erroneous and lacking in legal substance since it fails to contain the judicial reasoning which recognizes the distinction between the intent elements of murder and attempted murder. Consequently, it is sufficient only for us to say that we recognize the distinction between the alternative states of mind delineated in the definitional murder instruction, as well as the fact that only the specific intent to kill satisfies the intent element of the crime of attempted murder. We reverse Gentry's (D) conviction and sentence, and remand this cause for a new trial in front of a properly instructed jury.

Analysis:

Criminal attempts really involve two different "intents" that merge as a practical matter. The actor must first intentionally commit the acts that constitute the actus reus of an attempt. Secondly, the actor must perform the acts with the specific intent to commit the substantive crime. It is a peculiarity in the common law that an attempt is usually punished less severely, and never more severely, than the intended offense, yet the mental state required for attempted murder is of a higher culpability than that required for the completed offense. This anomaly has been justified on the basis that the person intending to kill another is more dangerous, because he may try again if unsuccessful the first time. Simply put, "the actor's unspent intent is a source of harm independent of his conduct."

■ CASE VOCABULARY

ACTUS REUS: The physical criminal deed.

CULPABLE: Intentional wrong-doing.

SPECIFIC INTENT: Knowing and desiring certain consequences for a particular crime.

Bruce v. State

(*Store Robber*) v. (*State*)
317 Md. 642, 566 A.2d 103 (1989)

THE STATE OF MARYLAND DOES NOT RECOGNIZE THE CRIME OF ATTEMPTED FELONY MURDER

■ **INSTANT FACTS** Bruce (D) was convicted of attempted felony murder, as well as other charges, for shooting a storekeeper he was attempting to rob at gunpoint.

■ **BLACK LETTER RULE** Attempted felony murder is not a crime in Maryland.

■ PROCEDURAL BASIS

Certiorari granted on appeal from defendant's conviction by a jury in the trial court.

■ FACTS

Bruce (D) and two other men entered Barry Tensor's shoe store. Bruce (D) was masked and armed with a handgun. He ordered Tensor to open the cash register. Upon finding it empty, Bruce (D) demanded to know where the money could be found. Tensor told Bruce (D) that that was all there was, and Bruce (D) aimed the gun at Tensor's head, telling him he was going to kill him. Tensor ducked down and moved forward. He testified that he thought he bumped into Bruce (D), and then Bruce (D) shot him [clearly self-defense]. Tensor was hospitalized for five weeks from a gunshot wound to his stomach. A jury found Bruce (D) guilty of attempted first degree felony murder, robbery with a deadly weapon, and two handgun charges. On appeal, Bruce (D) argued that attempted felony murder was not a crime in Maryland. The Court granted certiorari to consider the issue.

■ ISSUE

Is attempted felony murder a crime in Maryland?

■ DECISION AND RATIONALE

(Murphy, C.J.) No. To secure a conviction for first degree murder under the felony murder doctrine, the State is required to prove a specific intent to commit the underlying felony and that death occurred in the perpetration or attempt to perpetrate the felony; it is not necessary to prove a specific intent to kill or to demonstrate the existence of willfulness, deliberation, or premeditation. In determining whether attempted felony murder is a crime in Maryland, we note that criminal attempts are applicable to any existing crime, whether statutory or common law. Under Maryland law, a criminal attempt consists of a specific intent to commit the offense coupled with some overt act in furtherance of the intent which goes beyond mere preparation. Because a conviction for felony murder requires no specific intent to kill, it follows that because a criminal attempt is a specific intent crime, attempted felony murder is not a crime in Maryland.

Analysis:

The court in this case cites a previous decision holding that there is an offense of attempted voluntary manslaughter, but no offense of attempted involuntary manslaughter. The reasoning behind this ruling is that the intent to kill is present in the former, but not in the latter case. The outcome in this case follows from that rationale, because the court "recognizes" that an attempt crime requires specific intent (like the intent to kill in voluntary manslaughter), whereas felony murder involves an unintentional death (as does involuntary manslaughter).

■ CASE VOCABULARY

CERTIORARI: Writ issued by a superior court to one of inferior jurisdiction so that the proceedings may be inspected to determine issues of importance.

FELONY MURDER: An unintentional death which occurs during the commission or attempted commission of a felony.

United States v. Mandujano

(*Government*) v. (*Not Stated*)
499 F.2d 370 (5th Cir. 1974)

MERE PREPARATION IS NOT ENOUGH TO CONSTITUTE "ATTEMPT"

■ **INSTANT FACTS** The court clarifies the definition of "attempt" as used in Section 846 of Title 21.

■ **BLACK LETTER RULE** For the crime of attempt, preparation alone is not enough, there must be some appreciable fragment of the crime committed.

■ PROCEDURAL BASIS

None Stated.

■ FACTS

None Stated.

■ ISSUE

Is preparation enough to constitute an "attempt" under Section 846 of Title 21?

■ DECISION AND RATIONALE

(Rives, C.J.) No. Apparently there is no legislative history indicating exactly what Congress meant when it used the word "attempt" in Section 846. It seems to be well settled that mere preparation is not sufficient to constitute an attempt to commit a crime, however it is also equally clear that the semantical distinction between preparation and attempt is one incapable of being formulated in a hard and fast rule. What might, in one factual situation, constitute preparation, may not under different facts. We have previously addressed the issue and concluded that the following test has been "frequently approved": Preparation alone is not enough, there must be some appreciable fragment of the crime committed, it must be in such progress that it will be consummated unless interrupted by circumstances independent of the will of the attempter, and the act must not be equivocal in nature.

Analysis:

While it may be well settled that mere preparation is not enough to constitute an attempt, there really is no clear-cut distinction between mere preparation and perpetration. The courts in many jurisdictions have tried to distinguish between the two, and the federal courts have confronted this issue on a number of occasions. Judge Learned Hand set forth a test as to whether conduct still remains in the zone of mere preparation, or if it has passed over to constitute an attempt. Hand stated that the test is satisfied if the actor has done all that it is within his power to do, but has been prevented by outside intervention in short, he has passed beyond any locus poenitentiae. This doctrine, however, does not appear to be followed in our courts. Other courts have required that the objective acts of the defendant evidence commitment to the criminal venture and corroborate the mens rea. This way, the courts reason, it prevents the conviction of persons engaged in innocent acts on the basis of a mens rea proved through subjective, and thus less reliable, means. The line between preparation and perpetration is a "murky twilight zone."

■ CASE VOCABULARY

LOCUS POENITENTIAE: The opportunity for one to withdraw or renounce before the consummation of a crime.

MENS REA: The "guilty" mental state accompanying a criminal act.

Commonwealth v. Peaslee

(State) v. *(Arsonist)*
177 Mass. 267, 59 N.E. 55 (1901)

THE DEFENDANT MUST HAVE HIS HAND IN THE FINAL ACT TO BE GUILTY OF ATTEMPT

■ **INSTANT FACTS** Peaslee (D) concocted a plan to burn a building and all its contents, but he changed his mind before the plan was accomplished.

■ **BLACK LETTER RULE** Collection and preparation of materials in a room for the purpose of setting fire to them, accompanied with a solicitation of another to set the fire, is near enough to the accomplishment of the substantive offense to be punishable.

■ PROCEDURAL BASIS

Motion to quash the defendant's indictment and motion for a directed verdict for the defendant.

■ FACTS

Peaslee (D) constructed and arranged combustibles in a building in such a way that they were ready to be lighted, and if lighted would have set fire to the building and its contents. The plan would have required a candle which was standing on a shelf six feet away to be placed on a piece of wood in a pan of turpentine and lighted [not one to keep it simple apparently]. Peaslee (D) offered to pay a younger man in his employment if he would go into the building, seemingly some miles from the place of the dialogue, and carry out the plan. This was refused. Later, Peaslee (D) and the young man drove towards the building, but when within a quarter of a mile, Peaslee (D) said that he had changed his mind and drove away. This is as near as he ever came to accomplishing what he had in contemplation.

■ ISSUE

Do Peaslee's acts come near enough to the accomplishment of the substantive offense to be punishable?

■ DECISION AND RATIONALE

(Holmes, C.J.) No. The most common types of an attempt are either an act which is intended to bring about the substantive crime, and which sets in motion natural forces that would bring it about in the expected course of events, but for the unforeseen interruption, as, in this case, if the candle had been set in its place and lighted, but had been put out by police, or an act which is intended to bring about the substantive crime, and would bring it about but for a mistake of judgment in a matter of estimate or experiment, as when a pistol is fired at a man, but misses, or when one tries to pick a pocket which turns out to be empty. [That was a mouthful!] On the pleadings in this case, which failed to allege the solicitation of the employee to set the fire, a mere collection and preparation of materials in a room for the purpose of setting fire to them, unaccompanied by any present intent to set the fire, would be too remote. If Peaslee (D) intended to rely upon his own hands to the end, he must be shown to have had a present intent to accomplish the crime without much delay, and to have had this intent at a time and place where he was able to carry it out. On the other hand, if the offense is to be made out by showing a preparation of the room and a solicitation of someone else to set the fire, which solicitation, if successful, would have been Peaslee's (D) last act, the solicitation must be alleged as one of the overt acts. If the indictment had been properly drawn, we have no question that Peaslee (D) might have been convicted. As it was drawn, however, Peaslee's (D) exceptions must be sustained.

Analysis:

The proximity of the preparation to the accomplishment of the act determines whether it will constitute an attempt, but the degree held sufficient may vary with circumstances. The key in this case, which lets Peaslee (D) off the hook, is that the prosecution did a poor job in drafting the indictment. The prosecution omits the fact that Peaslee (D) solicited the young man to actually start the fire, and such omission is fatal to the State's (P) case. All of the acts Peaslee (D) did in preparation for the fire are futile without the final step of lighting the fire. Such first steps cannot be described as an attempt, because the acts alone are not sufficient to accomplish the end. If, however, the evidence of the solicitation had been included, it would have shown that Peaslee's (D) last act (the solicitation) was so close in proximity to the completed act that it would constitute attempt.

■ CASE VOCABULARY

SOLICITATION: Requesting or encouraging another to engage in criminal acts.

People v. Rizzo

(*State*) v. (*Payroll Robber*)
246 N.Y. 334, 158 N.E. 888 (1927)

ACTS CONSTITUTING AN ATTEMPT MUST COME VERY NEAR TO THE ACCOMPLISHMENT OF THE CRIME

■ **INSTANT FACTS** Rizzo (D) and three others planned and looked for a man to rob a payroll from, but they were unable to find him before being arrested.

■ **BLACK LETTER RULE** For an act to constitute an attempt it must come very near to the accomplishment of the crime.

■ PROCEDURAL BASIS

Appeal from the defendant's conviction and prison sentence.

■ FACTS

Rizzo (D) and three others planned to rob Charles Rao of a payroll he was carrying to the bank valued at about $1,200. The four men, two of whom had firearms, set out in an automobile to find Rao or the man who was carrying the payroll on that day. Rizzo (D) claimed to be able to identify the man and was to point him out to the others who were to do the actual hold-up. After going to the bank and several buildings looking for Rao, they attracted the attention of two police officers, who began following and watching the four men. As Rizzo (D) jumped out of the car and went into a building, the four men were arrested [who needs probable cause?]. Neither Rao nor the man who was to actually carry the payroll that day were in the building where Rizzo (D) was arrested. The four men had not found nor seen the man they intended to rob; no person with a payroll was at any of the places where they had stopped and no one had been pointed out or identified by Rizzo (D) [now there's an airtight case!].

■ ISSUE

Do the acts performed by Rizzo (D) constitute the crime of an attempt to commit robbery in the first degree?

■ DECISION AND RATIONALE

(Crane, J.) No. The past case law states that in order for an act to constitute an attempt it must come very near to the accomplishment of the crime. How shall we apply this rule of immediate nearness to this case? To constitute the crime of robbery the money must have been taken from Rao by means of force or violence, or through fear. The crime of attempt to commit robbery was committed if Rizzo (D) and the others did an act tending to the commission of this robbery. Rao was not found, the men were still looking for him when they were arrested. No attempt to rob him could even be made until he came in sight. In short, Rizzo (D) and the other men had planned to commit a crime and were looking around the city for an opportunity to commit it, but the opportunity fortunately never came. For these reasons, the judgment of conviction of Rizzo (D) must be reversed and a new trial granted.

Analysis:

The court has repeatedly held that an act amounts to an attempt when it is so near to the result that the danger of success is very great. "There must be dangerous proximity to success." Thus it is no surprise that this case was decided the way it was on the facts presented. The quizzical part of this decision involves the facts surrounding the arrest scenario. Why did the police follow the four men to begin with, and what constituted the probable cause necessary for the arrests? How did the police find out about the men's plan? Did they have prior knowledge? It seems there are gaps in the fact sequence, which makes it difficult to analyze and apply the ruling in this case to others.

■ CASE VOCABULARY

RULE OF IMMEDIATE NEARNESS: An act constitutes an attempt when it comes very near to the accomplishment of the crime.

People v. Miller

(*State*) v. (*Rifleman*)
2 Cal.2d 527, 42 P.2d 308 (1935)

DIRECT ACT IN EXECUTION OF THE CRIMINAL DESIGN IS REQUIRED TO PROVE ATTEMPT

■ **INSTANT FACTS** Miller (D) was convicted of attempted murder for threatening to kill Jeans and then later approaching him with a loaded rifle.

■ **BLACK LETTER RULE** Whenever the design of a person to commit crime is clearly shown, slight acts done in furtherance of this design will constitute and attempt.

■ PROCEDURAL BASIS

Appeal from jury's conviction of the defendant.

■ FACTS

On the day in question, Miller (D), somewhat under the influence of liquor and in the presence of others at the town post office, threatened to kill Albert Jeans [drunk and postal!]. Jeans was employed on the hops ranch of the town constable, Ginochio. Miller (D), carrying a .22-caliber rifle, entered the hops field while Jeans, Ginochio and others were planting hops. Miller walked in a direct line towards Ginochio, who was 250 or 300 yards away. Jeans was about 30 yards beyond him. After Miller (D) had gone about 100 yards, he stopped and appeared to be loading his rifle. At no time did he raise the rifle as if to take aim. As soon as Jeans saw Miller (D), he fled on a line at about a right angle to Miller's (D) line of approach. When Miller (D) reached Ginochio, Ginochio took the rifle away from him, with Miller (D) offering no resistance. The rifle was found to be loaded with a high-speed cartridge.

■ ISSUE

Did Miller (D) commit acts in furtherance of his plan such that he is guilty of attempted murder?

■ DECISION AND RATIONALE

(Shenk, J.) No. We are mindful of the fact that case law requires that whenever the design of a person to commit crime is clearly shown, slight acts done in furtherance of this design will constitute an attempt. The reason for requiring evidence of a direct act, however slight, toward consummation of the intended crime, is that in the majority of cases, up to the time of the conduct of the defendant, consisting merely of acts of preparation, has never ceased to be equivocal; and this is necessarily so, irrespective of his declared intent. It is that quality of being equivocal that must be lacking before the act becomes one which may be said to be a commencement of the commission of the crime, or an overt act, or before any fragment of the crime itself has been committed, and this is so for the reason that, so long as the equivocal quality remains, no one can say with certainty what the intent of the defendant is. In the present case, up to the moment the gun was taken from Miller (D), no one could say with certainty whether Miller (D) had come into the field to carry out his threat to kill Jeans or merely to demand his arrest by the constable. Under the authorities, therefore, the acts of Miller (D) do not constitute an attempt to commit murder.

Analysis:

The American Law Institute tries to justify the res ipsa loquitur rule of the unequivocality doctrine by viewing it entirely as a matter of procedure. Whether the requirement of unequivocality is considered part of the substantive definition of attempt or as a separate rule of evidence, it can be realistically administered only by means of a procedural mechanism, that is, by excluding from the jury the actor's incriminating representations of purpose. It seems difficult to understand how the court could find Miller's (D) actions in this case to be equivocal, given the facts mentioned.

■ CASE VOCABULARY

INFORMATION: Alternative to indictment as a means of starting a prosecution.

HOPS: A grain.

RES IPSA LOQUITUR: The thing speaks for itself.

UNEQUIVOCALITY DOCTRINE: An act does not constitute an attempt unless the actor's specific criminal purpose is evident from his conduct.

State v. Reeves

(*State*) v. (*Teacher Killer*)

916 S.W.2d 909 (1996)

JURY MAY FIND THAT AN ACTOR HAS TAKEN SUBSTANTIAL STEP TOWARD COMMISSION OF A CRIME WHEN THE ACTOR POSSESSES REQUIRED MATERIALS NEAR THE SCENE OF THE CRIME AND THE COURSE OF ACTION CORROBORATES THE CRIMINAL PURPOSE

■ **INSTANT FACTS** Reeves (D) and a friend devised and tried to carry out a plan to kill their homeroom teacher and steal her car.

■ **BLACK LETTER RULE** When an actor possesses materials to be used in the commission of a crime, at or near the scene of the crime, and where the possession of those materials can serve no lawful purpose of the actor under the circumstances, the jury is entitled, but not required, to find that the actor has taken a "substantial step" toward the commission of the crime if such action is strongly corroborative of the actor's overall purpose.

■ PROCEDURAL BASIS

Appeal from the Circuit Court's affirmance of the juvenile court's delinquency conviction and sentencing of the defendant.

■ FACTS

Tracie Reeves (D) and Molly Coffman, both twelve years old, talked on the telephone and decided to kill their homeroom teacher [what happened to talking about boys and crushes?]. The girls agreed that Coffman would bring rat poison to school the following day so that it could be placed in their teacher's drink. The girls also agreed that they would thereafter steal the teacher's car and drive to the Smoky Mountains [great getaway plan]. Reeves (D) then contacted Dean Foutch, a local high school student, informed him of the plan, and asked him to drive the car. Foutch refused this request. The next morning, Coffman placed a packet of rat poison in her purse and boarded the school bus. During the bus ride, Coffman told another student, Christy Hernandez, of the plan, and showed her the packet of rat poison. Upon their arrival at school, Hernandez told her homeroom teacher of the plan [tattle-tale]. The teacher then relayed the information to the principal, Claudia Argo. When Geiger entered her classroom that morning she saw Coffman and Reeves (D) leaning over her desk. When the girls noticed her, they giggled and ran back to their seats. At that time Geiger saw a purse lying next to her coffee cup on top of the desk. Shortly thereafter, Argo called Coffman to the principal's office. Rat poison was found in her purse and it was turned over to a Sheriff's Department investigator. Reeves (D) and Coffman were found to be delinquent by the Juvenile Court, and both appealed from that ruling to the Circuit Court. After a jury found that the girls attempted to commit second-degree murder, the trial court affirmed the juvenile court's order and sentenced the girls to the Department of Youth Development for an indefinite period. This appeal followed.

■ ISSUE

Does simply planning a crime and possessing materials required to commit such crime constitute a "substantial step" towards the commission of the crime?

■ DECISION AND RATIONALE

(Drowota, J.) Yes. Prior to the passage of reform legislation in 1989, the law of criminal attempt was judicially defined in *Dupuy v. State.* In *Dupuy* in order to submit an issue of criminal attempt to the jury, the State was required to present legally sufficient evidence of: (1) an intent to commit a specific crime; (2) an overt act toward the commission of that crime; and (3) a failure to consummate the crime. There was a sharp differentiation in *Dupuy* between "mere preparation" and "overt act," or the "act itself," which was characteristic of the pre-1989 attempt law. In 1989, however, the legislature enacted a general criminal attempt statute as part of its comprehensive overhaul of Tennessee's criminal law. The statute specifically requires, in part, that the conduct constitute a substantial step toward the commission of the offense. Furthermore, conduct will not constitute a *substantial step* unless the person's entire course of action is corroborative of the Intent to commit the offense. Our task is to determine whether Reeves' (D) actions constitute a "substantial step" toward the commission of second-degree murder under the new statute. While we concede that a strong argument can be made that the conviction conflicts with *Dupuy* because Reeves (D) did not place the poison in the cup, but simply brought it to the crime scene, we are also well aware that the *Dupuy* approach to attempt law has been consistently and effectively criticized. Distinguishing between "mere preparation" and the "act itself" in a principled manner is a difficult, if not impossible, task. The other principal ground of criticism of the *Dupuy* approach bears directly on the primary objective of the law—that of preventing inchoate crimes from becoming full-blown ones. Failure to attach criminal responsibility to the actor until the actor is on the brink of consummating the crime endangers the public and undermines the preventative goal of attempt law. After carefully weighing considerations of *stare decisis* against the persuasive criticisms of the *Dupuy* rule, we conclude that this artificial and potentially harmful rule must be abandoned. We hold that when an actor possesses materials to be used in the commission of a crime, at or near the scene of the crime, and where the possession of those materials can serve no lawful purpose of the actor under the circumstances, the jury is entitled, but not required, to find that the actor has taken a "substantial step" toward the commission of the crime if such action is strongly corroborative of the actor's overall purpose. For the foregoing reasons, the conviction is affirmed.

■ CONCURRENCE AND DISSENT

(Birch, J.) The entire course of action of these two girls was not "strongly corroborative" of the intent to commit second-degree murder and the evidence was insufficient as a matter of law. These are twelve-year-old girls, not explosive-toting terrorists. Accordingly, while I concur in the majority's abandonment of the rule stated in *Dupuy*, I dissent from the conclusion of the majority in this case.

Analysis:

A jury could easily find that the girls took "substantial steps" toward the commission of the crime they had planned, that of killing their teacher. However, even if their conduct does seem to constitute a substantial step, it must be determined that those actions were "strongly corroborative" of their purpose to commit the crime. It seems possible that an argument could be made that the girls' failure to actually put the poison in the coffee cup is indicative of a lack of genuine intent to kill their teacher. As the dissent points out, the girls are giggly and young; the plan to run off to the mountains seems particularly juvenile. Perhaps this was really more of a game to the girls than a seriously cold and calculated murder plot. On the other hand, the increased incidence of violence in schools is such that all threats and plans must be taken seriously. Times have changed and the law must as well in order to keep up.

■ CASE VOCABULARY

INCHOATE CRIME: Offense not yet completed or finished.

STARE DECISIS: Principles announced in former judicial decisions which are upheld and followed unless there is a showing of good cause.

United States v. Alkhabaz

(*Government*) v. (*Deviant Sex Freak*)

104 F.3d 1492 (6th Cir. 1997)

"THREATENING COMMUNICATIONS" [UNDER 18 U.S.C. § 875(c)] MUST CONTAIN AN INTENT TO INFLICT HARM AS WELL AS FURTHERANCE OF A GOAL THROUGH INTIMIDATION

■ **INSTANT FACTS** Alkhabaz (D) was arrested for posting fictional stories involving the abduction, rape, torture, mutilation, and murder of women and young girls on the Internet.

■ **BLACK LETTER RULE** To constitute "a communication containing a threat" under 18 U.S.C. Sec. 875(c), a communication must be such that a reasonable person (1) would take the statement as a serious expression of an intention to inflict bodily harm (the mens rea), and (2) would perceive such expression as being communicated to effect some change or achieve some goal through intimidation (the actus reus).

■ PROCEDURAL BASIS

Appeal from the judgment of the district court quashing the defendant's indictment.

■ FACTS

Over a period of about three months, Alkhabaz (D) (a.k.a. Jake Baker), and Gonda exchanged email messages over the Internet, the content of which expressed a sexual interest in violence against women and girls [a couple of real catches!]. Alkhabaz (D) used a computer in Michigan while Gonda (whose true identity and whereabouts remain unknown) used a computer in Ontario, Canada. Prior to this time, Alkhabaz (D) had posted a number of fictional stories to a popular Interactive Usenet news group. His fictional stories generally involved the abduction, rape, torture, mutilation, and murder of women and young girls [not one to take home to meet your mother!]. One story he posted described the torture, rape, and murder of a young woman who shared the same name as one of Alkhabaz's (D) classmates at the University of Michigan. Alkhabaz was arrested and charged with violating 18 U.S.C. Sec. 875(c), which prohibits interstate communications containing threats to kidnap or injure another person.

■ ISSUE

Do fictional stories describing the torture, rape, and murder of women constitute "a communication containing a threat" under 18 U.S.C. Sec. 875(c)?

■ DECISION AND RATIONALE

(Martin, Jr., J.) No. To determine what type of action Congress intended to prohibit, it is necessary to consider the nature of a threat. At their core, threats are tools that are employed when one wishes to have some effect, or achieve some goal, through intimidation. This is true regardless of whether the goal is highly reprehensible or seemingly innocuous. Although it may offend our sensibilities, a communication objectively indicating a serious expression of an intention to inflict bodily harm cannot constitute a threat unless the communication also is conveyed for the purpose of furthering some goal through the use of intimidation. Accordingly, to achieve the intent of Congress, we hold that, to constitute "a communication containing a threat" under 18 U.S.C. Sec. 875(c), a communication must be such that a reasonable person (1) would take the statement as a serious expression of an intention to inflict bodily harm (the mens rea), and (2) would perceive such expression as being communicated to effect some change or achieve some goal through intimidation (the actus reus). The dissent argues that Congress did not intend to include as an element of the crime the furthering of some goal through the use of intimidation. Emphasizing the term "any" in the language of the statute, the dissent maintains that Congress did not limit the scope of communications that constitute criminal threats. While we agree that Congress chose inclusive language to identify the types of threats that it intended to prohibit, we cannot ignore the fact that Congress intended to forbid only those communications that in fact constitute a "threat." The conclusion that we reach here is one that the term "threat" necessarily implies. Applying our interpretation of the statute to the facts before us, we conclude that the communications between Alkhabaz (D) and Gonda do not constitute "communications containing a threat" under Section 875(c). Even if a reasonable person would take the communications between the two as serious expressions of an intention to inflict bodily harm, no reasonable person would perceive such communications as being conveyed to effect some change or achieve some goal through intimidation. Quite the opposite, Alkhabaz (D) and Gonda apparently sent email messages to each other in an attempt to foster a friendship based on shared sexual fantasies. For the foregoing reasons, the judgment of the district court quashing the indictment is affirmed.

■ DISSENT

(Krupansky, J.) The words in Section 875(c) are simple, clear, concise, and unambiguous. The plain, expressed statutory language commands only that the alleged communication must contain *any threat* to kidnap or physically injure *any person*, made for *any reason* or no reason. Section 875(c) by its terms does not confine the scope of criminalized communications to those directed to identified individuals and intended to effect some particular change or goal. Consequently, a communication which an objective, rational observer would tend to interpret, in its factual context, as a credible threat, is a "true threat" which may be punished by the government. Accordingly, I would reverse the district court's judgment which dismissed the superseding indictment as purportedly not alleging "true threats," and remand the cause to the lower court.

Analysis:

People cannot be punished for their thoughts, but how much further must a person go before the criminal law steps in? In this case, the woman whose name was used in the story knew nothing of the fantasy until the University and law enforcement notified her of the situation. It seems difficult to imagine then, that this fantasy could be threatening toward her. But what is to ensure that the fantasy truly was nothing more than just a story? How can the criminal law deal with a person who seems to have a criminal disposition, but who may or may not ever act out his thoughts? It's a difficult line to walk, for as legislatures enlarge the scope of inchoate criminality, the risk of punishing innocent persons increases. This case shows one court's efforts to modify a statute to reach what it believes is a proper balance. The dissent underscores the immense controversy in this arena.

■ CASE VOCABULARY

INTERSTATE COMMUNICATIONS: Either telephone, email or snail-mail, across state lines.

People v. Thousand

(*Prosecution*) v. (*Internet Pedophile*)

465 Mich. 149, 631 N.W.2d 694 (2001)

DOCTRINE OF IMPOSSIBILITY DOES NOT PROVIDE DEFENSE TO ATTEMPT OFFENSE

■ **INSTANT FACTS** A Sheriff's Deputy logged into a chat room, posing as a 14–year-old female, and chatted with Thousand (D), who was later charged with attempted distribution of obscene materials to a minor.

■ **BLACK LETTER RULE** A defendant is guilty of attempt if he attempted to commit an offense prohibited by law and engaged in conduct in furtherance of the intended offense, whether or not an element of the underlying offense could not be satisfied due to legal or factual impossibility

■ PROCEDURAL BASIS

The prosecution appeals the trial court's dismissal of the attempt charges brought against the defendant.

■ FACTS

Deputy William Liczbinski worked as an undercover investigator for the Wayne County Sheriff's Department. In this capacity, Liczbinski posed as a minor and logged into chat rooms on the Internet for the purpose of identifying persons using the Internet to engage in criminal activity. On December 8, 1998, Chris Thousand (D), who identified himself as a 23–year-old male, contacted Liczbinski in the chat room. Thousand (D) sent Liczbinski a photograph of his face. At the time, Liczbinski was using the screen name "Bekka" and he told Thousand (D) that he was a 14–year-old female. Liczbinski, still posing as "Bekka," and Thousand (D) engaged in chat room conversation from December 9 through 16, 1998. The conversation became sexually explicit, and during one of the conversations, Thousands (D) sent "Bekka" a photograph of male genitalia. Thereafter, Thousand (D) asked "Bekka" to come to his house to engage in sexual activity. Thousand (D) acknowledged that they would have to be careful because he could go to jail for this activity, and he also informed "Bekka" that he would have to lie about her age to his roommates. The two planned to meet at a local McDonald's restaurant. Thousand (D) arrived at the specified McDonald's on December 17, 1998. Identified by Liczbinski from the photograph Thousand (D) had sent him, Thousand (D) was taken into custody and charged with attempt to distribute obscene materials to a minor. The trial court dismissed the charge, finding that because the existence of a child victim was an element of the offense, the evidence was legally insufficient to support the charge. The Court of Appeals affirmed the dismissal.

■ ISSUE

Does the doctrine of legal impossibility, based on the absence of a minor victim, provide a valid defense to a charge of attempt to disseminate or exhibit sexual material to a minor?

■ DECISION AND RATIONALE

(Young, J.) No. A defendant's assertion of legal or factual impossibility as to the existence of one of the elements of the underlying offense is irrelevant to the determination of his or her guilt for attempt to commit that offense because the offense of attempt only requires the prosecution to prove that a defendant attempted to commit an offense prohibited by law and that the defendant engaged in conduct in furtherance of the intended offense. Courts have invoked the doctrine of impossibility in situations where, because of a defendant's mistake of fact or law, the defendant's actions could not have resulted in the commission of the substantive crime underlying an attempt charge. At common law, legal impossibility was a defense to the charge of attempt, but factual impossibility was not. Factual impossibility exists when a defendant intends to commit a crime but fails only because of factual circumstances unknown to her or beyond her control. Pure legal impossibility exists when a defendant engages in conduct that he believes is criminal, but which is not actually prohibited by law. Most claims, however, involve a hybrid of both legal and factual impossibility, where a defendant's goal was illegal but the commission of the offense was made impossible due to a factual mistake as to the legal status of some factor relevant to the conduct. As the facts of this case illustrate, it is possible to view almost any example of "hybrid legal impossibility" as "factual impossibility." Indeed, a majority of jurisdictions have recognized that legal and factual impossibility are, for all practical purposes, indistinguishable and have abolished impossibility as a defense. This Court has never recognized impossibility, whether factual or legal, as a defense to a charge of attempt. In fact, our attempt statute only requires 1) an attempt to commit an offense prohibited by law, and 2) any act towards the commission of the intended offense. Moreover, the attempt statute does not indicate any legislative intent to allow impossibility as a defense to attempt. In this case, it is unquestioned that Thousand (D) could not be charged with the actual substantive crime of distributing obscene materials to a minor because he unknowingly distributed the material to an adult man. Instead, Thousand (D) is charged with the distinct offense of attempt, which requires only a showing that he possessed the requisite specific intent to commit the underlying offense of distributing obscene materials to minors, and that he engaged in some act towards the commission of that offense. Thousand's (D) actions satisfy these elements, and the nonexistence of a minor victim does not provide a viable defense to the attempt charge in this case. The lower court erred in dismissing this case on the basis of impossibility. Reversed and remanded.

■ DISSENT

(Kelly, J.) I disagree with the majority's conclusion that the doctrine of legal impossibility has never been adopted in Michigan. On the contrary, legal impossibility is a viable defense in this state and should be allowed as a defense to the attempt charge at issue. Even if legal impossibility were not a defense, I would still affirm the appellate court's dismissal of this case. The language of our attempt statute clearly indicates that it seeks to make illegal the attempt to commit an offense prohibited by law. Here, the dissemination of sexual materials requires a minor recipient for it to become a crime. Because there was no minor recipient in this case, Thousand's (D) dissemination of materials to Deputy Liczbinski did not result in an attempt to commit a crime prohibited by law. I would affirm the Court of Appeals decision.

Analysis:

Before determining that the doctrine of impossibility does not serve as a defense to an attempt offense, the *Thousand* court defined legal and factual impossibility. *United States v. Oviedo*, cited in Note 3 following the case, states that legal impossibility occurs when a defendant sets in motion actions that, even if fully performed, would not constitute a crime. Factual impossibility occurs when the objective that the defendant seeks would constitute a crime if fully executed according to plan, but circumstances unknown to the defendant prevent him from bringing about the objective. Under the definitions given by the *Oviedo* court, would Thousand's (D) actions constitute legal or factual impossibility? Does Justice Kelly's reasoning in her dissent convince you that, if recognized, the doctrine of impossibility would bar the attempt charge against Thousand (D)?

■ CASE VOCABULARY

FACTUAL IMPOSSIBILITY: Crime is impossible due to some physical impossibility unknown to the defendant (this is not a defense to attempt).

LEGAL IMPOSSIBILITY: Act is not criminal therefore criminal liability cannot attach for an attempt to commit the act.

Commonwealth v. McCloskey

(*State*) v. (*Prisoner*)

234 Pa.Super. 577, 341 A.2d 500 (1975)

PRISONER MAY ABANDON HIS ESCAPE PLAN AND EXONERATE HIS CRIMINAL LIABILITY IF HE HAS NOT ACTUALLY LEFT THE PRISON

■ **INSTANT FACTS** Prisoner planned a prison breach but abandoned the plan before leaving the prison and attempting the escape.

■ **BLACK LETTER RULE** A prisoner contemplating a prison breach, but still within a prison having not yet attempted the act, is in a position to abandon the criminal act voluntarily, thereby exonerating himself from criminal responsibility.

■ PROCEDURAL BASIS

Appeal from the defendant's conviction in a bench trial.

■ FACTS

McCloskey (D) was serving a one-to-three-year prison sentence for larceny. One early morning, at 12:15 a.m., James Larson, a Guard Supervisor at the Luzerne County Prison, heard an alarm go off that indicated that someone was attempting an escape in the recreation area of the prison. The alarm was designed so that it could be heard in the prison office, but not in the courtyard [can't let them know we're on to them]. Larson immediately contacted Guards Szmulo and Banik, who then checked the prison population but found no one missing. The three guards then checked the recreation area where the alarm had been tripped. They found one piece of barbed wire that had been cut, as well as a laundry bag filled with civilian clothing. A check revealed that the bag belonged to McCloskey (D). At approximately 5:15 a.m. that same morning, McCloskey (D) voluntarily approached Larson. He explained to Larson that he was going to make a break that night, but that he had changed his mind because he got scared and didn't want to shame his family any more [what a guy!]. The grand jury subsequently returned an indictment charging McCloskey (D) with prison breach. McCloskey (D) was found guilty in a bench trial of attempted prison breach.

■ ISSUE

Can a prisoner be convicted of attempted prison breach when he abandons the plan before ever leaving the prison?

■ DECISION AND RATIONALE

(Hoffman, J.) No. The evidence shows that McCloskey (D) scaled a fence within the prison walls that led to the recreation yard and then to the prison wall. The evidence supports McCloskey's (D) claim that he went only as far as the yard before giving up his plan to escape. Thus McCloskey (D) was still within the prison, still only contemplating a prison breach, and not yet attempting the act. He was thus in a position to abandon the criminal offense of attempted prison breach voluntarily, thereby exonerating himself from criminal responsibility. Judgment of sentence is vacated and McCloskey (D) ordered discharged on the conviction of attempted prison breach.

■ CONCURRENCE

(Cercone, J.) I agree that the conviction should not be permitted to stand, however I disagree with the basis for the majority's conclusion. If voluntary abandonment is to be given effect in attempt cases, it should not be done covertly.

Analysis:

McCloskey (D) was charged under the old Penal Code, which did not speak to whether voluntary abandonment was a defense to a charge of attempt. It has long been recognized that plans voluntarily abandoned are less likely to be found to be attempts than are plans carried to the same point, but interrupted by the apprehension of the perpetrators. Unfortunately, in jurisdictions where voluntary abandonment or renunciation of a criminal purpose has not been recognized as an affirmative defense, the courts have sought to give effect to the defendant's abandonment, *sub silentio*, by characterizing his conduct as "preparatory." This is what the concurrence claims the majority did in this case, and this is what the concurrence disagrees with. The concurring opinion asserts that this preparation-perpetration dichotomy breeds superficially inconsistent results, and thus voluntary abandonment must be recognized as an affirmative defense itself.

■ CASE VOCABULARY

BENCH TRIAL: Trial before a judge sitting without a jury.

SUB SILENTIO: Literally, under silence; a later opinion overrules a prior holding by necessary implication.

State v. Mann

(State) v. *(Not Stated)*

317 N.C. 164, 345 S.E.2d 365 (1986)

SOLICITATION SUGGESTED AS MORE DANGEROUS THAN CONSPIRACY OR ATTEMPT

■ INSTANT FACTS None Stated.

■ BLACK LETTER RULE The solicitor conceives the criminal idea and furthers its commission via another person by suggesting to, inducing, or manipulating that person.

■ PROCEDURAL BASIS

None Stated.

■ FACTS

None Stated.

■ ISSUE

None Stated.

■ DECISION AND RATIONALE

(Martin, J.) Solicitation involves the asking, enticing, inducing, or counseling of another to commit a crime. The solicitor conceives the criminal idea and furthers its commission via another person by suggesting to, inducing, or manipulating that person. A solicitor may be more dangerous than a conspirator, as a conspirator may merely passively agree to a criminal scheme, while the solicitor plans, schemes, suggests, encourages, and incites the solicitation. Further, the solicitor is morally more culpable than a conspirator; he keeps himself from being at risk, hiding behind the actor.

Analysis:

There are many criticisms of the crime of solicitation. First, solicitations are said to be not in themselves dangerous, because no harm will occur unless the person solicited agrees. In that case, the conspiracy is proven, and there is no need for charging solicitation. Second, contrary to the assertions in this case, a solicitor is ordinarily *less* dangerous because of his reluctance to actually commit the crime himself. Finally, if solicitation is used over-zealously, it has been said that it will chill First Amendment free-speech rights.

■ CASE VOCABULARY

SOLICITATION: Asking, enticing, or encouraging another to commit a crime.

State v. Cotton

(*State*) v. (*Sexually Abusive Stepfather*)
109 N.M. 769, 790 P.2d 1050 (1990)

TO BE CONVICTED OF SOLICITATION, THE MESSAGE MUST BE RECEIVED BY THE PERSON INTENDED TO BE SOLICITED

■ **INSTANT FACTS** Cotton (D) wrote letters to his wife, which she never received, trying to get her to convince his stepdaughter not to testify against him at trial.

■ **BLACK LETTER RULE** If a solicitor's message never reaches the person intended to be solicited, the act is criminal, but it must be prosecuted as an attempt to solicit.

■ PROCEDURAL BASIS

Appeal from criminal solicitation convictions.

■ FACTS

Cotton (D), his wife, five children and a stepdaughter moved to New Mexico. A few months later, Cotton's (D) wife and children moved back to Indiana. Shortly thereafter, the stepdaughter moved back to New Mexico to live with Cotton (D). The next year, Cotton (D) was investigated by the Department of Human Services for allegations of misconduct involving him and his stepdaughter. He was subsequently arrested and charged with multiple counts of criminal sexual acts with a minor. While in jail awaiting trial on those charges, Cotton (D) discussed with his cell-mate Dobbs his desire to persuade his stepdaughter not to testify against him. During his incarceration, Cotton wrote numerous letters to his wife discussing his strategy for defending against the charges. In one letter, Cotton (D) requested that his wife assist him in persuading his stepdaughter not to testify at his trial. He also urged his wife to contact his stepdaughter and influence her to return to Indiana or to give her money to leave the state so she would be unavailable to testify. After writing the letter, Cotton (D) gave the letter to Dobbs and asked him to obtain a stamp for it. Unknown to Cotton (D), Dobbs removed the letter from the envelope, replaced it with a blank sheet of paper, and returned the sealed stamped envelope to Cotton (D). Dobbs gave Cotton's (D) original letter to law enforcement authorities. Cotton (D) wrote another letter to his wife again telling her either to try to talk the stepdaughter out of testifying or to talk her into testifying favorably for Cotton (D). Cotton (D) also said his wife should warn his stepdaughter that if she did testify for the state "it won't be nice and she'll make the news." It is undisputed that neither letter was ever mailed nor received by Cotton's (D) wife.

■ ISSUE

Can a person be convicted of solicitation if the solicitor's message never reaches the person intended to be solicited?

■ DECISION AND RATIONALE

(Donnelly, J.) No. The offense of criminal solicitation is defined in part as: Except as to bona fide acts of persons authorized by law to investigate and detect the commission of offenses by others, a person is guilty of criminal solicitation if, with the intent that another person engage in conduct constituting a felony, he solicits, commands, requests, induces, employs or otherwise attempts to promote or facilitate another person to engage in conduct constituting a felony within or without the state. Cotton (D) contends that the record fails to contain the requisite evidence to support the charges of criminal solicitation against him because Cotton's (D) wife, the intended solicitee, never received the two letters. The state (P) reasons that proof of Cotton's (D) acts of writing the letters, and attempts to mail them, together with his specific intent to solicit the commission of a felony constitutes sufficient proof to sustain a charge of criminal solicitation. We disagree. As enacted by our legislature, the section defining criminal solicitation significantly omits one section of the Model Penal Code which pertains to the effect of an uncommunicated criminal solicitation. This omission, we conclude, indicates an implicit legislative intent that the offense of solicitation requires some form of actual communication from the defendant to either an intermediary or the person intended to be solicited, indicating the subject matter of the solicitation. We thus conclude that if the solicitor's message never reaches the person intended to be solicited, as where the intermediary fails to pass on the communication or the solicitee's letter is intercepted before it reaches the addressee, it does not constitute criminal solicitation. The act is criminal, however it may be that the solicitor must be prosecuted for an attempt to solicit on such facts. Cotton's (D) convictions for solicitation are reversed and the cause is remanded with instructions to set aside the convictions.

Analysis:

The Model Penal Code provides that conduct "designed to effect" communication of the culpable message is sufficient to constitute criminal solicitation and there is therefore no need for a crime of attempted solicitation. The New Mexico legislature deliberately omitted this language from its section regarding criminal solicitation, and the court interprets this to mean it specifically wanted some actual communication to take place before liability attaches. The prosecution in this case could have, however, seized upon the statutory language that reads "or otherwise *attempts* to promote or facilitate. . . ." This phrase could have been used to cover the fact situation in this case and support the claim that uncommunicated solicitations are punishable as solicitations.

■ CASE VOCABULARY

BONA FIDE: Good faith, genuine.

People v. Carter

(*State*) v. (*Not Stated*)

415 Mich. 558, 330 N.W.2d 314 (1982)

CONSPIRACY IS A CRIME SEPARATE AND DISTINCT FROM THE UNDERLYING SUBSTANTIVE CRIME

■ **INSTANT FACTS** None Stated.

■ **BLACK LETTER RULE** A defendant may be convicted and punished for both the conspiracy and the substantive crime.

■ PROCEDURAL BASIS

None Stated.

■ FACTS

None Stated.

■ ISSUE

May a defendant be convicted and punished for both a conspiracy and the substantive crime?

■ DECISION AND RATIONALE

(Moody, Jr., J.) Yes. Criminal conspiracy is a mutual agreement or understanding, express or implied, between two or more persons to commit a criminal act or accomplish a legal act by unlawful means. The crime is complete upon formation of the agreement; It is not necessary to establish any overt act in furtherance of the conspiracy as a component of the crime. However, a twofold specific intent is required for conviction: intent to combine with others, and intent to accomplish the illegal objective. It is a settled principle of black-letter law that conspiracy is separate and distinct from the substantive crime that is its object. A defendant may be convicted and punished for both the conspiracy and the substantive crime.

Analysis:

As the court points out, the guilt or innocence of a conspirator does not depend upon the accomplishment of the goals of the conspiracy. And, more importantly, a conviction for conspiracy does not merge with a conviction for the completed offense. This is why a defendant may be convicted of both the conspiracy as well as the underlying substantive offense. Additionally, while conspiracy is an inchoate offense, in most jurisdictions it also constitutes the basis for holding a person accountable for the completed crimes of others (co-conspirators).

■ CASE VOCABULARY

CONSPIRACY: A partnership in criminal purposes.

Pinkerton v. United States

(*IRS Scammer*) v. (*Government*)

328 U.S. 640, 66 S.Ct. 1180, 90 L.Ed. 1489 (1946)

PARTNERS IN CONSPIRACY CAN BE CONVICTED OF THE SUBSTANTIVE CRIME WITHOUT PARTICIPATION

■ **INSTANT FACTS** Two brothers were convicted of both conspiracy and the substantive offense even though only one actually participated in committing the offense.

■ **BLACK LETTER RULE** Participation in the conspiracy is enough to sustain a conviction for the substantive offense in furtherance of the conspiracy.

■ PROCEDURAL BASIS

Appeal from jury's conviction of the defendant.

■ FACTS

Walter and Daniel Pinkerton (D) are brothers who live a short distance from each other on Daniel's (D) farm. They were indicted for violations of the Internal Revenue Code. The indictment contained ten substantive counts and one conspiracy count. The jury found Walter guilty on nine of the substantive counts and on the conspiracy count. It found Daniel (D) guilty on six of the substantive counts and on the conspiracy count. A single conspiracy was charged and proved. Each of the substantive offenses found was committed pursuant to the conspiracy.

■ ISSUE

Is participation in a conspiracy enough to sustain a conviction for the substantive offense?

■ DECISION AND RATIONALE

(Douglas, J.) Yes. It is contended that there was insufficient evidence to implicate Daniel (D) in the conspiracy, but we think there was enough evidence for submission to the jury. There is, however, no evidence to show that Daniel (D) participated directly in the commission of the substantive offenses on which his conviction has been sustained, although there was evidence to show that these substantive offenses were committed by Walter in furtherance of the unlawful agreement or conspiracy existing between brothers. We take the view here that there was a continuous conspiracy which Daniel (D) never took any affirmative action to withdraw from. So long as the partnership in crime continues, the partners act for each other in carrying it forward. It is settled that an overt act of one partner may be the act of all without any new agreement specifically directed to that act. Thus we hold that Daniel's (D) participation in the conspiracy is enough to sustain his conviction for the substantive offense in furtherance of the conspiracy. Affirmed.

■ DISSENT

(Rutledge, J.) The judgment concerning Daniel Pinkerton (D) should be reversed. It is my opinion that it is without precedent here and is a dangerous precedent to establish. The result is a vicarious criminal responsibility as broad as, or broader than, the vicarious civil liability of a partner for acts done by a co-partner in the course of the firm's business.

Analysis:

The court's decision in this case, taken at face value, appears sound. However, the underlying facts make the judgment a bit harder to understand. The proof showed that Walter alone committed the substantive crimes, and there was no proof that Daniel (D) even knew that he had done so. In fact, Daniel (D) was in prison for other crimes when some of Walter's crimes were committed. Walter and Daniel (D) became partners in crime by virtue of their agreement and, without more on his part, Daniel (D) became criminally liable for everything Walter did thereafter so long as there was no proof of a clear withdrawal from or revocation of the agreement. The dissent correctly labels Daniel's (D) liability as vicarious, and it seems to be a better argument that vicarious liability should remain in the civil law and not be transferred to the criminal field.

■ CASE VOCABULARY

VICARIOUS LIABILITY: Imputing liability upon one person for the actions of another.

People v. Swain

(*State*) v. (*Drive-by Shooter*)

12 Cal.4th 593, 49 Cal.Rptr.2d 390, 909 P.2d 994 (1996)

INTENT TO KILL IS A REQUIRED ELEMENT TO PROVE CONSPIRACY TO COMMIT MURDER

■ **INSTANT FACTS** Swain (D) was convicted of conspiracy to commit murder after his friend killed a young boy in a drive-by shooting.

■ **BLACK LETTER RULE** A conviction of conspiracy to commit murder requires a finding of intent to kill, and cannot be based on a theory of implied malice.

■ PROCEDURAL BASIS

Appeal from defendant's conviction and sentence in a jury trial.

■ FACTS

A brown van passing through a neighborhood at about 2:00 a.m. one morning slowed down near the spot where Saileele, a 15-year-old Samoan boy, and his friends were listening to music on the street. A young black male was driving the van. Suddenly, several shots were fired from the front of the van. Chatman and another youth also fired guns from the rear of the van. One of the intended victims had yelled out "drive-by" as a warning of the impending shooting, so most of the people on the street ducked down [common occurrence in the neighborhood?]. Saileele, who was holding the radio from which the music was playing, was shot twice from behind. He died later in surgery. Afterward, Swain (D) was in jail boasting to jailmates about what good aim he had with a gun. He told them that he had shot the Samoan boy when they were in the van. At trial, Swain (D) testified that he had been in the van earlier in the evening, but that he had left prior to the incident because the smell of marijuana bothered him. At trial, Chatman admitted he had been in the van with his friends to retaliate for a car theft attributed to a neighborhood youth who was not the victim of the shooting. The original plan was allegedly to steal the car of the thief [that'll teach him!]. Chatman admitted he had fired shots, but claimed he fired wildly and only in self-defense [just a lucky shot]. He said he heard an initial shot and thought it was fired by someone outside the van shooting at him, so he returned fire. The jury returned a verdict finding Chatman guilty of second degree murder and conspiracy and, as instructed, made a finding that the target offense of the conspiracy was murder in the second degree. Several days later, the jury returned verdicts against Swain (D), finding him not guilty of murder or its lesser included offenses, but guilty of conspiracy.

■ ISSUE

Is intent to kill a required element of the crime of conspiracy to commit murder?

■ DECISION AND RATIONALE

(Baxter, A.J.) Yes. Swain (D) contends that the jury should have been instructed that proof of intent to kill is required to support a conviction of conspiracy to commit murder, whether the target offense of the conspiracy—murder—is determined to be in the first or second degree. More particularly, Swain (D) asserts it was error to instruct the jury on the principles of implied malice second degree murder in connection with the determination of whether he could be found guilty of conspiracy to commit murder, since implied malice does not require a finding of intent to kill. As we shall explain, we agree. Conspiracy is a specific intent crime. The specific intent required divides into two elements: (a) the intent to agree, or conspire, and (b) the intent to commit the offense which is the object of the conspiracy. To sustain a conviction for conspiracy to commit a particular offense, the prosecution must show not only that the conspirators intended to agree but also that they intended to commit the elements of that offense. We next turn to the elements of the target offense of the conspiracy here in issue. The crime of murder is defined as the unlawful killing of a human being with malice aforethought. The malice aforethought may be express or implied. This court has observed that proof of unlawful "intent to kill" is the functional equivalent of express malice. We have noted that conspiracy is a specific intent crime requiring an intent to agree or conspire, and a further intent to commit the target crime, here murder, the object of the conspiracy. Since murder committed with intent to kill is the functional equivalent of express malice murder, conceptually speaking, no conflict arises between the specific intent element of conspiracy and the specific intent requirement for such category of murders. Simply put, where the conspirators agree or conspire with specific intent to kill and commit an overt act in furtherance of such agreement, they are guilty of conspiracy to commit express malice murder. The conceptual difficulty arises when the target offense of murder is founded on a theory of implied malice, which requires no intent to kill. Implied malice murder, in contrast to express malice, requires instead an intent to do some act, the natural consequences of which are dangerous to human life. Hence, under an implied malice theory of second degree murder, the requisite mental state for murder—malice aforethought—is by definition "implied," as a matter of law, from the specific intent to do some act dangerous to human life together with the circumstance that a killing has resulted from the doing of such act. Stated otherwise, all murders require, at the core of the corpus delicti of the offense, a "killing." But only in the case of *implied malice* murder is the requisite mental state—malice aforethought—implied from the specific intent to do some act *other than* an intentional killing *and* the resulting circumstance: a killing has in fact occurred as "the direct result of such an act." We conclude that a conviction of conspiracy to commit murder requires a finding of intent to kill, and cannot be based on a theory of implied malice.

Analysis:

The Model Penal Code notes that the traditional definition of conspiracy said nothing about the actor's state of mind, except insofar as the concept of agreement itself carries certain implications about his attitude toward the crime. Perhaps this is because the intent to agree is difficult to distinguish from the agreement itself. It is not sufficient to show that the conspirators intended to agree. It must be proved that the conspirators intended to accomplish an unlawful objective, which is the object of the conspiracy. The elements of the unlawful objective must be met. Conspiracy to commit a particular substantive offense cannot exist without at least the degree of criminal intent necessary for the substantive offense itself. The court does a good job in this case of breaking down the crime committed versus the crime intended in order to arrive at a reasonable and just solution.

■ CASE VOCABULARY

CORPUS DELICTI: Body of the crime; proof a crime was committed.

IMPLIED MALICE: State of mind inferred from conduct and lacking in specific intent.

MALICE AFORETHOUGHT: Characteristic state of mind for murder; there is no justification or excuse, and no mitigating circumstances exist.

People v. Lauria

(*Government*) v. (*Telephone Answering Service Provider*)

251 Cal.App.2d 471, 59 Cal.Rptr. 628 (1967)

A PERSON WHO SUPPLIES A PRODUCT OR SERVICE TO ANOTHER KNOWING THAT IT WILL BE USED AS PART OF A CRIME, MAY BE CONVICTED FOR CONSPIRACY UNLESS ONLY A MISDEMEANOR IS INVOLVED

■ **INSTANT FACTS** Lauria (D) ran a telephone answering service, which he knew was used by several prostitutes in their business ventures; Lauria (D) was indicted with the prostitutes for conspiracy to commit prostitution.

■ **BLACK LETTER RULE** The intent of a supplier who knows his supplies will be put to criminal use may be established by (1) direct evidence that he intends to participate, or (2) through an inference that he intends to participate based on (a) his special interest in the activity, or (b) the felonious nature of the crime itself.

■ PROCEDURAL BASIS

Appeal by prosecution from order setting aside an indictment for conspiracy to commit prostitution.

■ FACTS

In a prostitution investigation, police focused their attention on three prostitutes who used Lauria's (D) telephone service. An undercover policewoman, Stella Weeks, signed up for Lauria's (D) services. Weeks hinted that she was a prostitute, and wanted to conceal that fact from the police. Lauria (D) assured her that his service was discreet and safe. A few weeks later, Weeks called Lauria (D) and complained that because of his operation she had lost two "tricks." Lauria (D) claimed that her tricks probably lied about leaving messages for her. Lauria (D) did not respond to Weeks' hints that she needed more customers, other than to invite her over to become better acquainted. A couple of weeks later Weeks again complained that she had lost two tricks, and the office manager said she would investigate. Two weeks later, Lauria (D) and the three prostitutes were arrested. Lauria (D) testified before the Grand Jury that he only had 9 or 10 prostitutes using his service, and he kept records for known or suspected prostitutes for the convenience of police. However, Lauria (D) did not volunteer the information, but would give it when asked about a specific prostitute. He claimed that he tolerated the prostitutes so long as they paid their bills. Lauria (D) admitted having personal knowledge that some of his customers were prostitutes. Lauria (D) and the three prostitutes were indicted for conspiracy to commit prostitution. The trial court set aside the indictment as having been brought without a showing of reasonable or probable cause. The Government (P) appeals claiming that a sufficient showing of an unlawful agreement to further prostitution was made. To establish agreement, the Government (P) need show no more than an implied mutual understanding, between co-conspirators, to accomplish an unlawful act.

■ ISSUE

Is a person criminally liable for conspiracy if he furnishes goods and services he knows will be used to assist in the operation of an illegal business?

■ DECISION AND RATIONALE

(Fleming, J.) No. *United States v. Falcone* held that a seller's knowledge of the illegal use of the goods was insufficient to make the seller a participant in the conspiracy. In *Direct Sales Co. v. United States,* by contrast, the conviction on federal narcotics laws of a drug wholesaler was affirmed on a showing that the company had actively promoted the sale of morphine. In both cases, however, the element of knowledge of the illegal use of the goods or services and the element of intent to further that use must be present in order to make the supplier a participant in a criminal conspiracy. Proof of knowledge is ordinarily a question of fact. Lauria (D) admitted he knew that some of his customers were prostitutes. He probably knew that some of his customers were subscribing to his service in order to further their trade. The Government argues that this knowledge serves as a basis for concluding that Lauria (D) intended to participate in the criminal activities. We note some characteristic patterns in precedent cases: (1) intent may be inferred from knowledge, when the purveyor of the legal goods for illegal use has acquired a stake in the venture; (2) intent may be inferred from knowledge, when no legitimate use for the goods or services exists; and (3) intent may be inferred from knowledge, when the volume of business with the buyer is grossly disproportionate to any legitimate demand. In response to the first pattern, we note that Lauria (D) had no stake in the venture, and was not charging higher prices to the prostitutes. As to the second pattern, we note that nothing in the furnishing of telephone service implies that it will be used for prostitution, since all sorts of persons might use the service for completely legal activities. Finally, no evidence suggests any unusual volume of Lauria's (D) business was with prostitutes. In all three of these patterns, it can be said that in one way or another a supplier has a special interest in the operation of the criminal enterprise. There are cases in which it cannot be said that the supplier has a stake in the venture, yet still may be held liable based on knowledge alone. Some examples of this would be supplying cutting equipment to be used in a bank robbery, or supplying telephone service to persons involved in the extortion of ransom. Still, we do not believe that an inference of intent drawn from knowledge should apply to misdemeanors. Thus, with respect to misdemeanors, we conclude that positive knowledge of a supplier that his products will be used for illegal activities does not in itself establish intent to participate in the misdemeanor. However, with respect to felonies, we hold that in all felony cases, knowledge of criminal use alone may justify an inference of intent. From this analysis we deduce the following rule: the intent of a supplier who knows of the criminal use to which his supplies are put to participate in the criminal activity connected with the use of his supplies may be established by (1) direct evidence that he intends to participate, or (2) through an inference that he intends to participate based on (a) his special interest in the activity, or (b) the felonious nature of the crime itself. Lauria (D) took no direct action to further the activities of the prostitutes. There is no evidence of a special interest in the prostitutes' activities. The offense with which he has been charged is a misdemeanor. Thus the charges of conspiracy against Lauria (D) fail, and since the conspiracy theory was built around the activities of Lauria's (D) business, the charges against his co-conspirators must also fail. The order is affirmed.

Analysis:

Some argue that conspiracy laws should apply to those with criminal goals, rather than seeking to sweep within the dragnet of conspiracy all those who have been associated to any degree whatsoever with the main offenders. They argue that the law should not be extended to punish "legitimate businessmen" like Lauria (D). On the other hand, some argue that persons should be convicted solely on the basis of their knowledge that they are contributing to a criminal enterprise, even if they do not intend the same goals as the conspiracy. They argue that business people should not be immunized from criminal responsibility under the guise of free enterprise.

Commonwealth v. Azim

(*State*) v. (*Co-conspirator Driver*)

313 Pa.Super. 310, 459 A.2d 1244 (1983)

CO-CONSPIRATORS ARE GUILTY OF THE CRIMINAL ACTS OF ALL MEMBERS OF THE CONSPIRACY IN FURTHERANCE OF THE AGREEMENT

■ **INSTANT FACTS** Azim (D) was the driver of a car which two friends jumped out of in order to beat and rob a man walking on the street.

■ **BLACK LETTER RULE** Once conspiracy is established and upheld, a member of the conspiracy is also guilty of the criminal acts of his co-conspirators.

■ PROCEDURAL BASIS

Appeal from jury's conviction of the defendant.

■ FACTS

Azim (D) drove a car in which two other men, James and Robinson, were passengers. Azim (D) pulled the car over to the side of the street, and Robinson called a passerby, Tennenbaum over to the car. When he refused, James and Robinson got out, beat and choked Tennenbaum, and took his wallet [nice guys]. Azim (D) sat at the wheel, with the engine running and lights on, and the car doors open, while the acts were committed in the vicinity of the car. He then drove James and Robinson from the scene. Robinson and Azim (D) were tried and convicted as co-defendants. Azim (D) argues in this appeal that because his conspiracy conviction was not supported by sufficient evidence against him, the charges of assault and robbery must also fail.

■ ISSUE

Can a driver of the getaway car be considered a member of the conspiracy and thus guilty of the criminal acts of his co-conspirators?

■ DECISION AND RATIONALE

(Per Curiam) Yes. This court has maintained that the essence of criminal conspiracy is a common understanding, no matter how it came into being, that a particular criminal objective was to be accomplished. Among those circumstances relevant to proving conspiracy are association with alleged conspirators, knowledge of the commission of the crime, presence at the scene of the crime, and, at times, participation in the object of the conspiracy. We find no merit in Azim's (D) claim that he was merely a hired driver, with no knowledge of his passengers' criminal activity. We hold that a rational factfinder could find, beyond a reasonable doubt, that Azim (D) conspired with James and Robinson to commit assault and robbery. Once conspiracy is established and upheld, a member of the conspiracy is also guilty of the criminal acts of his co-conspirators.

Analysis:

By its very nature, the crime of conspiracy is frequently not susceptible of proof except by circumstantial evidence. And although a conspiracy cannot be based upon mere suspicion or conjecture, a conspiracy may be inferentially established by showing the relationship, conduct, or circumstances of the parties, and overt acts on the part of the co-conspirators have been held adequate to prove that a wrongful alliance has in fact been formed.

Commonwealth v. Cook

(*State*) v. (*Rape Accomplice*)

10 Mass.App.Ct. 668, 411 N.E.2d 1326 (1980)

EVIDENCE TENDING TO SHOW COMPLICITY AS AN ACCOMPLICE IN THE COMMISSION OF A SUBSTANTIVE CRIME IS NOT ENOUGH IN ITSELF TO CONVICT A DEFENDANT OF CONSPIRACY

■ **INSTANT FACTS** Cook (D) and his brother met a girl and partied a bit, after which Cook's (D) brother forcibly raped her in the woods while Cook (D) watched.

■ **BLACK LETTER RULE** While proof of a tacit agreement to commit a crime may be enough to establish a conspiracy, a defendant cannot be convicted of conspiracy solely on evidence tending to show his complicity as an accomplice in the commission of the substantive crime.

■ PROCEDURAL BASIS

Appeal from the trial court's denial of the defendant's motion for a required finding of not guilty, and subsequent conviction and sentence on the indictment.

■ FACTS

Cook (D) and his brother, Maurice, were sitting in the common meeting area in a housing project, drinking and smoking marijuana. The victim, a seventeen-year-old girl, walked past them on her way to her boyfriend's home. The brothers tried to engage her in conversation, but she spumed their invitation to join them. Her boyfriend wasn't home, so on the way back past the brothers she decided to sit and talk to them while she waited for her boyfriend to return. The three sat for about forty-five minutes in the common area, several people were in the vicinity as well. The victim had a drink of beer but declined the marijuana. Cook (D) and his brother both identified themselves and told the girl where they worked; they even showed her their IDs, as she was having difficulty remembering their names. Maurice indicated that he was out of cigarettes and suggested the three walk to a convenience store located about a minute and a half away. The victim agreed. To reach the store, the trio proceeded along the street to a narrow path or trail located behind the project office. This path led down a hill through a wooded area to the rear of a well-lit service station adjacent to the convenience store. As they walked towards the path single file, the victim slipped and fell. She sat on the ground for a few seconds laughing when Maurice turned around and jumped on her. He told her she "was going to love it." After she screamed, Maurice covered her mouth with his hand, took off his belt and handed it to Cook (D), who was seated nearby. After some vile talk, Maurice forcibly raped her. During the assault the victim lost consciousness. She awoke a couple of hours later and went straight to her friends' home in the projects. The incident was reported to the police and the Cooks were arrested. Maurice was indicted for rape, and his brother (D), for accessory to rape and conspiracy to commit rape.

■ ISSUE

Can a defendant be convicted of conspiracy solely on evidence tending to show his complicity as an accomplice in the commission of the substantive crime?

■ DECISION AND RATIONALE

(Greaney, J.) No. Proof of a conspiracy may rest entirely or mainly on circumstantial evidence, but "some record evidence" is not enough, and an acquittal must be ordered if any essential element is left to surmise, conjecture or guesswork. We are of the opinion that the evidence, tested against the foregoing principles, was insufficient to establish a conspiracy. The circumstances under which the victim and Cook (D) met and socialized were not indicative of a preconceived plan between the brothers to commit a sexual assault. The brothers made special efforts to identify themselves to the girl, thus they could not be said to have attempted to lull her into a false sense of security. Moreover, since all the conversation took place in the victim's presence, no clandestine plan could have been formed. While openness will not automatically sanitize a conspiracy, highly visible conduct has to be considered inconsistent with the shadowy environment which usually shrouds the crime. The purpose for leaving the area was on its face innocuous and was suggested by Maurice, not Cook (D). The path was a short, reasonably direct route to a nearby, well-lit convenience store, visible from the hill. We do not think that the events up to the time the victim fell were sufficient to establish a criminal agreement or to warrant the jury in inferring the state of facts that the commonwealth (P) claims to have existed. As to the attack itself, the fact that Maurice's attack began immediately after the victim found herself in a compromising situation suggests spontaneity of action on his part rather than the purposeful execution of a predetermined plan. From that point on, Cook's (D) actions fit the classic paradigm of an accomplice adding encouragement to a crime in progress. The fact that Cook (D) may have aided and abetted the crime does not establish a conspiracy, particularly where the evidence shows that prior planning is not an inherent facet of the crime. In reaching our conclusion, we are mindful of the principle that proof of a tacit agreement to commit a crime may be enough to establish a conspiracy. But in this case it is just as reasonable to conclude that Cook (D) became implicated in the crime as an accomplice after it had commenced without any advance knowledge it was about to occur, as it is to infer that the minds of the parties had met in advance and agreed to commit the offense charged. The remaining question is whether Cook (D) can be convicted of conspiracy *solely* on evidence tending to show his complicity as an accomplice in the commission of the substantive crime. We think on the evidence in this case such a conclusion would be unjustified. Accomplice and conspiratorial liability are not synonymous, and one can be an accomplice aiding in the commission of a substantive offense without necessarily conspiring to commit it. Absent from the formulation of accomplice liability is the necessity of establishing an agreement or consensus in the same sense as those terms are used in describing the agreement or combination which hallmarks a conspiracy. Acts of aiding and abetting clearly make each actor a principal in the substantive offense but cannot, without more, also make each other a principal in the crime of conspiracy to commit such offense. We conclude that in this case the evidence of the confederation at the scene was insufficient to warrant Cook's (D) conviction of conspiracy.

Analysis:

The gist of conspiracy rests in the agreement between the conspirators to work in concert for the criminal, corrupt, or unlawful purpose, and it is that agreement that constitutes the criminal act and generally serves to manifest the requisite intent. When a defendant is convicted of conspiring with others to commit a crime, the conviction stems from, and is designed to punish, the unlawful agreement that preexists commission of the substantive offense. That is why proof of the conspiracy typically involves circumstantial evidence aimed at establishing a consensus prior to the commission of the target offense. Execution of the crime thus represents performance of the agreement, but the offense does not substitute for the agreement.

■ CASE VOCABULARY

CONFEDERATION: Alliance.

People v. Foster

(*State*) v. (*Robber*)

99 Ill.2d 48, 75 Ill.Dec. 411, 457 N.E.2d 405 (1983)

ILLINOIS LAW REQUIRES AT LEAST TWO PARTICIPANTS AGREE IN ORDER TO CONSTITUTE A CONSPIRACY

■ **INSTANT FACTS** Foster (D) devised a plan to rob an old man, however his co-conspirator really had reported him to the police and was just feigning agreement.

■ **BLACK LETTER RULE** The Illinois legislation encompasses the bilateral theory of conspiracy, which requires the actual agreement of at least two participants.

■ PROCEDURAL BASIS

Appeal from the appellate court's reversal of the defendant's conviction.

■ FACTS

Foster (D) initiated his plan to commit a robbery, approaching Ragsdale in a bar and asking him if he was "interested in making some money." Foster (D) told Ragsdale of an elderly man, Hedrick, who kept many valuables in his possession [not much of a challenge]. Although Ragsdale stated that he was interested in making money, he did not believe Foster (D) was serious until he returned to the bar the next day and discussed in detail his plan to rob Hedrick. In an effort to gather additional information, Ragsdale decided to feign agreement to Foster's (D) plan but did not contact the police. Two days later, Foster (D) went to Ragsdale's residence to find out if he was "ready to go." Since Ragsdale had not yet contacted the police, he told Foster (D) that he would not be ready until he found someone else to help them. Ragsdale informed the police of the planned robbery two days later [snitch!]. Foster (D) and Ragsdale met at Hedrick's residence the following day and were arrested. The appellate court determined that the Illinois conspiracy statute required actual agreement between at least two persons to support a conspiracy conviction. Reasoning that Ragsdale never intended to agree to Foster's (D) plan but merely feigned agreement, the court reversed Foster's (D) conviction. On appeal to this court, the State (P) argues that under the conspiracy statute it suffices if only one of the participants to the alleged conspiracy actually intends to commit the offense.

■ ISSUE

Did the Illinois legislature intend to adopt the unilateral theory of conspiracy?

■ DECISION AND RATIONALE

(Underwood, J.) No. The question is whether the Illinois legislature, in amending the conspiracy statute in 1961, intended to adopt the unilateral theory of conspiracy. Prior to the 1961 amendment, the statute clearly encompassed the traditional, bilateral theory. The former statute read in part "If any *two or more persons* conspire or *agree together* to do any illegal act they shall be deemed guilty of a conspiracy." The amended version provides that "*a person* commits conspiracy when, with the intent that an offense be committed, *he agrees* with another to the commission of that offense." The State (P) urges that the change in wording of the statute supports the argument that only one person need intend to agree to the commission of the offense. The unilateral/bilateral issue is not addressed in the comments to this statute, however, and we doubt that the drafters could have intended what represents a rather profound change in the law of conspiracy without mentioning it in the comments to the section. Illinois does have a solicitation statute which embraces virtually every situation in which one could be convicted of conspiracy under the unilateral theory. Moreover, the penalties for solicitation and conspiracy are substantially similar. There would appear to have been little need for the legislature to adopt the unilateral theory of conspiracy in light of the existence of the solicitation statute. We are also mindful of the rule of construction which requires us to resolve statutory ambiguities in favor of criminal defendants. For the above reasons, we conclude that the Illinois statute encompasses the bilateral theory of conspiracy.

Analysis:

The court found it significant that there was a statute for solicitation in Illinois; thus, unilateral conspiracy was considered unnecessary. This is an important point, for some states only punish specific forms of solicitation and, as such, some defendants could slip through the cracks and go free unless conspiracy is deemed to be a unilateral offense. In those states without solicitation statutes, unilateral conspiracy fills in the gaps. This reasoning, however, can be a problem in that, generally speaking, solicitation statutes punish one who "commands, encourages, or requests *another to commit*" a crime. Thus, if Foster (D) intended Ragsdale to actually commit the robbery, he would be guilty of solicitation; however, if he merely wanted Ragsdale to help *him* commit the crime, the State (P) would need a unilateral conspiracy statute to reach Foster (D).

■ CASE VOCABULARY

BILATERAL THEORY OF CONSPIRACY: Requires actual agreement of at least two parties.

UNILATERAL THEORY OF CONSPIRACY: Only one conspirator needs to agree to the commission of the offense.

Kilgore v. State

(*Freeway Shooter*) v. (*State*)
251 Ga. 291, 305 S.E.2d 82 (1983)

IN A "WHEEL CONSPIRACY" EACH "SPOKE" MAY BE UNAWARE OF THE OTHER "SPOKES" AND, ACCORDINGLY, EACH ACTOR MAY NOT BE LIABLE FOR THE ACTIONS OF THE OTHER "SPOKES"

■ **INSTANT FACTS** Kilgore (D) was convicted of shooting Norman twice in the head, killing him, while he was driving down the interstate.

■ **BLACK LETTER RULE** Hearsay testimony can only be admissible under the exception to the hearsay rule which provides that the out-of-court statements of one conspirator are admissible against all conspirators.

■ PROCEDURAL BASIS

Appeal from the defendant's conviction and life sentence.

■ FACTS

Roger Norman was driving home on the interstate in the early morning hours when he was shot twice in the head and killed. Kilgore (D) was arrested and tried for the crime. At trial, the state (P) introduced evidence of a conspiracy to kill Norman, including three previous attempts on Norman's life [third time's the charm!]. As to the first attempt, David Oldaker testified that earlier in the year, Greg Benton, his cousin, asked him to go with him to Norman's home. He testified that the purpose of the trip was to kill Norman for a crippled man named Tom who wanted Norman dead. This testimony was admitted over the hearsay objection of defense counsel. Tom Carden was Norman's brother-in-law, and a paraplegic, however he died before the case came to trial. Oldaker and Benton went to Norman's home, where they unsuccessfully tried to kill him. Kilgore (D) was in no way implicated in this attempt. Evidence did however directly connect Kilgore with the second attempt. Ed Williams, an employee of a truck stop located just off the interstate, testified that one month before the killing, he saw two cars traveling close to each other while crossing over a bridge. He heard sounds like a car backfiring, then Norman's car pulled into the truck stop while the other car turned north on the interstate. Norman, who had been on his way home from work, had been shot in the upper back [now might be a good time to go into hiding]. The police, based on what Norman told them, posted a lookout for a 1962 or 1963 Rambler with a dark bottom, white top, and Tennessee tags. Constance Chambers, Kilgore's (D) ex-girlfriend, testified that on that day, Kilgore (D) and his cousin, Lee Berry, borrowed her 1964 Rambler. It had a dark green body, white top, and Tennessee tags. She testified that Kilgore (D) returned to her apartment the next morning and told her they had killed a man. Later that day, Chambers testified that Kilgore (D) received a phone call from Tom Carden, during which she heard Kilgore (D) say "apparently we didn't get him." Chambers testimony further shows the continuation of a conspiracy to kill Norman. She testified to a phone call during which she heard Kilgore (D) tell Carden he needed more money to obtain a faster car and another man to help him. Shortly thereafter, Kilgore obtained the total of $16,500 from Carden. Chambers then drove Kilgore (D) to meet his friend, Bob Price, and the two drove off in Price's van after Kilgore (D) took his rifle from his car. Chambers testified that the day before the murder, Kilgore (D) and Price left her apartment in the evening driving separate vehicles [notifying the police would be out of the question?]. She next saw Kilgore (D) the next morning, and he was driving a blue Lincoln. Chambers testified that Kilgore told her that he and Price had killed a man on the interstate. Kilgore (D) was convicted and given a life sentence. He appeals from that judgment.

■ ISSUE

Was the hearsay testimony of Oldaker properly admitted in Kilgore's (D) trial as an exception to the hearsay rule which provides that the out-of-court statements of one conspirator are admissible against all conspirators?

■ DECISION AND RATIONALE

(Bell, J.) No. Kilgore (D) argues that the trial court erred in admitting over objection the hearsay testimony of Oldaker that Benton told him Tom was the man who wanted Norman killed. This testimony was the only evidence connecting Tom Carden to the attempt. For the reasons which follow, we find that this hearsay testimony was inadmissible. The testimony could only be admissible under the exception to the hearsay rule which provides that the out-of-court statements of one conspirator are admissible against all conspirators. Therefore, this testimony was only admissible if Oldaker, Benton, and Kilgore (D) were co-conspirators. To have a conspiracy, there must be an agreement between two or more persons to commit a crime. Here, there is no question that the evidence shows that Oldaker, Benton and Carden were co-conspirators in their attempt to kill Norman, and that Kilgore (D), Price and Carden were co-conspirators in the murder of Norman, but the question is whether Kilgore (D), who did not know of or communicate with Oldaker and Benton, and Oldaker and Benton, who likewise did not know of or communicate with Kilgore (D), can be considered to have agreed to and become co-conspirators in the murder of Norman. We find that they cannot. Limitations have been imposed upon the concept that persons who do not know each other can "agree" to commit a crime. An agreement, and thus one conspiracy, is more likely to be inferred in "chain" conspiracies usually involving drug distribution, in which there is successive communication or cooperation. It is more difficult to infer an agreement among the spokes of a "wheel" conspiracy because they are less likely to have a community of interest or reason to know of each other's existence since one spoke's success is usually not dependent on the other spokes' success, but instead on his dealings with the hub. In the instant case, we conclude that Kilgore (D) was not a co-conspirator of Benton and Oldaker. Here, there was no community of interests between Benton and Oldaker on the one hand and Kilgore (D) on the other. The success of Benton's and Oldaker's attempt to kill Norman was not dependent in any way on Kilgore (D). Likewise, the success of Kilgore's (D) attempt to kill Norman was not aided by Oldaker and Benton, especially considering that they did not assist in further efforts to kill Norman. In addition, Benton and Oldaker, as one spoke, and Kilgore (D), as another spoke, had no knowledge of and no reason to know of each other such that an agreement can be inferred between them. There was no reason for Kilgore to know of the previous attempt on Norman's life, as his success was not dependent on it. Likewise, Oldaker and Benton had no reason to know of another spoke. For the above reasons, we find that Kilgore and Oldaker and Benton were not co-conspirators. Consequently it was error to admit the hearsay testimony of Oldaker.

Analysis:

Kilgore contended that the State (P) did not prove he actually committed the murder, and that, consequently, it must have been proceeding on the theory that his guilt was based upon a conspiracy. Yet, he argues, the State (P) did not prove a conspiracy because it did not prove an overt act occurred in Georgia. However, the conspiracy was merely an evidentiary tool used by the State (P) to help prove Kilgore (D) guilty of the murder of Norman. In fact, Kilgore (D) could not have been tried for conspiracy, since the object of the conspiracy was completed. As for the conspiracy itself, the type of agreement necessary to form a conspiracy is not the "meeting of the minds" necessary to form a contract and may be a mere tacit understanding between two or more people that they will pursue a particular criminal objective. It is possible for various persons to be parties to a single agreement (and thus one conspiracy) even though they do not know the identity of one another, and even though they are not all aware of the details of the plan of operation.

■ CASE VOCABULARY

CHAIN CONSPIRACY: A conspiracy in which there is successive communication and cooperation.

HEARSAY: Out-of-court statement not admissible as evidence.

HUB: common source of the conspiracy.

SPOKE: Different persons involved in the conspiracy.

WHEEL CONSPIRACY: A conspiracy in which there is a single hub (conspiracy) and spokes (conspirators) who do not know each other.

Braverman v. United States

(*Moonshiner*) v. (*Government*)

317 U.S. 49, 63 S.Ct. 99, 87 L.Ed. 23 (1942)

SINGLE AGREEMENT TO COMMIT ACTS IN VIOLATION OF SEVERAL PENAL STATUTES MUST BE PUNISHED AS ONE CONSPIRACY

■ **INSTANT FACTS** Braverman (D) and others were convicted of violating several statutes in the illicit manufacture, transportation, and distribution of distilled spirits.

■ **BLACK LETTER RULE** A single agreement to commit acts in violation of several penal statutes must be punished as one conspiracy.

■ PROCEDURAL BASIS

Appeal from the Court of Appeals' affirmance of the trial court's conviction and sentence of the defendant after a jury trial.

■ FACTS

The trial evidence showed that for a considerable period of time Braverman (D), and others, collaborated in the illicit manufacture, transportation, and distribution of distilled spirits involving the violations of statutes mentioned in the several counts of the indictment [pass the moonshine!]. At the close of the trial, Braverman (D) renewed a motion which was made at the beginning to require the Government (P) to elect one of the seven counts of the indictment upon which to proceed, contending that the proof could not and did not establish more than one agreement. In response, the Government (P) took the position that the seven counts of the indictment charged as distinct offenses the several illegal objects of one continuing conspiracy, that if the jury found such a conspiracy it might find Braverman (D) guilty of as many offenses as it had illegal objects, and that for each offense the two-year statutory penalty could be imposed [throw the book at them!]. The trial judge submitted the case to the jury on the Government's (P) theory. The jury returned with a general verdict finding Braverman (D) guilty as charged, and the court sentence was eight years imprisonment. On appeal, the Court of Appeals for the Sixth Circuit affirmed.

■ ISSUE

Can a single agreement to commit acts in violation of several penal statutes be punished as several conspiracies?

■ DECISION AND RATIONALE

(Stone, C.J.) No. Both courts below recognized that a single agreement to commit an offense does not become several conspiracies because it continues over a period of time, and that there may be a single continuing agreement to commit several offenses. But they thought that in the latter case each contemplated offense renders the agreement punishable as a separate conspiracy. Where each of the counts of an indictment alleges a conspiracy to violate a different penal statute it may be proper to conclude, in the absence of a bill of exceptions bringing up the evidence, that several conspiracies are charged rather than one, and that the conviction is for each. But it is a different matter to hold, as the court below appears to have done in this case, that even though a single agreement is entered into, the conspirators are guilty of as many offenses as the agreement has criminal objects. Whether the object of a single agreement is to commit one or many crimes, it is in either case that agreement which constitutes the conspiracy which the state punishes. The one agreement cannot be taken to be several agreements and hence several conspiracies because it envisages the violation of several statutes rather than one. Thus we hold that a single agreement to commit acts in violation of several penal statutes must be punished as one conspiracy.

Analysis:

Once again, it is pointed out that the gist of the crime of conspiracy as defined by the statute is the agreement or confederation of the conspirators to commit one or more unlawful acts. When a single agreement to commit one or more substantive crimes is evidenced by an overt act, as the statute requires, the precise nature and extent of the conspiracy must be determined by reference to the agreement that embraces and defines its objects. It is tempting to look at all the statutory violations and attach individual liability, as the lower courts did, but this court correctly identified the bottom line, which is that the conspiracy is the crime that is being punished, and it is not relevant whether that agreement encompasses one or several substantive crimes. The single agreement constitutes a single conspiracy.

■ CASE VOCABULARY

BILL OF EXCEPTIONS: Writing submitted to a trial court stating for the record objections to rulings made and instructions given by the trial judge.

ENVISAGES: Conceives.

Iannelli v. United States

(*Gambling Businessman*) v. (*Government*)
420 U.S. 770, 95 S.Ct. 1284, 43 L.Ed.2d 616 (1975)

CERTAIN EXCEPTIONS TO WHARTON'S RULE PERMIT CONVICTION OF A SUBSTANTIVE OFFENSE AND THE UNDERLYING CONSPIRACY

■ **INSTANT FACTS** Iannelli (D) was convicted and sentenced under both the substantive and conspiracy counts for gambling violations.

■ **BLACK LETTER RULE** There is a recognized exception to Wharton's Rule which permits prosecution and punishment for both the substantive offense and the conspiracy.

■ PROCEDURAL BASIS

Appeal from the Court of Appeal's affirmance of the trial court's conviction and sentence of the defendant.

■ FACTS

Iannelli (D) was charged, along with seven others, seven unindicted co-conspirators, and six co-defendants, inter alia, with conspiring to violate and violating 18 U.S.C. Sec. 1955, a federal gambling statute making it a crime for five or more persons to conduct, finance, manage, supervise, direct, or own a gambling business prohibited by state law [too many cooks...]. Iannelli (D) and seven others were convicted of both offenses, and each was sentenced under both the substantive and conspiracy counts. The Court of Appeals for the Third Circuit affirmed, finding that a recognized exception to Wharton's Rule [rule that prohibits prosecution for conspiracy of crime that necessarily involves two or more persons] permitted prosecution and punishment for both offenses.

■ ISSUE

Is there a recognized exception to Wharton's Rule which permits prosecution and punishment for both the substantive offense of gambling and the conspiracy?

■ DECISION AND RATIONALE

(Powell, J.) Yes. The classic formulation of Wharton's Rule requires that the conspiracy indictment be dismissed before trial. Federal courts earlier adhered to this literal interpretation and thus sustained demurrers to conspiracy indictments. More recently, however, some federal courts have differed over whether Wharton's Rule requires initial dismissal of the conspiracy indictment. Federal courts likewise have disagreed as to the proper application of the recognized "third-party exception," which renders Wharton's Rule inapplicable when the conspiracy involves the cooperation of a greater number of persons than is required for commission of the substantive offense. The Courts of Appeals are at odds even over the fundamental question whether Wharton's Rule ever applies to a charge for conspiracy to violate Section 1955. This Court's prior decisions indicate that the broadly formulated Wharton's Rule has current vitality only as a judicial presumption, to be applied in the absence of legislative intent to the contrary. The conduct proscribed by Sec. 1955 is significantly different from the offenses to which the Rule traditionally has been applied. Wharton's Rule applies only to offenses that *require* concerted criminal activity, a plurality of criminal agents. In such cases, a closer relationship exists between the conspiracy and the substantive offense because *both* require collective criminal activity. The substantive offense therefore presents some of the same threats that the law of conspiracy normally is thought to guard against, and it cannot automatically be assumed that the Legislature intended the conspiracy and the substantive offense to remain as discrete crimes upon consummation of the latter. Thus, absent legislative intent to the contrary, the Rule supports a presumption that the two merge when the substantive offense is proved. But a legal principle commands less respect when extended beyond the logic that supports it. In this case, the significant differences in characteristics and consequences of the kinds of offenses that gave rise to Wharton's Rule and the activities proscribed by Sec. 1955 counsel against attributing significant weight to the presumption the Rule erects. More importantly, the Rule must defer to a discernible legislative judgment. Major gambling activities were a principal focus of congressional concern, as evidenced by passage of the Organized Crime Control Act of 1970. Large-scale gambling activities were seen to be both a substantial evil and a source of funds for other criminal conduct. We conclude, therefore, that the history and structure of the Organized Crime Control Act of 1970 manifest a clear and unmistakable legislative judgment that more than outweighs any presumption of merger between the conspiracy to violate Sec. 1955 and the consummation of that substantive offense. Affirmed.

Analysis:

Traditionally, the law has considered conspiracy and the completed substantive offense to be separate crimes. Conspiracy is an inchoate offense, the essence of which is an agreement to commit an unlawful act. Unlike some crimes, the conspiracy to commit an offense and the subsequent commission of that crime normally do not merge into a single punishable act. Thus it is well recognized that in most cases separate sentences can be imposed for the conspiracy to do an act and for the subsequent accomplishment of that end. Courts have even held that the conspiracy can be punished more harshly than the accomplishment of its purpose. Wharton's Rule first emerged at a time when the contours of the law of conspiracy were in the process of active formulation. The general question whether the conspiracy merged into the completed felony offense remained for some time a matter of uncertain resolution. That issue is now settled, however, and the Rule currently stands as an exception to the general principle that a conspiracy and the substantive offense that is its immediate end do not merge upon proof of the latter.

■ CASE VOCABULARY

DEMURRER: Request for dismissal of the action based only on the law.

INTER ALIA: Among other things.

PLURALITY: Significant number.

WHARTON'S RULE: Prevents conspiracy prosecution for a crime that necessarily involves the participation of two or more persons.

Gebardi v. United States

(*Amorous Mann Act Violator*) v. (*Government*)
287 U.S. 112, 53 S.Ct. 35, 77 L.Ed. 206 (1932)

IT IS IMPOSSIBLE FOR A MAN TO CONSPIRE WITH HIMSELF

■ **INSTANT FACTS** Gebardi (D) and a woman agreed to go across state lines for illicit purposes in violation of the Mann Act, and the two were charged with conspiracy to violate the Mann Act.

■ **BLACK LETTER RULE** A woman cannot be held criminally liable for conspiring to transport herself across state lines for illicit purposes, even where she consents to the substantive offense.

■ PROCEDURAL BASIS

Certiorari granted to review conviction of a couple for conspiracy to transport a woman across state lines for illicit purposes.

■ FACTS

Gebardi (D) and a woman agreed that Gebardi (D) would transport her across state lines for the purpose of having sexual intercourse. [No, other states weren't necessarily preferable for the purposes of sexual relations—Gebardi (D) was a mobster and when his girlfriend claimed they were out of town during the Valentine's Day Massacre of '29, in which Gebardi (D) allegedly supposedly was the gunman, the prosecutor pursued Mann Act charges against both of them.] Gebardi (D) purchased train tickets for at least one journey, though the couple went on several such trips together. Each time, in advance of the tickets' purchase, the woman voluntarily agreed to go on the trip in order to engage in illicit sexual relations. Gebardi (D) and the woman were both convicted of conspiracy to violate the Mann Act, which imposes a penalty on any person who knowingly transports any woman or girl for the purposes of prostitution or debauchery, or for any other immoral purpose. The trial court convicted on the authority of *United States v. Holte*, where the court argued that if a woman suggested the journey and carried out the journey by purchasing the tickets, in the hopes of blackmailing the man, the woman could be found guilty of conspiracy.

■ ISSUE

May a woman who consents to transportation across state lines for illicit purposes be convicted of conspiracy to violate the substantive offense of transporting herself across state lines?

■ DECISION AND RATIONALE

(Stone, J.) No. First, the circumstances where a woman might violate the Mann Act are not present here. She did not purchase the tickets, nor does she appear to be the active and moving force in conceiving or carrying out the transportation. For a woman to be liable for violating the statute she must aid and assist in her transportation, meaning she must do more than consent—she must take an active role in the transportation. Second, just as by consenting the woman has not violated the Mann Act, she also is not guilty of conspiracy to violate the Mann Act. An incapacity to commit the substantive offense does not necessarily insulate one from being convicted of conspiracy to commit the offense. However, although Congress set out to deal with cases in which the woman frequently, if not normally, consents to the transportation, the consent to transportation was not made a crime under the

Mann Act. The Mann Act does not condemn a woman's participation in transportation effected by her consent, so we take it as evidence that Congress meant to leave her acquiescence unpunished. On the evidence before us the woman has not violated the Mann Act, and is not guilty of conspiracy to do so. Since the man did not conspire with anyone else, his conviction on the conspiracy count must also be overturned. Judgments reversed.

Analysis:

Wharton's Rule states that where the very definition of a crime requires the agreement and voluntary participation of two persons, the two persons cannot be prosecuted as conspirators for the offense. For example, the crimes of bigamy, adultery, incest, and dueling are all crimes that require the willing participation of both parties. The rule is based on the premise that conspiracy laws seek to control the more dangerous nature of group criminality, yet these offenses require two people to commit them—there is no danger added by commission of the crime, and no extra need to control group criminality. There are some exceptions to the rule, however. A very important exception is the "third-party exception." The third-party exception provides that if more than the minimum number of persons needed to commit the offense agree to commit the offense, a conspiracy is formed, and Wharton's Rule does not apply.

■ CASE VOCABULARY

ILLICIT: Illegal, unlawful; typically used in reference to sexual relations.

People v. Sconce

(*State*) v. (*Murder Conspirator*)
228 Cal.App.3d 693, 279 Cal.Rptr. 59 (1991)

A CONSPIRACY IS COMPLETE AFTER AGREEMENT AND THE COMMISSION OF AN OVERT ACT, AND WITHDRAWAL IS NOT A VALID DEFENSE TO THE FORMATION OF THE CONSPIRACY

■ **INSTANT FACTS** Sconce (D) hired someone to kill a man but before the murder was carried out he changed his mind and called it off.

■ **BLACK LETTER RULE** Withdrawal from a conspiracy avoids liability only for the target offense, or for any subsequent act committed by a co-conspirator in pursuance of the common plan, but liability for forming the conspiracy remains.

■ PROCEDURAL BASIS

Appeal from the trial court's setting aside of the information charging the defendant.

■ FACTS

Sconce (D) offered Bob Garcia $10,000 to kill Elie Estephan, the estranged husband of Cindy Estephan [pretty cheap!]. Sconce (D) told Garcia that he, Cindy, and a man named Sallard were plotting the murder. Garcia agreed to find someone to kill Estephan or to do it himself. Garcia then contacted ex-convict Herbert Dutton and offered him $5,000 to carry out the killing [even more affordable, *and* an easy profit!]. Subsequently, Garcia and Dutton went to Estephan's house to inspect the area. They decided that Dutton would plant a bomb under Estephan's car. Approximately three weeks after Sconce's (D) initial conversation with Garcia, Sconce (D) "just called it off." He said to "just forget about it, disregard doing it." Garcia did not see Dutton after the night they drove to Estephan's house, and although Garcia did not know it at the time Sconce (D) told him not to kill Estephan, Dutton had been arrested on a parole violation. (The murder was not carried out.) The People (P) contend that the trial court erroneously set aside the information because Sconce's (D) withdrawal from the conspiracy, although it might insulate him from liability for future conspiratorial acts, does not constitute a defense to liability for the conspiracy itself.

■ ISSUE

Is withdrawal a valid defense to the completed crime of conspiracy?

■ DECISION AND RATIONALE

(Klein, P.J.) No. Under California law, withdrawal is a complete defense to conspiracy only if accomplished before the commission of an overt act, or where it is asserted in conjunction with the running of the statute of limitations. The requirement of an overt act exists to provide a locus poenitentiae to avoid punishment for the conspiracy. Obviously, the inverse of this rule is that once an overt act has been committed in furtherance of the conspiracy, the crime of conspiracy has been completed and no subsequent action by the conspirator can change that. Thus, even if it be assumed Sconce (D) effectively withdrew from the conspiracy, withdrawal merely precludes liability for subsequent acts committed by the members of the conspiracy. The withdrawal does not relate back to the criminal formation of the unlawful combination. In sum, conspiracy is complete upon the commission of an overt act. We are bound to follow the foregoing rule, and any change in the law is a matter for the legislature. The decision of the trial court is thus reversed.

Analysis:

Withdrawal from a conspiracy requires "an affirmative and bona fide rejection or repudiation of the conspiracy, communicated to the co-conspirators." The court speaks of communication to each and every co-conspirator, however this requirement appears to be onerous, and even impossible in the case of a large conspiracy where all members do not know each other. Thus, this requirement could remove any incentive the withdrawal defense may provide. This court, however, correctly recognizes that the rule remains that withdrawal from a conspiracy avoids liability only for the target offense, or for any subsequent act committed by a co-conspirator in pursuance of the common plan. However, the change of mind is ineffectual as to the conspiracy crime itself, as one cannot undo that which he has already done.

■ CASE VOCABULARY

LOCUS POENITENTIAE: An opportunity to withdraw from or terminate the agreement before the consummation of the crime.

CHAPTER ELEVEN

Liability for the Conduct of Another

State v. Ward

Instant Facts: The court distinguishes and defines the common law treatment of felony principals and accessories.

Black Letter Rule: An accessory cannot be tried, without his consent, before the principal, and an accessory cannot be convicted of a higher crime than his principal.

State v. Hoselton

Instant Facts: Hoselton (D) was charged and convicted as a principal in the first degree for acting as lookout while his friends broke into a boat's storage locker.

Black Letter Rule: The accused's response that "you could say" he was a lookout, standing completely alone, does not establish that the accused was an aider and abettor by participating in, and wishing to bring about the entering with intent to commit larceny.

People v. Lauria

Instant Facts: Lauria (D) ran a telephone answering service, which he knew was used by several prostitutes in their business ventures; Lauria (D) was indicted with the prostitutes for conspiracy to commit prostitution.

Black Letter Rule: The intent of a supplier who knows his supplies will be put to criminal use may be established by (1) direct evidence that he intends to participate, or (2) through an inference that he intends to participate based on (a) his special interest in the activity, or (b) the felonious nature of the crime itself.

Riley v. State

Instant Facts: Riley (D) and Portalla fired shots at a crowd of young people around a bonfire and seriously wounded two of the people, but at trial, the prosecution could not prove which man fired the wounding shots.

Black Letter Rule: In proving liability as an accomplice, the prosecution must only show that the accomplice had the required mental state for the underlying substantive offense, as opposed to proving intent to promote the actual forbidden result.

State v. Linscott

Instant Facts: Linscott (D) was convicted of murder, under a theory of accomplice liability, when his friend shot and killed a man the two had intended to rob.

Black Letter Rule: A rule allowing for a murder conviction under a theory of accomplice liability based upon an objective standard, despite the absence of evidence that the defendant possessed the culpable subjective mental state that constitutes an element of the crime of murder, does not represent a departure from prior Maine law and, as such, is constitutional.

State v. Vaillancourt

Instant Facts: The defendant challenged his indictment and conviction for burglary as he was merely present at the location of the crime and did not participate.

Black Letter Rule: Accompaniment and observation are not sufficient acts to constitute "aid" so as to satisfy the elements necessary for accomplice liability or for any other crime.

Wilcox v. Jeffery

Instant Facts: Reporter was convicted for aiding and abetting after he paid for and attended an illegal jazz concert to report on it for his jazz magazine.

Black Letter Rule: Presence and payment to attend an illegal performance in order to attain benefit for oneself can constitute aiding and abetting the criminal act.

State v. Helmenstein

Instant Facts: Helmenstein (D) was convicted of burglary after he and his friends drove to a nearby town and broke into a store and stole beer and food.

Black Letter Rule: A conviction may not be had upon the testimony of an accomplice unless his testimony is corroborated by such other evidence as tends to connect the defendant with the commission of the offense, and the corroboration is not sufficient if it merely shows the commission of the offense or the circumstances thereof.

People v. Genoa

Instant Facts: Genoa (D) was charged with aiding and abetting for giving money to an undercover agent to buy and then sell cocaine for a profit.

Black Letter Rule: A person cannot be convicted of aiding and abetting the commission of a crime when the underlying crime was never committed by anyone.

Bailey v. Commonwealth

Instant Facts: Bailey (D) was convicted of manslaughter when his neighbor was shot by police responding to reports from Bailey (D) regarding his neighbor's behavior, which he instigated.

Black Letter Rule: One who effects a criminal act through an innocent or unwitting agent is a principal in the first degree.

U.S. v. Lopez

Instant Facts: Lopez's (D) boyfriend broke her out of prison by helicopter because her life was being threatened by prison authorities.

Black Letter Rule: A defendant can be convicted of aiding and abetting even if the principal is not identified or convicted, however an aider or abettor may not be held liable absent proof that a criminal offense was committed by a principal.

People v. McCoy

Instant Facts: McCoy (D1) and Lakey (D2) were tried together for a murder arising out of a drive-by shooting. At trial, McCoy (D1), the person who actually shot the victim, claimed self-defense.

Black Letter Rule: An accomplice's *mens rea* may be deemed more culpable than that of the principal perpetrator of the crime, and thus, the accomplice may be convicted of a greater offense than the offense for which the principal perpetrator is convicted.

In re Meagan R.

Instant Facts: Minor girl was convicted of burglary for breaking into a house with her boyfriend so they could have sex.

Black Letter Rule: Where the Legislature has dealt with crimes which necessarily involve the joint actions of two or more persons, and where no punishment at all is provided for the conduct, or misconduct, of one of the participants, the party whose participation is not denounced by statute cannot be charged with criminal conduct on either a conspiracy or aiding and abetting theory.

People v. Brown

Instant Facts: Brown (D) and friends broke into a car dealership to steal a car, but changed their minds before actually entering the building and left.

Black Letter Rule: Withdrawal provisions of an accountability statute are ineffective to prevent liability for an attempted crime after the planning has already taken place.

Commonwealth v. Koczwara

Instant Facts: Tavern owner and operator was fined and imprisoned for violations of the Liquor Code committed by his employees without his presence, participation or knowledge.

Black Letter Rule: An employer cannot be imprisoned (but can be fined) under a theory of respondeat superior for the criminal acts of his employees committed on his premises without his presence, participation or knowledge.

State v. Christy Pontiac–GMC

Instant Facts: Car dealership was convicted of theft and forgery when its employees forged customer rebate forms and did not pass the rebates on to the customers.

Black Letter Rule: A corporation may be prosecuted and convicted for the crimes of theft and forgery.

State v. Ward

(*State*) v. (*Not Stated*)
284 Md. 189, 396 A.2d 1041 (1978)

ACCESSORY LIABILITY CANNOT BE DETERMINED PRIOR TO, AND CANNOT BE GREATER THAN, THE PRINCIPAL'S

■ **INSTANT FACTS** The court distinguishes and defines the common law treatment of felony principals and accessories.

■ **BLACK LETTER RULE** An accessory cannot be tried, without his consent, before the principal, and an accessory cannot be convicted of a higher crime than his principal.

■ PROCEDURAL BASIS

Not stated.

■ FACTS

Not stated.

■ ISSUE

May an accessory to a felony be tried prior to the principal's trial and be convicted of a higher crime than his principal?

■ DECISION AND RATIONALE

(Orth, J.) No. The doctrine of accessoryship applicable to felonies developed through the common law of England. Maryland has not changed this doctrine by legislation or judicial decision, and it is presently in virtually the same form as it existed in the 18th century. The guilty parties are divided into principals, first degree (perpetrators) and second degree (abettors), and accessories, before the fact (inciters) and after the fact (criminal protectors). At the common law, the abettor may be tried and convicted prior to the trial of the perpetrator, or even after the perpetrator has been tried and acquitted. Furthermore, an abettor may be convicted of a higher crime or a lower crime than the perpetrator. The common law took a different path with regard to accessories, however. An accessory cannot be tried, without his consent, before the principal, and an accessory cannot be convicted of a higher crime than his principal.

Analysis:

Two other principal-accessory distinctions developed in the common law era. An accessory could only be prosecuted in the jurisdiction where the accessorial acts took place, rather than where the crime was committed. This rule did not apply, however, to principals in the second degree (abettors). Additionally, strict rules of pleading and proof prevented a defendant charged as an accessory from being convicted as a principal, and vice versa. Almost all states have abrogated, through legislation, the distinction between principals and accessories before the fact. Other states have permitted accessories before the fact to be tried and punished without regard to the status of the principal's prosecution, which reaches substantially the same result. Generally, being an accessory after the fact is now treated as a separate and lesser offense, such as hindering prosecution or obstruction of justice, rather than as a party to the crime committed by a perpetrator.

■ CASE VOCABULARY

ABETTOR: Affirmative criminal conduct to assist in the commission of the felony.

ACCESSORY: The person who helps the perpetrator commit the felony. [Something added to spice up your wardrobe or placed on your dresser to make your room look nice.]

CRIMINAL PROTECTOR: Accomplice after the felony has been committed, who helps the felon in an attempt to prevent his apprehension or punishment.

INCITER: Accomplice not present during the commission of the felony, but who helped facilitate the crime.

PERPETRATOR: The person who actually commits the felony.

State v. Hoselton

(*State*) v. (*Boat Burglar*)
179 W.Va. 645, 371 S.E.2d 366 (1988)

DEFENDANT CANNOT BE LABELED "LOOKOUT" WHEN HE LACKS REQUISITE INTENT TO HELP COMMIT CRIME

■ **INSTANT FACTS** Hoselton (D) was charged and convicted as a principal in the first degree for acting as lookout while his friends broke into a boat's storage locker.

■ **BLACK LETTER RULE** The accused's response that "you could say" he was a lookout, standing completely alone, does not establish that the accused was an aider and abettor by participating in, and wishing to bring about the entering with intent to commit larceny.

■ PROCEDURAL BASIS

Appeal from the trial court's conviction and subsequent denial of the defendant's motions for acquittal and new trial.

■ FACTS

When Hoselton (D) was eighteen years old, he and several friends went to a barge they frequently trespassed upon for fishing [boys will be boys]. His friends broke into the storage locker on the barge while Hoselton stood out at the end of the barge. His friends stole several items from the locker and loaded them into their car. Hoselton (D) took no part in assisting the others to load the goods into the car, and he was then driven immediately home. Hoselton (D) was charged and tried as a principal in the first degree for either breaking and entering or entering without breaking with intent to commit larceny. At the trial, Hoselton (D) testified that he didn't go into the storage locker. He was asked if he was keeping a lookout, and he said "You could say that. I just didn't want to go down in there." [Not the best coaching from his attorney!] Hoselton (D) was subsequently convicted of entering without breaking based upon his statement, which was the only evidence used to link him to the crime.

■ ISSUE

May a defendant's statements at trial be sufficient evidence to establish that he was a lookout, thus sustaining a conviction for breaking and entering as a principal in the first degree?

■ DECISION AND RATIONALE

(Per Curiam) No. A lookout is one who is "by prearrangement, keeping watch to avoid interception or detection or to provide warning during the perpetration of the crimes and thereby participating in the offenses charged." This Court has consistently held that lookouts are aiders and abettors, principals in the second degree who are punishable as principals in the first degree under State statute. An aider or abettor must "in some sort associate himself with the venture, that he participate in it as something that he wishes to bring about, that he seeks by his action to make it succeed." The prosecution must demonstrate that he or she shared the criminal intent of the principal in the first degree. Therefore, if the State establishes evidence that an accused acted as a lookout, it has necessarily established the requisite act and mental state to support a conviction of aiding and abetting. In both his voluntary statement and his testimony at trial, Hoselton (D) stated that he had no prior knowledge of his friends' intentions to steal anything from the barge. He did not help remove the goods from the barge and he never received any of the stolen property. The accused's response that "you could say" he was a lookout, standing completely alone, does not establish that the accused was an aider and abettor by participating in, and wishing to bring about the entering with intent to commit larceny. Viewed in the light most favorable to the prosecution, the State did not prove that Hoselton (D) was a lookout. We therefore reverse and set aside Hoselton's (D) conviction for entering without breaking.

Analysis:

Both the requisite act and mental state must be present in order to support accomplice liability. That is, one must give assistance or encouragement in the commission of the crime *along with* the intent that the aid promote or facilitate the commission of the crime. The court focuses mostly on the idea that Hoselton's (D) statements show he did not have the requisite intent, but it is also important to the decision that he did not engage in any assistance of the crime. In fact, when he saw his friends removing the stolen items, he left the barge and waited in the car. Thus, neither prong was met in this case, and, as such, Hoselton (D) could not have been held liable for the crime.

■ CASE VOCABULARY

LARCENY: Theft.

PER CURIAM: Opinion of the court in which the author is not identified.

People v. Lauria

(*Government*) v. (*Telephone Answering Service Provider*)

251 Cal.App.2d 471, 59 Cal.Rptr. 628 (1967)

A PERSON WHO SUPPLIES A PRODUCT OR SERVICE TO ANOTHER KNOWING THAT IT WILL BE USED AS PART OF A CRIME, MAY BE CONVICTED FOR CONSPIRACY UNLESS ONLY A MISDEMEANOR IS INVOLVED

■ **INSTANT FACTS** Lauria (D) ran a telephone answering service, which he knew was used by several prostitutes in their business ventures; Lauria (D) was indicted with the prostitutes for conspiracy to commit prostitution.

■ **BLACK LETTER RULE** The intent of a supplier who knows his supplies will be put to criminal use may be established by (1) direct evidence that he intends to participate, or (2) through an inference that he intends to participate based on (a) his special interest in the activity, or (b) the felonious nature of the crime itself.

■ PROCEDURAL BASIS

Appeal by prosecution from order setting aside an indictment for conspiracy to commit prostitution.

■ FACTS

In a prostitution investigation, police focused their attention on three prostitutes who used Lauria's (D) telephone service. An undercover policewoman, Stella Weeks, signed up for Lauria's (D) services. Weeks hinted that she was a prostitute, and wanted to conceal that fact from the police. Lauria (D) assured her that his service was discreet and safe. A few weeks later, Weeks called Lauria (D) and complained that because of his operation she had lost two "tricks." Lauria (D) claimed that her tricks probably lied about leaving messages for her. Lauria (D) did not respond to Weeks' hints that she needed more customers, other than to invite her over to become better acquainted. A couple of weeks later Weeks again complained that she had lost two tricks, and the office manager said she would investigate. Two weeks later, Lauria (D) and the three prostitutes were arrested. Lauria (D) testified before the Grand Jury that he only had 9 or 10 prostitutes using his service, and he kept records for known or suspected prostitutes for the convenience of police. However, Lauria (D) did not volunteer the information, but would give it when asked about a specific prostitute. He claimed that he tolerated the prostitutes so long as they paid their bills. Lauria (D) admitted having personal knowledge that some of his customers were prostitutes. Lauria (D) and the three prostitutes were indicted for conspiracy to commit prostitution. The trial court set aside the indictment as having been brought without a showing of reasonable or probable cause. The Government (P) appeals claiming that a sufficient showing of an unlawful agreement to further prostitution was made. To establish agreement, the Government (P) need show no more than an implied mutual understanding, between co-conspirators, to accomplish an unlawful act.

■ ISSUE

Is a person criminally liable for conspiracy if he furnishes goods and services he knows will be used to assist in the operation of an illegal business?

■ DECISION AND RATIONALE

(Fleming, J.) No. *United States v. Falcone* held that a seller's knowledge of the illegal use of the goods was insufficient to make the seller a participant in the conspiracy. In *Direct Sales Co. v. United States*, by contrast, the conviction on federal narcotics laws of a drug wholesaler was affirmed on a showing that the company had actively promoted the sale of morphine. In both cases, however, the element of knowledge of the illegal use of the goods or services and the element of intent to further that use must be present in order to make the supplier a participant in a criminal conspiracy. Proof of knowledge is ordinarily a question of fact. Lauria (D) admitted he knew that some of his customers were prostitutes. He probably knew that some of his customers were subscribing to his service in order to further their trade. The Government argues that this knowledge serves as a basis for concluding that Lauria (D) intended to participate in the criminal activities. We note some characteristic patterns in precedent cases: (1) intent may be inferred from knowledge, when the purveyor of the legal goods for illegal use has acquired a stake in the venture; (2) intent may be inferred from knowledge, when no legitimate use for the goods or services exists; and (3) intent may be inferred from knowledge, when the volume of business with the buyer is grossly disproportionate to any legitimate demand. In response to the first pattern, we note that Lauria (D) had no stake in the venture, and was not charging higher prices to the prostitutes. As to the second pattern, we note that nothing in the furnishing of telephone service implies that it will be used for prostitution, since all sorts of persons might use the service for completely legal activities. Finally, no evidence suggests any unusual volume of Lauria's (D) business was with prostitutes. In all three of these patterns, it can be said that in one way or another a supplier has a special interest in the operation of the criminal enterprise. There are cases in which it cannot be said that the supplier has a stake in the venture, yet still may be held liable based on knowledge alone. Some examples of this would be supplying cutting equipment to be used in a bank robbery, or supplying telephone service to persons involved in the extortion of ransom. Still, we do not believe that an inference of intent drawn from knowledge should apply to misdemeanors. Thus, with respect to misdemeanors, we conclude that positive knowledge of a supplier that his products will be used for illegal activities does not in itself establish intent to participate in the misdemeanor. However, with respect to felonies, we hold that in all felony cases, knowledge of criminal use alone may justify an inference of intent. From this analysis we deduce the following rule: the intent of a supplier who knows of the criminal use to which his supplies are put to participate in the criminal activity connected with the use of his supplies may be established by (1) direct evidence that he intends to participate, or (2) through an inference that he intends to participate based on (a) his special interest in the activity, or (b) the felonious nature of the crime itself. Lauria (D) took no direct action to further the activities of the prostitutes. There is no evidence of a special interest in the prostitutes' activities. The offense with which he has been charged is a misdemeanor. Thus the charges of conspiracy against Lauria (D) fail, and since the conspiracy theory was built around the activities of Lauria's (D) business, the charges against his co-conspirators must also fail. The order is affirmed.

Analysis:

Taking account of the seriousness of the criminal objective is appropriate when striking a balance between the conflicting interests of vendors (in regard to their freedom to engage in gainful and otherwise lawful activities) and that of the community in preventing behavior that facilitates the commitment of crimes. Some believe that proof of purpose should be required, arguing that conspiracy laws should apply to those with criminal goals, rather than "seek[ing] to sweep within the dragnet of conspiracy all those who have been associated in any degree whatever with the main offenders." They argue that the law should not be extended to punish "legitimate businessmen" like Lauria (D).

Riley v. State

(Reckless Gun Shooter) v. *(Prosecution)*
60 P.3d 204 (Alaska Ct. App. 2002)

FINDING OF ACCOMPLICE LIABILITY DOES NOT REQUIRE PROOF OF INTENT TO BRING ABOUT ACTUAL HARM RESULTING FROM RECKLESS CONDUCT

■ **INSTANT FACTS** Riley (D) and Portalla fired shots at a crowd of young people around a bonfire and seriously wounded two of the people, but at trial, the prosecution could not prove which man fired the wounding shots.

■ **BLACK LETTER RULE** In proving liability as an accomplice, the prosecution must only show that the accomplice had the required mental state for the underlying substantive offense, as opposed to proving intent to promote the actual forbidden result.

■ PROCEDURAL BASIS

Riley (D) was convicted of two counts of first-degree assault and challenges his convictions in this appeal.

■ FACTS

Richard Riley (D) and Edward Portalla both fired at a crowd of young people who were socializing around a bonfire on the banks of a river in Alaska. Two of the young people were seriously wounded by the gunfire. Both Riley (D) and Portalla were indicted on two counts of first-degree assault. The men were tried separately. At their trials, the ballistics analyst failed to prove which of the men's weapons had fired the wounding shots; the analyst could only prove that the wounds were inflicted by one of the two men. The trial court instructed the jurors that, with respect to each count, they should decide whether Riley (D) acted as the principal, firing the wounding shot, or, if they could not decide which man fired the wounding shot, they should decide whether Riley (D) acted as an accomplice. The jurors convicted Riley (D) as an accomplice in the wounding of the two young people. Riley (D) appeals this conviction, arguing that the jury instruction on accomplice liability was in error, since it did not inform the jurors that the State had to prove that Riley (D) intended to have Portalla inflict serious physical injury on the victims (not simply that Riley (D) acted recklessly with respect to the possibility that Portalla's conduct would cause this result).

■ ISSUE

Does a conviction for accomplice liability require a finding that the accomplice intended that the principal cause the particular harm that resulted from his or her actions?

■ DECISION AND RATIONALE

(Mannheimer, J.) No. In proving liability as an accomplice, the prosecution must only show that an accomplice had the required mental state for the underlying substantive offense, as opposed to proving intent to promote the actual forbidden result. In this case, Riley (D) had the required mental state for a first-degree assault conviction: that is, recklessness as to the possibility that his conduct would cause serious physical injury. The prosecution did not have to prove that Riley (D) specifically intended that

Portalla seriously wound the victims. Our holding today overrules our decision in *Echols v. State*. At issue in *Echols* was an interpretation of Alaska's complicity statute, AS 11.16.110(2), which states that a defendant may not be held criminally responsible for another person's conduct unless the State proves that the defendant acted "with intent to promote or facilitate the commission of the offense." Based upon our interpretation of the complicity statute in *Echols*, we held that a defendant's culpability as an accomplice could not be premised on recklessness and instead, we required the prosecution to prove that the defendant acted intentionally with respect to the resulting injury. The *Echols* interpretation of this statute can lead to counterintuitive results. In the event that a homicide had occurred under the facts of this matter, the *Echols* interpretation would lead to a situation where the State would have to prove the defendants acted with intent to kill, rather than just recklessly, or the defendants would escape criminal liability. We do not believe that these were the type of results intended by the drafters of the complicity statute. Moreover, the complicity statute is based on Model Penal Code § 2.06(3), which also refers to acting with the purpose of "promoting or facilitating the commission of the offense." Section 2.06(4) states that in situations where causing a particular result is an actual element of the offense, an accomplice is guilty when he or she acts with the kind of culpability sufficient to bring about that result. In an explanatory note to Section 2.06, however, the drafters point out that in situations where the criminal result is unanticipated or unintended, but flows from the conduct and is a result prohibited by law, the accomplice's degree of guilt must be evaluated separately from any other defendant's culpable mental state. Because our interpretation of the complicity statute in *Echols* is contradicted by the pertinent Model Penal Code commentary, as well as most other courts with Model Penal Code-based complicity statutes, we find our holding in that decision to be in error. In the case at hand, the jury was only required to determine that Riley (D) shot a firearm into the crowd or that he acted with the intent to facilitate Portalla's shooting into the crowd to find Riley (D) guilty of first-degree assault as an accomplice. In either case, the applicable mental state remains recklessness as to the possibility that this conduct would cause serious injury. The jury did not need to find that Riley (D) actually intended that the young people sustain serious wounds. Affirmed.

Analysis:

As noted by the *Riley* Court, there is some division, even among states with a Model Penal Code-based complicity statute, regarding the degree of *mens rea* necessary to be considered an accomplice to an unintentional crime. Some courts have held that one cannot be an accomplice to a crime that is committed unintentionally, like involuntary manslaughter. In theory, this may seem like a logical policy decision, especially where there is a clear principal and accomplice involved in the case. The logic breaks down, however, in a case like *Riley*, where you cannot actually prove which participant was the principal and which one was the accomplice. In such a case, there is the risk that two reckless actors may escape all criminal liability for the injuries that they caused.

■ CASE VOCABULARY

ACTUS REUS: Guilty act.

INDICT: To charge with a crime.

State v. Linscott

(*State*) v. (*Robber*)
520 A.2d 1067 (1987)

MURDER CONVICTION UNDER THEORY OF ACCOMPLICE LIABILITY BASED UPON AN OBJECTIVE STANDARD RULED CONSTITUTIONAL

■ **INSTANT FACTS** Linscott (D) was convicted of murder, under a theory of accomplice liability, when his friend shot and killed a man the two had intended to rob.

■ **BLACK LETTER RULE** A rule allowing for a murder conviction under a theory of accomplice liability based upon an *objective* standard, despite the absence of evidence that the defendant possessed the culpable *subjective* mental state that constitutes an element of the crime of murder, does not represent a departure from prior Maine law and, as such, is constitutional.

■ PROCEDURAL BASIS

Appeal from trial court's conviction of the defendant following a jury-waived trial.

■ FACTS

Linscott (D), Willey, and Colby drove to Fuller's house to pick him up. Fuller came to the vehicle with a sawed-off shotgun in his possession. The four men next drove to Ackley's house, where Fuller obtained 12-gauge shotgun shells. Later that evening, Fuller suggested that the four men drive to the home of a reputed drug dealer, Norman Grenier, take Grenier by surprise, and rob him. Linscott (D) and the others agreed to the plan, reasoning that Grenier would be reluctant to call the police due to his being a reputed drug dealer. Fuller stated that Grenier had been seen with $50,000 in cash that day, and he guaranteed Linscott (D) $10,000 as his share of the proceeds of the robbery. The four men drove to Grenier's house and Linscott (D) and Fuller approached the house [the other two had a glimmer of sense]. Linscott (D) carried a hunting knife and switchblade, and Fuller was armed with the shotgun. Linscott (D) and Fuller walked around the back of the house; Grenier and his girlfriend were watching television in the front of the house. They wanted to break in the back door in order to place themselves between Grenier and the bedroom, where they believed Grenier kept a loaded shotgun. The back door was blocked by snow, however, so the men revised their plan and were to go in through the living room picture window [subtle]. Linscott (D) broke the living room window without otherwise entering the house. Fuller immediately fired a shot through the broken window, hitting Grenier in the chest. Fuller left through the broken window after having removed about $1,300 from Grenier's pants pocket [wow, jackpot!], later returning to the house to retrieve an empty shotgun casing. At a jury-waived trial, Linscott (D) testified that he knew Fuller to be a hunter and that it was not unusual for Fuller to carry a firearm. He stated that he had no knowledge of any reputation for violence that Fuller may have had, and that he had no intention of causing anyone's death in the course of the robbery. At the completion of the trial, the trial justice found Linscott (D) guilty of robbery and, on a theory of accomplice liability, found him guilty of murder. The court specifically found that Linscott (D) possessed the intent to commit the robbery, that Fuller intentionally or at least knowingly caused the death of Grenier, and that this murder was a reasonably foreseeable consequence of Linscott's (D) participation in the robbery. However, the court also found that Linscott did not intend to kill Grenier, and that he probably would not have participated in the robbery had he believed that Grenier would be killed in the course of the enterprise.

■ ISSUE

Does a rule allowing for a murder conviction under a theory of accomplice liability based upon an *objective* standard, despite the absence of evidence that the defendant possessed the culpable *subjective* mental state that constitutes an element of the crime of murder, represent a departure from prior Maine law and, as such, unconstitutionally violate a defendant's right to due process?

■ DECISION AND RATIONALE

(Scolnik, J.) No. The Due Process Clause protects the accused against conviction except upon proof beyond a reasonable doubt of every fact necessary to constitute the crime with which he is charged. Linscott (D) contends that the accomplice liability statute impermissibly allows the State to find him guilty of murder, which requires proof beyond a reasonable doubt that the murder was committed either intentionally or knowingly, without having to prove either of these two culpable mental states. Instead, Linscott (D) argues, the accomplice liability statute permits the State to employ only a mere negligence standard in convicting him of murder in violation of his right to due process. We find Linscott's (D) argument to be without merit. We have previously held that the "foreseeable consequence rule" of accomplice liability demands that accomplices be held liable for those crimes that were the reasonably foreseeable consequence of their criminal enterprise, *notwithstanding an absence on their part of the same culpability required for conviction as a principal to the crime.* We have consistently upheld this interpretation of the statute in issue here, and we discern no compelling reason to depart from this construction of the statute now. Furthermore, the foreseeable consequence rule merely carries over the objective standards of accomplice liability as used in the common law. Thus, a rule allowing for a murder conviction under a theory of accomplice liability based upon an *objective* standard, despite the absence of evidence that the defendant possessed the culpable *subjective* mental state that constitutes an element of the crime of murder, does not represent a departure from prior Maine law. We also do not find fundamentally unfair or disproportionate the grading scheme for sentencing purposes of murder premised on a theory of accomplice liability. The potential penalty of life imprisonment for murder under a theory of accomplice liability does not "shock the conscience." For the foregoing reasons, we find no constitutional defect in this statutory provision, nor any fundamental unfairness in its operation. Affirmed.

Analysis:

The "foreseeable consequence" or "natural and probable consequence" rule has been followed in many cases. The interpretation that this court alludes to is that liability for a "primary crime" (here, robbery) is established by proof that the actor intended to promote or facilitate that crime. Liability for any "secondary crime" (here, murder) that may have been committed by the principal is established upon a two-fold showing: first, that the actor intended to promote the *primary crime*, and second, that the commission of the secondary crime was a "foreseeable consequence" of the actor's participation in the primary crime. It seems a fair and logical result in the case at bar.

■ CASE VOCABULARY

FORESEEABLE CONSEQUENCE RULE: An accessory is liable for a criminal act which was the natural or probable consequence of the crime he intended, even though such consequence was not intended.

JURY-WAIVED TRIAL: Trial in front of a judge due to the defendant's exercising his right to waive a trial by jury.

State v. Vaillancourt

(*State*) v. (*Alleged Burglar*)
122 N.H. 1153, 453 A.2d 1327 (1982)

MERE PRESENCE AT A CRIME IS NOT SUFFICIENT TO CONSTITUTE "AID" TO SATISFY THE REQUIREMENTS FOR ACCOMPLICE LIABILITY

■ **INSTANT FACTS** The defendant challenged his indictment and conviction for burglary as he was merely present at the location of the crime and did not participate.

■ **BLACK LETTER RULE** Accompaniment and observation are not sufficient acts to constitute "aid" so as to satisfy the elements necessary for accomplice liability or for any other crime.

■ PROCEDURAL BASIS

Appeal from a jury's conviction of the defendant after his pre-trial motion to dismiss was denied.

■ FACTS

Vaillancourt (D) and a friend, Burhoe, were seen standing together on the O'Connors' front porch. The men were ringing the doorbell and conversing with one another [trick or treat?]. After remaining on the porch for approximately ten minutes, the neighbor who had seen them earlier became suspicious and began to watch them more closely [she obviously needs more excitement in her life]. She saw them walk around to the side of the house where Burhoe allegedly attempted to break into a basement window. Vaillancourt (D) allegedly stood by and watched Burhoe, talking to him intermittently while Burhoe tried to pry open the window. The neighbor called the police, who apprehended Vaillancourt (D) and Burhoe as they were fleeing the scene. Vaillancourt (D) was subsequently indicted and convicted for accomplice liability. He now contests the sufficiency of his indictment.

■ ISSUE

Are accompaniment and observation sufficient acts to constitute "aid" such as to satisfy the elements necessary for accomplice liability or for any other crime?

■ DECISION AND RATIONALE

(Per Curiam) No. Vaillancourt (D) bases his argument on the axiomatic principle that an indictment must allege some criminal activity. He specifically contends that his indictment was insufficient because, even if the facts alleged in it were true, they would not have satisfied the elements necessary for accomplice liability or for any other crime. We agree. The crime of accomplice liability requires the actor to have solicited, aided, agreed to aid, or attempted to aid the principal in planning or committing the offense. The crime thus necessitates some active participation by the accomplice. We have held that knowledge and mere presence at the scene of a crime could not support a conviction for accomplice liability because they did not constitute sufficient affirmative acts to satisfy the actus reus requirement of the accomplice liability statute. In the instant case, other than the requisite mens rea, the State alleged only that Vaillancourt (D) aided Burhoe by accompanying him to the location of the crime and watching. Consistent with our rulings with respect to "mere presence," we hold that accompaniment and observation are not sufficient acts to constitute "aid."

■ DISSENT

(Bois, J.) Although I agree that "mere presence" would be an insufficient factual allegation, the indictment in this case alleged more than "mere presence." While not a customary form of assistance "accompaniment with the purpose of aiding" implies the furnishing of moral support and encouragement in the performance of a crime, thereby "aiding" a principal in the commission of an offense.

Analysis:

It seems that the line between "mere presence," which does not constitute aiding, and presence combined with some other factor, which may constitute aiding, is a very fine one. However the case law has been very consistent that even an undisclosed intention to render aid if needed will not suffice, nor is mental approval enough to impose accomplice liability. Additionally, mere presence plus flight has often been held insufficient to constitute aiding and abetting. The courts have been quite clear that presence is only equated to aiding and abetting when it designedly encourages the perpetrator, facilitates the unlawful deed, or when it stimulates others to render assistance to the criminal act.

Wilcox v. Jeffery

(*Magazine Proprietor*) v. (*Not Stated*)
1 All England Law Reports 464 (1951)

BUYING A TICKET FOR AN ILLEGAL CONCERT CAN CONSTITUTE AIDING AND ABETTING

■ **INSTANT FACTS** Reporter was convicted for aiding and abetting after he paid for and attended an illegal jazz concert to report on it for his jazz magazine.

■ **BLACK LETTER RULE** Presence and payment to attend an illegal performance in order to attain benefit for oneself can constitute aiding and abetting the criminal act.

■ PROCEDURAL BASIS

Appeal from the judgment of conviction.

■ FACTS

Hawkins, an American saxophone player was invited by Curtis and Hughes to play at a jazz club in England. Curtis and Hughes applied for permission, as required by law, for Hawkins to "land," which was refused, but Hawkins nevertheless went to England with four other musicians [get out, Yank!]. Wilcox (D), who had no part in bringing the musicians to England, was at the airport when they arrived. He was there to report the arrival of these important musicians for the jazz magazine he wrote and sold for a living. Curtis and Hughes arranged for Hawkins to play a concert while he was in England (which was, apparently, illegal since Hawkins did not have permission to be in the country). Wilcox (D), along with many others, bought a ticket and attended the concert. He then wrote a most laudatory description of the concert in his magazine [uh oh, now you're in for it!].

■ ISSUE

Does one's presence at an illegal performance constitute aiding and abetting?

■ DECISION AND RATIONALE

(Lord Goddard, C.J.) Yes. Presence and payment to attend an illegal performance in order to attain benefit for oneself can constitute aiding and abetting the criminal act. There was not accidental presence in this case. Wilcox (D) paid to go to the concert and he went there because he wanted to report it. He must, therefore, be held to have been present, taking part, concurring, or encouraging, whichever word you like to use for expressing this conception. It was an illegal act on the part of Hawkins to play the concert. Wilcox (D) clearly knew that it was an unlawful act for Hawkins to play. Wilcox (D) had gone there to hear him; his presence and his payment to attend were encouragements for Hawkins to be there. He went there to make use of the performance to help sell his magazine. In those circumstances there was evidence on which the magistrate could find that Wilcox (D) aided and abetted, and for these reasons I am of the opinion that the appeal fails.

Analysis:

The court asserts that the result may have been entirely different if Wilcox (D) had gone to the concert and protested the illegality of the musicians playing there, and even perhaps attempted to stop the concert. The court goes on to say that if Wilcox (D) had "booed" at Hawkins it might have been evidence against the aiding and abetting charge. However, the court here appears to find the fact that Wilcox (D) used the unlawful performance to gain profit for his magazine to be the nail in his coffin. There were many other spectators who paid to attend the concert and who did not "boo" or create a disruption in protest, yet no one else was brought up on aiding and abetting charges. It seems that the case turns more on the fact that Wilcox profited from an illegal activity than the fact that he "encouraged" the performance, and aiding and abetting was simply the easiest way to prevent what the court viewed as spurious gain on the part of Wilcox (D).

■ CASE VOCABULARY

MAGISTRATE: England's version of a trial judge.

State v. Helmenstein

(*State*) v. (*Banana Burglar*)
163 N.W.2d 85 (1968)

ACCOMPLICE TESTIMONY MUST BE CORROBORATED BY INDEPENDENT EVIDENCE IN ORDER TO SUSTAIN A DEFENDANT'S CONVICTION

■ **INSTANT FACTS** Helmenstein (D) was convicted of burglary after he and his friends drove to a nearby town and broke into a store and stole beer and food.

■ **BLACK LETTER RULE** A conviction may not be had upon the testimony of an accomplice unless his testimony is corroborated by such other evidence as tends to connect the defendant with the commission of the offense, and the corroboration is not sufficient if it merely shows the commission of the offense or the circumstances thereof.

■ PROCEDURAL BASIS

Appeal from the judgment of conviction and from an order denying the defendant's motion for new trial.

■ FACTS

A group of young people were drinking beer in a town park. After a while, they all got into Helmenstein's (D) car and started driving around. Someone in the car suggested that they drive to a nearby town and break into a grocery store there. One girl in the party said she wanted some bananas [oh yummy, beer and bananas], and someone else expressed a desire for other items which could be obtained from the store. They drove to the town and parked the car some distance from the store. Three of the party, including Helmenstein (D), went to the store, broke in, and returned with beer, cigarettes, candy and bananas. They then drove back to their own town and, on the way, agreed on a story they would tell police if any of them was questioned [sure, that always works!]. They then divided the loot and separated. At trial, five of the people in the party testified against Helmenstein (D). The only witness other than those who were in the party on the night of the burglary was Harold Henke, the owner of the store that had been burglarized. His testimony in no way connected Helmenstein (D) with the offense, but merely established the fact that a crime had been committed. The trial court found Helmenstein (D) guilty and this appeal followed.

■ ISSUE

Is the testimony of an accomplice to a crime against another accomplice sufficient to sustain a conviction?

■ DECISION AND RATIONALE

(Strutz, J.) No. A conviction may not be had upon the testimony of an accomplice unless his testimony is corroborated by such other evidence as tends to connect the defendant with the commission of the offense, and the corroboration is not sufficient if it merely shows the commission of the offense or the circumstances thereof. To determine whether there was competent evidence against Helmenstein (D) sufficient to sustain the judgment of conviction, we must examine the record to determine the status of the witnesses the State called to testify against Helmenstein (D) who were members of the party on the night of the burglary. Carol Weiss was the one who wanted the bananas; we believe this makes her an accomplice. Janice Zahn admitted that she herself agreed to the burglary when it was suggested, thus she also is an accomplice. Kenneth Cahoon took part in the actual burglary with Helmenstein (D) so his status is clearly that of an accomplice. Glen Zahn was asleep in the car during the burglary, however he was awake when the three left for the store, and he helped make up the story to mislead the police. This makes him part of the offense as well. The record clearly shows that the burglary in this case was the result of a plan in which each of the parties had a part, and that each of these young people encouraged and countenanced the offense and that each of them was thus concerned with its commission. There is no evidence in this case, other than that of persons who are also accomplices, connecting Helmenstein (D) with the commission of the offense with which he is charged. Therefore the evidence against him is insufficient to sustain the judgment of conviction.

Analysis:

Most states have a rule similar to the corroboration rule in this case, or else require a jury instruction cautioning jurors to treat the testimony of accomplices with a cautious eye. It is important to note that the "assistance" of each of the accomplices does not need to involve a causal link to the offense. The courts have held that it is quite sufficient if the aid merely facilitated a result that would have transpired even without it. Some have criticized this approach, however, for in ignoring causation, persons are held accountable for the actions of others. As a result, although the accomplice is punished because of his own wrongful conduct, he is punished to the extent of another's. Sine qua non causation, on the other hand, ensures personal responsibility for crimes. It also is an assurance that those who are legally blameworthy are given their "just desserts."

■ CASE VOCABULARY

CORROBORATION: Affirmation.

COUNTENANCED: Approved.

SINE QUA NON: The act without which the harm would not have occurred.

People v. Genoa

(*State*) v. (*Drug Financier*)

188 Mich.App. 461, 470 N.W.2d 447 (1991)

COURT RULES IT LEGALLY IMPOSSIBLE TO AID AND ABET A CRIME WHICH WAS NEVER COMMITTED

■ **INSTANT FACTS** Genoa (D) was charged with aiding and abetting for giving money to an undercover agent to buy and then sell cocaine for a profit.

■ **BLACK LETTER RULE** A person cannot be convicted of aiding and abetting the commission of a crime when the underlying crime was never committed by anyone.

■ PROCEDURAL BASIS

Appeal from the lower court's order dismissing charges against the defendant.

■ FACTS

An undercover agent of the Michigan State Police met with Genoa (D) at a hotel and proposed that if Genoa (D) gave him $10,000 toward the purchase of a kilogram of cocaine, which the police agent claimed he would then sell, the agent would repay Genoa (D) the $10,000, plus $3,500 in profits and a client list [sounds like easy money!]. Genoa (D) accepted the proposal and later returned with the $10,000. After Genoa (D) left, the police agent turned the money over to the Michigan State Police, and Genoa (D) was subsequently arrested and charged with attempted possession with intent to deliver 650 grams or more of cocaine [I've been tricked!]. The district court judge dismissed the charge against Genoa (D) on the ground that because the police agent never intended to commit the contemplated crime and, indeed, never did commit it, Genoa (D), though he believed he was giving money for an illegal enterprise, financed nothing.

■ ISSUE

Can a person be convicted of aiding and abetting the commission of a crime when the underlying crime was never committed by anyone?

■ DECISION AND RATIONALE

(Shepherd, J.) No. The only theory by which Genoa (D) could be prosecuted was that he attempted to aid and abet the crime of possession with intent to deliver cocaine. Genoa (D) never attempted to constructively possess the cocaine himself, he simply helped to finance the proposed venture. While Michigan does not distinguish between principals and accessories for purposes of culpability, certain elements must be established to show someone aided and abetted the commission of a crime. One of those elements is that the underlying crime was committed by either the defendant or some other person. Thus, while the conviction of the principal is not necessary to a conviction of an accessory, the prosecution must prove that the underlying crime was actually committed. In the case at bar, it is clear that the underlying crime was never committed by anyone. The absence of this element made it legally impossible for Genoa (D) to have committed any offense. Affirmed.

Analysis:

Legal impossibility applies to situations where the actor performs an act that would otherwise be criminal, except that the facts render the crime impossible to commit. For example, it is impossible to murder someone who is already dead. It is impossible to commit the crime of receiving stolen property when the property was never stolen in the first place. It is impossible for Genoa (D) to have aided and abetted the crime of possession of cocaine when there was never any possession of cocaine. The court opines that the inability to charge or prosecute Genoa (D) results from a gap in legislation. However, the court never even addresses the topic of entrapment which, from the facts of the case, could also have been a viable defense to prosecution in this case, issues of accomplice liability aside. The undercover agent set up the offense and induced Genoa (D) to participate in its commission. The prevailing "subjective" test of entrapment requires a comparison of the defendant's predisposition to commit the offense against the police conduct to determine whether the police can be said to have caused the crime. The alternative "objective" test looks solely to the police conduct used to induce the defendant to commit the crime. If Genoa (D) could show that but for the police agent's encouragement he never would have violated the law, he could have successfully defended prosecution that way.

■ CASE VOCABULARY

ENTRAPMENT: Affirmative defense to a crime induced by governmental persuasion or trickery.

LEGAL IMPOSSIBILITY: Failure to commit a crime because of some underlying legal bar.

Bailey v. Commonwealth

(*Disgruntled Neighbor*) v. (*State*)

229 Va. 258, 329 S.E.2d 37 (1985)

A SECONDARY PARTY MAY BE CONVICTED AS A PRINCIPAL IN THE FIRST DEGREE UNDER THE INNOCENT AGENCY DOCTRINE

■ **INSTANT FACTS** Bailey (D) was convicted of manslaughter when his neighbor was shot by police responding to reports from Bailey (D) regarding his neighbor's behavior, which he instigated.

■ **BLACK LETTER RULE** One who effects a criminal act through an innocent or unwitting agent is a principal in the first degree.

■ PROCEDURAL BASIS

Appeal from the defendant's conviction in a jury trial.

■ FACTS

One night, Bailey (D) and Murdock, who were neighbors, were arguing over their citizens' band radios. They were both drunk and began cursing and threatening each other. Bailey (D) told Murdock he was coming over to Murdock's house to injure or kill him. Bailey (D), who knew Murdock was visually impaired, told him to arm himself with his handgun and wait on his front porch for Bailey (D) to come. Murdock told Bailey (D) he would be waiting and implied he was going to kill him. Bailey (D) then made an anonymous phone call to the police, telling them that Murdock was out on his porch waving around a gun. A police car went to Murdock's house, but they did not see anything. Bailey (D) called Murdock again and chided him for not being out on his porch. They threatened each other some more, and Bailey (D) told Murdock to go out on the porch and wait because he was on his way. Bailey (D) then called the police again and said Murdock was waving his gun and threatening to shoot up the neighborhood. Three officers were dispatched to Murdock's house, and when they got there, no one was on the porch. A few minutes later, Murdock came out with something shiny in his hand. He sat on the porch with the shiny object beside him. One of the officers approached the porch and told Murdock to leave the gun on the porch and walk away from it. Murdock just sat there. The officer repeated the command, and Murdock cursed him. Murdock then got up with the gun and advanced in the officer's direction, firing. All three officers returned fire, and Murdock was struck. Lying on the porch, he said several times, "I didn't know you was the police." He died from the gunshot wounds. The trial court told the jury it should convict Bailey (D) if it found that his negligence or reckless conduct was so gross and culpable as to indicate a callous disregard for human life and that his actions were the proximate cause or a concurring cause of Murdock's death. The jury convicted Bailey (D) of involuntary manslaughter, and this appeal followed.

■ ISSUE

Can a person be convicted as a principal in the first degree if he was not the immediate perpetrator of a crime?

■ DECISION AND RATIONALE

(Carrico, J.) Yes. Bailey (D) argues that his conviction can be sustained only if he was a principal in the first degree, a principal in the second degree or an accessory before the fact to the killing of

Murdock. The Attorney General agrees and maintains that he was a principal in the first degree. Bailey (D) counters that he could not be a principal in the first degree because only the immediate perpetrators of crime occupy that status, and the immediate perpetrators of Murdock's killing were the police officers who returned Murdock's fire. He was in his own home two miles away, Bailey (D) asserts, and did not control the actors in the confrontation at Murdock's home or otherwise participate in the events that occurred there. We have adopted the rule that one who effects a criminal act through an innocent or unwitting agent is a principal in the first degree. The question we must resolve is whether the police officers who responded to Bailey's (D) calls occupied that status, and, in resolving this question, we believe it is irrelevant whether Bailey (D) and the police shared a common scheme or goal. What is relevant is whether Bailey (D) undertook to cause Murdock harm and used the police to accomplish that purpose, a question which we believe must be answered affirmatively. Knowing Murdock was intoxicated, nearly blind and in an agitated state of mind, Bailey (D) orchestrated a scenario whose finale was bound to include harmful consequences to Murdock, either in the form of his arrest or his injury or death. Bailey (D) argues that Murdock's death was not the natural or probable result of Bailey's (D) conduct, but rather Murdock's own reckless and criminal conduct in opening fire upon the police. Alternatively he argues that the officers' return fire constituted an independent, intervening cause absolving Bailey (D) of guilt. We have held, however, that an intervening act which is reasonably foreseeable cannot be relied upon as breaking the chain of causal connection between an original act of negligence and subsequent injury. Here, under instructions not questioned on appeal, the jury determined that the fatal consequences of Bailey's (D) reckless conduct could reasonably have been foreseen and, accordingly, that Murdock's death was not the result of an independent, intervening cause, but rather arose out of Bailey's misconduct. Affirmed.

Analysis:

Bailey's (D) guilt in this case cannot be premised upon accomplice liability because of the fact that Bailey (D) could not be considered an accomplice of the police. The police were not guilty of any offense, therefore there is no guilt for Bailey (D) to derive from them. The police were justified in their actions: they returned fire in self-defense. Bailey (D) cannot take advantage of their self-defense claim, however, since he was the one who wrongfully created the emergency that required the police action. Bailey is guilty of an offense committed by his own conduct.

■ CASE VOCABULARY

INNOCENT AGENCY DOCTRINE: A secondary party is a principal in the first degree if his acts cause a crime to be committed through an innocent agent.

U.S. v. Lopez

(*Government*) v. (*Prison-Breaking Boyfriend*)

662 F.Supp. 1083 (N.D. Cal. 1987)

AIDER AND ABETTOR CANNOT BE CONVICTED ABSENT PROOF THAT THE PRINCIPAL COMMITTED A CRIME

■ **INSTANT FACTS** Lopez's (D) boyfriend broke her out of prison by helicopter because her life was being threatened by prison authorities.

■ **BLACK LETTER RULE** A defendant can be convicted of aiding and abetting even if the principal is not identified or convicted, however an aider or abettor may not be held liable absent proof that a criminal offense was committed by a principal.

■ PROCEDURAL BASIS

Excerpts from the trial court's ruling on the government's pretrial motion in limine.

■ FACTS

McIntosh (D) landed a helicopter on the grounds of a federal prison in order to effect the escape of his girlfriend, Lopez (D), whose life allegedly was unlawfully threatened by prison authorities [if you're gonna do it, do it big!]. The two were apprehended and prosecuted for various offenses, including prison escape [at least they can sell the movie rights!]. Prior to their trial, McIntosh and Lopez (D) indicated their intent to raise a "necessity/duress" defense based upon the threats to Lopez's (D) life. This writing comes from excerpts from the trial court's ruling on the government's (P) motion in limine for an order barring the presentation of evidence on the defense of necessity or duress.

■ ISSUE

If a principal is found not guilty as the result of a successful affirmative defense can another party be found liable of aiding and abetting the principal?

■ DECISION AND RATIONALE

(Lynch, D.J.) No. In response to the government's (P) motion, each defendant has filed a written offer of proof in camera. By these offers of proof, McIntosh and Lopez (D) seek to establish the prima facie case required to be shown before they are entitled to an instruction on the defense of necessity/duress. The parties agree that if Lopez (D) makes a prima facie showing of each element of the necessity/duress defense, she will be entitled to an instruction on that defense. McIntosh (D) requests a jury instruction stating if Lopez (D) is found not guilty because she acted under necessity/duress, then McIntosh must also be found not guilty of aiding and abetting her alleged escape. The government (P) contents that McIntosh can be convicted of aiding and abetting Lopez's (D) escape even if Lopez (D) succeeds on her necessity/duress defense. The general rule is that a defendant can be convicted of aiding and abetting even if the principal is not identified or convicted, however an aider or abettor may not be held liable absent proof that a criminal offense was committed by a principal. This Court must therefore determine whether Lopez (D) committed a criminal offense if her necessity/duress defense succeeds. This determination requires first classifying Lopez's (D) defense as either a justification or an excuse. Justification defenses are those providing that, although the act was committed, it is not wrongful. When a defense is classified as an excuse, however, the result is that, although the act is wrongful, the actor will not be held accountable. The classification of a defense as a justification or an excuse has an important effect on the liability of one who aids and abets the act. A third party has the right to assist an actor in a justified act. In contrast, excuses are always personal to the actor and a third party can be convicted of aiding and abetting an actor in that case. The defense of duress or coercion traditionally arises when a person unlawfully commands another to do an unlawful act using the threat of death or serious bodily injury. The defense of necessity may be raised in a situation in which the pressure of natural physical forces compels an actor to choose between two evils. The actor may choose to violate the literal terms of the law in order to avoid a greater harm. The defense of necessity is categorized as a justification. In the context of prison escapes, the distinction between duress/coercion and necessity has been hopelessly blurred. In fact, courts seem to use the two terms interchangeably. This Court believes, however, that the defense asserted by Lopez (D), under the facts of this case, most nearly resembles necessity, which is a justification to an alleged crime. In the present case, Lopez's (D) claim is not that the alleged threats overwhelmed her will so that her inability to make the "correct" choice should be excused. Instead, Lopez (D) claims that she, in fact, did make the correct choice. Accordingly, if the jury finds Lopez (D) not guilty of escape by reason of her necessity defense, her criminal act will be justified. No criminal offense will have been committed by a principal, therefore McIntosh (D) would be entitled to his requested jury instruction.

Analysis:

Traditionally, the courts have been reluctant to permit the defenses of duress and necessity by escapees. This reluctance appears to have been primarily grounded upon considerations of public policy. Several recent decisions, however, have recognized the applicability of these defenses to prison escapes. Determining whether the defense is classified as an excuse or justification holds significant importance to an accomplice of the principal. Basically, the important principle to take away from this case is that if the principal is acquitted on the basis of an excuse, the accomplice will not be protected from conviction. However, if the principal is acquitted because the action was justified, the accomplice cannot be convicted of aiding and abetting.

■ CASE VOCABULARY

IN CAMERA: Proceedings held in a judge's chambers or where the public is not present.

MOTION IN LIMINE: Motion before trial to exclude reference to anticipated objectionable evidence.

"NECESSITY/DURESS" DEFENSE: Affirmative defense raised by the defendant which shows a just cause for an act so as to excuse liability.

PRIMA FACIE: On its face; doesn't require further evidence.

People v. McCoy

(*Prosecution*) v. (*Drive-by Shooter*)

25 Cal.4th 1111, 108 Cal.Rptr.2d 188, 24 P.3d 1210 (2001)

AN ACCOMPLICE MAY BE CONVICTED OF A MORE SERIOUS OFFENSE THAN THAT OF THE PRIMARY PERPETRATOR

■ **INSTANT FACTS** McCoy (D1) and Lakey (D2) were tried together for a murder arising out of a drive-by shooting. At trial, McCoy (D1), the person who actually shot the victim, claimed self-defense.

■ **BLACK LETTER RULE** An accomplice's *mens rea* may be deemed more culpable than that of the principal perpetrator of the crime, and thus, the accomplice may be convicted of a greater offense than the offense for which the principal perpetrator is convicted.

■ PROCEDURAL BASIS

Appeal to California Supreme Court challenging the Court of Appeals' reversal of Lakey's (D2) murder conviction.

■ FACTS

Ejaan Dupree McCoy (D1) and Derrick Lakey (D2) were involved in a drive-by shooting, in which McCoy (D1) fired a shot that resulted in another's death. McCoy (D1) and Lakey (D2) were tried together on charges of first-degree murder. McCoy (D1) claimed self-defense, but the jury rejected his claim. Both McCoy (D1) and Lakey (D2) were convicted of first-degree murder. On appeal, the Court of Appeals reversed McCoy's (D1) conviction on the grounds that the jury was incorrectly instructed on the theory of imperfect self-defense. The Court of Appeals also reversed Lakey's (D2) conviction, holding that Lakey (D2), an aider and abettor, could not be convicted of an offense greater than the offense for which the actual perpetrator was convicted where the two were tried in the same trial.

■ ISSUE

Is it possible for an aider and abettor to be convicted of a greater offense than the crime for which the perpetrator was convicted?

■ DECISION AND RATIONALE

(Chin, J.) Yes. An accomplice's *mens rea* may be deemed more culpable than that of the principal perpetrator of the crime, and thus, the accomplice may be convicted of a greater offense than the offense for which the primary party is convicted. There is evidence in this matter that McCoy (D1) killed with an unreasonable, but good faith, belief that he had to act in self-defense. Thus, it is possible that on retrial, McCoy (D1) may be found guilty of manslaughter rather than murder. The question for us is then whether such a possibility requires also that Lakey's (D2) conviction for first-degree murder be reversed. While we recognize that the mental state of an aider and abettor is different than the mental state of the perpetrator, this does not mean that the aider and abettor is always less culpable than the primary actor. We are influenced by the notable scholar Professor Joshua Dressler, who has observed that there is no conceptual obstacle to convicting a secondary party of a more serious offense than the one proven against the primary party. Although both parties are tried together for the same *actus reus*, each participant's *mens rea* should be separately assessed. Professor Dressler has also noted that, with respect to a homicide conviction, it is quite possible that an accomplice may be convicted of first-degree murder when the primary party is convicted of voluntary manslaughter. This policy would certainly be warranted in a case where a drunk primary party killed, without premeditation, while the accomplice was completely sober and calmly assisted in the killing. This example shows how critical it is to evaluate the *mens rea* of the accomplice separately from that of the principal actor. In the present case, we do not find that Lakey's (D2) conviction must be reversed merely because the jury, on retrial, may find McCoy (D1) guilty of a lesser offense than first-degree murder. Reversed as to Lakey (D2).

Analysis:

Does it make sense to you that a single homicide offense could be deemed both voluntary manslaughter and first-degree murder, depending on the *mens rea* of the defendants? Do you think the rule should apply to non-homicide crimes? In footnote 3, the *McCoy* court indicated that it was not reaching any conclusions on how it would decide a case outside of the homicide setting. In *Regina v. Richards*, cited in the notes following the *McCoy* case, the court came to an opposite conclusion from *McCoy* in a non-homicide context. In that case, Richards hired two friends to beat up her husband. Richards was convicted of a more serious offense than the two men who beat him. On appeal, the *Regina* court held that where there is only one offense committed, the person who has requested that the offense be committed, or advised that it be committed, cannot be guilty of a graver offense than that which was in fact committed. The *Regina* decision, however, was widely criticized.

■ CASE VOCABULARY

ACTUS REUS: Guilty act.

MENTES REAE: Another term for *mens rea* or, guilty mind.

In re Meagan R.

(*State*) v. (*Teenage Girl*)

42 Cal.App.4th 17, 49 Cal.Rptr.2d 325 (1996)

TEENAGE GIRL CANNOT BE FOUND GUILTY OF AIDING AND ABETTING HER OWN STATUTORY RAPE

■ **INSTANT FACTS** Minor girl was convicted of burglary for breaking into a house with her boyfriend so they could have sex.

■ **BLACK LETTER RULE** Where the Legislature has dealt with crimes which necessarily involve the joint actions of two or more persons, and where no punishment at all is provided for the conduct, or misconduct, of one of the participants, the party whose participation is not denounced by statute cannot be charged with criminal conduct on either a conspiracy or aiding and abetting theory.

■ PROCEDURAL BASIS

Appeal from a judgment entered against the defendant in juvenile court.

■ FACTS

Oscar Rodriguez broke into his ex-girlfriend's home, with the assistance of 14-year-old Meagan R. (D), in order for the two to have sexual intercourse in violation of a California statute proscribing statutory rape. The state attempted to prosecute Meagan R. (D) for burglary.

■ ISSUE

Can a minor girl be convicted of burglary predicated upon a finding that she entered a residence with the intent to aid and abet her own statutory rape?

■ DECISION AND RATIONALE

(Work, A.P.J.) No. Within the context of being an aider or abettor, there is a rule that where the Legislature has dealt with crimes which necessarily involve the joint actions of two or more persons, and where no punishment at all is provided for the conduct, or misconduct, of one of the participants, the party whose participation is not denounced by statute cannot be charged with criminal conduct on either a conspiracy or aiding and abetting theory. So, although generally a defendant may be liable to prosecution for conspiracy as an aider or abettor to commit a crime even though he or she is incapable of committing the crime itself, the rule does not apply where the statute defining the substantive offense discloses an affirmative legislative policy that the conduct of one of the parties shall go unpunished. Moreover, when the Legislature has imposed criminal penalties to protect a specific class of individuals, it can hardly have meant that a member of that very class should be punishable as either an aider and abettor or as a co-conspirator. The California statute has a provision designed to criminalize the exploitation of children rather than to penalize the children themselves. A ruling to the contrary that a child could be held responsible on a theory of aiding and abetting for violating such a statute would be contrary to express legislative intent. Consequently, Meagan (D), as the victim of the statutory rape, cannot be prosecuted on that charge, regardless of whether her culpability be predicated upon being a co-conspirator, an aider and abettor or an accomplice, given her protected status. Accordingly, the juvenile court cannot rely on the crime of statutory rape to serve as the predicate felony in a finding that Meagan (D) committed burglary. When she entered the residence, she had no punishable intent, for she did not have the culpable state of mind required for burglary. The judgment is reversed.

Analysis:

The logic used in this case flows quite smoothly. The statutory rape statute was designed to punish only the male's criminal conduct, and the legislative intent was to protect the female. Therefore, a female may not be convicted of aiding and abetting her own statutory rape. Further, Meagan (D) could not be convicted of burglary, as she had no intent to commit a felony that could be punished.

■ CASE VOCABULARY

STATUTORY RAPE: Having sexual intercourse with a female under an age set by statute, regardless of her consent.

People v. Brown

(*State*) v. (*Car Thief*)

90 Ill.App.3d 742, 46 Ill.Dec. 591, 414 N.E.2d 475 (1980)

WITHDRAWAL ONLY EFFECTIVE IF IT OCCURS BEFORE THE CRIME IS COMPLETED

■ **INSTANT FACTS** Brown (D) and friends broke into a car dealership to steal a car, but changed their minds before actually entering the building and left.

■ **BLACK LETTER RULE** Withdrawal provisions of an accountability statute are ineffective to prevent liability for an attempted crime after the planning has already taken place.

■ PROCEDURAL BASIS

Appeal from a jury's conviction and sentence of four years imprisonment.

■ FACTS

Brown (D) and a friend, Schultz, were driving around town in Schultz's truck. They picked up another man, Babcock, who was unknown to Brown (D). Babcock suggested that the three steal a car and go out and wreck it [now that's doing it up big!]. He said he knew a place where they could steal a car. Brown (D) testified that he and Schultz didn't really want to steal the car, but that they went along to Hillside Motors, the place where the theft was to occur. When they arrived there, Babcock told Brown and Schultz to go around the back and kick in the door while he stood lookout in front [the big risk-taker]. Brown (D) and Schultz did as planned, and Brown (D) kicked at the door twice [no leniency for being a wimp]. The door did not open, so Schultz kicked it once and it came open. At this time, Brown (D) got scared and decided he didn't want to participate anymore. He and Schultz went around to the front of the building and told Babcock they were leaving. Babcock didn't want to leave, but the other two told him they were going and the truck was too, so Babcock got in the truck. As they were leaving the parking lot next to Hillside Motors, the police arrived and stopped them. After a jury trial, in which Brown (D) was found guilty of attempted burglary, the trial court sentenced him to four years imprisonment. On appeal, Brown (D) argues his conviction should be overturned because the evidence established that he voluntarily abandoned his criminal activity and purpose.

■ ISSUE

Can a defendant relieve himself of liability by renouncing his intent and withdrawing from the commission of a crime after the crime has been planned and begun, but before the crime is completed?

■ DECISION AND RATIONALE

(Alloy, P.J.) No. Brown (D) first argues that his acts in kicking the door were a mere preparation and did not constitute a substantial step toward the commission of the burglary. We find, without difficulty, that the kicking in of the door was *not* merely preparation to the burglary but that it was a substantial step toward its completion. Once the door was open, the only step remaining was the entry into the building. Brown (D) next argues that even if the evidence was sufficient to show attempted burglary, the conviction should not have been entered because of the fact that Brown (D) was not acting as a principal and because he effectively withdrew from the criminal enterprise, while at the same time preventing its completion. The Illinois accountability statute removes accountability if before the commission of the offense, the person terminates his efforts to promote such commission and makes a proper effort to prevent the commission of the offense. The question of withdrawal must focus upon the offense or offenses which Brown (D) aided or abetted in the planning or commission of. In the factual context of this case, both burglary and attempted burglary are possible referents under the statute. As to the burglary offense, Brown's (D) withdrawal would have been effective, in that it occurred prior to the commission of any burglary. However, as to the offense of attempted burglary, his withdrawal was ineffective to prevent application of accountability to his actions, for the reason that such withdrawal did not occur before the commission of the attempted burglary. We conclude that the withdrawal provisions of the accountability statute were not applicable to the attempted burglary charge in that the evidence supported a finding that the offense had occurred prior to the time of Brown's (D) withdrawal. Affirmed.

Analysis:

The withdrawal provision is designed to provide an incentive to accomplices to back out of their criminal activity and block the commission of the crime by the remaining actors. The way the court in this case interprets the statute, however, there was no way for Brown (D) to have avoided criminal liability for the attempted burglary once he and Schultz kicked in the door. This seems to be a flaw in the system, for unless there are two levels of punishment reserved for attempt vs. the completion, the court's reasoning appears to remove any incentive Brown (D) would have had to stop Babcock from completing the burglary. In fact, Illinois classifies burglary as a Class 2 felony, whereas attempted burglary is a Class 3 felony. Thus, there is a slight inducement to renounce in this case.

■ CASE VOCABULARY

WITHDRAWAL: The separating of oneself from the criminal activity.

Commonwealth v. Koczwara

(*State*) v. (*Tavern Owner*)
397 Pa. 575, 155 A.2d 825 (1959)

EMPLOYER CANNOT BE IMPRISONED FOR THE CRIMINAL ACTS OF HIS EMPLOYEES COMMITTED ON HIS PREMISES WITHOUT HIS PRESENCE, PARTICIPATION OR KNOWLEDGE

■ **INSTANT FACTS** Tavern owner and operator was fined and imprisoned for violations of the Liquor Code committed by his employees without his presence, participation or knowledge.

■ **BLACK LETTER RULE** An employer cannot be imprisoned (but can be fined) under a theory of respondeat superior for the criminal acts of his employees committed on his premises without his presence, participation or knowledge.

■ PROCEDURAL BASIS

Appeal from the judgment sentencing the defendant to three months in jail, a fine of $500 and the costs of prosecution.

■ FACTS

Koczwara (D) is the licensee and operator of an establishment known as J.K.'s Tavern. At that place he had a restaurant liquor license issued by the Pennsylvania Liquor Control Board. Koczwara (D) was indicted on four counts for violations of the Liquor Code. The first and second counts averred that Koczwara (D) permitted minors, unaccompanied by parents, guardians, or other supervisors, to frequent the tavern on two separate occasions [shocking!]. The third count charged Koczwara (D) with selling beer to minors, and the fourth charged him with permitting beer to be sold to minors. At the conclusion of the presentation of evidence, count three of the indictment was removed from the jury's consideration by the trial judge on the ground that there was no evidence that Koczwara (D) had personally participated in the sale or was present in the tavern when sales to the minors took place. Defense counsel demurred to the evidence as to the other three counts, but the demurrer was overruled. Koczwara (D) thereupon rested without presenting any evidence and moved for a directed verdict. The motion was denied, the case went to the jury, and the jury returned a verdict of guilty as to each of the remaining three counts.

■ ISSUE

Does a liquor code, which regulates and controls the use and sale of alcoholic beverages, intend to impose vicarious criminal liability on a licensee-principal for acts committed on his premises without his presence, participation or knowledge?

■ DECISION AND RATIONALE

(Cohen, J.) No. This case requires us to determine the criminal responsibility of a licensee of the Liquor Control Board for acts committed by his employees upon his premises, without his personal knowledge, participation, or presence, which acts violate a valid regulatory statute passed under the commonwealth's police power. While an employer in almost all cases is not criminally responsible for the unlawful acts of his employees, unless he consents to, approves, or participates in such acts, courts all over the nation have struggled for years in applying this rule within the framework of "controlling the sale of intoxicating liquor." At common law, any attempt to invoke the doctrine of respondeat superior in a criminal case would have run afoul of our deeply ingrained notions of criminal jurisprudence that guilt must be personal and individual. In recent decades, however, many states have enacted detailed regulatory provisions in fields which are essentially non-criminal. Such statutes are generally enforceable by light penalties, and although violations are labeled crimes, the considerations applicable to them are totally different from those applicable to true crimes, which involve moral delinquency and which are punishable by imprisonment or another serious penalty. It is here that the social interest in the general well-being and security of the populace has been held to outweigh the individual interest of the particular defendant. The penalty is imposed despite the defendant's lack of a criminal intent or mens rea. Because of the peculiar nature of the business, one who applies for and receives permission to carry on the liquor trade assumes the highest degree of responsibility to his fellow citizens. This is the quid pro quo the commonwealth demands in return for the privilege of entering the highly restricted and dangerous business of selling intoxicating liquor. Koczwara (D) argues that a statute imposing criminal responsibility should be construed strictly, with all doubts resolved in his favor. While he is entirely correct, we must remember that we are dealing with a statutory crime within the state's plenary police power. The question here raised is whether the legislature intended to impose vicarious criminal liability on the licensee-principal for acts committed on his premises without his presence, participation or knowledge. The language of the statute specifically omits the use of such words as "knowingly, wilfully, etc." This omission is highly significant and it indicates a legislative intent to eliminate both knowledge and criminal intent as necessary ingredients of such offenses. We find that the intent of the legislature in enacting this Code was not only to eliminate the common law requirement of a mens rea, but also to place a very high degree of responsibility upon the holder of a liquor license to make certain that neither he nor anyone in his employ commit any of the prohibited acts upon the licensed premises. However, in this case, the trial court, of its own accord, imposed imprisonment as well as a fine for Koczwara's (D) violations of the Liquor Code. Such sentence of imprisonment in a case where liability is imposed vicariously cannot be sanctioned by this Court consistent with the State Constitution. Although to hold a principal criminally liable might possibly be an effective means of enforcing law and order, it would do violence to our more sophisticated modern-day concepts of justice. Liability for all true crimes, wherein an offense carries with it a jail sentence, must be based exclusively upon personal causation. It can be readily imagined that even a licensee who is meticulously careful in the choice of his employees cannot supervise every single act of the subordinates. A man's liberty cannot rest on so frail a reed as whether his employee will commit a mistake in judgment. We are holding that so much of the judgment as calls for imprisonment is invalid, and we are leaving intact the fine imposed in the lower court.

■ DISSENT

(Musmanno, J.) The Majority's opinion is so novel, so unique, and so bizarre that one must put on his spectacles, remove them to wipe the lenses, and then put them on again in order to assure himself that what he reads is a judicial decision. Without any justification anywhere, the Majority sustains the conviction of a person for acts admittedly not committed by him, not performed in his presence, not accomplished at his direction, and not even done within his knowledge. The Majority introduces into its discussion a proposition which is shocking to contemplate. Such a concept of "vicarious criminal liability" is as alien to American soil as the upas tree.

Analysis:

Strict liability allows for criminal liability without the element of mens rea found in the definition of most crimes. In contrast, vicarious liability eliminates the requirement of the actus reus and imputes the criminal act of one person to another. Vicarious liability is based solely on the relationship of the parties, as opposed to accomplice liability, where the justification for holding a secondary party liable for the actions of the primary party is that the accomplice has willingly participated in the criminal acts. This case is one of the earliest appellate decisions to consider the validity of vicarious liability, which helps to explain the vehement dissent.

■ CASE VOCABULARY

DEMURRER: Request for dismissal because the opponent's argument is legally insufficient.

DIRECTED VERDICT: Verdict entered by the court, without consideration by the jury, because the facts presented during the trial make it clear that there is only one verdict which could reasonably be reached.

PLENARY POLICE POWER: Absolute power of the state to impose restrictions upon the public's private rights.

QUID PRO QUO: That which you get for that which you give.

RESPONDEAT SUPERIOR: Employer is responsible for the acts of his employees.

State v. Christy Pontiac–GMC

(*State*) v. (*Car Dealership*)

354 N.W.2d 17 (1984)

CORPORATIONS CAN BE HELD CRIMINALLY LIABLE FOR SPECIFIC INTENT CRIMES

■ **INSTANT FACTS** Car dealership was convicted of theft and forgery when its employees forged customer rebate forms and did not pass the rebates on to the customers.

■ **BLACK LETTER RULE** A corporation may be prosecuted and convicted for the crimes of theft and forgery.

■ PROCEDURAL BASIS

Appeal from bench trial resulting in the defendant's four convictions.

■ FACTS

Christy Pontiac (D) is a car dealership owned by James Christy, a sole stockholder, who serves as president and as director. In the spring of 1981, General Motors (GM) offered a cash rebate program for its dealers. A customer who purchased a new car delivered during the rebate period was entitled to a cash rebate, part paid by GM and part paid by the dealership. GM would pay the entire rebate amount initially and later charge back, against the dealer, the dealer's portion of the rebate. Apparently it was not uncommon for the dealer to give the customer the dealer's portion of the rebate in the form of a discount on the purchase price. Phil Hesli, a salesman and fleet manager for Christy Pontiac (D), sold two cars to different customers past the dates of the rebate periods. He told the customers they would not be able to get the rebate on the cars. Subsequently, it was discovered that Hesli had forged the customers' signatures on the rebate forms, backdated the forms to within the rebate period, and submitted the forms to GM [sure he's not a *used* car salesman?]. Both purchasers learned of the forged rebate applications when they received a copy of the application in the mail from Christy Pontiac (D). Both purchasers complained to James Christy, and in both instances the conversations ended in angry mutual recriminations. Christy did tell one of the customers that the rebate on his car was a "mistake" and offered half the rebate amount to "call it even." [or what others call "cover your a___"] After the Attorney General's office made an inquiry, Christy Pontiac (D) contacted GM and arranged for cancellation of one of the rebates that had been allowed to Christy Pontiac (D). Subsequent investigation disclosed that of 50 rebate transactions, only two sales involved irregularities [see, not *too* shady!]. In a separate trial, Phil Hesli was acquitted of three felony charges but found guilty on one count of theft and was given a misdemeanor disposition. An indictment against James Christy for theft by swindle was dismissed for lack of probable cause. Christy Pontiac (D), the corporation, was also indicted, and the appeal here is from the four convictions on those indictments (two counts of theft by swindle and two counts of aggravated forgery).

■ ISSUE

Can a corporation be prosecuted and convicted for the crimes of theft and forgery?

■ DECISION AND RATIONALE

(Simonett, J.) Yes. Christy Pontiac (D) argues that a corporation cannot be held criminally liable for a specific intent crime because the statutes refer only to natural persons and define a crime as "conduct which is prohibited by statute and for which the actor may be sentenced to imprisonment, with or without a fine." A corporation cannot be imprisoned, and cannot entertain a mental state so as to have the specific intent required for theft or forgery, Christy Pontiac (D) asserts. We are not persuaded by these arguments. The legislature has not expressly excluded corporations from criminal liability and, therefore, we take its intent to be that corporations are to be considered persons within the meaning of the Code, absent any clear indication to the contrary. We do not think the statutory definition of a crime was meant to exclude corporate criminal liability; rather, we construe that definition to mean conduct which is prohibited and, if committed, *may* result in imprisonment. We also have no trouble assigning specific intent to a corporation for theft or forgery. There was a time when the law declared that a legal fiction could not be a person for purposes of criminal liability, at least with respect to offenses involving specific intent, but that time is gone. Particularly apt candidates for corporate criminality are types of crime, like theft by swindle and forgery, which often occur in a business setting. We hold, therefore, that a corporation may be prosecuted and convicted for the crimes of theft and forgery. If a corporation is to be criminally liable, it is clear that the crime must not be a personal aberration of an employee acting on his own; the criminal activity must, in some sense, reflect corporate policy so that it is fair to say that the activity was the activity of the corporation. What must be shown is that from all the facts and circumstances, those in positions of managerial authority or responsibility acted or failed to act in such a manner that the criminal activity reflects corporate policy, and it can be said, therefore, that the criminal act was authorized or tolerated or ratified by the corporation. We also hold that the evidence in this case is sufficient to sustain Christy Pontiac's (D) convictions. Hesli, the forger, had authority and responsibility in the business, and Christy Pontiac (D), not Hesli, received the rebate money; therefore Hesli was acting in furtherance of the corporation's business interests. The rebate money was obtained by Christy Pontiac (D) and kept by Christy Pontiac (D) until somebody blew the whistle. We conclude the evidence establishes that the theft by swindle and the forgeries constituted the acts of the corporation. Affirmed.

Analysis:

Most courts today recognize that corporations may be guilty of specific intent crimes. It is a logical conclusion, for if corporations can be liable in civil tort for both actual and punitive damages for libel, assault and battery, or fraud, it seems they should also be criminally liable for conduct requiring specific intent. As the court stated, for the corporation to be criminally liable, the crime must not be based on an employee acting on his own; it must, in some sense, reflect corporate policy so that it is fair to say that the crime was the activity of the corporation. The evidence here showed that James Christy, as an individual, tried to negotiate a settlement when the customer complained, and that he did not contact GM headquarters about the problems until after the Attorney General's inquiry. The court's logic seems to indicate that if James Christy had tried to correct the situation as soon as he learned of the wrongful conduct, the corporation may not have been liable, as that would have demonstrated that the corporation did not authorize, tolerate, or ratify the employee Hesli's actions.

■ CASE VOCABULARY

CORPORATE CRIMINAL LIABILITY: A corporation can commit a crime.

LEGAL FICTION: Assumption that certain facts exist, whether or not they actually do, so that a principle of law may be applied to achieve justice on the facts as they do exist.

THEFT BY SWINDLE: Stealing through trickery or deception.

CHAPTER TWELVE

Theft

Lee v. State

Instant Facts: None stated.

Black Letter Rule: Larceny is the trespassory taking and carrying away of personal property of another with intent to steal the same and may include the misappropriation of property by the person receiving the property, even if it was obtained by the consent of the owner.

Rex v. Chisser

Instant Facts: A person in a jewelry store asks the storekeeper to hand him some rings to inspect, but, instead of inspecting and paying for them, he runs off with the rings in hand.

Black Letter Rule: A person with limited or temporary control over another's property merely has custody of it.

United States v. Mafnas

Instant Facts: An armored car guard was arrested for taking money out of bank money bags while delivering them.

Black Letter Rule: Where an employer furnishes property to an employee in furtherance of the employment relationship, the employee has mere custody of the employer's goods.

Topolewski v. State

Instant Facts: A person was charged with stealing three barrels of meat from his employer, a meat packing company.

Black Letter Rule: A trespassory taking, for the purposes of larceny, does not take place where the taking is facilitated by the owner or at the owner's request.

Rex v. Pear

Instant Facts: A person rented a horse for the stated purpose of making a trip, but never returned it.

Black Letter Rule: Possession obtained by fraud is a trespassory taking for the purposes of larceny.

Brooks v. State

Instant Facts: A person found a wad of $200 in bills that someone else had lost a month earlier and spent the money for himself.

Black Letter Rule: Larceny of lost property does not take place unless the finder had a reasonable ground for finding the true owner and had an intent to steal the property at the time he or she takes possession of it.

Lund v. Commonwealth

Instant Facts: A student used the computer services of his university without authorization or permission.

Black Letter Rule: Traditional common law does not prohibit the wrongful taking of labor or services.

People v. Brown

Instant Facts: A boy took a bicycle from another boy intending to return it the same day.

Black Letter Rule: A felonious taking requires that the taking be with the intent to permanently deprive the owner of possession.

People v. Davis

Instant Facts: A customer in a department store took a shirt off a rack, carried it to a sales counter, claimed it to be his own, and asked for a refund of cash or credit.

Black Letter Rule: An intent to steal is established where the taker's conduct creates a substantial risk of permanent loss.

Rex v. Bazeley

Instant Facts: A bank teller decides to pocket a customer's deposit.

Black Letter Rule: An employee who receives property from a third person for delivery to the employer takes lawful possession upon delivery.

People v. Ingram

Instant Facts: A definition of the crime of false pretenses.

Black Letter Rule: Theft by false pretenses occurs when the defendant makes a false representation of an existing fact with the intent to cheat or defraud the owner of his or her property.

People v. Whight

Instant Facts: Knowing that his bank account was no longer valid, a person continued to use his ATM card to obtain cash at several local grocery stores.

Black Letter Rule: A misrepresentation can be explicit or implicit, and the misrepresentation must have caused the victim to transfer the property to the defendant.

United States v. Czubinksi

Instant Facts: An employee of the IRS looked through the personal taxpayer information of several people using unauthorized computer access.

Black Letter Rule: For the purposes of the federal wire and computer fraud statutes: 1) A scheme to defraud is shown where the defendant has a dishonest intent to deprive a person of their property by causing the owner some articulable harm or by intending to use the property for some gainful use; 2) A deprivation of honest services is found where the defendant fails or intends to fail to carry out his official tasks adequately for an employer or the public; 3) Computer fraud is found where the defendant makes an unauthorized access of a federal computer and gains anything of value in order to further an intent to defraud.

Lee v. State

(*Accused*) v. (*State*)
59 Md.App. 28, 474 A.2d 537 (1984)

LARCENY IS THE TRESPASSORY TAKING AND CARRYING AWAY OF PERSONAL PROPERTY OF ANOTHER WITH INTENT TO STEAL THE SAME

■ **INSTANT FACTS** None stated.

■ **BLACK LETTER RULE** Larceny is the trespassory taking and carrying away of personal property of another with intent to steal the same and may include the misappropriation of property by the person receiving the property, even if it was obtained by the consent of the owner.

■ PROCEDURAL BASIS

None stated.

■ FACTS

None stated.

■ ISSUE

What is the *actus reus* of larceny?

■ DECISION AND RATIONALE

(Bell, J.) Originally, common law courts designed theft-related offenses out of concern for crimes of violence and for protecting society against breaches of the peace. This then grew to include nonviolent takings of property such as larceny, the trespassory taking and carrying away of personal property of another with intent to steal the same. A trespassory taking under traditional common law focused on the physical taking and possession of property, making larceny a crime against possession. Thus, if the owner willingly transferred property to another, the receiving party had "possessorial immunity" against punishment for receiving possession, misappropriation, or using the property in a manner inconsistent with the owner's expectations. However, courts gradually expanded the definition of larceny by manipulating the concept of possession to include misappropriation by the person receiving the property, even if the owner consented to the possession.

Analysis:

This opinion provides a brief outline of larceny's historical evolution. Originally, the common law only punished the taking of property that included the use of force. Larceny was created to include nonforcible, nonconsensual taking of property. This shifted the concept of theft away from being a crime against a person to being a crime against possession. Thus, it became a crime to nonviolently take the property of another without the owner's consent. However, this definition proved too narrow, as those entrusted with property often misused it to the dismay of the owner. As a result, courts had to tinker with the concept of possession to include such misuse as a violation.

■ CASE VOCABULARY

ASPORTATION: Where property has been moved.

BAILEE: A person who receives personal property of another but with no transfer of ownership.

CAPTION: Where a taking has occurred.

LARCENY: The trespassory taking and carrying away of personal property of another with an intent to steal.

MISAPPROPRIATION: Where someone dishonestly uses the property of another to his or her own benefit.

POSSESSION: Where someone has dominion (or authority) *and* control over a piece of property.

TRESPASSORY: An act or instance done wrongfully.

Rex v. Chisser

(*State*) v. (*Accused*)

T. Raym. 275, 83 Eng.Rep. 142 (1678)

A PERSON WITH LIMITED OR TEMPORARY CONTROL OVER ANOTHER'S PROPERTY MERELY HAS CUSTODY OF IT

■ **INSTANT FACTS** A person in a jewelry store asks the storekeeper to hand him some rings to inspect, but, instead of inspecting and paying for them, he runs off with the rings in hand.

■ **BLACK LETTER RULE** A person with limited or temporary control over another's property merely has custody of it.

■ PROCEDURAL BASIS

A jury found the following facts to be true, and the court turned to the issue of whether the defendant's conduct was criminal.

■ FACTS

Abraham Chisser (D) came to the jewelry store of Anne Charteris and asked her to show him two rings. Charteris placed the rings into Chisser's (D) hands, and Chisser (D) asked her their price. Charteris stated that the price was 7s, but Chisser (D) offered her 3s and then immediately ran out of the store with the rings in hand. He was caught [obviously Chisser (D) was no criminal mastermind] and brought to trial. A jury found the above facts to be true, and the court turned to the issue of whether the Chisser's (D) conduct was criminal.

■ ISSUE

Is mere custody of property enough to establish physical possession by a defendant for the purposes of larceny?

■ DECISION AND RATIONALE

(Court) No. Although the owner gave the property to Chisser (D), they were not out of her possession (and would not have been until they completed a contract for sale). In this case, no contract was concluded. Therefore, when Chisser (D) ran away with the goods, he committed a felony.

Analysis:

In this opinion, the accused is trying to argue that before he fled, he already had possession of the rings, so his subsequent flight was not trespassory. After all, he didn't break into the display case and run off with the rings. The shopkeeper actually gave them to him. The court, therefore, had to fill a gap in larceny law and did so using the concepts of custody and constructive possession. For legal purposes, the accused did not have possession of the rings while he inspected them in the store. Despite her actions, the shopkeeper retained constructive possession of the rings, even though she handed them over to the accused. This is because Charteris gave him the rings, but did not intend to give him possession unless he paid for them. Therefore, she retained constructive possession of the rings, but gave the accused temporary custody of them for inspection. Consequently, at the moment he fled, he asserted control *and* dominion over the rings, and his actions became a trespassory taking. As a result, Chisser (D)'s custody of the rings converted into a wrongful possession as he fled. After fleeing, he had committed both a trespassory taking and a carrying away of property, making him guilty of larceny.

■ CASE VOCABULARY

CONSTRUCTIVE POSSESSION: Where an owner of property may not have physical control over her property at that moment, but still retains dominion over it.

CREVATS: An old english word used for jewelry, especially rings.

United States v. Mafnas

(*State*) v. (*Accused*)
701 F.2d 83 (9th Cir. 1983)

EMPLOYEES HAVE MERE CUSTODY OF THEIR EMPLOYER'S PROPERTY

■ **INSTANT FACTS** An armored car guard was arrested for taking money out of bank money bags while delivering them.

■ **BLACK LETTER RULE** Where an employer furnishes property to an employee in furtherance of the employment relationship, the employee has mere custody of the employer's goods.

■ PROCEDURAL BASIS

Appeal from a district court for violation of a federal larceny statute.

■ FACTS

Mafnas (D) was an employee of the Guam Armored Car Service whom the Bank of Hawaii and the Bank of America hired to deliver bags of money. On three occasions, Mafnas (D) opened the money bags and took money while making his deliveries. Mafnas' (D) [kleptomaniacal tendencies] were put to an end after he was caught. He was convicted in a district court under 18 U.S.C. § 2113(b) [which prohibits the taking "with intent to steal ... any money belonging to ... any bank"]. Mafnas (D) appealed to the United State's Court of Appeals for the Ninth Circuit.

■ ISSUE

Does an employee who receives property belonging to the employer during the scope of employment and converts the property to the employee's personal use commit larceny?

■ DECISION AND RATIONALE

(Court) Yes. If a person receives property for a temporary or limited purpose, that person is only acquiring custody, not possession in the legal sense. The owner retains constructive possession. Thus, a person hired to deliver the employer's property to another only has custody over the property in the course of the delivery. As a result, the decision of the employee to take the property for his own use is beyond the consent of the owner and constitutes larceny. See United States v. Pruitt [Larceny found where the defendant was a messenger who staged a fake robbery while he was delivering money for the bank]. However, Mafnas (D) distinguishes Pruitt by claiming he was an agent of the bank, not an employee, making him a bailee who had lawful possession over the money bags. See Lionberger v. United States [Holding that a bailee exists where the owner, while retaining title, gives property to the bailee for "some particular purpose upon an express or implied contract."]. Bailees are treated differently and are considered to have possession over their employer's goods. Nevertheless, a bailee may still commit larceny where the bailee "breaks bulk". Under this doctrine, the bailee-carrier is given lawful possession of a package, but not its contents. Thus, breaking open the package and taking a portion or all its contents is an act of larceny. As a result, under either theory, Mafnas (D) has committed larceny. In addition, the argument that the theft was from the service and not the banks has no merit. The money stolen was within the meaning of § 2113(b) since it was money "in the care, custody, control, management, or possession of any bank". Conviction is affirmed.

Analysis:

In the case at hand, Mafnas (D) tries to argue that he was a bailee in lawful possession of both the package and its contents. However, the "breaking bulk" doctrine defeats that argument. Nevertheless, the doctrine has its faults. For example, if Mafnas (D) had taken the bags of money unopened and brought them to his own bank for deposit, there would be no larceny. Mafnas (D) has lawful possession of the bags and did not break them open. His bank would not be guilty of larceny either. The bank will open the bags to make the deposit; but, at that point, the bank has lawful possession of the bags and its contents. This is because it received consensual possession of the bag from Mafnas (D), the bank is not a bailee, and the bank lacks the intent to steal. A better approach may be to treat the bailee as holding the package and its contents custodially, or at least accept the notion that there may be persons with "possession" that nonetheless do not have total dominion over the property and can defraud others entitled to the property or its benefits.

■ CASE VOCABULARY

CONVERSION: The use or possession of another's property as if it were one's own.

Topolewski v. State

(*Accused*) v. (*State*)
130 Wis. 244, 109 N.W. 1037 (1906)

A TRESPASSORY TAKING DOES NOT TAKE PLACE WHERE THE TAKING IS FACILITATED BY THE OWNER OR AT THE OWNER'S REQUEST

■ **INSTANT FACTS** A person was charged with stealing three barrels of meat from his employer, a meat packing company.

■ **BLACK LETTER RULE** A trespassory taking, for the purposes of larceny, does not take place where the taking is facilitated by the owner or at the owner's request.

■ PROCEDURAL BASIS

The defendant was found guilty of larceny. The defendant appealed.

■ FACTS

Topolewski (D) was an employee of the Plankinton Packing company. Topolewski (D) wanted to collect a debt owed to him by a former employee of the meat packing company named Mat Dolan. Topolewski (D) approached Dolan for payment of the debt. However, Dolan was unable to make payment. Topolewski (D) conjured up a scheme for Dolan to satisfy his debt by helping Topolewski (D) steal some of the company's meat products. Topolewski (D) discussed the plan with Dolan, but Dolan [was a snitch and told the company about the scheme]. Dolan and the company agreed to set up Topolewski (D), so that he could be caught red handed. After Topolewski (D) and Dolan discussed a variety of possible schemes, the two arranged to meet and discuss the plan while an employee of the company listened in hiding. Dolan and Topolewski (D) agreed to a plan where Dolan would order some packages of meat to be placed on one of their loading platforms that was normally used to deliver meat to customers. Topolewski (D) would then arrive, pretending to be a customer, and pick up the meat. Dolan would make this arrangement at the company through Mr. Layer, the person in charge of its wholesale department. Mr.Layer was informed about the scheme and the plan to trap Topolewski (D). Mr.Layer ordered four barrels of meat to be packed and placed on the loading platform for Topolewski (D) to pick up. Mr.Layer notified the person in charge of the platform, Ernst Klotz, that a customer was to pick up the barrels. Topolewski (D) arrived, on schedule, to pick up the meat. Klotz allowed Topolewski (D) to load the barrels onto his wagon. Klotz consented to Topolewski's (D) actions, but did not actually help Topolewski (D) load the barrels onto the wagon. Topolewski (D) did not pick up the fourth barrel but told Klotz that he wanted it marked and sent to him with a bill. Topolewski (D) also told Klotz that he had ordered the barrels the night before through Dolan. Topolewski (D) then drove away with his [grand prize of] three barrels of meat, worth $55.20 while leaving the meat packing company [high and dry]. Topolewski (D) was caught and found guilty of having stolen three barrels of meat from the Plankinton packing company. Topolewski (D) appealed.

■ ISSUE

Is a person guilty of larceny where the owner of the property actually or constructively aids in the commission of the offense, as intended by the wrongdoer, by performing or rendering unnecessary some act in the transaction essential to the offense?

■ DECISION AND RATIONALE

(Marshall) No. The question in this case is whether the meat packing company consented to the taking of the barrels such that the element of trespass or nonconsent is not satisfied for the crime of larceny. The plan for stealing the property did originate with Topolewski (D). Nonetheless, the plan was impossible to achieve without the property being placed on the loading platform and Topolewski (D) being allowed to take it. However, neither Dolan nor the company explicitly consented to the misappropriation of the property. This case "is very a near the borderline, if not across it, between consent and nonconsent to the taking of the property." Larceny does not take place where property is delivered by a servant to a defendant under the direction of the master, regardless of the defendant's purposes. See *Reg v. Lawrence,* 4 Cox C.C. 438. This case is similar. The company placed the barrels on the loading platform with the knowledge that Topolewski (D) would arrive to pick it up. While Klotz did not assist Topolewski (D) in taking the barrels, he stood by and allowed Topolewski (D) to pick up the barrels, assisted him in arranging the wagon, and made provision for the fourth barrel. In addition, Klotz was instructed and had every reason to believe that Topolewski (D) had a right to take the property. His conduct amounted to a delivery of the three barrels to Topolewski (D). In *Rex v. Egginton,* 2 P. & P. 508, [a servant informed his master that he had been approached to assist in the robbing of the master's house. The master instructed the servant to open the house to the thieves and allow them to steal certain items. The master intended to have the thieves arrested after they achieved their goal. However the court held that the crime of larceny was complete because the master did not direct the servant to deliver the property to the thieves or consent to its taking. The thieves "were neither induced to commit the crime nor was any act essential to the offense done by anyone but themselves."] The element of trespass is absent in this case. The company intended to set a trap for Topolewski (D), but the setting of the trap went too far by actually placing the company in the position of having consented to the taking. There can be no larceny without a trespass. Therefore, "where the owner of property by himself or his agent, actually or constructively, aids in the commission of the offense, as intended by the wrongdoer, by performing or rendering unnecessary some act in the transaction essential to the offense, the would be criminal is not guilty of all the elements of the offense." If Topolewski (D) had merely agreed with Dolan to improve the opportunity for the accused to steal the barrels of meat from the loading platform, then this case would have had a different result. Conviction reversed.

Analysis:

In this case, while the accused clearly had the proper *mens rea* for larceny, his *actus reus* was insufficient. The company allowed him to pick up the barrels, effectively allowing him to steal them. However, the company did not, in actuality, intend to give the barrels to the accused. In fact, it intended to temporarily give the accused the barrels, and then subsequently have him apprehended for his actions. Presumably, the company would then have its barrels returned. So, given that the company did not actually intend to give the accused the barrels permanently and he had the requisite *mens rea,* why let Topolewski (D) off? Criminal law is designed to prevent crime, not facilitate the commission of crime. Presume, for example, that without the company's assistance, it would be impossible for Topolewski (D) to take the barrels. In this case, Topolewski (D), while having criminal intentions, would never have been able to carry out his intent to steal. No crime would have taken place. If the court had found that Topolewski (D) had committed larceny in this case, this would give private persons the power to trap individuals into committing crime by encouraging and facilitating criminal behavior on the part of both the company and the accused. Instead of preventing crime, the law would encourage people to create crimes where they would not have otherwise existed. To thwart this undesirable result, the court applies a strict, literal meaning to the element of trespass. While the company did not actually intend or consent to a permanent deprivation of its property, its temporary consent, for the purpose of incriminating Topolewski (D), was not sufficient for larceny.

Rex v. Pear

(*State*) v. (*Accused*)
1 Leach 212, 168 Eng.Rep. 208 (1779)

POSSESSION OBTAINED BY FRAUD IS A TRESPASSORY TAKING

■ **INSTANT FACTS** A person rented a horse for the stated purpose of making a trip, but never returned it.

■ **BLACK LETTER RULE** Possession obtained by fraud is a trespassory taking for the purposes of larceny.

■ **PROCEDURAL BASIS**

A jury found the following facts to be true, and the court turned to the issue of whether the defendant's conduct was criminal.

■ **FACTS**

Samuel Finch was a stable keeper who rented a horse to Pear (D) on July 2, 1779. Pear (D) hired the horse telling the owner that he intended to ride to Surry, that he lived at 25 King-street, and that he would return with the horse at about 8 o'clock that same evening. Pear (D) did not go to Surry and did not return the horse. In fact, the very same day [after some horsing around], he sold the horse to someone else. Also, he was not living at the address that he gave to the owner. A jury found that the above facts were true and also found that Pear (D) had hired the horse with the fraudulent intention of selling it immediately. The case was then referred to the judges who had to decide whether Pear's (D) actions were a mere breach of trust or a felony.

■ **ISSUE**

Does possession obtained by fraud constitute larceny?

■ **DECISION AND RATIONALE**

(Court) Yes. The question of whether, at the time of the hiring, Pear (D) intended to steal and sell the horse, was decided by the jury. If no such intent existed, he must be acquitted. The jury concluded that Pear (D) hired the horse under the "mere pretense" to obtain possession and sell it. The judges found that the question regarding Pear 's (D) original intentions had been properly left to the jury. The judges then decided whether the pretense constituted a breach of trust or a felonious conversion. The judges concluded that the possession was obtained fraudulently and the true owner remained in possession at the time of the conversion. As a result, Pear (D) is guilty of a felony.

Analysis:

This is another opinion that deals with the element of trespass in larceny. This case is different because, while the owner did consent to Pear 's (D) possession of the horse, this consent was obtained fraudulently. This offense is now known as "larceny by trick". The opinion focuses on the timing of the intent of the accused. If the accused had no intention to steal and sell the horse at the time the owner gave it to him, than he could not be guilty of larceny. However, if the accused had the intent to steal and sell the horse at the time he obtained possession from the owner, then he could be held accountable. The opinion takes this approach because it needs to fit the facts of the case within the confines of traditional larceny law. Larceny is defined only as a crime of possession. Punishment is merited only if possession is wrongfully obtained. If Pear (D) was not lying when he asked to rent Finch's horse, then he used no fraud to obtain the horse and possession passed lawfully. At transfer, neither Pear (D) nor Finch had any knowledge about any "horseplay," unless, of course, Pear (D) later changed his mind and decided to steal it. However, does it make sense to allow a person who later develops the intention to steal the property to go free? Clearly, the law of larceny may be inadequate to cover this kind of behavior.

■ CASE VOCABULARY

SERIATIM: When something occurs successively, one after another.

Brooks v. State

(*Accused*) v. (*State*)
35 Ohio St. 46 (1878)

LARCENY OF LOST PROPERTY DOES NOT TAKE PLACE UNLESS THE FINDER HAS A REASONABLE MEANS FOR FINDING THE TRUE OWNER AND HAD AN INTENT TO STEAL THE PROPERTY AT THE TIME HE OR SHE TAKES POSSESSION OF IT

■ **INSTANT FACTS** A person found a wad of $200 in bills that someone else had lost a month earlier and spent the money for himself.

■ **BLACK LETTER RULE** Larceny of lost property does not take place unless the finder had a reasonable ground for finding the true owner and had an intent to steal the property at the time he or she takes possession of it.

■ PROCEDURAL BASIS

Appeal of a jury verdict that found the defendant guilty of larceny.

■ FACTS

Charles B. Newton, on October 24, 1878, rode into the city of Warren in a buggy to attend some business. He hitched his horse to a post and went to attend to his business matters. Later that afternoon, as he returned home, he discovered that he had lost a package of bank bills totaling $200. After an unsuccessful search for the money, Newton published an advertisement in two Warren newspapers regarding the missing money. On November 20, George Brooks (D), a resident of the city of Warren, found the roll of bank bills a few feet from the hitching post while he was working with several other laborers. None of the other laborers saw Brooks (D) find the money. However, to ward off any suspicion, Brooks (D) showed to the laborers a dollar bill which was wet and muddy. He then offered to sell the dollar bill to one of them for $0.25. A half-hour past his dinner break, he quit work and was paid off. Brooks (D) then spent part of the money that same day to buy a pair of boots and other items and gave $50.00 to Mrs. Lease to purchase furniture and other items for his wife. Brooks (D) and his wife, shortly afterward, then tried to sneak quietly out of town. The evidence does not show that Brooks (D) saw any of the newspaper notices regarding the lost money or that he knew of Newton's loss at the time he found the money. A jury found Brooks (D) guilty of larceny. Brooks (D) appealed.

■ ISSUE

Does a person commit larceny where he or she finds lost goods and takes them for his or her own use but has good grounds to believe that the owner can be found?

■ DECISION AND RATIONALE

(White, J.) Yes. Larceny may be committed of lost property. Constructive possession still remains in the owner, unless the circumstances reveal that the owner abandoned the property. According to Baker v. The State, 29 Ohio St. 184, ["when a person finds goods that have actually been lost, and takes possession with intent to appropriate them to his own use, really believing, at the time, or having good ground to believe, than the owner can be found, it is larceny"]. This rule does not require the finder "to use diligence or to take pains" in finding the true owner. Lost property may be the subject of larceny if the finder has reasonable ground to believe, from the nature of the property, or the circumstances under which it is found, that if he deals with the item openly and honestly the owner will be discovered. In addition, the finder will be guilty of larceny if an intent to steal existed at the time he took the item into his possession. The case was properly submitted to the jury and the evidence reveals no ground to interfere with their decision. The judgment of the court below is affirmed.

■ DISSENT

(Orey, J.) I do not think the accused was properly convicted. The evidence fails to show that the accused had any information that someone had lost money or any information regarding the owner. The money had been left undiscovered for several weeks and its owner had stopped searching for it. The accused may have had been morally bound to take steps to find the owner, "but in violating the moral obligation, I do not think that the plaintiff incurred criminal liability." The obligation of dealing "honestly" with the money is far too indefinite with no guidance to the jury. "What one jury might think was honest dealing, another jury might think was the reverse."

Analysis:

An intent to steal can develop in only two ways. First, the finder may have a greedy propensity and, upon seeing a twenty-dollar bill, immediately think, "That's my twenty bucks now," irrespective of any clues as to ownership. If there are good clues as to ownership, the finder would be guilty of larceny. Second, the finder may find the twenty-dollar bill with a neutral intent and later discover good clues as to ownership, but still decide to keep it. This person could not be criminally punished. The finder only developed an intent to steal *after* taking possession. Are you convinced that Brooks (D) had a wrongful intent at the moment he picked up the bills, or did he develop it later? This question reveals loopholes in larceny law. What if Brooks (D) found the bills wrapped in brown paper, picked them up with a neutral intent, later unwrapped the paper to reveal the cash, and then decided to keep it? Because he lacked the intent to steal when he picked up the package, he would not be guilty of larceny. What if Brooks (D) found only an anonymous dollar bill blowing in the wind, picks it up not intending to steal it but knowing that there is no clue as to ownership, and learns five minutes later that a co-worker had just lost a dollar bill? Again, if he decided to keep the dollar bill, this would not be larceny because the intent to steal occurred after possession as a result of a new clue. However, is not his decision to keep the money just as deceptive and fraudulent as if he had picked up the bill with the intent to steal it in the first place?

Lund v. Commonwealth

(*Accused*) v. (*State*)
217 Va. 688, 232 S.E.2d 745 (1977)

COMMON LAW LARCENY DOES NOT PROHIBIT THE WRONGFUL TAKING OF LABOR OR SERVICES

■ **INSTANT FACTS** A student used the computer services of his university without authorization or permission.

■ **BLACK LETTER RULE** Traditional common law does not prohibit the wrongful taking of labor or services.

■ PROCEDURAL BASIS

The accused was found guilty of grand larceny and sentenced to two years and the accused appealed.

■ FACTS

Charles Walter Lund (D) was a graduate student in statistics studying for his Ph.D. at Virginia Polytechnic Institute and State University. His dissertation required him to use a computer. The university had a computer center, but Lund's (D) faculty adviser neglected to arrange for Lund's (D) use of the computer facilities. [So, in the interests of science and earning that Ph.D.,] Lund (D) used the campus computer facilities without obtaining the proper authorization. The computers used by Lund (D) are leased by the university from IBM Corporation. The rental cost of the computers is shared by various departments within the university and is charged to the budget of each department. These departments are allocated computer credits based on a proportion of their budget. These departments receive a monthly statement showing the amount of computer time used to by each department and the remaining balance for each department. Each department receives their own account number and a key to a post office box where the computer center personnel store any printing jobs made under the account. Lund (D) came under surveillance on October 12, 1974 after complaints from departments of unauthorized charges to their computer accounts. Lund (D) was confronted by the university's investigator and initially denied use of the services, but later made an admission. He turned over seven keys for four post office boxes assigned to other persons. Lund (D) stated that he had received the keys from another student. In addition, a large number of computer cards and printouts were recovered from his apartment. The director of the computer center testified that the unauthorized use of the accounts totaled $ 5,065, and that Lund (D) used as much as $26,384,16 in unauthorized computer time, and furthermore, he stated that Lund's (D) computer cards and printouts had a value worth no more than scrap paper. Lund (D) testified that he used the computer without authorization, but he believed he did not do anything wrong because he was working on his dissertation. Four faculty members also testified in Lund's (D) behalf stating that the computer time used "probably would have been" or "would have been" given to Lund (D) if he had sought the proper authorization. Lund (D) was convicted under § 18.1–100 and § 18.1–118. § 18.1–100 [defines grand larceny as a taking from another of money or an item that is greater than $5 in value, or the taking not from the person of another goods and chattels greater than $100 in value]. § 18.1–118 [defines the crime of larceny by false pretense as a taking from another person money or other property through a false representation of an existing fact with knowledge of its falsity and with the intent to defraud]. Lund (D) argued that his conviction should be overturned because there was no evidence that articles were stolen or that they had a value of $100 or more and the computer time and services are not the subject of larceny under § 18.1–100 or 18.1–118.

■ ISSUE

Can the taking of labor or services be the subject of the crime of false pretense or larceny?

■ DECISION AND RATIONALE

(I'Anson, J.) No. Under common law, larceny is a taking and carrying away of goods and chattels of another with intent to permanently deprive the owner of possession. Our statutes are no different. The phrase "goods and chattels" cannot be interpreted to include labor or services such as computer time. Criminal statutes must be strictly construed. Some jurisdictions have amended their criminal codes specifically to include the taking of labor or services by false pretense. However, no such amendments have been made to our statutes. Furthermore, the unauthorized use of the computer time cannot be the subject of larceny. Neither statute prohibits the use of the property of another. The statutes only refer to a taking and carrying away of a concrete piece of property. Labor, services, and the unauthorized use of property cannot be construed to be subjects of larceny under § 18.1–100 and 18.1–118. The commonwealth argues that even though the computer printouts have no market value, their value can be determined by the value of the computer time use to produce them. However, the cost of producing the printouts is not the proper method to ascertain the value here. If an article has no market value, the better rule is that the article's actual value should be proved. The evidence shows that the printouts had no monetary value to the university or the computer center and had no more value than scrap paper. As a result, the evidence was insufficient to convict under either § 18.1–100 or § 18.1–118. The judgment of the trial court is reversed and the indictment is quashed.

Analysis:

Traditional common law protected "goods and chattels." Intangible personal property was not protected under criminal law. Takings of intangible property were not the subject of criminal law because they were the subjects of contract and equity. If a person "stole" labor or services, the victim could recover under equitable theories of quasi-contract or unjust enrichment. However, as the economy evolved, labor and services became more or as valuable as tangible property, and pressure increased to include the "taking" of such intangibles within the scope of larceny. In this case, the accused stole intangibles valued at over $30,000. Recognizing the problem, the opinion refused to expand its statutory definition of larceny, under § 18.1–100, or false pretense, under § 18.1–118, to include the use of computer services. Note, however, that the false pretense statute, § 18.1–118, does not use the language "taking and carrying away of the goods and chattels of another" found in § 18.1–100. Instead, the statute uses the language "*obtain*... money or other property which may be the subject or larceny" (emphasis added). This statute does not refer to a taking or carrying away, which may signify a legislative intent to include intangibles.

■ CASE VOCABULARY

FALSE PRETENSE: A statement or conduct expressing a fact that is actually untrue.

People v. Brown

(*State*) v. (*Accused*)
105 Cal. 66, 38 P. 518 (1894)

A FELONIOUS TAKING REQUIRES THAT THE TAKING BE WITH THE INTENT TO PERMANENTLY DEPRIVE THE OWNER OF POSSESSION

■ **INSTANT FACTS** A boy took a bicycle from another boy intending to return it the same day.

■ **BLACK LETTER RULE** A felonious taking requires that the taking be with the intent to permanently deprive the owner of possession.

■ PROCEDURAL BASIS

The defendant was convicted by a jury trial of the crime of burglary with intent to commit grand larceny and the defendant appealed.

■ FACTS

Brown (D) was a seventeen-year-old boy who had been in an argument with another boy named Yount. Yount had thrown oranges at Brown (D), and Brown (D) wanted to get back at him. Brown (D) entered Yount's house and tried to take his bicycle, but took Frank's bicycle instead. Brown (D) claimed that he took the bicycle to get back at Yount, but intended to return the bike the next day. Brown (D) drove the bicycle into a grove, placed it on the ground, covered it with brush, and hid under it so that no one could find him until the evening when he planned to return the bike. However, Frank found him hiding under the bicycle and the brush. The trial court instructed the jury that larceny may take place even though the party taking the property only intended to temporarily deprive the owner of it. The trial judge compared the case to a man who takes a horse, not with the intent to take permanent possession of it, but only to ride to a particular destination, and then abandon it. The judge said this example was an example of conversion of property to one's own use, making the act a felony. The jury found Brown (D) guilty. Brown (D) appealed.

■ ISSUE

Does an intent to temporarily deprive the owner of his or her property constitute larceny?

■ DECISION AND RATIONALE

(Garoutte, J.). No. The jury instruction was erroneous. The court instructed the jury that larceny may take place if the accused only intended to temporarily deprive the owner of the property. However, judicial authorities "form an unbroken line" holding that the felonious intent must be the intent to permanently deprive the owner of the property. The judge's example regarding the man taking the horse is too broad to accurately state what the law is. Under the judge's example, the man may or may not be guilty of larceny, and it would be a question of fact for the jury to decide. For there to have been felonious intent, the accused must have intended to permanently deprive the owner of his property and not just to convert the property to his own use. Judgment reversed.

Analysis:

This opinion illustrates the requisite *mens rea* for larceny. If a person takes another person's bicycle for a joyride and returns it, the joyrider cannot be guilty of larceny. However, in terms of the *actus reus*, a trespassory taking has still taken place. Nonetheless, the joyrider cannot be convicted of larceny because he lacked the required *mens rea.* The trial judge confused the concept of *animus furandi*, the intent to permanently deprive, with *lucria causa*, "for the sake of gain." If a joyrider takes a bicycle for a day to run his newspaper route, he may have gained from the taking, but his intent to return the bicycle does not create a felonious intent. On the other hand, if the joyrider takes the bicycle with the intent to wreck it beyond repair, he may not have received any pecuniary gain, but his intention to destroy it is *animus furandi.* Under traditional larceny law, a person who takes property temporarily, but later decides to permanently deprive the owner of it, could not be found guilty of larceny because the proper *mens rea* did not exist at the time of taking. However, courts remedied this loophole by developing the legal fiction of "continuing trespass." Thus, if a person takes a bicycle intending to return it the next day, but decides the next day to keep the bicycle, then the initial trespass continues and the crime of larceny takes place at the moment the joyrider changes his mind.

People v. Davis

(*State*) v. (*Accused*)

19 Cal.4th 301, 79 Cal.Rptr.2d 295, 965 P.2d 1165 (1998)

AN INTENT TO STEAL IS ESTABLISHED WHERE THE TAKER'S CONDUCT CREATES A SUBSTANTIAL RISK OF PERMANENT LOSS

■ **INSTANT FACTS** A customer in a department store took a shirt off a rack, carried it to a sales counter, claimed it to be his own, and asked for a refund of cash or credit.

■ **BLACK LETTER RULE** An intent to steal is established where the taker's conduct creates a substantial risk of permanent loss.

■ PROCEDURAL BASIS

Appeal to the state supreme court of a conviction of petty theft.

■ FACTS

Davis (D) entered a Mervyn's department store carrying a Mervyn's shopping bag. As he entered the store, he was placed under surveillance by a store security agent, named Carol German. German observed Davis (D) take a shirt off a rack and carry it to a sales counter in the women's department. Davis (D) told the cashier, Heather Smith, that he had previously bought the shirt for his father and that he wanted to return it now because it did not fit. Smith asked for a receipt, but Davis (D) said that he did not have one because "it was a gift." Smith informed Davis (D) that the store policy was not to issue cash refunds without a receipt for an amount more than $20.00, but she could issue a credit voucher. At this point, Smith was interrupted by a telephone call from the German who told Smith to issue Davis (D) a credit voucher. Smith issued the voucher which Davis (D) signed using a false name. German detained him as he walked away from the counter with the voucher. Davis (D) was convicted under penal code § 484 [which uses the common law definition of larceny]. Davis (D) appealed the conviction to the state supreme court.

■ ISSUE

Can an intent to steal exist if the primary purpose in taking the property is not to permanently deprive the owner of it?

■ DECISION AND RATIONALE

(Mosk, J.) Yes. Davis (D) argues that the elements of trespass and intent to steal are lacking. First, Davis (D) argues that the element of trespass is not satisfied because the store, knowing how Davis (D) came into possession of the shirt, still consented to the issuance of the voucher. Davis (D) confuses the issue of consent. The issue is not consent regarding the voucher, but whether Mervyn's consented to Davis (D) taking the shirt. A department store impliedly consents to customers picking up, handling, and carrying to a sales counter an item for sale provided they have an intent to purchase the item. However, the store does not consent to a customer removing an item from a display with the intent to steal it. Second, Davis (D) argues that he lacked the intent to steal because he had no intent to permanently deprive Mervyn's of the shirt. He only intended to have the shirt long enough to receive a refund. Our research of case law reveals that the intent to steal may be found even though Davis' (D) purpose was not permanent deprivation. These cases are: (1) when the defendant intends to "sell" the property back to its owner, (2) when the defendant intends to claim a reward for "finding" the property, and three (3) when, as here, the defendant intends to return the property to its owner for a "refund". The "sale" cases offer three rationales for finding permanent deprivation. The first is that the deprivation would have been permanent unless the owner agreed to buy the property. The second rationale is that defendant's claim of the right to sell the property is also an assertion of the right of ownership and evidence of an intent to permanently deprive. Third, the act creates a substantial risk of permanent loss, because if the owner does not buy back his property the defendant will have "a powerful incentive to keep it in order to conceal the theft". See Perkins & Boyce, Criminal Law (3d ed 1982, at p. 329. The second line of cases involves a defendant who takes property for the purpose of later claiming a reward for "finding" the property. Courts, in these cases, have affirmed convictions of larceny on the theory that felonious intent existed because the defendant intended to deprive the owner of "a portion of the value of the property". The "portion of the value" in question involves the reward money paid. A second rationale is that the defendant makes the return of the property hinge on the offer of a satisfactory reward, and without the reward, the defendant would keep the property. Perkins, again, applies the rationale of a substantial risk of permanent loss to this scenario because a failure to give or offer a reward will also result in the permanent loss of the property. The third class of cases involves refunds much like the case at issue. Although these cases are similar factually, the opinions are less useful than the "sale" or "reward" cases. However, many of the rationales used in the "sale" and "reward" cases are also applicable to the "refund" cases. First, claiming a right to return an item, like claiming a right to sell an item, is an assertion of a right of ownership. Also, an intent to return an item to a store only if the store provides a refund is no less conditional than an intent to return an item based on the owner's reward. Therefore, a person "who takes an item from a store display with the intent to claim its ownership and restore it only on condition that the store pays a 'refund' must be deemed to intend to permanently deprive the store of the item within the meaning of the law of larceny." Second, the situation creates a substantial risk of permanent loss if the attempt to receive a refund of fails. Davis (D) has a strong incentive to keep the item in order to avoid drawing attention to the theft and avoid detection. As a result, we conclude that Mervyn's did not consent to Davis (D) taking possession of the shirt with the intent to steal it. Davis' (D) conduct was a trespassory taking. Furthermore, Davis' (D) intent to claim ownership of the shirt and to return it on condition of a payment of a refund is a felonious intent to permanently deprive Mervyn's within the meaning of larceny. Judgment of the court of appeal is affirmed.

Analysis:

As this opinion illustrates, there are situations where it is difficult to fit a defendant's conduct under the rubric of the intent to permanently deprive another of property. The "sale," "reward," and "refund" cases reveal new methods of theft. To deal with these new methods, courts created the doctrine of "a substantial risk of permanent loss." In these cases, an intent to permanently deprive is said to exist if the defendant knew that his conduct would create a substantial risk of permanent loss. Therefore, if a person takes an automobile only for the purpose of driving it to a particular location, but abandons the automobile, then that person may create a substantial risk of permanent loss. Though the person may have an intent for the automobile to be eventually returned to its owner, by abandoning it the person creates the risk that the automobile may be stolen again. However, this risk does not necessarily lay on third parties; it may also lay on the person taking the property in the first place. In the "sale," "reward," and "refund" cases, the substantial risk of permanent loss rests on the taker. If the resale, reward, or refund is unsuccessful, the taker's temporary possession may turn into a permanent possession. In this case, it is highly likely that if Davis (D) was not able to obtain a refund, he would have walked out of the store with the shirt in his Mervyn's shopping bag. After all, he was claiming to own it. Finally, it is worth noting that the *mens rea* in this case is, in actuality, different than the *mens rea* of the intent to permanently deprive another of property. A person who shoplifts by pocketing an item and walking out of the store does have the intent to permanently deprive. However, a person who takes an item from the shelf and tries to receive a refund at the sales counter does not have the intent to permanently deprive at the time of taking.

■ CASE VOCABULARY

ANIMUS FURANDI: Where one intends to permanently deprive another of his or her property.

Rex v. Bazeley

(*State*) v. (*Accused*)

2 Leach 835, 168 Eng.Rep. 517 (1799)

AN EMPLOYEE WHO RECEIVES PROPERTY FROM A THIRD PERSON FOR DELIVERY TO THE EMPLOYER TAKES LAWFUL POSSESSION

■ **INSTANT FACTS** A bank teller decides to pocket a customer's deposit.

■ **BLACK LETTER RULE** An employee who receives property from a third person for delivery to the employer takes lawful possession upon delivery.

■ PROCEDURAL BASIS

The defendant is charged with larceny.

■ FACTS

Bazeley (D) was the principal teller at a bank run by Esdaile & Hammet. In January 1799, he received bank notes and cash for deposit from William Gilbert through his employee, George Cock. Bazeley (D) credited Gilbert's account, but placed a bank note directly into his pocket. As is permitted in England, Esdaile & Hammet brought a criminal prosecution against Bazeley (D). Bazeley (D) was charged with larceny.

■ ISSUE

Does an employee who receives property from a third person for delivery to his employer take lawful possession upon delivery, thereby not constituting a trespassory taking?

■ DECISION AND RATIONALE

(Court) Yes. Defense counsel makes four different arguments. First, the argument is that the bank did not have constructive possession of the bank note at the time Bazeley (D) converted it to his own use. It is clear that at the time of taking the bank did not have actual possession of the note; therefore, we must decide whether the bank had constructive possession of the bank note. Sir William Blackstone defines possession as "both the right to, and also the occupation of, the property ". The bank may have had a right to possess the bank note; however, it was never under its custody *or* control. If, for example, Bazeley (D) had the bank note in his own custody and refused to turn it over to his employers, they could have recovered it by filing an action of trover or detinue. However, such actions assume that the person obtained possession of the property by lawful means, and that the right of possession of the property rests with the person bringing the action. In the case at hand, the note was delivered into Bazeley's (D) possession upon the bank's implied confidence that he would later deliver it into the bank's possession. If Bazeley (D) had deposited the bank note in the drawer kept for the receipt of deposits, it would have been a delivery of possession into the bank, but no such deposit was made. The facts support this. Second, the defense argues that, even assuming that the bank had possession of the note, Bazeley (D) did not have a felonious intention to steal it. The facts reveal no evidence that Bazeley (D) had any such intention at the time the note came into his hands. In addition, Bazeley (D) had given the bank a bond to insure the deposits he was handling. He also was the agent of a trading company and had the means to repay the bank the money that he took for his own use. In any case, Bazeley (D) must have had an intent to steal when the property came into his hands, but if he develops the intent afterwards, it is not larceny. Third, the defense argues that the situation at hand represents only a breach of trust between Bazeley (D) and the bank. Fourth, the defense argues that this is a breach of trust that has not been made punishable by the legislature. It is a settled point "that a breach of trust cannot by the rules of common law be converted into a felonious taking." There are only four statutes that convert such breaches of trust into a felony. Two of these statutes apply only to breaches of trust committed by employees of the post office. The third statute applies only to employees of the Bank of England. The fourth statute only applies to goods delivered by the employer to the employee. Therefore, none of these statutes are applicable to this case. The prosecution argues that the deposit made with Bazeley (D) was, in reality, a payment to the bank itself, not to Bazeley (D). The depositor entered the bank, and Bazeley (D), employed within the walls of the bank, was merely "one of the organs" of the bank who received the bank notes. Thus, payment to Bazeley (D) was, in effect, a payment to the bank. However, we disagree. Bazeley (D) should be pardoned.

Analysis:

This opinion highlights a gap in traditional common law and led to the development of the laws of embezzlement. Under traditional common law, an employee who takes property from a third person for delivery to the employer takes lawful possession of the property. This is different than an employee who is given property of the employer in furtherance of the working relationship. In this case, the employee merely takes custody of the property from the employer-owner. Thus, the employee may have temporary control of the property, but the employer had established dominion over the property before it was given to the employee and retains dominion over it while the employee uses it. However, if a third person gives property to the employee to hold and deliver to the employer, it is not possible to say that the employer has possession. Instead, the third party has voluntarily given up possession and transferred it to the employee. Thus, the employee's holding cannot be described as custodial. During delivery, the employee is the only person with dominion and control over the property. The employer may have a right to the property, as the opinion states, but it simply never managed to obtain possession over it.

■ CASE VOCABULARY

DETINUE: An action against a person to recover wrongfully taken property.

EO INSTANTER: At that moment.

TROVER: An action against a person for damages due to the wrongful conversion of property.

People v. Ingram

(*State*) v. (*Accused*)

76 Cal.Rptr.2d 553 (1998)

THEFT BY FALSE PRETENSES OCCURS WHEN THE DEFENDANT MAKES A FALSE REPRESENTATION OF AN EXISTING FACT WITH THE INTENT TO CHEAT OR DEFRAUD THE OWNER OF HIS OR HER PROPERTY

■ **INSTANT FACTS** A definition of the crime of false pretenses.

■ **BLACK LETTER RULE** Theft by false pretenses occurs when the defendant makes a false representation of an existing fact with the intent to cheat or defraud the owner of his or her property.

■ PROCEDURAL BASIS

None stated.

■ FACTS

None stated.

■ ISSUE

What is the crime of false pretenses?

■ DECISION AND RATIONALE

(Haller, J.) At issue here are two different forms of theft: larceny by trick and false pretenses. The crime of larceny by trick requires a trespassory taking where the defendant obtains possession, but not title to, another's property by fraud or trick. The fraud invalidates the consent, making the action a trespass. However, if the defendant obtains both possession and title through false representations with an intent to steal, there is no common law larceny. "The statutory crime of theft by false pretenses was created to fill the gap". The crime of false pretenses, while similar to larceny by trick, is a crime against *both* title and possession. "Theft by false pretenses occurs where the defendant makes a false representation with the intent to defraud the owner of his or her property, and the owner is in fact defrauded."

Analysis:

The crimes of larceny, embezzlement, and false pretenses may all take place as a result of fraud. However, the distinction between larceny by trick and false pretenses, as it relates to fraud, is a bit more difficult. As the opinion states, the primary difference between the two crimes is that false pretenses is a crime against title. A person may commit larceny by trick if she claims she wishes to rent a car but really intends to steal it. However, she drives off with possession of the car, but not with title to it. Title remains with the rental company. On the other hand, if she goes to a gas station with the intent to steal gas, fills up the tank, gives the station a bad check, and drives off, then she is guilty of the crime of false pretenses. The gas station gave her "ownership" to the gas free and clear, assuming that her check was good. As a result, since she fraudulently obtained title to the gas with a misrepresentation, she is guilty of false pretenses.

■ CASE VOCABULARY

TITLE: The legal right to use, control, or dispose of property.

People v. Whight

(*State*) v. (*Accused*)

36 Cal.App.4th 1143, 43 Cal.Rptr.2d 163 (1995)

A MISREPRESENTATION MUST CAUSE THE OWNER TO TRANSFER THE PROPERTY TO THE DEFENDANT

■ **INSTANT FACTS** Knowing that his bank account was no longer valid, a person continued to use his ATM card to obtain cash at several local grocery stores.

■ **BLACK LETTER RULE** A misrepresentation can be explicit or implicit, and the misrepresentation must have caused the victim to transfer the property to the defendant.

■ PROCEDURAL BASIS

Appeal of a conviction of four counts of false pretenses.

■ FACTS

Theodore Whight (D) opened a checking account at Tri-Counties Bank in January 1991. With this account, he was issued an ATM card which had no expiration date and was linked to his checking account. Whight (D) began the account with a deposit of $3,750.99. By June 1991 the account was overdrawn by $6.17. The bank mailed Whight (D) a letter notifying him that his account was overdue and that it would be closed if no deposits were made to make up for the overdraft. On July 10, 1991, with no deposits, the bank closed Whight's (D) account along with his ATM card. However, despite the cancellation, Whight (D) discovered that his ATM card continued to be valid at local Safeway stores. Safeway allows customers to make payments for items and receive cash back by using ATM cards. Safeway had a computer system that was used to verify ATM cards. Wells Fargo Bank operated this computer system. When a customer uses an ATM card at the Safeway check stand, a machine reads the magnetic strip on the back of the card. The information about the card is then sent by modern through telephone lines to Wells Fargo. Wells Fargo then sends the information to a banking network which links up with the customer's bank to verify the card. After the card is checked, a code is sent back to Safeway approving or disapproving the card. However, in some cases, Wells Fargo could not link up with the customer's bank or there would be a substantial delay in verifying the card. If this delay lasted more than 30 seconds, Wells Fargo would provide a "stand-in" code that would allow the transaction to take place without actually verifying the customer's information from the bank. Safeway would then automatically re-send the account information later in order to verify the account status. Safeway used "stand-in" codes for better customer service in order to speed transactions at the check stand. However, it also took the gamble that there would ultimately be a positive verification of the customer's account status. With Whight's (D) card, there was an error in the Wells Fargo computer system, which repeatedly returned a code to Safeway indicating that Whight's (D) bank could not be contacted. As a result, Safeway would repeatedly issue a "stand-in" code for Whight's (D) transactions. Whight (D) quickly realized that his ATM card was the modern-day equivalent of the "goose that laid the golden egg" and used the card on four different occasions to rack up a total of $19,000.00 [whoa!] in cash. After being caught [whew!], he admitted that he knew that his checking account had been closed. Whight (D) was convicted of four counts of false pretenses. Whight (D) appealed.

■ ISSUE

Can an implicit misrepresentation of fact cause the owner of property to transfer the property to the defendant for the purposes of the crime of false pretenses?

■ DECISION AND RATIONALE

(Sparks, J.) Yes. Whight (D) argues that his convictions for theft under false pretenses should be reversed because Safeway did not rely on Whight's (D) implicit misrepresentation that his ATM card was valid, but did rely on the code issued by Wells Fargo Bank in approving Whight's (D) transactions. "This leaky contention cannot hold water". A conviction of theft by false pretenses must be supported by three elements: (1) the defendant made a misrepresentation or false pretense, (2) the defendant had an intent to use the representation to defraud the owner of his property, and (3) the owner is in fact defrauded because he gave up his property in reliance upon the misrepresentation. In this case, we are concerned with the issue of causation or reliance. The misrepresentation does not need to be expressed, oral, or written, but may involve conduct calculated and intended to deceive. Therefore, when Whight (D) offered his ATM card, he was making an implicit representation that it was valid. However, if the victim did not rely on the false pretense, a conviction cannot be made. Such reliance may be lacking in three typical situations: "(1) Where the complainant knew the representation was false, or did not believe it to be true. (2) Where, even if he believed it, he did not rely on it, but investigated it for himself or sought and relied on other advice. (3) Where, although some false representations are proved, the complainant parted with his money or property for other reasons or in reliance on other representations not shown to be false." In addition, the false pretense or misrepresentation does not need to be the sole reason causing the victim to part with his property, it must have materially influenced the owner. As long as the victim does not rest completely upon his own investigation, "sufficient reliance is shown if the victim relied in part upon the defendant's representations." Whight (D) claims that Safeway relied upon the computer authorization as opposed to his implicit representation that his ATM card was valid. This issue would normally be a question of fact for the jury to decide. However, the evidence establishes that Safeway did not rely upon the computer authorization. The facts establish that Safeway had nothing to rely upon except Whight's (D) implicit representation that his ATM card was valid. Due to the glitch in the Wells Fargo computer system, Whight's (D) bank was not contacted and his account status was not verified. In fact, Wells Fargo kept returning a code to Safeway indicating that there was no response from Whight's (D) bank. As a result Safeway issued a "stand-in" code in order to facilitate the transaction. Consequently, the computer system never had the opportunity to verify Whight's (D) account. Therefore, it cannot be said that Safeway relied upon the computer system to verify the validity of his ATM card. "On this record, the element of reliance or causation was indisputably established." Conviction affirmed.

Analysis:

This opinion focuses on the elements of misrepresentation and reliance for the crime of false pretenses. According to the opinion, the misrepresentation can be implicit, based on words or conduct, as long as it was made with an intent to deceive. The reliance element requires that the victim actually rely on the misrepresentation. In other words, it must cause the victim to give up his or her property. If the victim knew the misrepresentation to be true or relied on evidence independent of the misrepresentation and still decided to give the property to the defendant, then the victim did not rely on the misrepresentation. Even if other independent evidence is used in the victim's decision, as long as the victim materially relied on the misrepresentation, the crime has been committed. In other words, the misrepresentation does not need to be the sole factor in the victim's decision to give up the property, but it should be the primary reason. In essence, the law only wants to punish the defendant's deceit to the extent that it causes another to do what they would not have otherwise done.

United States v. Czubinski

(*State*) v. (*Accused*)

106 F.3d 1069 (1st Cir. 1997)

A SCHEME TO DEFRAUD IS SHOWN WHERE THE DEFENDANT HAS A DISHONEST INTENT TO DEPRIVE A PERSON OF THEIR PROPERTY BY CAUSING THE OWNER SOME ARTICULABLE HARM OR BY INTENDING TO USE THE PROPERTY FOR SOME GAINFUL USE

■ **INSTANT FACTS** An employee of the IRS looked through the personal taxpayer information of several people using unauthorized computer access.

■ **BLACK LETTER RULE** For the purposes of the federal wire and computer fraud statutes: 1) A scheme to defraud is shown where the defendant has a dishonest intent to deprive a person of their property by causing the owner some articulable harm or by intending to use the property for some gainful use; 2) A deprivation of honest services is found where the defendant fails or intends to fail to carry out his official tasks adequately for an employer or the public; 3) computer fraud is found where the defendant makes an unauthorized access of a federal computer and gains anything of value in order to further an intent to defraud.

■ PROCEDURAL BASIS

Appeal of jury conviction on nine counts of wire fraud and four counts of computer fraud.

■ FACTS

Richard Czubinski (D) was employed in the Boston office of the Internal Revenue Service ("IRS"). Czubinski (D) acted as a Contact Representative who answered questions from taxpayers regarding their returns. To retrieve information for inquiring taxpayers, Czubinski (D) routinely accessed information from one of the IRS computer systems known as the integrated Data Retrieval System ("IDRS"), a database of taxpayer information. Czubinski (D) used a password (given to all IRS Contact Representatives), special search codes, and taxpayer social security numbers to retrieve the information of taxpayers on his computer screen in Boston. This information is permanently stored in a master file located in a computer in West Virginia. IRS rules prohibit an employee from accessing taxpayer information outside of the course of their official duties. In 1992, Czubinski (D) made unauthorized access of the IDRS files. He did so knowingly disregarding IRS rules. Internal IRS auditors discovered that Czubinski (D) made several unauthorized accesses of the IDRS. These unauthorized accesses involved information regarding: the tax returns of two David Duke presidential campaigners, the joint tax return of an assistant district attorney (who was prosecuting Czubinski's (D) wife on an unrelated charge) and his spouse, the tax return of a Boston city counselor or who had defeated Czubinski (D) in the previous election for a seat on the council, the tax return of one of his brother's instructors, the tax return of a police officer and his wife, and the tax return of a woman whom Czubinski (D) had dated a few times. Czubinski (D) also accessed the tax return information of other social acquaintances without authorization. [While Czubinski (D) was an electronic, peeping-tom IRS agent by day, at night he was the head of his own local invisible knights of the Ku Klux Klan chapter, no doubt making mom proud]. Neither the evidence nor the government argued that Czubinski (D) ever disclosed the information he accessed to any third party. The government's only evidence demonstrating an intent to use the confidential information for "nefarious ends" was the testimony of William A. Murray. Murray was briefly a member of Czubinski's (D) Klan chapter and worked with Czubinski (D) on the David Duke campaign. Murray testified that Czubinski (D) in early 1992 told a group that "he intended to use some of that information to build dossiers on people" who are involved in "the white supremacist movement". However, there was no evidence that Czubinski (D) created any dossiers or took any steps to create dossiers. In addition, he did not share any information in the following years with anyone. Czubinski (D) did not perform unauthorized accesses after 1992. He remained a Contact Representative for the IRS until June 1995 when a grand jury indicted him. The jury convicted him of nine counts of wire fraud and four counts of computer fraud under federal statutes. Czubinski (D) appealed to the First Circuit Court of Appeals.

■ ISSUE

Is merely accessing confidential information a sufficient deprivation of property for the purposes of wire fraud?

■ DECISION AND RATIONALE

(Torruella, J.) No. In order to establish a conviction for wire fraud, the government must prove beyond a reasonable doubt: (1) the accused participated knowingly and willingly in a plan to defraud with the specific intent to defraud, and (2) used interstate wire communications in furtherance of the plan. We find the first element dispositive of the case and conclude that the government failed to prove that Czubinski (D) participated in a plan to defraud within the meaning of the wire fraud statute. The government's case rested on two theories of wire fraud. The first is that Czubinski (D) defrauded the IRS of its property under section 1343, [which prohibits the transmission in interstate or foreign commerce "any writings, signs, signals, pictures, or sounds" for the purpose of carrying out a "scheme or artifice" (already created or intended to be created) to defraud or for obtaining money or property by false pretenses, representations, or promises], by acquiring confidential information for Czubinski's (D) intended personal use. The second is that Czubinski (D) defrauded individuals of their intangible right to honest government services under section 1346. Under the first theory, confidential information and its unauthorized distribution is "property" that an accused may deprive the owner of. Where the deprivation takes place through dishonest or deceitful means, a "scheme to defraud", is found within the meaning of the new wire fraud statute. As a result, it is necessary to show that Czubinski (D) intended to deprive another of this protected right. The government, however, fails to prove that a mere access of confidential information without any further use or intended use is sufficient to constitute a deprivation of IRS property, as it did in *Carpenter v. United States* [the court found a deprivation of property where the accused used confidential information regarding the contents of a newspaper article to his own benefit]. In contrast, Czubinski's (D) unauthorized browsing is not a deprivation within the meaning of the federal wire fraud statutes. In order to prove a deprivation of property, the owner must suffer some articulable harm from the unauthorized use or the accused must intend to have "some gainful use" of the information. While the government can prove that Czubinski (D) viewed the information deceitfully and without authorization, they cannot prove that Czubinski (D) gained from access to the information by using the information or that he intended to use the information. The only evidence regarding Czubinski's (D) intent to use any of the information rests on the testimony of Murray. Nevertheless, following Czubinski's (D) remark to Murray, Czubinski (D) did not create dossiers or even take steps to create such dossiers. Czubinski (D) did not record or print any of the taxpayer information nor did anyone else to testify as to Czubinski's (D) intent to use such confidential information. Therefore, since the evidence shows that Czubinski (D) never used, intended to use, or shared the information with anyone else, no rational jury could have found, beyond a reasonable doubt, that Czubinski (D) was browsing taxpayer files in furtherance of a scheme to use the information for his private gain. Regarding the second theory, Congress responded to a Supreme Court decision by enacting section 1364, [which expanded the term "scheme or artifice to defraud" to include "a scheme or artifice to deprive another of the intangible right of honest services"]. We hold that this section applies to the scope of the mail and wire fraud statutes. In *United States v. Sawyer*, we first noted that the definition of honest services is uncertain, but should include instances of serious corruption of public officials such as embezzlement of public funds, bribery of public officials, or failure of public decision makers to disclose certain conflicts of interest. Second, we warned that deprivation of honest services should not include every instance of official misconduct that may result in the official's personal gain. Third, our holding in *Sawyer* found that the conduct of the official must intend to or actually deprive the public of its right to the official's honest services. Applying *Sawyer* to Czubinski's (D) case, "it is clear that his conviction cannot stand." First, his case falls outside of the class of fraud that is protected such as bribery, embezzlement, or disclosure of a conflict of interest. Second, finding Czubinski (D) culpable in this case would open the "threat" of "transforming governmental workplace violations into felonies." Czubinski's (D) conduct may have been troubling, but he received no indication that this workplace violation would be punishable by anything more than dismissal. Therefore, without a clear Congressional mandate, we cannot presume that Congress intended "to create what amounts to a draconian personnel regulation." Third, as discussed previously, there is no evidence that Czubinski (D) used the information or intended to use the information in a scheme to defraud. Czubinski (D), while committing wrongdoing in searching confidential information, did not deprive or intend to deprive the public of their right to his honest services. Czubinski (D) was also charged with four counts of computer fraud based on § 1030(a)(4) [which prohibits the fraudulent, unauthorized access of a federal interest computer that furthers an intended fraud and obtains anything of value]. While Czubinski (D) did make unauthorized access, the government failed to prove that he obtained anything of value. There is no evidence of an "end" to achieve other than Czubinski's (D) satisfaction of his curiosity. The legislative history of the statute further emphasizes that the statute was intended to include the theft of information for a specific use, rather than a mere unauthorized access. Finally, as a cautionary note, the broad language of the mail and wire fraud statutes makes them adaptable to new forms of criminal conduct, but also may result in the prosecution of behavior that may be "offensive to the morals or aesthetics of federal prosecutors". This should not be the basis of a federal felony. There is troubling evidence that this prosecution may have been motivated by Czubinski's (D) views, but the "wire fraud statute must not serve as a vehicle for prosecuting only those citizens whose views run against the tide, no matter how incorrect or uncivilized such views are". The convictions of nine counts of wire fraud and four counts of computer fraud are reversed.

Analysis:

As the previous opinions have revealed, the laws of theft are a patchwork of imperfectly constructed rules that are often too rigid to cover new forms of dishonest conduct or present loopholes that wrongdoers may exploit. The wire fraud statute in this case was an attempt to deal with these problems. This federal statute essentially prohibits a person from defrauding or intending to defraud another using an electronic instrumentality of interstate commerce. The term "defraud" carries with it two concepts: deceit and loss. A person who defrauds another is actually doing two things. The defrauder is tricking the victim, and the victim, as a result of the deceit, is deprived of something or is injured. Therefore, while the wire fraud statute itself does not include the term "deprivation," the court rightfully understands that it is a necessary element of the term "defraud," which is used in the statute.

■ CASE VOCABULARY

A FORTIORI: By great force of logic.

ARTIFICE: A ruse, deception, or trick.

DEFRAUD: An act of deceit or dishonesty that causes the victim loss or injury.